In the early 1960s, Britain and the United States were still trying to come to terms with the powerful forces of indigenous nationalism unleashed by the Second World War. The Indonesia–Malaysia confrontation – a crisis which was, as Macmillan remarked to Kennedy, 'as dangerous a situation in South East Asia as we have seen since the war' – was a complex test of Anglo-American relations. As American commitment to Vietnam accelerated under the Kennedy and Johnson Administrations, Britain was involving herself in an 'end-of-empire' exercise in state-building which had important military and political implications for both nations. Matthew Jones provides a detailed insight into the origins, outbreak and development of this important episode in international history; using a large range of previously unavailable archival sources, he illuminates the formation of the Malaysian federation, Indonesia's violent opposition to the new state and the Western powers' attempts to deal with the resulting conflict.

MATTHEW JONES is a Lecturer in International History at Royal Holloway College, University of London. His previous publications include *Britain, the United States and the Mediterranean War, 1942–44* (1996).

Conflict and Confrontation in South East Asia, 1961–1965

*Britain, the United States and
the Creation of Malaysia*

Matthew Jones

CAMBRIDGE
UNIVERSITY PRESS

PUBLISHED BY THE PRESS SYNDICATE OF THE UNIVERSITY OF CAMBRIDGE
The Pitt Building, Trumpington Street, Cambridge, United Kingdom

CAMBRIDGE UNIVERSITY PRESS
The Edinburgh Building, Cambridge CB2 2RU, UK
40 West 20th Street, New York, NY 10011-4211, USA
10 Stamford Road, Oakleigh, VIC 3166, Australia
Ruiz de Alarcón 13, 28014 Madrid, Spain
Dock House, The Waterfront, Cape Town 8001, South Africa

http://www.cambridge.org

© Matthew Jones 2002

First published 2002

Printed in the United Kingdom at the University Press, Cambridge

Typeface Plantin 10/12 pt.   *System* LaTeX 2$_\varepsilon$ [TB]

A catalogue record for this book is available from the British Library

Library of Congress Cataloguing in Publication Data
Jones, Matthew, 1966–
Conflict and confrontation in South East Asia, 1961–1965 : Britain, the
United States and the Creation of Malaysia / Matthew Jones.
    p.   cm.
Includes bibliographical references and index.
ISBN 0 521 80111 7 hardback
1. Asia, Southeastern – Foreign relations – Great Britain.   2. Great
Britain – Foreign relations – Asia, Southeastern.   3. Asia, Southeastern –
Foreign relations – United States.   4. United States – Foreign relations – Asia,
Southeastern.   5. Indonesia – Foreign relations – Malaysia.   6. Malaysia –
Foreign relations – Indonesia.   I. Title.
DS525.9.G7 J66   2001
327'.0959'09046 – dc21   2001025561

ISBN 0 521 80111 7 hardback

For Anya and Alexander

Contents

Maps

Preface and acknowledgements

The Vietnam War, particularly for scholars of American foreign relations, has dominated studies of Western involvement in South East Asia during the 1960s. The destructiveness and significance of that conflict makes this entirely understandable, yet this emphasis has led to comparative neglect for the major events and upheavals taking place elsewhere in the region. Above all, another destabilizing conflict erupted during the course of 1963, as a new state, the Federation of Malaysia, was brought into being under the protective wing of its British patron, in the face of the hostility of its vast neighbour, Indonesia. The resulting Malaysian–Indonesian *konfrontasi* (confrontation) saw a low-intensity guerrilla war fought out across the inhospitable terrain of Borneo, punctuated by raids into peninsular Malaya itself, as Jakarta tried to undermine the fledgling Federation before it could take root. An official agreement ending hostilities and resuming normal diplomatic relations between the two states was eventually concluded in August 1966, but in the meantime both had also witnessed profound internal transformations. Singapore's rancorous departure from Malaysia in August 1965 spelt the end of the original conception of the Federation, while an attempted coup in Indonesia at the beginning of October gave the Army the opportunity it required to assert a dominance over national political life that was to last until the end of the century. While the public face of confrontation has been the subject of notable scholarly study (the leading work in the field, based on open sources, is J. A. C. Mackie, *Konfrontasi: The Indonesia–Malaysia Dispute, 1963–1966* (Kuala Lumpur, 1974)), less attention has been paid to the British role in the conflict. As the Americans committed ever greater resources (and eventually manpower) to the fighting in Vietnam, the British were simultaneously engaged with substantial forces in supporting Malaysia against the Indonesian military threat. By late 1964 and early 1965, at a time when domestic pressures for reductions in defence spending were intense and imperial contraction almost complete, the British found themselves maintaining around 68,000 service personnel, 200 aircraft and 80 ships in the South East Asian theatre. As one study of the end of empire has remarked, 'Two centuries of expansion into Asia had reached a bizarre finale' (John Darwin, *Britain and Decolonisation* (London, 1988), 287).

My interest in the British role in the origins and outbreak of confrontation, combined with the opening during the 1990s of official British government records under the thirty-year rule, and the absence of any major archive-based study of this crucial phase of Western involvement in South East Asia, drew me into research for this book. It soon became apparent, however, that the study would need to be expanded and deepened to encompass the inevitable connections that existed between British policies, attitudes and perceptions of the South East Asian scene and their American equivalents, particularly if one was to appreciate conflicting Western responses to the regime of President Sukarno in Indonesia. Therefore, it would be necessary to extend my researches into American archives and the policies and attitudes of the administrations of John F. Kennedy and Lyndon B. Johnson. Another perspective that would also need to be more fully developed was an understanding of the process by which Malaysia was created. In this context, it was required that aspects of British colonial policy should be explored through the newly available primary source material and some fresh views offered on the negotiating and bargaining process, both internal and international, that resulted in the inauguration of the new Federation in September 1963.

Hence, in the work that follows, an initial chapter introduces post-war British and American policies in their South East Asian setting, building up to the arrival in office of the Kennedy Administration. Part I of the book goes on to trace two strands of Western policy, beginning with US efforts to cultivate closer relations with Indonesia under Kennedy, and then moving on to examine the scheme for a 'Greater Malaysia' which began to gather momentum from the spring of 1961 onwards. By the end of 1962, when Part I closes, both Britain and the United States displayed some satisfaction with their policies in the region. A major Dutch–Indonesian dispute had been settled by American mediation, substantial US aid to Jakarta was under consideration, and Sukarno's regime showed signs of moderating its behaviour. In Vietnam, the counter-insurgency effort appeared to be making progress, and Kennedy might consider that a sought-after but elusive post-colonial regional stability was nearer in sight. From London's perspective, the plans to form Malaysia were well advanced and there were expectations of an orderly exit from colonial responsibilities and a reduction of burdensome commitments.

During 1963, these British and American hopes received severe blows as Indonesian objections to Malaysia's formation became clear, and the situation in South Vietnam steadily deteriorated. Part II follows the diplomacy that accompanied the creation of Malaysia during this pivotal year, and highlights the way Anglo-American policies came into conflict over how to respond to Indonesian belligerency. By the time of Kennedy's assassination, sharp disagreements had arisen, with Washington pressing for a political solution to the dispute, while London resisted the notion of making concessions to the Indonesian position and argued that more pressure should be put on Jakarta to desist from its attempts to subvert Malaysia.

As Part III demonstrates, Lyndon Johnson's assumption of the presidency, combined with the imperatives of the struggle in Vietnam, helped to resolve some of the earlier tensions in Anglo-American relations. With the British offering support for US policies, and opposition to contemporary French calls for the neutralization of South East Asia, the Americans were ready to adopt a tougher attitude to Indonesia and affirm their backing for the British effort to defend Malaysia. Meanwhile, the diplomacy and tactics of confrontation continued, and in September 1964 the conflict threatened to spill over into a full-scale war as military clashes multiplied. Although they entertained doubts over the increasingly offensive posture assumed by Washington towards North Vietnam, and began to see the advantages that neutrality for the region might bestow, the British felt they had little choice but to back US escalation in Vietnam. When British plans were thrown awry by the sudden departure of Singapore from Malaysia in August 1965, and London contemplated a negotiated settlement to the dispute, it was the Americans who now insisted that confrontation with Indonesia be continued, so great had their aversion to Sukarno's international orientation become. Within a few months, however, dramatic upheaval in Indonesia heralded a gradual transformation in Jakarta's foreign policy, from strident anti-imperialism to one far more conducive to Western Cold War interests. Soon after, with the end of confrontation, Britain was able to take overdue steps to reduce and eventually remove its military presence from the region altogether, at just the time the American commitment was reaching its peak.

As indicated, the focus throughout the book is on the roles and behaviour of Britain and the United States, but their actions were invariably mediated through the key regional players, and hence I have tried also to convey the essence of significant developments in Malaya, Singapore, the Borneo territories and Indonesia bearing on the external scene, as well as to chart the course of confrontation itself. In this way, the present study differs in scope and approach from John Subritzky's *Confronting Sukarno: British, American, Australian and New Zealand Diplomacy in the Malaysian–Indonesian Confrontation, 1961–5* (London, 2000), a work which appeared just as this book was consigned for publication, and which concentrates primarily on the period 1963–5. Finally, in a conclusion to the study which looks at the overall experiences of Britain and the United States in South East Asia during the 1960s, the point is emphasized that their policies had to work to accommodate the emergence of powerful local voices and impulses, increasingly suspicious of Western 'advice' and determined to chart their own course in international affairs. Indeed, this period marks a stage where both powers were having to adapt and adjust their positions, and where a formal and visible presence 'on the ground' was becoming positively harmful to the preservation of influence and interests. As the United States assumed even more onerous tasks in its mantle of global policeman, one of the chief sources of tension in Anglo-American relations during the 1960s was Washington's pressure on Britain to maintain a world-power role when British political leaders were finally coming to appreciate the urgent need to shed an imperial past and release themselves from their formal commitments, particularly in the area 'east of Suez'.

I have incurred many debts over the past few years in the research and writing of this book. For stimulating and good-humoured discussions, I would like to thank Tony Stockwell, whose own documentary study of the creation of Malaysia will soon be appearing. As ever, Philip Murphy offered ideas on British colonial policy and much encouragement throughout. Among friends in the United States who provided support and hospitality during two research trips, John Parachini stands out for his generosity. Correspondence with the late George McT. Kahin enhanced my feel for American views of Indonesia in the early 1960s. Of contemporary participants, I am grateful to Sir James Cable, Walt W. Rostow and the late Lord Perth for sharing their recollections of the period with me. Crown copyright material in the Public Record Office is reproduced by permission of The Controller of Her Majesty's Stationery Office, while the Trustees of the Macmillan Archive allowed use of quotations from the Macmillan diaries. Parts of an article published in *Journal of Imperial and Commonwealth History* were derived from chapters 2, 3 and 4, while parts of an article for *Diplomatic History* were also drawn from material used in chapters 9 and 10. Financial assistance for travel was forthcoming from the John F. Kennedy Foundation, as well as from the History Department at Royal Holloway College, University of London, where many colleagues have been supportive and encouraging. I have been fortunate in having Elizabeth Howard and Sophie Read as my editors at Cambridge University Press, as well as Margaret Berrill as copy-editor. Thanks are also due to the staff of the archives and libraries, listed in the bibliography, that I have used in the preparation of this study. As with my previous work on Anglo-American relations, I am indebted to the late Christopher Thorne, who as my undergraduate tutor at Sussex University first sparked my interest in Western approaches, attitudes and policies in the Far East. On a more personal note, I would like to thank my wife, Amir, who has again helped to sustain me through this project with love and advice. Providing a welcome and demanding distraction to the task of writing-up has been the arrival of two children, and it is to Anya and Alexander that this book is lovingly dedicated.

Brighton, 1997–2000   MATTHEW JONES

Abbreviations

ANZUS	Australia–New Zealand–United States
CAB	Cabinet (Cabinet papers at the PRO)
CCO	Clandestine Communist Organization (in Sarawak)
C-in-C	Commander-in-Chief
CIA	Central Intelligence Agency
CO	Colonial Office
COS	Chiefs of Staff
CRO	Commonwealth Relations Office
DO	Dominions Office
DOS	Department of State
FO	Foreign Office
HMG	Her Majesty's Government
ICJ	International Court of Justice
IMF	International Monetary Fund
ISC	Internal Security Council
JCS	Joint Chiefs of Staff
JIC	Joint Intelligence Committee
MCA	Malayan Chinese Association
MCP	Malayan Communist Party
MSCC	Malaysia Solidarity Consultative Committee
NATO	North Atlantic Treaty Organization
NSC	National Security Council
NSF	National Security File
OECD	Organization of Economic Cooperation and Development
PAP	People's Action Party
PKI	Partai Kommunis Indonesia (Indonesian Communist Party)
PRC	People's Republic of China
PREM	Premier (Prime Minister's Office files at the PRO)
PRO	Public Record Office

PRRI	PEMERINTAH REVOLUSIONER REPUBLIK INDONESIA (REVOLUTIONARY GOVERNMENT OF THE REPUBLIC OF INDONESIA)
RG	RECORD GROUP
SEA	SOUTH EAST ASIA
SEATO	SOUTH EAST ASIA TREATY ORGANIZATION
SUPP	SARAWAK UNITED PEOPLE'S PARTY
TNKU	TENTARA NASIONAL KALIMANTAN UTARA (NORTH BORNEO LIBERATION ARMY)
UMNO	UNITED MALAYS NATIONAL ORGANIZATION
UN	UNITED NATIONS
UPP	UNITED PEOPLE'S PARTY
USNA	US NATIONAL ARCHIVES
WNG	WEST NEW GUINEA

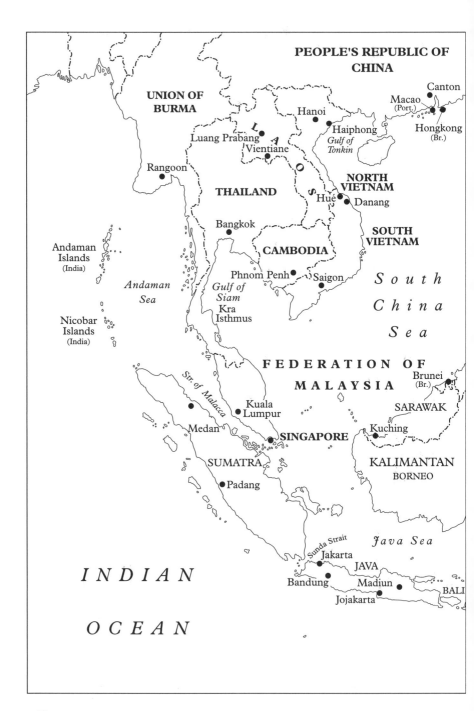

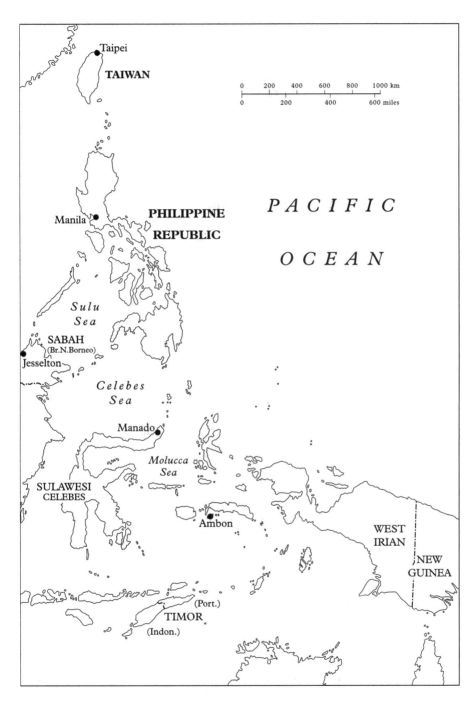

Taipei

TAIWAN

0   200   400   600   800   1000 km

0   200   400   600 miles

PACIFIC

Manila   **PHILIPPINE**
         REPUBLIC

OCEAN

Sulu
Sea

SABAH
(Br.N.Borneo)
Jesselton

Celebes
Sea

Manado

Molucca
Sea

SULAWESI
CELEBES

Ambon

WEST
IRIAN

NEW
GUINEA

(Port.)
TIMOR
(Indon.)

xix

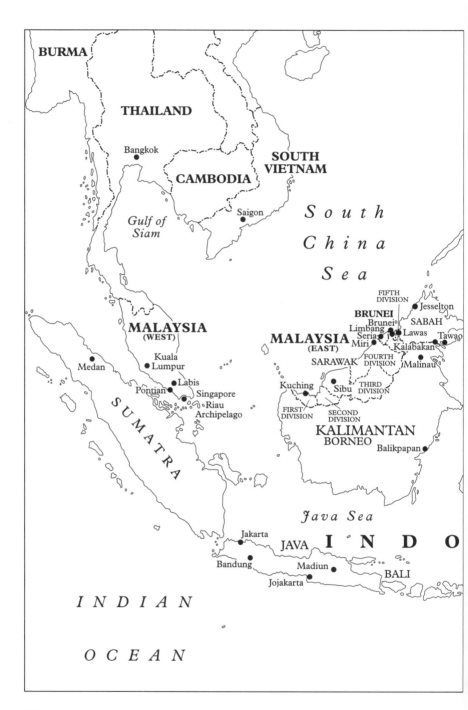

BURMA

THAILAND

Bangkok

CAMBODIA

SOUTH
VIETNAM

Saigon

Gulf of
Siam

S o u t h

C h i n a

S e a

FIFTH
DIVISION

Jesselton

BRUNEI

MALAYSIA
(WEST)

Brunei
Limbang
Seria
Miri

SABAH

Lawas
Kalabakan

Tawao

MALAYSIA
(EAST)

Kuala
Lumpur

SARAWAK

FOURTH
DIVISION

Malinau

Medan

Labis
Pontian
Singapore
Riau
Archipelago

Kuching

Sibu

THIRD
DIVISION

FIRST
DIVISION

SECOND
DIVISION

KALIMANTAN
BORNEO

Balikpapan

J a v a   S e a

Jakarta

JAVA

I   N   D   O

Bandung

Madiun

Jojakarta

BALI

I N D I A N

O C E A N

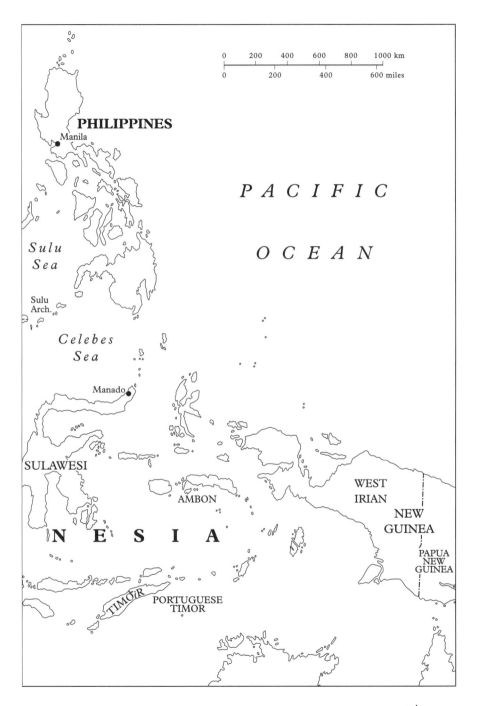

PHILIPPINES

Manila

PACIFIC

OCEAN

Sulu
Sea

Sulu
Arch.

Celebes
Sea

Manado

SULAWESI

AMBON

WEST
IRIAN

NEW
GUINEA

PAPUA
NEW
GUINEA

N E S I A

TIMOR

PORTUGUESE
TIMOR

0   200   400   600   800   1000 km

0   200   400   600 miles

Introduction: Britain, the United States and the South East Asian setting

During the late 1950s and early 1960s, both Britain and the United States were still trying to adjust and come to terms with the tumultuous changes brought to South East Asia by the effects of the Second World War. The dramatic events of 1941–2, when Japan, an Asian and non-white power, had confronted Western dominance in the region, had provided a powerful new spur to local nationalist and revolutionary feeling and helped to undermine previous perceptions of European omnipotence and superiority. As the struggle between Japan and her Occidental adversaries was played out, the states and societies of South East Asia found themselves afflicted by the direct effects of the fighting, a complete disruption of the pre-war social order, economic dislocation, occupation and the eventual return of the colonial powers in 1945 (the latter being seen by many as a second occupation).[1] Moreover, the Japanese had brought with them an ideology of Asian liberation from Western imperialism that struck a chord throughout the whole area.[2] By the end of the war, local resistance to Japan's own imperial and racial pretensions had also emerged in such areas as Indochina, Malaya and the Philippines. In the window of opportunity accorded by the sudden Japanese surrender in August 1945, nationalist leaders came forward to assert claims of independence and statehood, transforming the local scene for the returning and much weakened European powers, who despite all the signs that a reversion to pre-war patterns of control and domination was no longer tenable, sought to further exploit the economies of the region and rediscover the grandeur of an imperial past that had now run its course.[3]

In French Indochina and the Netherlands East Indies the result was bitter conflict that merely served to feed the impulses of revolutionary

---

[1] For a recent and penetrating analysis of the turmoil brought to one society by the experience of war and its aftermath, see T. N. Harper, *The End of Empire and the Making of Malaya* (Cambridge, 1999).

[2] These themes are conveyed in Christopher Thorne, *The Issue of War: States, Societies, and the Far Eastern Conflict of 1941–1945* (London, 1985), 144–72.

[3] See e.g. David J. Steinberg (ed.), *In Search of Southeast Asia: A Modern History* (Honolulu, 1987), 349–55 and *passim*.

nationalism and make for a violent and divisive removal of formal colonial rule. Having done their best through the use of military force to extinguish the Republic proclaimed by Sukarno in August 1945, and under steady international pressure, the Dutch reluctantly conceded independence to Indonesia in December 1949, though still trying to blur the issue by leaving behind them an elaborate federal structure (that was promptly removed by Indonesia's new leaders in 1950). In an even more protracted manner, the French were faced with a ferocious struggle with the Communist forces of the Viet Minh, being eventually driven out of the northern part of Vietnam in 1954, but with international agreement on a temporary partition of the state at the Geneva Conference, leaving behind a precarious non-Communist governmental structure in the south.

Despite transferring power to nationalist elites in India, Pakistan and Ceylon in 1947, and Burma the following year, the British had no intention of abandoning their own valuable colonial possessions in South East Asia. The pragmatic philosophy that guided the British approach to colonial affairs made concessions to well-established and moderate nationalist movements preferable to the blatant use of coercion, but there was no inclination among officials or ministers (either Conservative or Labour) to embark on a wholesale retreat from empire or to renounce a world-power role after 1945.[4] The inescapable fact was that Britain had global interests and responsibilities, nowhere more so than in South East Asia, and these could not be easily discarded, even had this been desired. One of those responsibilities was to help provide for the defence of Australia and New Zealand, a task so manifestly neglected, at least in the eyes of most Antipodean observers, in the run-up to the Japanese victories of 1941–2. Reliance on the United States for their security during the war in the Far East was reflected by the fact that Australia and New Zealand chose to conclude an exclusive defence pact with Washington in 1951, in the form of the ANZUS Treaty. This was the cause of some umbrage in London, though not sufficient to offset the strong desire to preserve close connections with Canberra and Wellington, and to devise common policies towards security issues in South East Asia, shown in the liaison built up between military staffs after 1949 and the later establishment, in 1955, of a Commonwealth Strategic Reserve in Malaya.[5]

In the colonial sphere, there was a marked tendency on the part of British officials to highlight the different rate of political, economic and

---

[4] See the authoritative discussion in John Darwin, *Britain and Decolonisation: The Retreat from Empire in the Post-War World* (London, 1988), 122–31.

[5] See Philip Darby, *British Defence Policy East of Suez, 1947–1968* (London, 1973), 23, 29; also, Peter Edwards, *Crises and Commitments: The Politics and Diplomacy of Australia's Involvement in Southeast Asian Conflicts, 1948–1965* (Sydney, 1992), 163–9.

social development in each colonial territory, making some more ready for the demands of self-government and eventual independence than others. None of the prior conditions for rapid political advance, it was believed, were as yet apparent in the territories for which the British held responsibility in South East Asia. Moreover, in the minds of many British observers, economic recovery and the expansion of British commercial activity after the ravages of the war were inextricably linked with the preservation and development of investments and trade in the area east of Suez. In this connection, Malaya assumed pride of place, with its production and export of tin and natural rubber making it a vital source of dollar earnings for the Sterling area.[6] Thus the British expended considerable efforts developing post-war plans for a new Malayan Union, with a centralized administration in Kuala Lumpur and citizenship rights extended to the substantial Chinese and Indian populations, only to be forced into hasty reappraisal upon the scheme's introduction in April 1946 by the resultant uproar in the Malay community. The subsequent emergence of the United Malays National Organization (UMNO) set the stage for the development of communal politics in Malaya, and in February 1948 the British exhibited their flexibility by substituting a Federation for the Union, restoring some of the authority of the old Malay sultans over the individual states and removing the controversial extension of citizenship rights to non-Malays.[7] Nevertheless, eventual self-government for Malaya within the Commonwealth, though promised, remained in the far distance, while the outbreak of a large-scale insurrection by the Malayan Communist Party (MCP) in June 1948, backed by sections of the discontented rural Chinese community, gave the British authorities a pressing new challenge and made early departure seem unlikely. Beyond Malaya, North Borneo was accorded crown colony status in 1946 (having been run since 1881 by a chartered company), and Sarawak was similarly transferred from the reign of the Brooke dynasty despite a violent campaign of local Malay opposition. Also administered separately as a colony was the great commercial and strategic centre of Singapore, where the new (and grand-sounding) post of Commissioner General for South East Asia was created in 1948, with the job of coordinating regional foreign, colonial and defence policies. With this new imperial dispensation came the return in even greater numbers of colonial officials, military officers

---

[6] See A. J. Stockwell, 'Colonial Planning during World War Two: the Case of Malaya', *Journal of Imperial and Commonwealth History*, 2, 3, 1974.

[7] Principal works on this subject include J. de V. Allen, *The Malayan Union* (New Haven, 1967), A. J. Stockwell, *British Policy and Malay Politics during the Malayan Union Experiment, 1942–1948* (Kuala Lumpur, 1979), Albert Lau, *The Malayan Union Controversy, 1942–1948* (Singapore, 1991).

4 Conflict and confrontation in South East Asia

and technical experts to South East Asia, adding to the impression that the British were consolidating and extending their position in the region. Entertaining many of the same condescending and racially charged attitudes and assumptions about their role in the area as the Europeans had previously shown, many Americans after 1945 felt a reinvigorated sense of mission in the Far East. Emerging from the war against Japan with its power and reach incomparably enhanced, the United States exhibited a new confidence in the justness of its cause and the perfectibility of its institutions and values. Anti-imperialist sentiment during the war years fuelled the idea that the United States was distinct and different in what it had to offer the region from the fading European powers (a self-image greatly reinforced by the grant of independence to the Philippines in 1946).[8] The American idea that it was now their turn to offer leadership in Asia, with all the political and commercial advantages that this might bestow, was manifested most immediately in the semi-regal occupation regime that General Douglas MacArthur introduced in Japan, and the project of political and social reform that accompanied it, but could also be observed in the unsuccessful attempts made to mediate in the Chinese Civil War. The collapse of the Marshall Mission by early 1947 led to the Truman Administration's forlorn (and ambivalent) efforts to affect the outcome of the subsequent fighting through large-scale aid to the ailing Chinese Nationalist forces. Although Washington's core priority remained containing Soviet power in Europe, the failings of American China policy only underscored the importance of promoting stability and opposing Communist penetration elsewhere in Asia, a point the Administration's domestic critics pushed repeatedly as the implications of the Chinese Communist victory in October 1949 were absorbed. Moreover, by the late 1940s, State Department analysts themselves were coming to appreciate that the markets and raw materials of South East Asia (as in the pre-war era) were essential to the economic recovery and future prosperity of Japan, while a strong and secure Japan, firmly in the Western camp, was seen as a fundamental component of the extension of containment to eastern Asia as a whole.[9]

Having exhibited a hearty disdain and in many cases hostility to the European colonial presence in South East Asia during the Second World War, official American policy now had to balance its urgent desire for

---

[8] Though the status of the Philippines remained, as one of Stanley Karnow's chapter headings terms it, one of 'dependent independence', see his *In Our Image: America's Empire in the Philippines* (New York, 1989). On the sense of an American destiny rooted in the affairs of Asia, see Thorne, *The Issue of War*, 203–6.

[9] See e.g. Andrew J. Rotter, *The Path to Vietnam: Origins of the American Commitment to Southeast Asia* (Ithaca, 1987), 35–48, 127–40.

regional stability against the indigenous efforts being made to expel Western imperialism.[10] In Malaya, the fact that the British counter-insurgency campaign was directed against the Chinese Communist guerrillas of the MCP made it relatively straightforward to take a supportive approach. In Indonesia, on the other hand, the Dutch were active in suppressing a republican nationalist movement that had widespread popular backing. Moreover, Sukarno and his supporters had demonstrated their anti-Communist credentials by defeating an attempted uprising by the Indonesian Communist Party (PKI) at Madiun in September 1948. By early 1949, and after the Dutch had defied the United Nations (UN) by launching a second military offensive against republican forces, the Truman Administration, fearful that Dutch belligerence was doing harm to the West's image as a whole, belatedly began to put pressure on The Hague to negotiate terms for full independence. Threatened with the denial of Marshall aid funds, the Dutch were faced with little choice but to accede. Nevertheless, the American moderator at the subsequent conference sweetened this bitter pill by insisting that the new Indonesian government accept the external debt of the old East Indies, and allowed the Dutch to hold onto a remnant of their former empire in the form of the western portion of New Guinea (West Irian), a matter, as we shall see, of great offence to Indonesian nationalists.[11] In French Indochina, the Communist nature of the leading Vietnamese nationalist movement obviated any support by Washington for early independence, and by early 1950 the United States found itself extending military and economic aid to French efforts to contain the Viet Minh insurgency.[12] With the People's Republic of China (PRC) also beginning to supply assistance to the Vietnamese Communists, Vietnam became a front-line state as the Cold War and the doctrine of containment was extended to Asia, the latter phenomenon confirmed by the outbreak of the Korean War in June 1950, and the subsequent sharp escalation of US commitment to the whole region.

---

[10] For a useful overview see George McT. Kahin, 'The United States and the Anticolonial Revolutions in Southeast Asia', in Yonosuke Nagai and Akira Iriye (eds.), *The Origins of the Cold War in Asia* (Oxford, 1977), 338–61. Standard works stressing this theme include Gary R. Hess, *The United States' Emergence as a Southeast Asian Power, 1940–1950* (New York, 1987), Lloyd C. Gardner, *Approaching Vietnam: From World War II through Dienbienphu* (New York, 1988) and Robert J. McMahon, *The Limits of Empire: The United States and Southeast Asia since World War II* (New York, 1999).

[11] It is worth recalling the conclusions of one major study of these events: 'To infer . . . that American policy towards the Indonesian revolution was motivated by a historic opposition to colonialism would grossly misrepresent the American record in the East Indies during the immediate post-war years', see Robert J. McMahon, *Colonialism and Cold War: The United States and the Struggle for Indonesian Independence, 1945–1949* (Ithaca, 1981), 304.

[12] See Gardner, *Approaching Vietnam*, 85–7; Rotter, *Path to Vietnam*, 199–203.

French failings in Vietnam provided a salutary lesson for the British, but they faced several key advantages when tackling their own problems in Malaya, foremost of which was the geographical isolation of the insurgents from outside means of support, the hostility of the socially conservative Malay nationalist leadership to the aims of the MCP, and the failure of the Communists to extend their reach beyond the minority Chinese community. By 1952, the security situation was under control, but the pace of political change was beginning to accelerate as UMNO formed an alliance with two other parties, the moderate Malayan Chinese Association (MCA), and the Malayan Indian Congress, and began to demand greater powers of self-government. With the worst period of the Emergency having passed, the anti-Communism of the UMNO Alliance evident, and its popular support demonstrated by conclusive victory at the July 1955 Legislative Council elections (winning 51 out of 52 available seats), the British no longer felt it necessary to delay a progressive handover of colonial controls. Indeed, such concessions were advisable if more radical voices within UMNO were to be stifled, or if the UMNO leadership was to be stiffened in its responses to the MCP's overtures for peace talks, made in late 1955.[13] At the constitutional conference held in London in January–February 1956, the British were ready to agree a rapid advance to independence for Malaya, even though the communal basis of the territory's politics had not been surmounted and the guerrilla war continued, with the transfer of power to be complete by the end of August 1957. This concession was undoubtedly made easier by the fact that the Alliance, under the leadership of Tunku Abdul Rahman, was ready to see Britain continue to provide for Malayan internal and external security under new treaty arrangements, to preserve its Commonwealth links, and to offer a secure environment for British investments. Explaining to his Cabinet colleagues that constitutional change could not be deferred any longer, the Colonial Secretary, Alan Lennox-Boyd, argued in January 1956: 'The tide is still flowing in our direction, and we can still ride it; but the ebb is close at hand and if we do not make this our moment of decision we shall have lost the power to decide. Not far off the French have shown us what can happen if such a tide is missed.'[14]

British readjustment to the threat to their Far Eastern interests presented by the emergence of the PRC (including worries over the anomalous position of Hong Kong) was reflected in their decision to recognize,

---

[13] See A. J. Stockwell (ed.), *Malaya, Part I: The Malayan Union Experiment, 1942–1948* (London, 1995), lxxii–lxxvii.

[14] Extract from Cabinet memorandum by Colonial Secretary, January 1956, CAB 134/1202, reproduced in David Goldsworthy (ed.), *The Conservative Government and the End of Empire, 1951–1957, Part II: Politics and Administration* (London, 1994), 389.

maintain contacts with and if possible accommodate the new regime in Beijing, in stark contrast to the attitude adopted by the Truman Administration.[15] Despite the need to keep in general step with US policy, American off-shore and nuclear power being the ultimate guarantor of the Western position if a major offensive were launched by the Chinese, during the 1950s the British also felt the need to distance themselves from their allies when imprudent and bellicose positions were adopted by Washington. Clouding Anglo-American relations for much of the decade, above all, were concerns that the Eisenhower Administration, armed with its rhetoric of 'massive retaliation', might choose to escalate local conflicts into a full-scale confrontation with either Communist China or even the Soviet Union itself, with all the catastrophic consequences that might ensue. This difference in emphasis was shown in most graphic fashion during the Dien Bien Phu crisis of 1954, where British opposition to forceful American ideas for concerted intervention, and their subsequent role at the Geneva Conference in promoting an agreement that confirmed Communist control of North Vietnam and 'neutralized' Laos and Cambodia under international supervision, was resented by many in Washington as a prime example of appeasement.[16] Post-war Anglo-American relations in South East Asia had been brought to their lowest point, but in September 1954 the Americans received some compensation with the formation of the South East Asia Treaty Organization (SEATO), the United States, along with Britain, France, Australia, New Zealand, the Philippines, Thailand and Pakistan, all now ready to subscribe to the notion of collective defence against future instances of overt aggression.[17]

Nevertheless, SEATO, though claiming to bring together Western and Asian perspectives on the security problems of the region, soon became a potent target for Asian and neutral critics of the militarized forms of containment that had been practised by the United States since the Korean War, and helped to antagonize the PRC. British attitudes towards SEATO were ambivalent. Following the trauma of the Suez crisis, Harold Macmillan's premiership from January 1957 placed the highest priority on reestablishing and then maintaining close relations with Washington by demonstrating Britain's continuing usefulness in upholding the global pattern of containment. In this context, membership of SEATO was felt to be a good marker with Washington that, after the

[15] See e.g. Peter Lowe, *Containing the Cold War in East Asia: British Policies towards Japan, China and Korea, 1948–53* (Manchester, 1997), 99–122.
[16] See e.g. Lawrence S. Kaplan, Denise Artaud and Mark R. Rubin (eds.), *Dien Bien Phu and the Crisis of Franco-American Relations, 1954–1955* (Wilmington, 1990) and James Cable, *The Geneva Conference of 1954 on Indochina* (London, 1986).
[17] See Leszek Buszynski, *SEATO: The Failure of an Alliance Strategy* (Singapore, 1983).

uncertainties generated over Anglo-American relations in the Far East by the Indochina crisis, the British were still prepared to play their part in providing for regional security. The alliance was assumed to provide some deterrent power and might allow greater access to closely guarded US military planning and thinking towards the whole region (and where a restraining British voice might be heard), while membership also broke into the exclusive ANZUS club. On the other hand, SEATO entailed potentially onerous (and ambiguous) obligations to respond to future crises in Indochina, where threats were often subversive and ill defined, and where Britain might find itself tied to the chariot-wheels of precipitate American action, especially if the other members were supportive of Washington's position. Moreover, British aspirations to appeal to moderate and non-aligned Asian nationalism, where friendship with India was considered vital, tended to be undercut by membership of SEATO and association with the policies of the US Secretary of State, John Foster Dulles, whose portrayal of neutralism in the Cold War as nothing short of a moral evil clung to perceptions of US attitudes throughout the period.[18]

The suspicions reserved for SEATO by much Asian opinion, that it was an intrusive military power bloc that served as another example of the West's desire to establish the framework for how independent nations should order their external relations, raised immediate problems for British relations with Malaya. Prior to independence, Tunku Abdul Rahman had offered private assurances to British ministers that he intended to take his country into the alliance at an early date.[19] Nevertheless, within UMNO there was grass-roots neutralist sentiment that was liable to be strongly opposed to any such action, and after August 1957 the Malayan Prime Minister preferred not to mention the subject at all.[20] More difficult was the domestic reception accorded the Anglo-Malayan Defence Agreement, which came into operation in October 1957, and allowed British and Commonwealth forces to retain their bases on Malayan soil to assist with external defence, but also to fulfil 'Commonwealth and international obligations', a catch-all phrase that the British anticipated would cover SEATO-related activities.[21] By the end of 1957, the British High Commission in Kuala Lumpur was noting the strong voices

[18] See the discussion in Anita Inder Singh, *The Limits of British Influence: South Asia and the Anglo-American Relationship, 1947–56* (London, 1993), 177–9.
[19] See e.g. Lennox-Boyd minute for Eden, PM(56)43, 28 June 1956, PREM 11/4763.
[20] See May 1957 paper, 'The outlook in Malaya up to 1960', prepared in the Commissioner General's office, D1051/8G, FO 371/129342; see also Tory to Macmillan, no. 3, 12 October 1957, PREM 11/1767.
[21] 'Note on the Malayan Defence Agreement', Appendix A to PM(57)39, 12 August 1957, reproduced in A. J. Stockwell (ed.), *Malaya, Part III: The Alliance Route to Independence, 1953–1957* (London, 1995), 408–12.

of disapproval for the Defence Agreement apparent among the Malay rank and file of UMNO, and that it was

obvious that there is an influential group in UMNO who are Indonesian both in origin and outlook and favour a policy of neutralism on the Afro-Asian model. Their views are reflected in important sections of the Malay language press. Cleavages are, therefore, appearing among the Malays themselves and this is a source of worry and weakness to the Tunku and his more responsible colleagues.[22]

There was some annoyance in London when the Malayan Government subsequently insisted that the Defence Agreement committed the British to consult with the authorities in Kuala Lumpur over the movement of British forces in Malaya and the operational use of their bases. The result was a private understanding that if British forces were engaged in SEATO operations (such as deployment exercises to Thailand), they would have to be routed through Singapore first before continuing on their missions. The Malayans later tried to reduce the sense of British irritation by maintaining that in a genuine emergency they would be prepared to turn a blind eye to such technical niceties, but the British were concerned that if Malayan reservations became widely known, the credibility of their military commitment in the eyes of other SEATO members would be reduced.[23] In addition, and much to the disapproval of the Commanders-in-Chief (Cs-in-C) Far East, the British Government also agreed that official Malayan permission would have to be sought before British forces equipped with nuclear weapons could be stationed on Malayan soil.[24]

The powerful currents of neutralism in Asia, and the attractions of the non-aligned movement, were also on the minds of policy-makers in Washington as they contemplated the state of their relations with Indonesia by the mid-1950s. Hopes that the American role in the final process that led to Indonesian independence would be acknowledged by the formation of a close relationship with the United States were quickly dashed. Jakarta's strong preference for a policy of non-alignment was conclusively demonstrated when in early 1952 the Sukiman Cabinet was displaced under the pressure of public opinion after having accepted US economic aid on terms which implied association with American Cold War policies.[25] This was a worrying sign for the Eisenhower

[22] Brief prepared by UK High Commissioner, Kuala Lumpur, 13 December 1957, D1051/1, FO 371/135652.
[23] For Malayan reassurances discussed by the Cabinet, see CC(61) 17th mtg, 23 March 1961, CAB 128/35.
[24] This arrangement arose when the British Minister of Defence, Duncan Sandys, was indiscreet enough to inform a journalist during this sensitive period that British forces in Malaya retained a nuclear capability; see material in PREM 11/1767.
[25] See McMahon, *Colonialism and Cold War*, 321.

Administration, which acknowledged the vital strategic and economic place held by Indonesia in South East Asia, and the importance of denying it to Communist control; at one meeting of the National Security Council (NSC) in late 1954, when Dulles was explaining that the country should be considered an 'essential element' in the off-shore island chain of containment, the President exclaimed, '... why the hell did we ever urge the Dutch to get out of Indonesia?'[26] Unease continued with Indonesia's hosting of the Bandung Conference of non-aligned states in April 1955, and was also exhibited over the domestic political instability that afflicted the Republic as it strove to build national unity and satisfy the expectations for social and economic change that had been unleashed by the revolutionary period of 1945–9. During the early 1950s, Indonesia laboured to superimpose a Western-style parliamentary system on a highly complex and diverse society spread across a vast archipelago. A string of fragile, inefficient and corrupt coalition governments in Jakarta, keen rivalry and feuding between the Indonesian Nationalist Party (PNI) and the Islamic, loosely organized Masjumi party, and a lack of consensus over how Indonesia was to address the legacies of colonial rule helped to create a wave of disappointment, especially among the young who had been so central to the vitality of the independence movement. To add to the fissures within the Indonesian political scene, in 1952 Masjumi split, with the conservative Nahdatul Islam breaking off to form another party, and taking with it much of Masjumi's base in central and eastern Java. Meanwhile, the PKI, under the leadership of Dipa Nusantara Aidit, was staging a remarkable resurgence after its abortive 1948 rising and building a mass base among the *abangan* villagers on Java. In the 1955 parliamentary elections none of the main parties managed to achieve a majority, only adding to popular disillusionment with the political process. Separatist tendencies in the Outer Island provinces were also being fuelled by growing Javanese dominance of the expanding bureaucracy of the Indonesian state, imbalances in the distribution of economic resources, and the resistance of regional commanders to efforts to create a modern, professional and centrally controlled Indonesian Army.[27]

Although he stood at the apex of the political system, and was the embodiment of Indonesian national pride and sentiment having led the

---

[26] Memorandum of discussion of 226th meeting of the NSC, 1 December 1954, *Foreign Relations of the United States, 1952–1954, vol. XII: East Asia and the Pacific, part 1* (Washington, 1984), 1005. Volumes in the *Foreign Relations of the United States* series are hereafter indicated by *FRUS*.

[27] Background on the Indonesian scene can be found in Herbert Feith, *The Decline of Constitutional Democracy in Indonesia* (Ithaca, 1962), and in J. D. Legge, *Sukarno: A Political Biography* (London, 1972), 240–78.

anti-colonial struggle, President Sukarno's executive role was constrained by the terms of the Provisional Constitution of 1950, and he grew increasingly restless with inter-party squabbling, signs of disunity and the limits on his own powers. Following visits to the Soviet Union and the PRC, in October 1956 Sukarno began to attack the parliamentary system, calling for the burying of all the parties and a new approach of 'Guided Democracy' more suitable to Indonesian traditions. With many Indonesians looking for firm presidential leadership as assertions of regional autonomy spread on Sumatra and Sulawesi, in March 1957 the last party-based government collapsed and amid a swirl of political uncertainty was eventually succeeded by one headed by Dr Djuanda Kartawidjaja, with its members selected as individuals. At the same time, the Army's Chief of Staff, General A. H. Nasution, managed to persuade Sukarno to declare martial law in response to the regional unrest. Henceforth the Indonesian Army, itself a divided and faction-ridden body, was to play a direct role in political affairs, with extensive powers being exerted over the bureaucracy and economy. As Sukarno moved also to extend his prerogatives and articulate his vision of Indonesia's political future built around a return to a consensual style of decision-making, in July 1957 provincial elections on Java saw the PKI returned as the largest party with 27.4 per cent of the vote.[28]

Officials in the Eisenhower Administration were alarmed by these developments, and the clear signs that Sukarno, far from acting to curb the rapid growth of the PKI, was ready to play for its organizational backing in his efforts to refashion Indonesia's governing institutions and to counteract the influence of the Army. The next general election was due in 1959, and observers predicted even greater gains for the PKI. When the NSC reviewed the Indonesian picture in August 1957, Allen Dulles, the head of the CIA, was asked 'whether Sukarno had gone past the point of no return'; he 'replied in the affirmative, saying that Sukarno had been impressed by his trip to Moscow, had concluded that the party system did not work, and would henceforth play the Communist game'. Eisenhower told the meeting, 'The best course would be to hold all Indonesia in the Free World. The next best course would be to hold Sumatra if Java goes Communist. We should also consider what to do if all Indonesia votes Communist.' Reflecting the tone of the discussion was Admiral Arthur W. Radford, the Chairman of the Joint Chiefs of Staff (JCS), who remarked that 'Indonesia was important enough to warrant drastic action by the United States to hold it in the Free World.'[29] The result of

---

[28] Most informative on this period is Daniel S. Lev, *The Transition to Guided Democracy: Indonesian Politics, 1957–1959* (Ithaca, 1966).
[29] Record of 333rd mtg of NSC, 1 August 1957, NSC series, box 9, Ann Whitman File, Dwight D. Eisenhower Library.

such deliberations was a decision by the Administration to begin a CIA effort to provide covert support to the local anti-Communist military commanders on Sumatra and Sulawesi behind the movement for Outer Island autonomy.[30] The intentions behind backing the Outer Island leaders were notably confused. They included the hope that exerting general pressure on the government in Jakarta would induce it to take stronger measures against the PKI, the belief that the authority of Sukarno himself could be challenged from the regions, and the expectation that if Java should fall under Communist control a pro-Western fall-back position in the Outer Islands might be created. By the end of 1957, US officials had managed to enlist the active support of Britain and Australia at the highest level for this clandestine intervention in the internal politics of Indonesia, and secret working groups were formed to coordinate their joint efforts.[31]

Events began to spin out of control in February 1958 when the rebels in the Outer Islands declared a Revolutionary Government of the Republic of Indonesia (PRRI), prompting the authorities on Java to begin military operations against the dissident strongholds on Sumatra and Sulawesi. Over the next few months, covert aid continued to reach the PRRI rebels from Western sources, but the Indonesian Government responded swiftly and effectively to this threat to national unity, and by May 1958 serious resistance in the Outer Islands was in the process of collapsing.[32] Covert action had comprehensively failed to undermine Sukarno's regime and made it very uncomfortable for Indonesians who favoured closer contacts with the United States, while the capture after a rebel bombing raid over Ambon of Allen Lawrence Pope, an American pilot on the CIA payroll, compromised the posture of neutrality towards the civil conflict that Washington had been publicly maintaining. Moreover, it was becoming plain that the rebellion had actually elevated the status of the PKI, which had strongly supported the Jakarta Government's military response. With all these considerations in mind, and guided by the advice of its new Ambassador to Indonesia, Howard P. Jones, the Eisenhower Administration

---

[30] These developments have been traced in Audrey R. Kahin and George McT. Kahin, *Subversion as Foreign Policy: The Secret Eisenhower and Dulles Debacle in Indonesia* (New York, 1995).

[31] See record of conversation at British Embassy, Paris, 14 December 1957, N.A.(57)(Del)(Secret)1, CAB 133/304. The present author has combined British and American sources in his own account of these events, see ' "Maximum Disavowable Aid": Britain, the United States and the Indonesian Rebellion, 1957–58', *English Historical Review*, 114, 459, 1999.

[32] The latest, and most revealing, ground-level account of the CIA's efforts to bolster the rebels is given by Kenneth Conboy and James Morrison, *Feet to the Fire: CIA Covert Operations in Indonesia, 1957–1958* (Annapolis, 1999).

undertook a major turnaround.[33] Direct assistance to the rebels was cut off, while new channels of dialogue were opened to the Indonesian Army, which after its recent successes against the rebels was now seen as the best bulwark against the dangers posed by Communism in Indonesia. Responding to the overtures of anti-Communist Army leaders (and the prompting of the Pentagon), in the summer of 1958 US officials initiated a modest military assistance programme. Nevertheless, opinion in the State Department was still sharply divided over how far to extend aid, with John Foster Dulles, above all, concerned that Sukarno's prestige should not be enhanced by such shipments.[34]

When, in September 1958, Djuanda's Government, probably under Army pressure, announced that the national elections due for the following year were to be postponed, it appeared that the new approach of the Eisenhower Administration was reaping some reward.[35] Over the next two years, the United States continued to supply small quantities of military equipment to the Indonesian armed forces, and to cultivate inter-service ties with the Army. Such efforts were spurred by the knowledge that since early 1958 the Soviet Union had also begun to negotiate credits with the Indonesians for the supply of military equipment, with a particular emphasis on the Air Force and Navy (the former held by US officials as being the arm most susceptible to Communist influence). Yet in this developing competition for influence, US policy-makers faced one overriding handicap: the unwillingness of the Eisenhower Administration to support the Indonesian position in the ongoing dispute with the Netherlands over the status and disposition of the territory of West Irian, an issue left unresolved by the negotiations surrounding independence in 1949. As it had been an intrinsic part of the Netherlands East Indies Empire, Indonesians regarded themselves as the rightful heirs to the territory, while West Irian had acquired an emotive significance as the place where many pre-war nationalist agitators had been interned and suffered at the hands of the colonial authorities.[36] The Dutch, however, preferred to point to the ethnic differences between the population of the New Guinea interior and the predominantly Malay peoples of the rest

---

[33] See Howard P. Jones, *Indonesia: The Possible Dream* (New York, 1971), 147–54.
[34] See Robertson to Dulles, 30 July 1958, and attachments, Lot 62 D 68, RG 59 (this and all subsequent references to RG 59 are from the Department of State Records at the US National Archives); see also memorandum of conversation, 1 August 1958, *FRUS, 1958–1960, vol. XVII, Indonesia* (Washington, 1994), 255–6; Special National Intelligence Estimate, 'The Outlook in Indonesia', 12 August 1958, *ibid.*, 258–9; Department of State (DOS) to Jakarta, 20 August 1958, *ibid.*, 269–70.
[35] See *FRUS, 1958–1960, XVII*, 283.
[36] See Benedict O. Anderson, *Imagined Communities: Reflections on the Origin and Spread of Nationalism* (London, 1991), 176–7.

of the Indonesian archipelago, and maintained that a nascent Papuan self-consciousness should be left to develop free from incorporation in Indonesia (though the Dutch case was hardly helped by the minimal efforts made to develop self-governing institutions or indigenous political parties in West Irian, at least until 1960). Dutch refusal to reopen talks on sovereignty throughout the 1950s, and the backing they received from Australia over maintaining a colonial foothold in South East Asia, was a continual affront to Indonesian national pride and was effectively exploited for populist ends by both Sukarno and the PKI.[37] The Americans, however, preferred not to break with their European NATO ally on this crucial matter, and as a result it proved more difficult for them to win favour among ruling circles in Jakarta.

The British had also extended considerable assistance to the CIA's covert operations in Indonesia during 1958, the Chiefs of Staff (COS) at one point instructing the Cs-in-C Far East 'to give all possible aid within the policy of "maximum disavowable support" to the rebels'.[38] Among other forms of assistance, base facilities in Singapore had been furnished for some of the American resupply missions flown over Sumatra. This was done in the overall interest of Anglo-American relations rather than through any confidence in American reading of the local Indonesian scene (though the then Commissioner General for South East Asia, Sir Robert Scott, was an enthusiast for bringing about Sukarno's downfall).[39] British officials did feel concern over the expansion of PKI influence within Indonesia, but had no desire to see the territorial integrity of the state destroyed, which might leave behind a Communist-dominated Javanese rump. Instead, reflecting a belief close to the Prime Minister's heart, intimate cooperation with the Americans would again allow, it was hoped, the injection of alternative and moderating voices through joint consultation, which could act as a counter to the more extreme views that tended to emanate from some quarters in Washington. Clandestine assistance was, moreover, extended to the Outer Island rebels with the misgiving that if news should leak, the delicate situation in Singapore might be affected, where radical left-wing political activity and trade union militancy was a cause of increasing alarm to the British colonial authorities in the middle and late 1950s.

The main base for the deployment of British naval, air and military forces in the region, Singapore had been made a full crown colony in April 1946. Maintenance of the Singapore base was seen as essential to

[37] The Australian position is covered in Glen St J. Barclay, *Friends in High Places: Australian–American Diplomatic Relations since 1945* (Melbourne, 1985), 101–5.
[38] See confidential annex to COS(58) 34th mtg, 15 April 1958, DEFE 32/6.
[39] See Scott to Macmillan, no. 702, 12 December 1957, DH1051/23G, FO 371/129531.

meet SEATO obligations, provide for the close defence of Malaya and surrounding sea communications, and demonstrate a continuing commitment to Australia and New Zealand. With a population that was 80 per cent Chinese, and possessing a well-organized labour movement, Singapore was, however, considered vulnerable to Communist subversion and left-wing influence, and the Governor held tight control over internal security. The Rendel constitution of 1955 introduced a largely elected assembly to the colony, but British hopes that moderate voices of political reform would prevail were confounded with the rapid emergence of David Marshall's Singapore Labour Front, and its principal socialist rival, the People's Action Party (PAP). Both held strong anti-colonial views and competed for the allegiance of an increasingly radicalized Chinese-educated mass electorate. Marshall's victory at the 1955 elections was followed by immediate demands for full self-government on terms that London found impossible to accept, as they effectively involved transferring control of internal security to Singapore ministers.[40] The breakdown of subsequent constitutional talks in London in April–May 1956 led to Marshall's resignation as Chief Minister, and his place was taken by Lim Yew Hock. The new Chief Minister was willing to act forcefully against alleged Communist united front organizations in Singapore's Chinese middle schools and in some of the trade union organizations, and in March 1957 a delegation from the colony travelled once more to London for another constitutional conference. This time a compromise agreement was reached which gave full internal self-government to Singapore, with Britain retaining control over questions affecting external affairs and defence. An Internal Security Council (ISC) would be formed to handle this most sensitive of issues, to be composed of three British and three Singapore representatives, while an additional Malayan member would hold a crucial casting vote. The ISC was to be chaired by a new British Commissioner for Singapore (a role filled by the existing Commissioner General for South East Asia) and its decisions on appropriate measures to tackle subversion and unrest were binding on the local government. In an extreme case, the British still reserved the right to suspend the new constitution and reimpose direct rule.[41]

Although they recognized the odium they might incur by refusing to meet the demands coming from Singapore for independence, and the threat to law and order that failure to make timely concessions could

---

[40] See 'Singapore' memorandum by the Colonial Secretary for the Cabinet, CP(56)97, 14 April 1956, CAB 129/80, reproduced in Goldsworthy (ed.), *The Conservative Government and the End of Empire 1951–1957, Part II*, 396–402.

[41] Singapore developments are covered at first hand and in revealing fashion by Lee Kuan Yew, *The Singapore Story* (Singapore, 1998), 224 and *passim*.

provoke, British ministers were not prepared to prejudice their free use of the colony's base facilities in the constitutional talks of 1956–7. Yet they had gone far in meeting the needs of the new group of Singapore politicians that had appeared in the mid-1950s. Such movement had been made easier by the fact that leaders such as Lim Yew Hock, and the dynamic young head of the rising PAP, Lee Kuan Yew, were committed anti-Communists aware of the dangers that a more radical switch to Chinese chauvinism could entail. They also, in common with much local political opinion, shared the British view that separate independence for Singapore was not a viable proposition, and that the key to ensuring the territory's future political stability and economic prosperity lay in a merger with Malaya.[42] Since the Second World War, British officials in the region (with Malcolm MacDonald probably the most prominent) had promoted the idea of merger in a low-key manner. During the discussions over Singapore's future in 1956 it had come to the fore as a key prerequisite before London would agree to give up sovereignty over the island. In March of that year, Lennox-Boyd was arguing: ' "Independence" for Singapore is a delusion. A trading centre and port, however important, at the mercy of world economics, with a large population and no natural resources, could have no viable place as a full member of the Commonwealth or as a State on its own.'[43]

The immediate problem for any scheme of merger, however, was adamant Malayan opposition. Viewed from Kuala Lumpur, Singapore seemed plagued by strikes, riots and radicalism, while Malay (and UMNO) political dominance of the Federation could be threatened if it were enlarged to incorporate Singapore's predominantly Chinese population.[44] The everleftward drift of Singapore politics was indicated by the results of the May 1959 Legislative Assembly elections, which saw Lee Kuan Yew's PAP winning 43 of the 51 available seats. Whereas the British greeted Lee's victory and the formation of a PAP government with some equanimity, and quickly saw that the new Prime Minister was determined to tackle Communist subversion, the authorities in Kuala Lumpur were

---

[42] See Mohamed Noordin Sopiee, *From Malayan Union to Singapore Separation: Political Unification in the Malaysia Region, 1945–65* (Kuala Lumpur, 1974), 125 and *passim*.

[43] See Colonial Office (CO) minute on closer association between the Federation of Malaya and Singapore, 10 December 1952, CO 1022/86, reproduced in Goldsworthy, *The Conservative Government and the End of Empire, Part II*, 376–7, and 'Singapore' memorandum by the Colonial Secretary for the Cabinet, CP(56)85, 23 March 1956, CAB 129/80, *ibid.*, 393. See also Brook memorandum for Eden, 19 April 1956, PREM 11/1802.

[44] Of Malaya's population of almost 7 million, about 3.4 million could be classed as Malays, about 800,000 as Indian, and over 2.5 million as Chinese, while there were approximately 1.2 million Singapore Chinese; figures are for December 1959 and derived from undated (but c. 26 June 1961) memorandum SR(050)304, PREM 11/3418.

less convinced.[45] Not only did they distrust the PAP's brand of pragmatic socialism, but they recognized that the PAP harboured many disparate elements, and that while its current leadership was moderate in character, its trade union wing was riddled with Communist sympathizers. Malayan leaders, and Tunku Abdul Rahman in particular, doubted that Lee would ultimately stand up to the radicals in his own party. The fragility of the PAP was indeed underlined during 1960, as Lee's domestic policies, particularly in the housing and employment fields, proved none too successful; a harbinger of problems to come was the expulsion from the party in June of Ong Eng Guan along with two other PAP members of the Assembly.[46] There were increasing signs that many in the PAP were unhappy with the leadership's lack of militancy and their unwillingness to press for full independence. To the Malayan Government these were alarming signs. The last thing they wanted to see was an independent, vulnerable and potentially Communist and Chinese-aligned Singapore on the Federation's door-step, and they looked to the British to step in to take the necessary repressive internal security measures to prevent any such eventuality.

On the part of the British there was widespread recognition that further pressures for change were unlikely to relent, especially when the new constitutional arrangements came up for scheduled review (set for 1963). This was coupled with an awareness that repressive action, though still perhaps needed as a last resort and if access to the base facilities were jeopardized, was becoming increasingly difficult to justify in the highly charged anti-colonial atmosphere of the late 1950s. In the spring and summer of 1959, the Macmillan Government had passed through the dual crises in colonial policy of the Hola Camp massacre, where in Kenya several detainees were beaten to death, and the highly critical Devlin Report on the state of emergency that had been declared in Nyasaland.[47] At the same time, the British were in the process of resolving through international agreement one of their most intractable colonial problems of the period, the controversial and bitter guerrilla war waged on Cyprus

---

[45] See the very favourable comments on the new PAP Government by the outgoing Governor, where ministers are described as 'obsessed by the threat of Communism'; Singapore to CO, no. 7, 26 June 1959, PREM 11/2659. In 1963, the Commissioner General would tell the Prime Minister: 'The important thing to remember about [Lee Kuan Yew] is, for all his twists of character and inhibitions, that he has basically absorbed the British framework of thinking through his education at Cambridge', Selkirk to Macmillan, 3 September 1963, PREM 11/4146.

[46] Sopiee, *Malayan Union to Singapore Separation*, 119–23; Lee Kuan Yew, *Singapore Story*, 351–2.

[47] For a brief summary see Alistair Horne, *Macmillan, 1957–1986* (London, 1989), 174–82. The Colonial Secretary had offered to resign over both matters.

since 1955 by elements of the Greek majority population aiming to secure union with the mainland (with London generally unwilling to make
concessions that could jeopardize the future use of their military bases
on the island). The government had no wish to incur more international
and domestic opprobrium through a further crackdown in Singapore. A
brief prepared for the Commonwealth Secretary in November 1960 explained such dilemmas when it highlighted the Malayan Prime Minister's
resistance to merger:

The Tunku's mind seems to be closed to any reasoned argument on the subject as
if he felt that Singapore could remain perpetually isolated from Malaya as a British
colony. In fact time is not on our side. If discouragement from the Federation
continues, the pressure towards an independent Singapore will be strengthened
and Mr Lee Kuan Yew will either have to give way or be overthrown. The result to
be feared would be the emergence of a more Left-wing Government and probably
an outbreak of violence. Faced with a 'Cyprus situation' the United Kingdom
Government would have difficult decisions to make on whether it should hold on
to the base by repression or leave the island. This sort of situation would help the
Malayans least of all.[48]

Some officials were even coming to believe that the only long-term answer
to the problem of Singapore's future lay with a drastic scaling-back of
the British military presence in South East Asia, obviating the need to
maintain the base in its present form.

In April 1956, Sir Robert Scott had put forward the notion to the
Prime Minister, Anthony Eden, that 'the main British contribution to
the maintenance of Commonwealth and Free World interests in South
East and Eastern Asia should take the form of a vigorous peace-time and
cold war policy rather than concentrations of forces'. The Commissioner
General doubted that extensive depots and bases, 'the cost of which in
peacetime cripples our policy in other fields', were an efficient deployment
of resources, particularly as they were 'at the mercy of local political crises
and labour agitators and are liable to be denied to us by the turn of the
electoral wheel'.[49] An emphasis on economic development and technical assistance rather than the maintenance of expensive bases and large
military forces was certainly welcome to those in Whitehall anxious to
relieve the pressures on the economy that spending on external policy,
particularly in the defence field, was imposing by the mid-1950s. In May
1956, Macmillan, then the Chancellor of the Exchequer, had registered
his mounting concern with Eden: 'I must tell you how anxious I am
about the state of the economy. We are like a man in the early stages of
consumption, flushed cheek and apparent health concealing the disease.

[48] Brief for Commonwealth Secretary, 14 November 1960, D1061/14, FO 371/152145.
[49] Scott to Eden, 15 April 1956, PREM 11/1778.

I do not think we can stand what is being put upon us much longer.'[50] Eden was fully conversant with such problems, and the major policy review he launched in the summer of 1956 had at its heart the need to cut military expenditure. When it came to the Far East, officials of the Foreign Office, Ministry of Defence and Treasury echoed Scott's earlier comments, by concluding that, as the Chinese threat was primarily political rather than overtly military, Britain should 'concentrate our available resources on a more vigorous and effective peacetime policy rather than on preparation for war'. It was recommended that studies should be initiated on the reduction of forces in Malaya and Singapore and whether large bases could continue to be held in places where the political future was so uncertain.[51]

Such proposals almost always faced objections, however, from those who argued that Britain must demonstrate its clear intention to uphold its responsibilities in South East Asia, while any attempt to construct alternative base facilities at new and less vulnerable locations in northern Australia ran into the prohibitive initial costs that would be involved. Moreover, the Commonwealth Relations Office (CRO), which after August 1957 also handled relations with Malaya, was anxious to stifle any open planning of a retreat from the forward defence of the area, not least for fear of exciting the ever-present suspicions of the Australians and New Zealanders (with memories still fresh of the events of 1941–2) that Britain was intending a full-scale withdrawal from east of Suez.[52] The Foreign Office, for their part, pointed to the effect on Anglo-American relations of any reduction in the British defence effort, as Washington looked on security in the Malaya/Singapore area as primarily a Commonwealth responsibility. The difficulties of thinking through this kind of policy shift were exacerbated by the problems of departmental coordination within Whitehall when it came to South East Asian issues, where overlapping jurisdictions in the colonial, Commonwealth relations, defence and foreign policy fields inhibited long-term planning.[53]

The emphasis among British military chiefs and defence planners remained on Singapore as the hub of Britain's continuing presence well into the foreseeable future. To some, indeed, the existence of a defence system in the Far East created a rationale for its own preservation, becoming an interest in itself, despite the growing realization that within the

---

[50] Macmillan minute for Eden, 1 May 1956, *ibid.*
[51] 'The future of the United Kingdom in world affairs', PR(56)3, 1 June 1956, CAB 134/1315, reproduced in David Goldsworthy (ed.), *The Conservative Government and the End of Empire, 1951–1957, Part I: International Relations* (London, 1994), 72.
[52] See e.g. Carrington to Scott, 9 December 1958, FO 1091/91.
[53] A point raised by Darby, *British Defence Policy East of Suez*, 135–9. See also official discussions of these problems in late 1958, ZP18/2G, FO 371/135632.

space of a few years the British position might be impossible to sustain. In early 1959, Scott reported that at the annual Eden Hall conference in Singapore, where Britain's military, diplomatic and colonial officials gathered to discuss common issues, there had been the usual 'stress on the key importance of Singapore as the main base on which Britain must for the next decade at least rely for naval, military or air operations east of Suez and in the Pacific area, and as a Chinese city open to Chinese and communist subversion because of its racial composition and looming unemployment problem'.[54] The following year, Scott's successor as Commissioner General, Lord Selkirk, again expressed to the Prime Minister the worries of British officials in the region over the implications of the grant of full self-government to the colony, 'not so much for what is happening now, but for the belief that our position in Singapore would be untenable at a time of tension between the West and Communist China, and that, in due course, the British would "scuttle again" '. Macmillan did his best to defend the Government's Singapore policy, arguing that the present arrangements meant that it was

less likely that we shall have to decide soon whether to stay or go. If we had not given internal self-government we should by now have a Cyprus situation in Singapore with the Chinese playing the role of the Greeks. As it is, we at least have a Government in Singapore which is not pro-China. That Government is conducting our battle for us and although it may lose, we shall at least have gained time. The real difficulty is how to help the Singapore Government without appearing to do so.[55]

Nevertheless, it was becoming increasingly evident to many observers that the mere fact of the presence of the base facilities was an anachronistic liability that provided a focus for indigenous resentment and Communist exploitation of inflamed local feeling. By July 1960, Selkirk was telling the Prime Minister that 'colonial' was such a hated word in South East Asia it should be removed from any office dealing with Singapore, and that Whitehall responsibility for the colony should be even transferred to the CRO. Moreover, he asserted that most defence planning for the area was essentially flawed, based as it was on the supposition that current base rights in Singapore could be maintained for at least another ten years; Selkirk felt that holding on for another three years would be difficult enough.[56]

Also fundamental to the problems of a major reorientation in British policy in the late 1950s was the SEATO obligation to provide for collective

[54] Scott to Macmillan, 18 January 1959, and see R. P. Heppel minute for Foreign Office dissent, 23 March 1959 (original at D1051/9), PREM 11/3276.
[55] Selkirk to Macmillan, 17 February 1960; Macmillan to Selkirk, 17 March 1960, *ibid.*
[56] Selkirk to Macmillan, 22 July 1960, PREM 11/3737.

defence in the area. During his bitter resignation speech to the Singapore Legislative Assembly in June 1956, Marshall had accused the British government of making the colony 'a live offering to their god of brass, SEATO'.[57] Preserving the Singapore base was essential if British forces (and voices) were to be involved in the organization's defence planning, which had become focussed on responding to a direct Communist attack from the north against Cambodia, Laos or South Vietnam (included in the SEATO area by an attached protocol to the Manila Treaty).[58]

It was the situation in Laos that caused most concern to British policy-makers, as civil insurgency and conflict threatened to draw in the great powers to what by 1959–60 was the principal battleground of the Cold War in South East Asia. Ever since the bruising experiences of 1954, the Eisenhower Administration had been alarmed at the unwillingness of its British ally to show sufficient nerve in confronting what it saw as examples of Communist aggression. In March 1955, Eisenhower had complained to Churchill:

> Although we seem always to see eye to eye with you when we contemplate any European problem our respective attitudes towards similar problems in the Orient are frequently so dissimilar as to be almost mutually antagonistic... The conclusion seems inescapable that these differences come about because we do not agree on the probable extent and the importance of further Communist expansion in Asia. In our contacts with New Zealand and Australia, we have the feeling that we encounter a concern no less acute than ours; but your own government seems to regard Communist aggression in Asia as of little significance to the free world future.[59]

Following the Geneva Conference, and convinced that further losses to the Communist 'bloc' of the countries of mainland South East Asia would precipitate a wholesale rout, with country after country succumbing like so many falling dominoes, the Eisenhower Administration had quickly moved to replace the French as the main prop of the South Vietnamese Government in Saigon. By 1959 the Americans were supporting the anti-Communist regime of President Ngo Dinh Diem to the tune of $250 million a year in economic and military aid, as well as providing several hundred military advisers for the army. But while Diem's repressive rule showed at least some signs of stabilizing the situation in South Vietnam in this period, and the 17th parallel offered a notional 'border'

---

[57] Quoted in Darby, *British Defence Policy East of Suez*, 88.

[58] Article IV of the South East Asia Collective Defence Treaty provided for members to 'act to meet the danger' posed by 'aggression by means of armed attack'. This carefully worded document also included a special clause which limited US action under Article IV to instances of Communist aggression only, see Wilfrid Knapp, *A History of War and Peace, 1939–1965* (Oxford, 1967), 255–6.

[59] Eisenhower to Churchill, 29 March 1955, PREM 11/1310.

that might be defended from an overt attack from the north, the situation in neighbouring Laos was far more ambiguous.

The Americans had never been happy with the provisions of the Geneva agreements that assigned Laos a flimsy neutrality and allowed the Communist Pathet Lao, with backing from North Vietnam, to continue to play a significant role in national political life. By the end of 1955, Washington had begun to channel discreet aid to the Royal Laotian Army, and soon set about frustrating attempts to form a coalition government of national unity in Vientiane while making efforts to direct Laos firmly into the Western camp.[60] A real turning point, however, and one that was to have a major effect on the politics of the whole region, was the military coup in Thailand in October 1958 that consolidated the hold on power of Marshal Sarit Thanarat.[61] Colluding closely with the United States (or more accurately with the local CIA, and US military officers attached to the Defense Department's advisory missions), the Thais stepped up their involvement in Laos, as right-wing forces within the army were built up. In the summer of 1959, the Pathet Lao began guerrilla action to tighten their grip over the two northern provinces of the country, and the Americans, in turn, responded with more covert intervention and began to consider the possibility of joint action by SEATO to head off further gains by the Pathet Lao on the grounds that North Vietnamese involvement with their operations was a clear example of externally directed aggression.[62] Although by late 1959 the situation in Laos had stabilized, an even more serious crisis flared up towards the end of 1960, as a US-backed right-wing government took power in Vientiane and proceeded to advance north against the Communist strongholds. In early 1961, a successful Pathet Lao counter-offensive, with help from the North Vietnamese and some supplies from the Soviet Union, brought to a head calls from the Thais, and from factions within the American government, for Western intervention to prevent a complete collapse in Laos.

British thinking on Laos, as in the Indochina crisis of 1954, was dominated by concerns that Western intervention would trigger an even more forceful Communist response, possibly involving the introduction of Chinese 'volunteers' in a rerun of the scenario that had occurred in the Korean War. In such circumstances, the use of nuclear weapons against

---

[60] See R. B. Smith, *An International History of the Vietnam War, vol. I: Revolution versus Containment, 1955–1961* (London, 1983), 36–49 and *passim*.

[61] A point Smith emphasizes, see *ibid.*, 163.

[62] The development of the Laotian crisis can be followed in Roger Hilsman, *To Move A Nation: The Politics of Foreign Policy in the Administration of John F. Kennedy* (New York, 1967), 92–130. For the British side see material in PREM 11/2657–8, 2961, while the American documentary record (though somewhat sanitized) is in *FRUS, 1958–1960, vol. XVI, East Asia–Pacific Region; Cambodia; Laos* (Washington, 1992).

Chinese targets would again appear as an attractive option to many on the American side, with consequences that few could foresee.[63] The British emphasis, in the dying days of the Eisenhower Administration, was to continue to search for a political solution to the fighting in Laos that would involve a return to the concept of Laotian neutrality and the formation of a coalition government of national unity. But a reconvening of the Geneva Conference as favoured by the British, where the great powers, including the Soviet Union, could underwrite a new Laotian settlement, was not at this stage acceptable in Washington, and there was much irritation within the Eisenhower Administration at British reluctance to react forcefully to the prospect of a Communist takeover. By early 1961, the differences over how to respond to the deteriorating situation in Laos had raised fears, as one official in the Washington Embassy put it, that South East Asia 'should become a festering sore in Anglo-American relations'.[64] For his part, Lord Selkirk felt, 'Whatever special relationship we may have in the Atlantic, I very much doubt whether any really exists in this part of the world.' Among some British officials in the region there was talk of adopting a more independent approach:

This might lead to our assuming the position of a third force between the Americans and the Communists. I do not think this dangerous line has as yet taken a clear form because we are all very conscious how much the position in South East Asia depends on the [US] Seventh Fleet. But these ideas are latent in a good many people's minds and there is a growing barrier between our Missions and the United States.

The Prime Minister was inclined to agree with Selkirk's analysis, noting, 'The success of their "brinkmanship" policy over the offshore islands led the Eisenhower Administration to believe that they could adopt this policy throughout South East Asia', but Macmillan expressed confidence that under the new Kennedy Administration, which assumed office on 20 January 1961, it would be 'easier to re-establish good and frank relations'.[65]

Macmillan's belief that Kennedy's arrival in the White House signalled a change in American policy over Laos was borne out by the actions and policies of the US Administration in its first few months. The President

---

[63] See memorandum for the Cabinet by the Foreign Secretary, where Lord Home reported that if North Vietnamese and Chinese troops intervened in any numbers the COS estimate was that 'the best we could hope for would be a stalemate and there would be every likelihood of defeat without using nuclear tactical weapons [sic]', 'Situation in Laos', C(61)4, 6 January 1961, CAB 129/104.

[64] Ledward to Warner, 15 March 1961, and see also Caccia to Hoyer Millar, 2 February 1961, D103145/3, FO 371/159712.

[65] Selkirk to Macmillan, 23 January 1961; de Zulueta minute for Macmillan, 26 January 1961; Macmillan to Selkirk (draft), 22 March 1961, the final version of this letter was sent on 23 March, and omitted the line about 'brinkmanship', PREM 11/3276.

was always highly dubious about the emphasis placed by some of his advisers on the strategic importance of Laos, and was notably sceptical over the plans for large-scale intervention put forward by the JCS.[66] After the Bay of Pigs debacle in April 1961, he was even more confirmed in his inclination not to be rushed into precipitate action. Kennedy's preference, as he indicated quite clearly at his famous televized press conference of 23 March, was for a neutral and independent Laos; this was a departure from the American policies of 1958–60 that was greeted with evident relief in London. Macmillan's cautious optimism over the new Administration was vindicated by his first encounters with Kennedy at Key West in Florida on 26 March 1961, where he had been summoned by the President at short notice specifically to discuss Laos.

Here Kennedy confirmed that 'the United States had recently changed their policy with regard to Laos. They now considered that they had been mistaken in the past in trying to encourage a state that would be of military support to them. They now thought that it was right to go for a genuinely neutral country.' Nevertheless, a cease-fire was still required in order to prevent an outright Pathet Lao victory and before any international conference to discuss the future of Laos could be held. In the meantime, the United States had to consider the final option of a military intervention, though the President made clear he envisaged this as a common SEATO effort, and action would have to be of a limited nature as it had now been accepted, 'unlike the previous Administration, that they would not get any military success in that area'. Realizing the pressure that Kennedy was under from the JCS and the legacy of Eisenhower's approach, Macmillan was ready to offer full moral and diplomatic support if the United States had to go into Laos at the request of SEATO, but advised that the action should be justified to the UN first, while he would have to secure Cabinet approval for the commitment of any British forces: '... whatever happened there must not appear to be a war between Europeans and Asiatics'.[67] The reluctance of Kennedy to sanction a unilateral American intervention was obvious throughout, as was the Prime Minister's evident desire to pursue every diplomatic route to a settlement before SEATO obligations were invoked. Accordingly, the British made concerted efforts to enlist Russian help in securing a Laotian cease-fire throughout April, and the following month it proved possible

[66] See e.g., Kennedy's questioning of the JCS at his conference of 9 March 1961, *FRUS, 1961–1963, vol. XXIV, Laos Crisis* (Washington, 1994), 72–9; a general account is provided by Arthur M. Schlesinger Jr, *A Thousand Days: John F. Kennedy in the White House* (London, 1965), 299–303.

[67] See 'Record of discussion at US naval base at Key West, Florida, 26 March 1961', PREM 11/3313. This is apparently the account that has been withheld from *FRUS, 1961–1963, XXIV*, 103. See also Harold Macmillan, *Pointing the Way, 1959–1961* (London, 1972), 335–8.

for representatives to gather at Geneva for a full-scale international conference on Laos. Subsequent negotiations were tortuous, and dragged on into 1962, but from a British point of view it was better to be talking than fighting as the Dulles-era voices in Washington calling for military intervention were steadily muted.

At the same time as the crisis situation in Laos began to ease, the British moved to demonstrate their full support for the Kennedy Administration's efforts to counter the rapidly developing Communist insurgency in South Vietnam. Indeed, it was widely recognized that the more aggressive noises now coming from Washington regarding Vietnam were necessary to fend off the Administration's critics over the neutralization solution that was being sought in Laos, while, as the British Ambassador in Washington and Selkirk described it, a 'Maginot Line' concept of containment in South East Asia still persisted.[68] The practical side of British support for US policy was the formation and despatch to Saigon in the summer of 1961 of a British Advisory Mission under Sir Robert Thompson, which was to lend the combined experience of its four civilian members in the counter-insurgency field, derived primarily from Malaya, to the Diem Government.[69] The arrival of Averell Harriman in the key post of Assistant Secretary for Far Eastern Affairs at the State Department in November 1961 (examined in the next chapter) was also welcomed at the Foreign Office. The head of the South East Asia Department, Fred Warner, was pleased, 'firstly because [Harriman] takes a broad and reasonable view of how much it is possible to achieve in the Far East without recourse to atom bombs, and secondly because when he embraces a policy he sticks to it and does not shift from one policy to another the whole time as so many well-intentioned Americans seem to do'.[70] By December 1961, Warner could reflect that relations with the Americans were 'immeasurably better' than when last surveyed earlier in the year: 'This is chiefly because the Americans have moved very close to our policy on Laos, and we have tried as hard as we can to move close to theirs on Vietnam.'[71]

[68] See Washington to FO, no. 100, 24 May 1961, D103145/11, FO 371/159712.
[69] The initiative for the use of Thompson in South Vietnam had, in fact, come from the Malayan Government, see Sandys to Lloyd, 25 July 1961, PREM 11/3736; see Ian F. W. Beckett, 'Robert Thompson and the British Advisory Mission to South Vietnam, 1961–1965', Small Wars and Insurgencies, 8, 3, 1997. The British Ambassador noted how British moves to lend assistance in South Vietnam had been warmly welcomed in the White House and State Department, and helped to offset Pentagon criticism over Laos, Washington to FO, no. 132, 10 July 1961, D103145/11, FO 371/159712.
[70] Warner to Ledward, 30 November 1961, D103145/25, FO 371/159713.
[71] Warner minute, 13 December 1961, D103145/27, ibid. Though here one should note that Selkirk remained sceptical that there had been any real improvement, particularly bearing in mind underlying differences over China policy, see Selkirk to Home, 21 December 1961, D103145/30, ibid.

The possibility that Britain might have either become embroiled in a dangerous conflict over Laos through its membership of SEATO, or taken a course that could have led to opposition to American intervention and an open breach in Anglo-American relations, helped to influence some of the debates then taking place between senior British policymakers over their whole posture in the Far East. Selkirk had written to the Prime Minister in May 1961, confessing that he had 'come to wonder whether SEATO's irritation to places like India is a greater disadvantage than the benefits attained by the existence of the organization as an anticommunist club'. By August he was complaining that

> in this area we are still finding it difficult to get away from the traditions of our past and in particular from what other people expect of us . . . we are stretched to a point where we might snap under the strain, and indeed our present position would be perilous were it not for our basic dependence on the USA. This fact does not seem to be adequately recognised. It is the more regrettable that we have not been able to achieve the close understanding and pooling of ideas with the Americans over China and the Pacific which we have in a fair measure succeeded in attaining across the Atlantic.

Pointing out that Malaya and Singapore could no longer be considered secure bases for military operations, and that Britain's ability to act depended on the 'consent and acquiescence' of the local populations there, Selkirk went on to state flatly:

> Whether we like it or not we have to recognise that China, both militarily and ideologically, is becoming increasingly the dominant force throughout South East Asia. The only long-term effective answer to Communist China is nationalism, coupled with a recognition by each State that it has an obligation to defend its own territory. I was glad to note recently that this idea seems to be more readily recognised in Washington than it was. We must clearly do everything we can to promote nationalism as a counter to communism and avoid policies (especially with an imperialistic flavour) which may lead nationalists and communists to join forces against us.

The problem was that SEATO was so closely bound up with Western rather than local interests, it was proving counter-productive to such goals, as Malayan reactions to the organization tended to show. The only solution Selkirk could see was for Britain to undertake a 'gradual redefinition of our position in SEATO which, while identifying us more closely with the defence of Malaya, would make fewer demands on us for other forms of support'. The long-term attraction of this course would be a reduction of the defence burden in the Far East. Moreover, Selkirk put forward his ideas regarding SEATO in the context of the plans that were then moving ahead for a 'Greater Malaysia', a merger of Malaya and Singapore that would also draw into a new independent federation Britain's remaining colonial outposts of Sarawak, North Borneo and Brunei.[72]

That the Prime Minister was attracted to such a readjustment of policy, involving embracing the notion of a Greater Malaysia, which would allow Britain to relinquish many of its remaining colonial responsibilities in South East Asia, and reducing the level of commitment to SEATO operations, was shown by his contributions to the ministerial deliberations over future policy that took place in the autumn of 1961. In June 1961, the Chancellor of the Exchequer, Selwyn Lloyd, had called for major cuts in spending to keep overseas defence expenditure within a £200 million ceiling, and the Future Policy Committee convened to consider the matter identified the internal security burden in Singapore as an area where savings might be made through the withdrawal of major units.[73] In September, Macmillan produced his own paper on future overseas policy, where he argued that any review of commitments in South East Asia should be 'radical and imaginative'. Support for the concept of a Greater Malaysia was seen as the best course to follow, but this raised the question of the future use of the Singapore base for SEATO purposes, and whether the UK should make any land contribution to SEATO at all.[74] Subsequent discussion by the Cabinet's committee on Future Policy revealed that after the formation of Greater Malaysia, Singapore would have to be considered a so-called 'Class II' base, where freedom of action was subject to local susceptibilities. Under such new conditions, there was a need to consider whether the Commonwealth Brigade Group in Malaya (earmarked for SEATO operations in Thailand and Laos) should not be relocated, possibly to a new base in Australia.[75]

Such ideas were only tentative, and in the Prime Minister's formal reply to Selkirk's wide-ranging proposals he chose to emphasize that although 'the need to readjust our policy is clear in the light of our reduced resources, ... as you yourself say, any solution to the problems of the area can only come about gradually'. Moreover, relations with Australia and New Zealand would need to be considered as 'we must not give them any cause to blame us for leaving them precipitately in the lurch'.[76] Nevertheless, it is clear that by the summer of 1961, as Anglo-American relations in South East Asia were restored by the new degree of understanding over Laos and the Geneva Conference process, Macmillan and other senior

[72] Selkirk to Macmillan, 14 August 1961, PREM 11/3737.
[73] See CC(61) 32nd mtg, 16 June 1961, CAB 128/35; FP(A)(61), 1st mtg, 24 July 1961, CAB 134/1932.
[74] 'Our Foreign and Defence Policy for the Future', memorandum by Macmillan, 29 September 1961, CAB 134/1929.
[75] FP(61) 1st mtg, 6 October 1961, *ibid.*
[76] Macmillan to Selkirk, 17 October 1961, PREM 11/3737.

ministers were considering a scaling-back of British responsibilities in the region.[77] A settlement in Laos would allow the British to rethink their future role within SEATO, and perhaps to withdraw somewhat from its military aspects. As a counterpart to this, developments within Singapore and Malaya made it possible to push forward long-held British desires to form a Greater Malaysia that would wrap up their formal colonial empire in South East Asia and provide a stable and secure federation friendly with the West and a welcome home for British investments and influence.

This 'Grand Design' for the Far East overlooked, however, the significant local impact such a reordering of states and peoples would necessarily produce. In particular, it was to generate opposition from an Indonesia afflicted by chronic domestic political instability and sensitive to signs that the Western powers were again meddling in regional affairs. Alienating Sukarno's Indonesia also brought British policy into increasing conflict with the new approaches that the Kennedy Administration sought to pursue in its relations with the non-aligned world, and threw fresh elements of doubt and uncertainty into the Far Eastern scene as the conflict in Vietnam gathered pace. It is appropriate, then, that our examination of the immediate origins of confrontation should begin by turning to the chequered history of US relations with Indonesia in the late 1950s and early 1960s.

[77] Some of these defence issues have recently been lucidly analysed by David Easter, 'British Defence Policy in South East Asia and the Confrontation, 1960–66,' unpublished PhD thesis, London School of Economics and Political Science, 1998, see especially 32–44.

Part I

Build-up

1   The Kennedy Administration, Indonesia and the resolution of the West Irian crisis, 1961–1962

Improving the state of relations with Jakarta occupied an important place in the foreign policy agenda of the Kennedy Administration. Indonesia's size, possession of natural resources, including oil, rubber and tin, strategic location astride lines of communication in the south west Pacific, and the fact that it was home to a significant level of US commercial investment, meant that in the late 1950s and early 1960s the state was often seen as a key prize in the Cold War competition for influence in the non-aligned world. The evident interest that the Soviet Union, under Khrushchev's energetic new leadership, exhibited during this period in cultivating ties with Jakarta, necessarily seemed to enhance Indonesia's importance to American eyes. Sukarno's visit to Moscow in September 1956 was accompanied by the extension of a $100 million long-term credit, while in early 1958 an arms deal totalling $250 million was negotiated, with Poland and Czechoslovakia acting as Soviet intermediaries. President K. I. Voroshilov's state visit to Jakarta in May 1957 had been followed up, even more significantly, by a ten-day tour of Indonesia by Khrushchev in February 1960.[1] When put alongside other initiatives in Russian policy during this period, many American observers came to the conclusion that a Soviet economic offensive was under way in the Third World, with Indonesia one of the prime targets.

Trends within Indonesia's own complex polity did little to reassure the Americans that external Communist influence would not find a welcome audience. The PKI had managed to further boost its domestic standing by its support for the central government during the Outer Island rebellion of 1958, while it was prepared to back Sukarno's own attempts to dismantle the Western-style parliamentary system that seemed such a

---

[1] See Steven I. Levine, 'Breakthrough to the East: Soviet Asian Policy in the 1950s', in Warren I. Cohen and Akira Iriye (eds.), *The Great Powers in East Asia, 1953–1960* (New York, 1990), 304; Justus M. van der Kroef, 'Soviet and Chinese Influence in Indonesia', in Alvin Z. Rubinstein (ed.), *Soviet and Chinese Influence in the Third World* (London, 1975), 54–5.

divisive source of Indonesia's problems. Indeed, as Sukarno moved more decisively in 1959 to implement his vision of 'Guided Democracy', by returning to the 1945 Constitution which gave him greatly increased executive powers and by acting as the overall arbitrator between the competing forces in Indonesian society, he also recognized that the PKI served as a useful and necessary counterweight to the potentially dominating influence of the Army.[2]

By the late 1950s, Washington's approach to Indonesia was marked by ambiguity and uncertainty. The Eisenhower Administration's efforts to undermine Sukarno's regime in 1958 through support for the Outer Island rebels was a constant background influence throughout the period, serving to sow suspicions in Indonesian minds of ultimate American intentions (it is worth noting in this regard that some American policy-makers continued into 1959 to toy with the notion of reviving covert backing for the remnants of the PRRI, while dissident groups were still at large as late as 1961). Although, as we have seen, the Eisenhower Administration had turned to providing limited amounts of military assistance to the Indonesian armed forces in the wake of the rebellion's failure, and in an effort to encourage anti-Communist feeling within the higher echelons of the Army, Jakarta still bridled at the inadequacies of American policy. Compared to the aid now coming from the Communist bloc, the military equipment offered by the Americans seemed meagre. Moreover, in the wider realm of American public opinion, Sukarno enjoyed a generally low reputation in the media due to the increasingly personalized nature of his rule, his good relations with the PKI, and what were seen as his dubious personal morals.[3] From his own point of view, Sukarno felt personally slighted that Eisenhower omitted Indonesia from his itinerary when visiting Asia both at the end of 1959 and in June 1960 (and this following repeated invitations and the premium the Indonesian President was known to place on personal forms of diplomacy).[4] However, of overriding importance in the relationship was the fact that the United States could provide no assistance in persuading the Dutch to relinquish their hold over West Irian. The issue of recovering West Irian had become the central preoccupation of Indonesia's foreign policy by the late 1950s, and an emotive symbol of patriotic sentiment on the internal

---

[2] See Legge, *Sukarno*, 301–16.

[3] Dulles, for one, could never quite seem to overcome his distaste for the Indonesian President's fondness for a variety of female company, see e.g. Kahin and Kahin, *Subversion*, 77.

[4] See Jakarta to Department of State (DOS), 18 November 1959, *FRUS, 1958–1960, XVII*, 450–51.

political scene. Sukarno maintained that the Indonesian revolution was incomplete while West Irian remained in alien hands, and the belligerence of the rhetoric surrounding Jakarta's demands steadily increased in line with Dutch intransigence; meanwhile, the new supplies of arms from the Communist bloc, including advanced jet aircraft and naval vessels, also opened up the prospect that force might eventually be used to resolve the claim.[5]

The dispute over West Irian raised some awkward dilemmas for the United States. As early as October 1952, Dean Acheson had made clear that Washington was not going to become involved with the argument, and this position of 'neutrality' was maintained under Eisenhower. The relationship with the Netherlands and the need to preserve solidarity within NATO was accorded a high priority, and certainly Dulles, for all the distractions of crises in the Middle and Far East during his tenure as Secretary of State, viewed European considerations as fundamental.[6] With the reputation and weight of the State Department's Bureau of Far Eastern Affairs relatively weak in this period, and continual Dutch pressure for some clear indication of US support in the event of an Indonesian use of force (accompanied by powerful backing from the Australians for a firm stand, who feared for their own position in Papua New Guinea), it was unlikely that the Administration would become a convert to Indonesian arguments. Washington's preferred position of non-involvement was, nonetheless, inherently problematic, as Jakarta saw commitment to the status quo as, in effect, support for the Dutch position. Moreover, the military assistance now being offered to Indonesia was deeply disturbing to both Dutch and Australian officials, who could only greet with scepticism Indonesian assurances that the arms they received from Western sources would not be used for aggressive purposes. Hence Dulles, and his successor from April 1959, Christian Herter, were not prepared to sanction an expanded programme of arms sales beyond those items deemed necessary for internal security, or to make a long-term commitment to the Indonesian military.[7]

For US officials in both the Far East Bureau of the State Department and the Pentagon concerned to improve relations with Indonesia, and for the US Ambassador in Jakarta, Howard P. Jones, Washington's refusal to move on the West Irian issue was intensely frustrating. Convinced

[5] Legge, *Sukarno*, 248–50, 291–2.
[6] See e.g. Richard H. Immerman (ed.), *The Diplomacy of John Foster Dulles* (Princeton, 1990), 43, 79–80, 235, 279–80.
[7] See e.g. Frederick P. Bunnell, 'The Kennedy Initiatives in Indonesia, 1962–1963', unpublished PhD thesis, Cornell University, 1969, 61–3.

that the Dutch would inevitably have to leave the territory, Jones argued:

Colonialism is finished and the longer we continue [to] support small western enclaves in Asia the longer we delay winning Asians to our cause, the more we intensify [the] danger of major explosion over minor issue. Even if it be argued that transfer [of] West Irian to Indonesia is to substitute Asian for western colonialism, [the] fact is that it is combination of white west over colored east that Asians are fighting, rather than imperialism or colonialism per se.[8]

Despite such advice, neutrality was maintained as Dutch–Indonesian tensions climbed throughout 1960, with Jakarta breaking off diplomatic relations with The Hague in August, while private affirmations were somewhat grudgingly repeated to the Dutch that US political and logistical support would be provided in the event of an Indonesian attack.[9] Faced with their continuing refusal to back Indonesia's claim to the territory, Sukarno would pointedly remark that the US was 'like [a] tight rope walker trying to balance its support of [the] West in Europe with support [of the] Asian nations in the East'.[10] In contrast to the United States, the Soviet Union could offer the Indonesians unreserved diplomatic and propaganda support over West Irian, as well as generous supplies of military aid, while adding to their anti-imperialist credibility in the developing world. At the end of December 1960, in the final few weeks of the Eisenhower Administration, the NSC met to discuss and approve a new draft statement on policy towards Indonesia. This paper, NSC 6023, held that 'domestic instability, burgeoning Sino-Soviet Bloc economic and military aid, and substantial local Communist strength may lead to a Communist takeover or to a policy increasingly friendly towards the Sino-Soviet Bloc on the part of whatever regime is in power'. There would need to be a 'vigorous US effort to prevent these contingencies'. Yet there was no recommendation to shift away from neutrality over West Irian, despite the admission: 'Not to support Indonesia on this issue is to leave this key gambit to the Communist Bloc.'[11]

The clearest sign that the Soviet Union was moving to bolster its position with Jakarta came at the very time when the newly elected President Kennedy was about to enter office. In early January 1961, General Nasution, the Indonesian Minister of Defence and Army Chief of Staff, along with Dr Subandrio, the Foreign Minister, visited Moscow where they were received by Khrushchev and signed agreements for the

---

[8] Jakarta to DOS, 23 January 1959, *FRUS, 1958–1960, XVII*, 323–5.
[9] See e.g. Jones, *Indonesia*, 189–90.
[10] Jakarta to DOS, 17 November 1959, *FRUS, 1958–1960, XVII*, 449.
[11] NSC 6023, 19 December 1960, *ibid.*, 571–83; and see memorandum of discussion at 472nd mtg of the NSC, 29 December 1960, *ibid.*, 590–2.

purchase of a further $400 million of military hardware, announcing that this was a response to the Dutch military build-up around West Irian.[12] This was a particularly bitter blow as Nasution was a strong anti-Communist and seen by US officials as an important bulwark against the domestic influence of the PKI. While the implications of the arms deal were being digested by interested observers in Washington, on 6 January Khrushchev delivered his now-famous speech at the Institute of Marxism–Leninism in Moscow, where he talked of the anti-colonial revolutions convulsing Asia and Africa (and the triumph of Castro's insurgency in Cuba) as marking a pivotal stage in the Cold War, with new post-colonial leaders emerging to reject the continuing tutelage and example of the West, turning instead to support from the Soviet Union and its Communist ideals. While the concept of peaceful coexistence with the capitalist West would continue to govern Soviet policies, Moscow would do all it could to further revolutionary tendencies in the Third World through the provision of economic and military assistance and by vigorous diplomatic and propaganda support for wars of national liberation that were still ongoing against the forces of Western imperialism. Khrushchev looked forward with overwhelming confidence to the coming ideological and political struggle on this new and promising stage. Evidently impressed with this statement of Soviet attitudes, Kennedy had Khrushchev's speech distributed among his foreign policy advisers with an exhortation for them to study it closely; the new President would regard meeting the Communist challenge in the Third World as the principal task facing the West for the 1960s.[13]

One of the most trenchant criticisms put forward by Kennedy of the previous Republican Administration had been its inability to respond to the needs and concerns of the developing world, and the way its very public rejection of the concept of neutrality in the Cold War had done much to alienate opinion among newly independent states. Rather than emphasize adherence to regional and Western-led alliances, in December 1959 Kennedy maintained that the trend towards countries taking a neutralist stance in foreign policy was 'inevitable'. 'The desire to be independent and free carries with it the desire not to become engaged as a satellite of the Soviet Union or too closely allied with the United States', the then Senator had argued. 'We have to live with that, and if neutrality

---

[12] *FRUS, 1961–1963, vol. XXIII, Southeast Asia* (Washington, 1994), 308, n1.
[13] See M. R. Beschloss, *Kennedy v. Khrushchev: The Crisis Years, 1960–1963* (London, 1991), 60–4; Schlesinger, *Thousand Days*, 274–6. As late as the following January, the President was still describing Khrushchev's remarks to an NSC meeting as 'possibly one of the most important speeches of the decade'. Kennedy comments to 496th mtg of the NSC, 18 January 1962, *FRUS, 1961–1963, vol. VIII, National Security Policy* (Washington, 1996), 240.

is the result of a concentration on internal problems, raising the standard of living of the people and so on, particularly in the underdeveloped countries, I would accept that ... '[14] Many members of the new Kennedy Administration assumed that in future competition with the Communist bloc, the United States would need to work with the changes that were transforming the Third World, and to open up a sympathetic dialogue with regimes that had thrown off old imperial controls and where hostility to excessive Western influence often went hand in hand with the anti-colonial struggle.[15] This apparent willingness to tolerate diversity was intended to be a key component in the Kennedy strategy of winning over the allegiance of what the President had called in the Senate in 1957 the 'uncommitted millions in Asia and Africa'.[16] Speaking to students at Berkeley in March 1962, Kennedy asserted that 'diversity and independence, far from being opposed to the American conception of world order, represent the very essence of our view of the future of the world'.[17] Leaders of the non-aligned world were to be given generous and understanding assistance and aid, while being gently coaxed into US patterns of economic development and into the anti-Communist camp. Over the long term, Kennedy believed that the encouragement of pluralism and strong national independence would serve US interests, and would in fact be the most effective response to the monolithic vision it was charged that Communism represented.

Yet there were significant qualifications to this vision of tolerating diversity. In his inaugural address, Kennedy sounded a note of warning:

> To those new states whom we welcome to the ranks of the free, we pledge our word that one form of colonial control shall not have passed away merely to be replaced by a far more iron tyranny. We shall not always expect them to be supporting our view. But we shall always hope to find them strongly supporting their own freedom – and to remember that, in the past, those who foolishly sought power by riding the back of the tiger ended up inside.[18]

As in the 1950s, the Kennedy Administration viewed its relations with the developing world through the pervasive prism of the all-consuming struggle against Communism; on the part of the President himself, both from personal inclination and from his awareness of what the American

---

[14] Interview conducted 9 December 1959, see John F. Kennedy, *The Strategy of Peace* (New York, 1960), 218.

[15] See e.g. Schlesinger, *Thousand Days*, 446–7.

[16] Senate speech, 2 July 1957, in Kennedy, *Strategy of Peace*, 66.

[17] Address to University of California at Berkeley, 23 March 1962, *The Public Papers of the Presidents: John F. Kennedy, 1962* (Washington, 1963), 265. On the background and drafting of the Berkeley speech see, Schlesinger, *Thousand Days*, 534–9.

[18] Inaugural address, 20 January 1961, *The Public Papers of the Presidents: John F. Kennedy, 1961* (Washington, 1962), 1.

public would tolerate, there was no desire to deviate from the assumptions that had underpinned all US policy since the enunciation of the Truman Doctrine. As one noted critic of the period has warned us: 'One can easily get caught up in the eloquent phrasing and noble appeals to human uplift and overlook contradictions between word and deed or the coercive components of American foreign policy.'[19] Instability in the Third World, or evidence of major social or political change, was all too readily seen as evidence of external Communist influence or intrigue, and as a possible challenge that necessitated a vigorous response. Washington still found it difficult to regard local regimes as anything but pieces to be moved and manipulated by their Soviet or American masters in a global power game, rather than as autonomous actors with their own priorities. In January 1963, the President can be found telling the National Security Council, 'We cannot permit all those who call themselves neutrals to join the Communist bloc. Therefore, we must keep our ties to . . . neutralists even if we do not like many things they do because if we lose them, the balance of power could swing against us.'[20] Then again, US officials would frequently complain that 'genuine' national independence was missing in many developing countries. In this world view there were different brands and varieties of neutral, with suspicion and hostility still being reserved for those who maintained friendly ties with Moscow or Beijing. In the wake of the Belgrade conference of non-aligned states in September 1961, Dean Rusk, the US Secretary of State, could be heard to remark, 'It is high time that they decided what side of the Cold War they were on.'[21] Over Vietnam, Kennedy was irritated at the often isolated position of the United States, stating in one meeting that 'the time had come for neutral nations as well as others to be in support of US policy *publicly* . . . we should aggressively determine which nations are in support of US policy and that these nations should identify themselves'.[22]

Throughout the Administration there was also a strong emphasis on the need for the United States to exercise global leadership, McGeorge Bundy, Kennedy's Special Assistant for National Security Affairs, memorably explaining that he had 'come to accept what he had learned from Dean Acheson – that, in the final analysis, the United States was the locomotive at the head of mankind, and the rest of the world was the

---

[19] Thomas G. Paterson, 'Bearing the Burden: a Critical Look at John F. Kennedy's Foreign Policy', *The Virginia Quarterly Review*, 54, 2, 1978, 194.
[20] Record of 508th mtg of the NSC, 22 January 1963, *FRUS, 1961–1963, VIII*, 460.
[21] Chester Bowles, *Promises to Keep: My Years in Public Life, 1941–1969* (New York, 1971), 359.
[22] Notes on the NSC mtg of 15 November 1961, *FRUS, 1961–1963, vol. I, Vietnam 1961* (Washington, 1988), 610.

caboose'.[23] Doubt and indecision were to be banished, as precise, cool-
headed memoranda, based on snap analysis and judgements, or the quan-
titative data flowing from Robert McNamara's Pentagon machine, were
issued by the 'action intellectuals' who came to be associated with the new
regime. The United States could not afford to be a passive onlooker,[24]
and this overwhelming desire for activism (which was supposed to provide
a contrast with the alleged lethargy and drift of the Eisenhower Administration) would lead along several uncertain and destructive paths. The
desire to assert credibility with allies, and the need to show strength when
changes appeared to threaten perceptions of the balance of global power,
meant that stability would often be more highly valued than a tolerance
of diversity; nowhere was this aversion to change better shown than in regard to Vietnam and Cuba.[25] The belief that all problems were capable of
solution, given only the application of sufficient expertise and resources,
could often result in a disturbing interventionism that did much to limit
the independence of many states in the developing world.

Kennedy had initially hoped that the new directions he was hoping
to set might come from within the bureaucracy of the State Department. In the final years of the Eisenhower Administration much anxiety had been expressed by commentators (and some participants) over
the elaborate and baroque structure of the NSC system, with its net-
work of coordinating committees. To those keen to promote initiative
and ideas, the round of endless discussions and approval of long policy
papers was cumbersome and stifling, merely serving to excuse inaction
and lethargy. Such matters received greater public comment due to the
work of Senator Henry M. Jackson's congressional subcommittee on government operations which began its hearings in the summer of 1959. Its
critical and influential reports were disseminated from the autumn of
1960, at the moment when President-elect Kennedy was also studying
how he should mark a sharp departure from the approach of his predecessor. The Jackson subcommittee made a strong case for pruning back
the NSC structure, and putting authority once more into the hands of the
State Department, with an emphasis on the importance of forceful personnel at the Assistant Secretary level, heading the Department's regional
bureaux.[26]

---

[23] Quoted in George C. Herring, *America's Longest War: The United States and Vietnam,
1950–75* (London, 1979), 74.

[24] Note Kennedy's pronouncement in his second State of the Union address in January
1962: '... our Nation is commissioned by history to be either an observer of freedom's
failure or the cause of its success', *Public Papers, Kennedy*, 1962, 5.

[25] On this point see John L. Gaddis, *Strategies of Containment* (Oxford, 1982), 201–3.

[26] See Hilsman, *To Move a Nation*, 18–25.

The new President took up such ideas in his first month in office, abolishing the Operations Coordinating Board of the NSC, effectively suspending the Planning Board, and investing increased authority, planning and coordination tasks in the State Department. At the same time a slimmed-down NSC Secretariat, under Bundy's direction, would function as a personal advisory staff for the President, while meetings of the full NSC would be kept to a minimum. For an energetic and knowledgeable chief executive such as Kennedy, who liked to rely more on direct, personal communication, the streamlined machinery seemed the best method of dealing with the packed agenda that he confronted.[27] However, Kennedy's choice of the conventionally minded and reticent Rusk to lead the State Department proved to be unfortunate. Under the detached guidance of Rusk, the Department's regional bureaux did not generate the fresh thinking and drive that was expected of the New Frontier.[28] By the middle of 1961, there was considerable disillusionment at the generally lacklustre performance of the Department across a wide area of policy. On too many occasions, from the Bay of Pigs episode to the Berlin crisis to Vietnam, it seemed that other agencies were playing the lead role in offering advice and developing policy.[29] Irrespective of the problems at the State Department, Kennedy was determined to stamp his own imprint on foreign policy. This was increasingly accomplished by the channelling of high-level decision-making and policy discussion through the close retinue of regional experts on Bundy's NSC staff, a group that exuded the youth, vigour and assertiveness that best personified the Kennedy style.[30]

Over the first year of the Administration some of the conflicts between the glacial thinking present within the State Department, particularly by the Bureau of European Affairs with its inclination not to challenge NATO allies over colonial issues, and the desire of Bundy's staff to forge a new relationship with the developing world, became very apparent over policy towards Indonesia and the West Irian dispute. From Jakarta, Jones tried to catch the mood of the new Administration by arguing that

[27] See notes of Secretary of State's daily staff meeting, 14 February 1961, *FRUS, 1961–1963, VIII*, 34, and 15n1.

[28] On Kennedy Administration personnel and appointments see David Halberstam, *The Best and the Brightest* (London, 1972), 4–77; Beschloss, *Kennedy v Khrushchev*, 46, 70–6, 463–5.

[29] See Hilsman, *To Move a Nation*, 34–9; Schlesinger, *Thousand Days*, 365–6, 384–7. For a stinging contemporary critique, see Galbraith to Kennedy, 15 August 1961, in John K. Galbraith, *Ambassador's Journal* (Boston, 1969), 186–9.

[30] On the operation of Kennedy's NSC staff see John Prados, *The Keepers of the Keys: A History of the National Security Council from Truman to Bush* (New York, 1991), 99–132, and Robert W. Komer Oral History.

neutrality should be abandoned and a solution developed that was accept-able to the Indonesians. An Indonesian resort to arms, with the possibil-ity that the United States might find itself lending support to the Dutch, would be a disastrous outcome, alienating neutral opinion throughout Asia, and driving Indonesia irretrievably into the waiting arms of the Communists. The Ambassador made clear that Sukarno was 'in well nigh absolute control of [the] destiny of Indonesia for [the] time being' and 'To ignore, snub, punish or attempt to wish away Sukarno are all equally futile pastimes. Like Nasser and Nehru he is there, and we must learn to live with him as a fact of life.' The coldness of the previous Administra-tion and general hostility to Sukarno in the American press meant that he 'believes we not only do not like him but that we are in fact out to get him'. The Ambassador recommended that a personal invitation for Sukarno to visit Washington for talks with the President should be made as soon as possible.[31]

Despite such entreaties, the Secretary of State was inherently sceptical over any move to alter the US stance over West Irian. During the final years of the Truman Administration, Rusk had served as Assistant Sec-retary for Far Eastern Affairs, and had shown no predilection to pressure the Dutch in their abortive negotiations with Indonesia in 1950–1 over the territory. With many more immediately pressing problems in early 1961, Rusk was dubious about pursuing ideas that had earlier surfaced in the Far East Bureau over the idea of replacing Dutch rule with a UN trusteeship for West Irian.[32] Rusk probably also had domestic consid-erations in mind. Although not significant in the early part of the year, by late 1961, in the wake of the Belgrade conference, where Indonesia played a prominent role, there was considerable opposition emerging in Congress to the whole notion of extensive foreign aid to neutrals. This opposition would grow more pronounced in the following year and help to convince Rusk, who had been in government during the assaults of the McCarthy years and was acutely conscious of the dangers of losing support within Congress, of the risks in swinging too far to accommodate a regime headed by such a controversial figure as Sukarno.[33]

Towards the end of February 1961, Jones had his request of the pre-vious month met, when the State Department confirmed that Kennedy

[31] Jakarta to DOS, nos. 2154 and 2164, 25 January 1961, 611.98/1–2561, RG 59. Sukarno himself also appears to have been ready to establish a new relationship with Kennedy, attracted by the latter's idealism and earlier criticisms of French colonialism in North Africa, see e.g. Jones, *Indonesia*, 191, 193.
[32] See memorandum from Rusk to Bowles, 18 February 1961, *FRUS, 1961–1963, XXIII*, 313–14.
[33] See Bunnell, 'Kennedy Initiatives', 166 and *passim*; Hilsman, *To Move a Nation*, 375–7.

would invite Sukarno for informal talks at the White House in April.[34] The prospect of a Sukarno visit generated fresh debates about how the West Irian issue could be resolved, with significant voices in the CIA expressing strong doubts that backing the Indonesian position would reap any benefits for the West.[35] The State Department's eventual position was to maintain that the Dutch must eventually leave the territory, but rather than a direct transfer to Indonesian control, a UN trusteeship could be introduced, with Malaya acting as the trustee, while a direct UN trusteeship was a fall-back position.[36] This kind of compromise was considered profoundly inadequate by members of the NSC staff, where Walt W. Rostow, Bundy's deputy, Robert H. Johnson, who held the brief for the Far East as a whole, and Robert W. Komer who, though specializing in the Middle East, interested himself in the non-aligned world generally, emerged as the champions of a more positive approach that would pressure the Dutch to simply hand over control of West Irian to Indonesia. Rostow was told by Komer that:

If the prime reason for a policy shift is to keep Indonesia from sliding away, we must come up with a solution which is broadly satisfactory with the Indonesians. If we do not, we merely let ourselves in for a pack of trouble without gaining the advantage which led us to move in the first place. Of course, if we are proposing trusteeship not only as graceful out for the Netherlands but as cover operation for eventually giving WNG [West New Guinea] to the Indonesians, it might make sense. But if this is the case, why not tell the President? [. . .] I'm sure we all agree that Indonesia will eventually get WNG, that we cannot afford to buck Sukarno on this issue while the Soviets back him, and that the Dutch will have to give. But we always enter these painful transactions with a little move that stirs up a ruckus and leads us from crisis to crisis before the issue is resolved in the way we knew it would be in the first place, but with all parties mad at us.[37]

Some of Kennedy's own views came across when he saw the Dutch Foreign Minister, Joseph Luns, prior to Sukarno's visit. As well as highlighting recent Dutch moves to prepare the inhabitants of West Irian for local self-government, Luns was eager for the President to deliver a warning to Sukarno over any resort to force, but Kennedy preferred to emphasize: 'When the United States shoots across Sukarno's bow, increased Soviet influence and efforts would be an inevitable result.' Moreover, the

[34] Jakarta to DOS, 23 February 1961, *FRUS, 1961–1963, XXIII*, 314–16.
[35] See e.g. Frederick P. Bunnell, 'The Central Intelligence Agency–Deputy Directorate for Plans 1961 Secret Memorandum on Indonesia: a Study in the Politics of Policy Formulation in the Kennedy Administration', *Indonesia*, 1981.
[36] Memorandum from Rusk to Kennedy, 3 April 1961, *FRUS, 1961–1963, XXIII*, 336–9.
[37] Komer memorandum for Rostow, 5 April 1961, Staff Memoranda, Robert Komer, 4/1/61–4/16/61, Meetings and Memoranda series, NSF, JFKL.

President was mystified as to why the Dutch attached such importance to retaining their position in West Irian, and with the United States so heavily engaged in both Laos and Vietnam, expressed his reluctance to take on any more commitments in South East Asia.[38] In subsequent talks with Rusk, and to the irritation of the NSC staff, Luns was told that he hoped no impression was received that the US attitude to the use of force had in any way changed, softening somewhat the earlier effect of the President's stonewalling on this question. Though sceptical it would gain the necessary support in the General Assembly, the Dutch were happy for the Americans to pursue ideas for an eventual UN trusteeship over West Irian, as long as the principle of self-determination was not lost.[39] In direct contrast to the prevailing State Department view, Johnson and Komer argued that (in the former's words):

> our principal objective is to improve the outlook for a non-Communist Indonesia and only secondarily to satisfy Dutch emotional needs ... our approach must be quite clearly directed toward an Indonesian takeover of WNG at a reasonably early date. While we need a formula that will save face for the Dutch by making a bow in the direction of self-determination, we should not in the process delude ourselves or confuse the Indonesians as to our real objective.[40]

Sukarno's visit to Washington was an amicable affair, and seemed for the Indonesian President, regarding Kennedy as an impressive leader who was sympathetic to the aspirations of Asian nationalism, to signify a fresh start in his relations with the United States.[41] Sukarno arrived at a difficult time for the President, only a few days after the failure of the Bay of Pigs expedition, and Kennedy himself found Sukarno personally distasteful (due, apparently, to the latter's brazen requests for US officials to procure him some female company while in the capital). When the key matter of West Irian was raised in the official talks on 24 April, Sukarno's appeals for clear American support for the Indonesian claim were unproductive, while Kennedy 'expressed the hope that the Indonesian Government would not consider the use of force' and that 'the problem would be made more complex and difficult a solution [sic] if there were military action in the area'.[42] This was somewhat less than a 'warning' as desired by the Dutch, but was also hardly the swing to a pro-Indonesian policy that the NSC staff had been lobbying for. As a

---

[38] Memorandum of conversation, 10 April 1961, *FRUS, 1961–1963, XXIII*, 345–51.
[39] See memoranda of conversations, 10 and 11 April 1961, and Johnson memorandum for Rostow, 17 April 1961, *ibid.*, 352–64.
[40] Johnson memorandum for Rostow, 18 April 1961, *ibid.*, 364–7.
[41] Jones, *Indonesia*, 195–7.
[42] Memorandum of conversation, 24 April 1961, *FRUS, 1961–1963, XXIII*, 382–90.

positive gesture towards Indonesia's future economic stability, Kennedy offered to provide help with Indonesia's recently announced Eight Year Development Plan through the despatch of a team of economists led by Professor Don D. Humphrey, which would report on how the US could best lend assistance. The President was still keen, at this stage, to try to retain a balance between his need for a friendly and reliable Netherlands in Europe, and the central role played by Indonesia both in fulfilling US goals in South East Asia and in overall strategy towards the non-aligned world.

During the summer of 1961 the prospects for a peaceful resolution of the dispute remained uncertain. After Sukarno's trip to Moscow in June, deliveries of Soviet aircraft and military equipment began to gather pace, adding to Indonesian confidence. Moreover, the last remnants of the Outer Island rebels began to give themselves up to the Army in the spring, and in August 1961, Sukarno announced a general amnesty for those who agreed to surrender before October, allowing the military to concentrate on the possibility of a campaign against the Dutch.[43] Meanwhile, with the Netherlands Government having indicated that they would eventually need to disengage from the territory, the State Department had begun a series of secret bilateral talks with Dutch officials to discuss proposals for either a trusteeship for West Irian or some form of investigative UN committee which would make recommendations. In August, Jones was authorized to begin his own dialogue with the Indonesians on possible formulas for a solution, though Subandrio held that before the issue was taken to a UN forum, the Indonesians would need some prior assurances over the real Dutch attitude. As the sixteenth annual session of the UN General Assembly approached, there was considerable American pessimism that any trusteeship proposal would be acceptable in the light of the UN's ongoing Congo experience, while ideas for a UN committee of investigation had run into both British and (more significantly given its administration of Papua New Guinea) Australian objections, both fearing that its membership would be dominated by Afro-Asian states.

The Dutch came to the General Assembly in New York with the announcement that they were prepared to hand over West Irian to a UN administration with a view to preparing the territory for self-determination. Their draft resolution called for a UN commission of enquiry which could organize a plebiscite on the territory's future, while the UN took West Irian under its trusteeship, though some Dutch administrators would stay on as UN accredited officials. Appealing for American help to find a solution based on Jakarta's claims to sovereignty, the Indonesians made

[43] See Kahin and Kahin, *Subversion*, 214–15.

clear they found the Dutch resolution unacceptable. At this stage, Robert Johnson's efforts to secure Rusk's intervention to change the Dutch position proved fruitless, the latter fearing that the Americans would be blamed if a negotiation failed.[44] Hence, before he left for his important trip to Vietnam in mid-October 1961, Rostow presented a memorandum to Kennedy which maintained that Indonesian control of West Irian was the only possible permanent solution to the dispute and argued that Dutch tactics at the UN showed that 'they are playing a double game with us', as the United States would either have to side with the Dutch resolution, and so antagonize Indonesia, or oppose it, and appear to reject the principle of self-determination. Subandrio had taken the tabling of the Dutch resolution as a 'declaration of war'. Rostow felt that the Dutch had to be told plainly that their proposals were inadequate, could not be endorsed and should be withdrawn if they were not prepared to modify them. The President was encouraged to take the subject up with Rusk so that the necessary pressure could be put on the Dutch at the UN.[45]

Although the NSC staff finally managed to elicit from Kennedy the view that the USA should 'lean gently' on the Dutch while avoiding direct involvement, there was palpable frustration that this message was not getting across to the State Department.[46] The US delegation to the UN was busy preparing its own alternative resolution to the Dutch proposal which tried to reach a compromise formula by leaving the final arrangements for the territory's status an open issue and toning down all references to self-determination. Yet all such efforts seemed futile exercises considering the increasingly belligerent language coming from the Indonesians and their rejection of both the Dutch- and US-drafted resolutions.[47] Nevertheless, Rusk took the decision to push forward the US compromise resolution and oppose all others proposed, despite the strong likelihood that Indonesia would find it impossible to support and that they could muster the necessary General Assembly votes to block it. Johnson was exasperated by Rusk's unwillingness to consult the President on tactics at the UN, and now felt that 'the end result of all of the months of work has been to put us in a worse position vis-à-vis the Indonesians on this issue than we have ever been in the past'. The Americans would now be actively opposing the Indonesians at the UN, while the pressures for a military solution from within Indonesia were likely to increase.[48] At the end of

---

[44] Memorandum by Johnson for Rostow, 29 September 1961, *FRUS, 1961–1963, XXIII*, 435–7.
[45] Memorandum from Rostow to Kennedy, 13 October 1961, *ibid.*, 440–2.
[46] See memorandum from Johnson to Bundy, 6 November 1961, *ibid.*, 447–52.
[47] Memorandum from Johnson to Rostow, 15 November 1961, *ibid.*, 455–7.
[48] Memorandum from Johnson to Rostow, 16 November 1961, *ibid.*, 458–60.

November, the US-conceived resolution failed to receive the necessary two-thirds majority from the General Assembly, and the Americans voted against an Indian resolution calling for direct bilateral talks, which also failed. This was, as Rostow expressed it, 'a fiasco', with the US delegation having voted against the Indonesians twice, the second time reversing the previous American record of abstaining when Indonesian resolutions calling for direct talks on West Irian had been introduced in the 1950s. While they pressed on with belated measures to promote political development in the territory, the Dutch were taking every opportunity to highlight the fact that their position on the issue of self-determination had received American backing. In the view of the NSC staff, the State Department would now need to change its whole approach to the problem; the only paradoxical consolation of the recent UN debates was that the US resolution had failed. 'It is the feeling of all of us on your staff', Rostow informed Kennedy, 'that the Western world has got to consider this problem somewhat less in terms of the pure diplomacy of West Irian and more in terms of a common interest in frustrating communism in Indonesia.'[49] There was still time, Komer felt, before the Indonesians decided to use force: ' . . . we have to get the President personally to weigh in on State. Now that the UN gambit has failed, time has come for him to press Rusk on why we shouldn't now lean on Aussies and Dutch.'[50] The President was in turn advised by McGeorge Bundy that

most of the specialists in the area believe that the Secretary's respect for the Australians and dislike of Sukarno has led him to take a position in the UN debate which, if continued, can only help the Communists. Sukarno, I know, is not your own favourite statesman, but the real point is that at the moment we seem to be working against the interest of the Indonesian moderates – our one reliance against eventual Communist take-over there.[51]

Reports from CIA sources at this time pointed to the awkward position faced by Nasution, and that he was a voice holding out for a negotiated solution to the problem in the face of the belligerence of other figures close to Sukarno.[52]

The difficulties being encountered over formulating policy towards Indonesia were bound up, in many eyes (including the President's), with

---

[49] Memorandum from Rostow to Kennedy, 30 November 1961, *ibid.*, 463–5.
[50] Memorandum from Komer to Rostow, 30 November 1961, *ibid.*, 469–70.
[51] Memorandum from Bundy to Kennedy, 1 December 1961, *ibid.*, 462–3.
[52] CIA information report, TDCS–3/494, 341, 'General Nasution's attitude towards the West Irian problem', 28 November 1961, National Security File (NSF), countries file, West New Guinea, 12/1/61–12/5/61, JFKL.

the failure of the State Department adequately to respond to the demands it had faced throughout a crisis-laden year. Kennedy was re-
spectful of the prerogatives of the Secretary of State, but press criticism of Rusk's alleged indecisiveness had gathered pace in the summer,
while Administration insiders such as Arthur Schlesinger were ready
to talk about his shortcomings.[53] The perception of shambolic organization and lack of leadership at the State Department made a sharp
and painful contrast with McNamara's energetic and assertive manage-
ment of the Defense Department, already being marked out as one of
the early successes of the Administration. The President-elect had not
known Rusk before selecting him in December 1960, and had in fact
hoped to appoint J. William Fulbright, but this had been opposed by
Robert Kennedy, who was concerned that the Arkansas Senator's identification with southern segregation would handicap the Administration's
approach to the developing world. Instead, the strong recommendations of Acheson and Robert Lovett secured the job for Rusk.[54] Now
Kennedy, despite all the reservations over Rusk's performance held by
many, including his own brother, was reluctant to displace the Secretary
of State, as this would reflect badly on his initial judgement in making the appointment.[55] Hence, when the anticipated State Department
shake-up occurred at the end of November 1961 (the so-called 'Thanks-
giving Day Massacre'), Rusk was spared. Instead, Chester Bowles, the
Under-Secretary who had also been disparaged by the Kennedys for his
verbosity, indecisiveness and after-the-event wisdom over the Bay of Pigs
episode, was removed. Upgraded to become Rusk's deputy was the highly .
regarded figure of George Ball, while Rostow was brought over from the
NSC staff to head a more grandly titled Policy Planning Council at the
State Department.[56]

Of overriding significance for policy towards Indonesia, however, was
the arrival of Averell Harriman as the new Assistant Secretary for Far
Eastern Affairs. The previous incumbent, Walter McConaughy, had been
appointed by Rusk in April (having previously acted as Ambassador to
South Korea), but had failed to invigorate the Far East Bureau. Harriman
had gained credibility with the President and his advisers during the
summer of 1961 by his skilful handling of the Geneva negotiations over

---

[53] Schlesinger memorandum for Bundy, 11 August 1961, box WH–3A, Schlesinger papers;
see also Schlesinger, *Thousand Days*, 384–90, Hilsman, *To Move a Nation*, 35–6.
[54] See Walter Isaacson and Evan Thomas, *The Wise Men: Six Friends and the World They
Made: Acheson, Bohlen, Harriman, Kennan, Lovett, McCloy* (New York, 1986), 592–
5; Edwin O. Guthman and Jeffrey Shulman (eds.), *Robert Kennedy In His Own Words*
(London, 1988), 36–7.
[55] Robert F. Kennedy Oral History.
[56] Schlesinger, *Thousand Days*, 392–4; Hilsman, *To Move a Nation*, 50–1.

the conflict in Laos and his clear-sighted pursuit of the neutralization solution that Kennedy advocated.[57] It was Bowles who had first suggested Harriman for the Far East assignment, hoping the latter's sympathy for nationalist aspirations in the developing world made him a good candidate for the task. Schlesinger spoke to Harriman about the idea in early October, and though the latter felt more at home with European affairs, he indicated he would be prepared to serve the President wherever it was thought he might be helpful, though he would need to be assured of his 'operating authority', and that he should not have to report through U. Alexis Johnson, the Deputy Under Secretary for Political Affairs (and an official closely associated with the previous Administration's controversial policies in Laos, while serving as the US Ambassador to Thailand, January 1958–April 1961).[58] On 15 November, Harriman's seventieth birthday, Kennedy met the veteran diplomat and offered him the position, Schlesinger advising the President that 'Averell has strong views on the people who have been shaping our policy in Southeast Asia. He will not volunteer these views in his talk with you; but he will probably respond with alacrity to any questions you might wish to ask him about his judgment of the people involved.'[59] Later that day, Bundy saw Rusk to argue that the President felt the 'need to have someone on this job that is wholly responsive to [his] policy, and that [he] really did not get that sense from most of us'. When Bundy put forward Harriman's name for the Far East Bureau, the Secretary of State countered by saying that Harriman was still needed at the Geneva talks and that 'Alexis would loyally carry out any policy [the President] directed.' Bundy was far from convinced and advised Kennedy that 'Averell is your man, as Assistant Secretary', and pushed for a 'general game of musical chairs' at the State Department, but that Rusk 'won't do this till you tell him to'. Within a few hours, the President was seeing the Secretary of State and issuing the necessary instructions.[60]

Harriman's long experience of government service and international diplomacy won him automatic respect, while he was possessed of a natural

---

[57] See Isaacson and Thomas, *The Wise Men*, 618–19.

[58] Schlesinger memorandum for Kennedy, 9 October 1961, President's Office Files, box 65, JFKL.

[59] Schlesinger memorandum for Kennedy, 15 November 1961, President's Office Files, box 30, JFKL.

[60] See Bundy memorandum for Kennedy, 15 November 1961, NSF, Departments and Agencies series, Department of State, 11/13/61–11/21/61, JFKL. See also Bundy's handwritten note of 15 November 1961: 'Sec/State. Would take Averell for this [Far East Bureau] and have discussed it with him – perhaps adding India and Pak to Far East Area. Averell for McConaughy would be *major* gain. The way to do this is to get Averell back here and in charge – RIGHT AWAY.' President's Office Files, box 88, JFKL. See also the lengthier memorandum in *FRUS, 1961–1963*, I, 612–14.

authority and power of command, and was intensely loyal to the office of President. What most impressed and surprised his younger colleagues, moreover, was his enthusiasm for unconventional ideas and willingness to learn. On his arrival, Harriman was determined to change the culture and prestige of the Far East Bureau, which during the McCarthy era had suffered the loss of some of its finest Asia specialists and was felt by many to be the most conservative section of the State Department. Taking over the Bureau, Harriman would comment that it was a 'wasteland... It's a disaster area filled with human wreckage... Perhaps a few can be saved. Some of them are so beaten down, they can't be saved. Some of those you would want to save are just finished. They try and write a report and nothing comes out. It's a terrible thing.'[61] One consequence of Harriman's arrival was to be a greater tone of scepticism towards prevailing Vietnam policy, a trend which was to culminate in the desire to dissociate the USA from the Diem regime in the south, and ultimately, towards the end of 1963, to advocate its overthrow. Another area where a new approach was more immediately displayed was over policy towards Indonesia. A sign of the change in tenor was provided soon after his appointment by Harriman's reaction to the comments of a television presenter about 'that Communist, Sukarno', the Assistant Secretary snapping back in characteristic style, 'He is not a Communist, he's a nationalist!'[62]

By late 1961, following the inconclusive UN debates, there was certainly a need to smooth ruffled Indonesian feathers through such greater identification with an Asian perspective. On 8 December, Sukarno had told Jones that he had been 'shattered' by the US stance at the UN, believing that the Americans had abandoned neutrality and were now actually supporting the Dutch in the dispute. Above the Ambassador's protests, the Indonesian President indicated that a forceful resolution to the problem seemed his only option, while his public speeches of the period were suffused with inflammatory rhetoric. At this critical juncture, Kennedy despatched a conciliatory message to Sukarno, emphasizing that the American attitude remained neutral, and that only small differences now seemed to exist between the Dutch and Indonesian positions. The President offered the services of the USA as a direct mediator, but went on to gently caution against any resort to force.[63] India's invasion of Goa on 17 December, along with the other remaining Portuguese enclaves on its territory, heightened the tense atmosphere

---

[61] Harriman quoted in Halberstam, *Best and the Brightest*, 189, and see also, 188–99.

[62] Quoted in Hilsman, *To Move a Nation*, 378; see also Jones, *Indonesia*, 203.

[63] See telegram from Bundy to Kennedy, 8 December 1961; telegrams from DOS to Jakarta, 9 December 1961, *FRUS, 1961–1963, XXIII*, 473–8.

by underlining the impression that the last vestiges of European colonialism in Asia were now on the back foot; two days later Sukarno announced a concentration of forces in eastern Indonesia, and small-scale infiltration of West Irian by amphibious raiding parties began soon after.

Both the Americans and the Indonesians had strong doubts that Dutch public opinion was prepared to face a full-scale conflict in the Pacific, especially if no assistance could be expected from other parties; indeed, Luns was often pictured as pursuing a personal crusade over West Irian, with the government in The Hague following rather uncomfortably behind. The NSC staff felt that the best way to encourage some flexibility in the Dutch position, and to shake them out of their complacency, was to let it be known they could expect no US support in the event of a major conflict erupting with the Indonesians. Harriman immediately made his influence felt on this issue when he informed Dutch officials that no assistance could be expected if the Indonesians attacked; the Dutch also agreed to drop Indonesian acceptance of the principle of self-determination as a precondition for starting negotiations.[64]

From 19–23 December 1961, Kennedy and Macmillan met on Bermuda for talks which dealt primarily with the subjects of Berlin and nuclear testing, though West Irian also featured. It would seem that just prior to these discussions the President had told Rusk that Dutch requests for even token levels of support should be refused. During the Anglo-American talks, the Secretary of State outlined his own belief that the Indonesians were not serious about launching a large-scale attack in the short term, while the President began to define American policy more closely in his meetings with Macmillan. Asserting that it would be a mistake to become involved in supporting the Dutch in the defence of West Irian, Kennedy made clear that his Administration had made no commitment to helping the Dutch in the event of an attack, and had no intention of doing so. Military operations would simply strengthen the PKI internally, and the right policy should be to persuade the Dutch to accept arrangements which would allow for them to leave the area. The Australians would also need to be impressed with the need to avoid a military clash over West Irian, and it was agreed by both leaders that 'it would be preferable that the Western Powers should refrain from offering to support the Dutch in resisting any Indonesian attack on this territory'.[65]

---

[64] Memorandum of conversation, 22 December 1961, *ibid.*, 495–8.
[65] Notes of conversation between Rusk and Home, 21 December 1961; and record of meeting at Government House, Bermuda, between Kennedy and Macmillan, 22 December 1961, PREM 11/3782.

By mid-January 1962, the naval tensions between the Netherlands and Indonesia had intensified, with clashes in the waters around West Irian, leading Komer to predict that without an even bigger shift in policy, 'we may be heading for a really major defeat in SEA [South East Asia] – one which would dwarf the loss of Laos'.[66] Shortly after, the President mirrored such concerns over the crisis, when he informed a full gathering of the NSC that:

> The area is a most unsuitable one for a war in which the United States would be involved. We would not wish to humiliate the Dutch, but on the other hand it would be foolish to have a contest when the Dutch really do want to get out if a dignified method can be found. We should recognize that this territory was likely eventually to go to Indonesia, even though we ourselves might deeply dislike Sukarno as an individual. The real stake here is not West Irian but the fate of Indonesia, the most rich and populous country in the area and one which was the target of energetically pursued Soviet ambitions.[67]

Meanwhile, from Jakarta Sukarno was signalling that he was prepared to enter into direct talks with the Dutch, but only if there was advance understanding that the purpose of such negotiations was to provide for a transfer to Indonesian administration of West Irian.[68] Sukarno and Subandrio also indicated, however, that they would be prepared to make some public declaration on self-determination prior to talks as a face-saving device for the Dutch. Despite the narrowing of the differences between the two sides, Indonesian patience with the laboriousness of the process of organizing direct talks was wearing thin.

One way to push forward the momentum behind the negotiating process was suggested by the fact that the Attorney General was due to pass through Jakarta as part of a wider trip to Asian capitals in mid-February. Robert Kennedy was well received, winning goodwill for his frank expression of earnest American desires to see a peaceful resolution of the dispute, and his open pronouncements of friendship towards the Indonesian people. In his talks with Sukarno, the Attorney General pressed the Indonesians to drop their preconditions for negotiations, while also coming close to hinting that the USA would use its influence behind the scenes with the Dutch to assure that any negotiation resulted in an outcome acceptable to the Indonesians.[69] When the Attorney General turned to

---

[66] Komer memorandum for Kaysen, 15 January 1962, NSF, Meetings and Memoranda, Komer memos, 1/62, JFKL.

[67] Kennedy remarks to 496th mtg of the NSC, 18 January 1962, *FRUS, 1961–1963, VIII*, 241.

[68] Jakarta to DOS, 27 December 1961, *FRUS, 1961–1963, XXIII*, 500–1.

[69] Jakarta to DOS, 14 February 1962, *ibid.*, 523–5. Robert Kennedy certainly did not emerge from this and his later Indonesian visit with any great liking for Sukarno; in April

Washington for advice on whether he could give an explicit assurance that the USA would put pressure on the Dutch to ensure that transfer of the administration of West Irian to Indonesia was part of a final settlement, the response was negative. Concerned that the Indonesians would leak such a statement of intent (and so harden the Dutch stance), or that it might be used by the Indonesians to argue that they had been betrayed by the Americans if eventual negotiations were to break down, the President, who was following the progress of the trip closely, did not feel that this final step could be taken. Such an assurance would entail the USA taking upon itself the entire responsibility for resolving the dispute when the result could not be guaranteed. In addition, the Attorney General was also busy in Jakarta securing the release from Indonesian captivity of Allen Pope, and the Americans did not want it to appear as though they were trading Pope's freedom for pressure on the Dutch (Sukarno had indeed floated this possibility). Robert Kennedy was authorized, though, to tell the Indonesians that the USA would use its influence with both sides to reach a successful resolution.[70] In turn, the Indonesians agreed to drop their preconditions, provided that secret talks were held with the Dutch on the agenda for the formal negotiations: it was understood that transfer of administration would be a leading agenda item in these preliminary discussions.

Travelling on to The Hague at the end of February, the Attorney General was given leave to explain that the USA would only be prepared to act as the third-party moderator in any secret agenda-setting talks if the Dutch would agree in advance to concede the issue of an ultimate transfer of West Irian to Indonesian administration. In the event, the Attorney General did not press this point, but this was, as Bundy commented, the furthest the USA had yet gone, and provoked some dissenting comment within the State Department, including from a sceptical Rusk.[71] With Luns due in Washington, Komer felt that the only way to make more progress was to put further pressure on the Dutch: ' . . . if Bobby couldn't move him, I'm sure [State] Department can't. *Therefore I see no alternative to JFK intervention*, either directly to Luns or by telling Rusk to do it.'[72] On 2 March, the President met Luns at the White House to impress on him the need to get the talks process under way, only to be told that while the Dutch were prepared to negotiate they also felt the need to reinforce

1964 he asserted, 'I don't have respect for him. I think that he's bright. I think he's completely immoral, that he's untrustworthy . . . I think he's a liar. I think he's got very few redeeming features', Robert F. Kennedy Oral History.

[70] *Ibid.*, 525–32.

[71] See State Department to Bonn, 23 February 1962, and footnotes, *ibid.*, 538–42.

[72] Komer memorandum for Bundy, 27 February 1962, NSF, Meetings and Memoranda, Komer memos, 2/62, JFKL.

their naval presence in the Far East. Kennedy was none too pleased and reminded the Dutch Foreign Minister that the USA

was not indifferent to the difficulties the Dutch face but in our opinion the problem is not a basic cold war issue. The President noted the extensive effort the United States is making in Viet Nam to prevent the Communists from taking over and that, while we have no confidence in Sukarno, if Indonesia goes to war the chances of a Communist take over in that country are greatly improved. This would be a disaster for the free world position in Asia and would force us out of Viet Nam.

When Luns tried to raise the moral obligation the Dutch owed to the Papuan people of West Irian, Kennedy countered by mentioning the moral obligation to prevent further Communist gains and urged that such matters 'be kept in perspective. The President noted that we have all the potential wars we need at the moment, and we do not consider it useful to become involved in this dispute.'[73]

The secret agenda-setting talks were finally convened at Middleburg, Virginia, just outside Washington on 20 March 1962, with the experienced US diplomat Ellsworth Bunker acting as a UN-appointed moderator. Over the next few months, the Dutch and the Indonesians stuck stubbornly to their original positions, as talks proceeded in a lacklustre manner, interspersed with naval and air clashes around New Guinea, and with American calls for restraint on both sides. Within Indonesia the PKI continued to agitate for a military solution, and Sukarno insisted that the Dutch concede that the ultimate result of any negotiations was that West Irian would be delivered to Indonesia. With the President's personal approval, at the end of March Bunker proposed his own formula to give a basis for substantive negotiations and revive the talks process.[74] The formula called for the Netherlands to transfer the administration of West Irian to a 'temporary executive authority' under the UN Secretary General, with the territory to be administered for a minimum of one and a maximum of two years. During the second year Indonesians would be introduced into the administration, with full control passing to Indonesia by the end of the second year; Indonesia would make arrangements with the assistance of the UN for an opportunity for the people of the territory to exercise their freedom of choice, but at a set time after Indonesia had taken over. Although still wary about the idea of a self-determination exercise, Sukarno was ready to accept the proposal. The first reaction of the Dutch was outright rejection, finding particularly objectionable the

---

[73] Memorandum of conversation, 2 March 1962, *FRUS, 1961–1963, XXIII*, 549–52.
[74] Robert H. Komer Oral History.

notion that a plebiscite should be held only after the introduction of Indonesian administration, when its results could patently be rigged.[75]

With the Dutch Cabinet eventually asking for 'modifications and clarifications' to the Bunker formula, in early May 1962 Rusk was due to meet Luns at a NATO Council ministerial meeting in Athens. The Secretary of State was instructed by the President (in a message actually drafted by Komer) that he should tell Luns quite firmly that if Dutch procrastination continued, the USA would withdraw the services of Bunker and publish his proposals, leaving the Dutch completely isolated.[76] In Athens, Luns conceded that talks could be reopened on the basis of the Bunker formula, but with the important understanding that other items could be raised if desired. Harriman later recalled that this outcome was not viewed very favourably by those anxious to resolve the dispute.[77] For their part, the Indonesians refused to resume the Middleburg talks as long as the Dutch continued to qualify their acceptance of the Bunker formula. With Bunker himself concluding that 'Luns is playing us for suckers', Harriman and Komer felt that the formula had to be made public in order to put domestic political pressure on the Dutch Government and its querulous Foreign Minister.[78] Luns finally accepted a negotiation based solely around the Bunker formula on 26 May, after it had been released through UN channels, but it took until mid-July to resume the Middleburg talks in the face of Indonesian suspicions of Dutch intentions. By that stage, the Indonesians had stiffened their position further by arguing that UN administration of West Irian should only last until the end of 1962 before the territory was passed to Indonesian control, while watering down the UN's involvement in any self-determination exercise. Kennedy met Subandrio at the end July, and this time pressure was put on the Indonesians to draw back, the President impressing on the Indonesian Foreign Minister that though the USA had been on the side of Indonesia thus far, if military action was taken with a peaceful settlement in sight, US support would have to be transferred to the Dutch.[79] Soon after, on 15 August 1962, agreement on terms for a final settlement of the dispute was reached between the Indonesian and Dutch negotiators: as soon as the UN General Assembly gave its approval a UN administration would be introduced to West Irian, which would begin to turn over the territory

---

[75] See *FRUS, 1961–1963, XXIII*, 566–71.
[76] DOS to Rusk, 2 May 1962, *ibid.*, 586–7.
[77] Averell Harriman Oral History.
[78] Memorandum from Komer to Kaysen, 22 May 1962, *FRUS, 1961–1963, XXIII*, 594.
[79] See Jones, *Indonesia*, 211, and Jakarta to DOS, 3 August 1962 (for Subandrio's own account of this meeting), *FRUS, 1961–1963, XXIII*, 624–5.

to Indonesian administration from 1 May 1963, while arrangements
would be made, with UN advice and assistance, for a self-determination
exercise no later than 1969.[80]

The resolution of the West Irian dispute demonstrated where the
Kennedy Administration's priorities lay. Despite a close and usually warm
relationship with the Netherlands, and the objections of some sections
of opinion within the State Department, including the Secretary of State
himself, it had been necessary to tilt quite decisively to the Indonesian
position during the long crisis. With the USA more heavily engaged than
ever in fighting Communist insurgency in South Vietnam, and the cease-
fire in Laos still tenuous at best, the outbreak of another full-scale conflict in the region, with its clear potential to pull in the United States,
had to be avoided, even at the cost of a temporary disruption to an
established alliance relationship. Siding with the Dutch in a clash over
the retention of a colonial backwater, moreover, was guaranteed to dissipate the goodwill that the Administration was attempting to accrue
in the Third World. The view that came to predominate by early 1962
was that the West Irian dispute, through its inflammation of Indonesian
nationalist feeling and PKI agitation, had the effect of pushing Indonesia
further under the influence of the Communist bloc. Sukarno's regime
was also being distracted from turning its attention to stabilizing and
developing the Indonesian economy with Western assistance and aid.
It is also possible to argue that by the summer of 1962 Kennedy believed he was beginning to implement the wider strategy he had expressed during the previous year's bruising encounters with Khrushchev
in Vienna, involving a stabilization of the balance of power between the
United States and the Soviet Union, and the avoidance of direct conflict in the developing world.[81] The removal of the prospect of an East–
West clash over West Irian could be viewed as one step in this intricate
process.

For those Americans who had worked tirelessly for better relations with
Indonesia, and had watched with apprehension the growth of Soviet interest and PKI influence in that country since West Irian had come to
dominate national life, the resolution of the dispute was viewed as a major
diplomatic achievement. Having gained, they supposed, considerable
capital with Jakarta, US officials were now intent on following up with a
series of overtures to assist in the economic development of Indonesia. On
1 August, as the Dutch–Indonesian negotiations were reaching a climax,
Jones presented a carefully sanitized copy of the Humphrey Report on

---

[80] See Hilsman, *To Move a Nation*, 379–80.
[81] See Beschloss, *Kennedy v Khrushchev*, 201, 217.

Indonesian economic development to President Sukarno, the conclusions of the American economic team despatched to Indonesia in the summer of 1961 having been circulating in US Government circles for several months beforehand. The Report's qualified endorsement of Indonesia's Eight Year Development Plan was intended to bolster the position of the economic technocrats surrounding Djuanda, the Indonesian Prime Minister.[82] That American initiatives on economic assistance might fall on fertile ground was indicated by Sukarno's Independence Day speech on 17 August 1962 where he recognized the sufferings endured by the Indonesian people and maintained that with the conclusion of the West Irian campaign more resources could now be devoted to economic development.[83]

Not surprisingly, it was Komer, one of the chief advocates on the NSC staff of a pro-Indonesian line over West Irian, who pressed for planning to begin on measures for economic assistance. Estimating that US funding of $250 million would be needed for a long-term economic stabilization programme, along with $80 million of support from the International Monetary Fund (IMF), Komer told a receptive President, 'Capital of the sort we've gained is a transitory asset to be used while it's still good. Moreover, Indonesia is one of the truly big areas of East–West competition; having invested so much in maneuvering a WNG [West New Guinea] settlement for the express purpose of giving us leverage in this competition, we'd be foolish not to follow through.'[84] On 16 August 1962, Kennedy issued National Security Action Memorandum 179, which called for new and better relations with Indonesia, and for a review of US aid programmes in the anticipation of new requests. The Joint Chiefs of Staff responded enthusiastically to this instruction, and, as was in vogue during the 1960s, were anxious to stress the anti-Communist potential of a civic action programme led by the Indonesian military, where Americans would offer training, advice and equipment to assist the Indonesian armed forces in a variety of projects in rural areas, such as improvements to irrigation or transportation.[85] The US military were also eager to build on their ongoing officer-training programme, that had seen a high proportion of the Indonesian Army's upper cadre receive instruction from Americans and attend courses at US military colleges.

In mid-October 1962, a full set of recommendations for action in Indonesia was delivered to the President. As coordinator of the review, the State Department adopted a cautious tone, emphasizing that too

---

[82] See Bunnell, 'Kennedy Initiatives,' 203 and passim.
[83] Jones, *Indonesia*, 212–13.
[84] Komer memorandum for Kennedy, 15 August 1962, *FRUS, 1961–1963, XXIII*, 626.
[85] JCS memorandum for McNamara, 5 September 1962, *ibid.*, 628–31.

insistent an American approach could be construed as interference by the Indonesians:

They must show an awareness of their economic needs and express a desire to receive Free World assistance. Only they can take the initiative in dealing with the problems of inflation, inadequate foreign exchange and shortages of food and critical materials. Until they take effective measures in their own behalf, Free World assistance of major proportions would be wasted. Our assistance should be related to their actions.

Several immediate measures were suggested, including $60 million to $70 million of PL-480 aid (allowing purchases in local currency of surplus US food and materials), $17 million of technical education and public administration assistance, an augmented military aid programme with an emphasis on civic action, more Peace Corps activity, and a $15 million to $20 million grant to facilitate purchases of spare parts and raw materials for industry. For the longer term, Indonesia should be persuaded to adopt an IMF-sponsored stabilization plan, backed by a multilateral group of international donors, who would also have to relieve Indonesia's heavy burden of foreign debt (servicing of which was adding to the huge problems in the country's balance of payments). In the area of US developmental assistance, the Humphrey mission's recommendations were included in the report and involved grants totalling $52 million to $62 million and loans of $105 million to $110 million over a three- to five-year period in order to strengthen the industrial and transportation infrastructure of Indonesia.[86]

The long-term aspects to the review, and the involvement of the USA in retrieving Indonesia's severe balance of payments position through an IMF stabilization programme, were greeted with some scepticism by Michael V. Forrestal, who had replaced Robert Johnson as the NSC staffer with prime responsibility for Far Eastern matters earlier in the year. Forrestal felt that 'it would take something of a political revolution to get a meaningful program through Congress if our object is to tackle their balance of payments problem', and moreover he questioned 'whether Indonesia presently has the kind of Government with whom we could fruitfully cooperate in achieving fiscal stability and economic reform. My impression from the cables is that attempts by us to cajole and induce the Indonesian Government to follow classic policies towards monetary reform would not only be met with resistance, but also with suspicion.' Nevertheless, Forrestal believed that the short-term measures should be given the go-ahead, and gave such advice to the President.[87]

[86] Memorandum from Ball to Kennedy, 10 October 1962, *ibid.*, 634–43.
[87] Memorandum from Forrestal to Harriman, 25 September 1962; memorandum from Forrestal to Kennedy, 11 October 1962, *ibid.*, 633–4, 643–4.

Also impressing on Kennedy the need to implement the emergency assistance outlined in the review was Howard Jones, who had been recalled to Washington for consultations. The President indicated to Jones his own recognition of the importance of the civic action programme with the Indonesian military when the subject was raised, while Jones could also see the problems that too close a connection between the USA and an interfering IMF programme might have on attitudes in Indonesia.[88] Formal presidential approval of the short-term assistance to Indonesia soon followed (with the exception of the $15 million to $20 million grant), with deliveries of rice under the provisions of PL-480 due to arrive in Indonesia in February or March 1963; Komer remembered Kennedy as saying, 'Go ahead with the emergency actions, but let's hold off on the larger investment till we see.'[89]

The President's reluctance to endorse more extensive measures of assistance to Indonesia probably derived from a mixture of his reading of congressional opinion and the uncertainties that still surrounded Indonesia's future external policies. During the summer of 1962 the Administration had suffered a series of stinging setbacks from Congress over its ambitious foreign aid bill, and would have to approach with caution future financial commitments. The main congressional impediment to the Administration's plans during 1962 had lain in the attacks on foreign aid to neutrals which emanated from the Subcommittee on Foreign Operations of the House Appropriations Committee, under its formidable Chairman, Representative Otto Passman (Democrat, Louisiana). Passman's Subcommittee had managed to secure cuts in the Administration's overall aid requests of about 20 per cent, and incorporated in its final report of September 1962 was particular criticism of aid to 'so-called neutral nations' who had taken part in the Belgrade conference of non-aligned states and indulged in attacks on American policy.[90] Grumbles about 'appeasement' of Sukarno over West Irian were also heard with increasing frequency in congressional circles from the spring of 1962 onwards. The Indonesian President's bellicose anti-imperialist rhetoric, toleration of the PKI's prominent role in Indonesian society, his acceptance of large-scale arms supplies from the Soviet Union and the widespread knowledge of his liking for the nocturnal (and female) pleasures of such places as Tokyo, did little to enhance his public reputation in the United States. Sukarno's most vociferous opponent emerged in the shape of Representative William S. Broomfield, the senior Republican on the House Foreign Affairs Committee. Broomfield was wont to characterize Sukarno as a

[88] Memorandum of conversation, 11 October 1962, *ibid.*, 644–6.
[89] Robert H. Komer Oral History.
[90] Bunnell, 'Kennedy Initiatives,' 182–94.

'despot', a 'Hitler' and an 'international juvenile delinquent'.[91] In such a hostile congressional environment, the President realized he would have to progress very carefully with efforts to give aid to Sukarno's regime.

Nonetheless, with the despatch of an IMF team to Jakarta in November 1962 to examine the practicalities of a stabilization programme, the Administration formed an inter-agency group drawn from the Policy Planning Council at the State Department, the Bureau of the Budget and the Agency for International Development, to formulate a response to its report. At the end of the year, Kennedy gave his blessing to a $17 million loan for raw materials and spare parts to assist Indonesian industry, an initiative approved on Harriman's advice in order to encourage the Indonesians to accept any conditions that the IMF were likely to place on its proposed assistance, and to make clear that the USA was serious in its desire to assist in Indonesia's peaceful economic development.[92] In all this, the Americans were also maintaining an insurance policy with their maturing links with the Indonesian Army, furthered in particular by the efforts of the US military attaché at the Jakarta Embassy, Lieutenant Colonel George Benson. Indeed, in October 1962 Benson learned of the Army's contingency planning if Sukarno were to be removed from power (whether by death through natural causes, assassination, accident or coup), and the domestic crackdown on the PKI that this involved.[93] In December, the Pentagon's civic action programme in Indonesia was given final approval, with projects set to begin in early 1963, while Indonesian officers continued to be sent on training courses at military establishments in the United States, providing more opportunities for service ties to be developed and American anti-Communist strictures to be delivered.

By late 1962, it appeared that Kennedy's goal of stabilizing the situation in South East Asia was some way to being realized. The Philippines, Thailand and South Vietnam represented a solid group of states firmly aligned with the United States. The conflict in Laos had been defused by the international agreement on neutralization finally reached with the Soviet Union and China at Geneva in July 1962. The Cambodian situation was problematic, as Washington felt Chinese Communist influence on Sihanouk's neutrality was increasing, while Cambodian tensions with its traditional rivals and neighbours, Thailand and Vietnam, were increasing the dilemmas faced by US officials. During the summer of 1962 a steady stream of optimistic reports began to flow from the recently established Military Assistance Command Vietnam in Saigon, which indicated that the decisions reached in November 1961 to increase the numbers

[91] See Hilsman, *To Move a Nation*, 376.
[92] See *FRUS, 1961–1963, XXIII*, 650–4.
[93] Telegram from Army attaché, Jakarta to DOS, 19 October 1962, 798.00/10–1962, RG 59.

of US advisers with the South Vietnamese forces and to supply much needed equipment, such as new helicopters, to help in counter-insurgency operations, were having their desired effect. At the July Honolulu conference, McNamara could even confidently look forward to the withdrawal of US personnel by the end of 1965.[94] Of course, the reality was that the National Liberation Front in the south had barely demonstrated its full potency or resilience, while the Diem regime was built on very fragile foundations and was busy eroding what little basis of popular support it had managed to accumulate in the late 1950s.

The development of US relations with Indonesia was another dimension to add to this picture. However, just as with the other elements in this overall design, the following year would see them begin to unravel. There were several ways in which US hopes that Sukarno might content himself with a path of neutrality and peaceful development were over-optimistic. For one, the Indonesian President's domestic political position was far from stable. The delicate balancing act between the Army and the mass organization of the PKI that helped to sustain his personal authority as the arbiter of internal tensions required also the distraction of foreign campaigns where he could arouse popular passions behind nationalistic causes. Neither the Army or the PKI were standing still under the ambit of Guided Democracy, and both jockeyed for a greater influence over national policy, and prepared themselves for their own showdown. By 1962, the Indonesian President was probably too reliant on the latter to be able to repudiate its role. Moreover, Sukarno possessed his own predilection for adventure and drama; projects for economic development were simply not stimulating enough, and in any event Sukarno's knowledge of economics was rudimentary. Although Sukarno had maintained that the acquisition of West Irian would complete the Indonesian revolution, there were some who believed that Indonesia's desire for territorial expansion had not been satiated, pointing, for example, to his calls in 1945 for a Greater Indonesia, including all of Borneo, Portuguese Timor, Malaya and Singapore.[95]

Developments in Sino-Soviet relations also served to complicate Washington's response to the Indonesian scene. The autumn of 1962 had witnessed the resurgence of tensions between Moscow and Beijing, as the Chinese began to adopt a more assertive line in their dealings with other Asian powers.[96] The most obvious manifestation of this trend

---

[94] See record of sixth Secretary of Defense Conference, Camp Smith, Hawaii, 23 July 1962, *FRUS, 1961–1963, vol. II, Vietnam 1962* (Washington, 1990), 548–50.

[95] See Gareth Jones, 'Sukarno's Early Views on the Territorial Boundaries of Indonesia,' *Australian Outlook*, 18, 1964, 31.

[96] See R. B. Smith, *An International History of the Vietnam War, vol. II: The Struggle for South-East Asia, 1961–65* (London, 1985), 80–9.

was the opening on 20 October of a Chinese military offensive across its disputed borders with India, a state whose ties with Moscow had become increasingly pronounced since the late 1950s. The success of this offensive proved a boost to China's status in Asia, and marked a setback for Khrushchev's policies in the subcontinent as Nehru turned to the West for support. Sino-Soviet tension was also apparent over the political situation in Mongolia, Soviet readiness to enter into nuclear test-ban talks with the USA and Britain, and Khrushchev's handling of the Cuban Missile crisis. A further indication that the Chinese now felt the need to push forward the revolutionary struggle in the Third World was given by the enhanced backing being accorded to the North Vietnamese regime in their attempts to promote the armed struggle in the south.[97] From the perspective of Beijing, the pursuit of a firmer anti-imperialist line might well find ready support in Indonesia, and from September 1962 onwards the Chinese seem to have begun a determined effort to improve their relations with Sukarno, and to foster closer contacts with the PKI. This was met, on the part of the PKI, by general support for Beijing's line in its polemics with Moscow, and the process was to culminate in the visit to Indonesia of the chairman of the PRC, Liu Shaoqi, in April 1963.

A final and decisive source of disruption to US aspirations for forging a closer relationship with Indonesia during 1963 came from British and Malayan plans for the creation of a new federation of Malaysia. Although the Indonesians had professed that they were indifferent to the formation of a Greater Malaysia when the scheme had first surfaced in the course of 1961, by the end of 1962 there were indications that tensions between Jakarta and Kuala Lumpur were on the increase, as the territories of Brunei, Sarawak and British North Borneo were readied for incorporation into the federation. Accusations of neo-colonialism from Indonesian observers began to flow, while there were signs that Jakarta was about to embark upon another West Irian-style campaign, with the British playing the role of the reviled European interloper in South East Asia. A collision between US policy towards Indonesia, British plans to withdraw from formal empire in South East Asia, and Indonesia's own fears, concerns and ambitions was imminent. To understand how this arose, it is necessary both to look at the background of relations between Indonesia, Malaya and Britain from the time of the West Irian crisis through to the end of 1962, and to examine the implementation of the scheme for a Greater Malaysia, the last a subject to which we will now turn.

---

[97] See e.g. Michael Yahuda, *China's Role in World Affairs* (London, 1978), 113–14, 120, 155–6.

2   The Greater Malaysia scheme I: the move towards merger

When speaking to a Singapore luncheon gathering of the Foreign Correspondents Association of South East Asia on 27 May 1961, Tunku Abdul Rahman, the Prime Minister of Malaya, made a seemingly casual reference to the need for a 'closer understanding' between the peoples of Malaya, Singapore, North Borneo, Brunei and Sarawak. The Tunku went on to say, '... it is inevitable that we should look ahead to this objective and think of a plan whereby these territories could be brought closer together in political and economic cooperation'.[1] The Malayan Prime Minister had carefully considered his remarks before delivering them, though even he could have had little realization that his speech would trigger a series of events that had such a profound effect on the future development of South East Asia. Taken at face value it seemed a modest enough proposal, but the Tunku's views represented a stark contrast with his earlier adamant and very public opposition to any closer association between Malaya and Singapore, and served to galvanize the political leaders and groups who saw the creation of a Greater Malaysia as satisfying their varying needs. Over the next eighteen months the plans and arrangements for a new federation would march on in a steady and seemingly inexorable fashion, though behind the scenes players from Britain, Malaya, Singapore and the Borneo territories engaged in a complex set of bargains and manoeuvres, as they sought to secure their essential interests in the new arrangements that would accompany the demise of formal colonial rule. We can now see that the process was far from smooth, and that the prospect of a complete collapse of the scheme, with all its unwelcome consequences, was perhaps the key ingredient that drove it forward to completion.

During the 1950s, the concept of a Greater Malaysian federation had occasionally been floated by British officials as a way to neatly organize their disparate colonial holdings in South East Asia, and offer the participants a degree of political stability, security and economic viability. Deep

---

[1] See Lee Kuan Yew, *Singapore Story*, 365.

reservations in Kuala Lumpur over any restructuring that could threaten Malay political paramountcy within the existing Malayan Federation had helped to stifle any progress being made with such ideas. Hence it was with some surprise that in June 1960 Lord Perth, the Minister of State at the Colonial Office, heard the Tunku talk favourably of an enlargement of the Federation while on a visit to London, saying he was 'prepared to face such a happening although it would give him a great number of headaches'. Perth was inclined to reinforce the Tunku's innate caution, pointing out that 'Indonesia recently had disclaimed any territorial ambition [in Borneo] and that at the moment it seemed wise to let sleeping dogs lie. If there was any hint of a move such as he mentioned I could imagine all sorts of agitation by other potential claimants.' There was also the state of development in the Borneo territories to consider, Perth noting that they were 'backward and how it was clearly important that they should learn the art of ruling themselves before they were asked to face decisions on their ultimate future'.[2]

Lord Selkirk, with his concerns for the future status of Singapore figuring heavily, was quick to pick up on Perth's account of his talks. He pressed the Foreign Secretary to give the proposals a speedy examination, having concluded that 'some association of this sort is the only evolution which I could envisage which can give a measure of stability to the area'. Selkirk felt that Singapore and Brunei (the latter with its overwhelming Malay and Muslim population of around 80,000) would quickly agree to the idea of a closer association, but in North Borneo and Sarawak there would undoubtedly be difficulties. Sarawak had about 750,000 inhabitants, of whom only 130,000 were classed as Malay in the 1960 census, while 230,000 were Chinese, and the remainder indigenous peoples, including 238,000 Sea Dyaks (Ibans) and 58,000 Land Dyaks. North Borneo had a population of 450,000, of whom 104,000 were Chinese and the remainder largely indigenous peoples.[3] It would be necessary to convince these differing populations that a closer association with Malaya did not entail subordination to the whims of Kuala Lumpur and Malay domination. The Commissioner General recognized that extending the Federation raised 'very big questions with regard to the protection of the more primitive people of the Borneo territories', though new arrangements over defence to protect the British right to use the Singapore base as they wished could probably be reached with the Tunku.[4] Lord Home,

---

[2] Perth note on talks with Tunku Abdul Rahman, 10 June 1960, PREM 11/3418.
[3] For the 1960 census figures, see *Report of the Commission of Enquiry, North Borneo and Sarawak, 1962*, Cmnd 1794 (London, 1962) (hereafter *Cobbold Report*), Appendix B, 83.
[4] Selkirk to Lloyd, 17 June 1960, PREM 11/3418.

the Commonwealth Relations Secretary, took more seriously the Tunku's wish to join only with the Borneo territories, and rather discounted the idea that he would be willing to bring Singapore in as a full partner; Perth had himself mentioned the Tunku's 'pretty deep-rooted suspicion of all that the Singapore Government stands for'. On the matter of closer ties between Malaya and the Borneo territories, Home noted that the Tunku had raised such ideas before, 'but always in the context of defence against Indonesia. He feels, and rightly, that we must be prepared for trouble, which will probably start in Borneo and that a plan to meet it ought to be on paper.'[5]

The Prime Minister had been following the exchange of ministerial views that had resulted from the Perth talks, and solicited the opinion of Sir Norman Brook, the Cabinet Secretary, with the thought, 'All this seems to me rather doubtful but I suppose it is worth considering.' Brook was more enthusiastic, noting: 'We had always hoped that Malaya might federate with the other British territories in the area. For the smaller ones, the only hope of constitutional advance lies in federation with Malaya.' The Tunku's fears of facing an overall Chinese majority if Malaya joined with Singapore could be allayed if the non-Chinese peoples of the Borneo territories were brought into the equation. The Colonial Office response was to commend the scheme as welcome in the long term, but to highlight the difficulties in the Borneo territories that would need to be overcome.[6] Brook ensured that the matter was placed on the agenda of the Cabinet's Colonial Policy Committee, and a paper was brought before the Committee by Iain Macleod, the Colonial Secretary, in July 1960. Here it was argued that a wider Malaysian federation offered considerable advantages, including some solution to the constitutional status of the Borneo territories, a more stable defensive framework for those territories in case of Indonesian or Philippine threats, the prospect of lessening the chance that Singapore would fall under Chinese Communist influence, and a reduction for the British of their internal security responsibilities. However, the Colonial Office was keen to apply the brakes. It was emphasized that the Tunku would probably be unwilling to join with Singapore (at least initially), that detailed new Treaty arrangements would be required to safeguard access to the British base facilities, and that the peoples of the Borneo territories would not welcome the idea of an early federation before their own political development had been completed. Macleod recommended that '... our attitude to the Tunku in this matter should be one of benevolent neutrality. He ought to be left in no doubt that this

[5] Home to Lloyd, 21 June 1960, *ibid.*
[6] Macmillan minute for Brook, M.214/60, 19 June 1960; Brook minutes for Macmillan, 27 June 1960, 6 July 1960, *ibid.*

is a matter where the Borneo peoples have got to have their own say in due course and in which we are not going to try to force them.'[7] This line was endorsed, with Selkirk instructed to further sound out opinions in the Borneo territories and the region as a whole.

Selkirk's efforts resulted in a Borneo Inter-Territorial Conference, held at Kuching on 20 October 1960, involving the Governors of North Borneo and Sarawak, the High Commissioner for Brunei and Lord Perth. Such scouting of official opinion on the question led to a formal recommendation from Selkirk that London should adopt the concept of a political association of Malaya, Singapore and the Borneo territories as the ultimate aim of policy. However, this would have to be secured through working with the support of local interests and developing a closer association between the Borneo territories themselves. Moreover, by late 1960, relations between the Federation and Singapore had become particularly strained, with the Tunku far from convinced that Lee Kuan Yew was determined to fight the internal threat from Communist subversion.[8] A visit to Malaya by Duncan Sandys, the new Commonwealth Relations Secretary, and the Tunku's presence in London for a Commonwealth Prime Ministers' conference in the first few months of 1961, gave British officials some insight into the Malayan Prime Minister's hostility to any premature merger with Singapore.[9] It was not until mid-April 1961 that the Colonial Policy Committee considered a further paper from Macleod on a closer association of Malaya with Singapore and the Borneo territories. Although the proposals received very general and tentative backing, the Colonial Secretary was not in favour of any public statements to this effect and emphasized the need to approach the idea slowly; the Cabinet Secretary agreed with Macleod's line and was concerned that the British should not be seen as imposing any wider scheme of federation on the peoples concerned. Highlighted also was the fact the Tunku, while willing to take the Borneo territories fully into a new federation, was still opposed to any closer relationship with Singapore.[10] Indeed, at about the same time the Committee met, Sir Geofroy Tory, the British High Commissioner in Kuala Lumpur, was reporting that the Tunku

---

[7] CPC(60)17, 15 July 1960, CAB 134/1559.
[8] CRO brief, 14 November 1960, DO 169/10.
[9] Notes of Secretary of State's discussions with Malayan ministers, 13–16 January 1961, *ibid.*, and see Sopiee, *Malayan Union to Singapore Separation*, 137–8.
[10] CPC(61)9, 14 April 1961; CPC(61)4th mtg, 18 April 1961, CAB 134/1560; Brook memorandum for Macmillan, 17 April 1961, PREM 11/3418. Objections to possibly prejudicing the free use of the Singapore base had also come from defence planners and the Air Secretary, Julian Amery, see Easter, 'British defence policy,' 38–9.

showed no signs of softening. He said we could prove to him as often as we liked that Malaya should assume responsibility for Singapore, but the fact remained that the bulk of the Chinese in Singapore were incapable ever of adopting a truly Malayan viewpoint and therefore of being assimilated safely into the Federation. He said 'they will never be Malaya's friends in a thousand years'.[11]

Within a few weeks the Malayan position had been transformed as a political crisis engulfed Singapore and seemed to herald the emergence of a more radical alternative party that would soon eclipse PAP rule in the colony. Ong Eng Guan, the ex-minister who had left the PAP the previous year, was not content with desultory opposition, and his continued sniping at Lee's Government culminated in his resignation from his seat in the Hong Lim constituency in order to fight a by-election and demonstrate the popularity of his anti-colonial message. At the beginning of April, Lee confessed to Selkirk that if the PAP's candidate was defeated, '. . . he had considered going into opposition and would be happy to do so if a right-wing government would take over. But he feared that was impossible and any new government would be much further to the left. He would be to-tally strung on a lamp-post.' When asked what sort of merger with Malaya he was now prepared to accept, he replied that 'he would accept anything; he was prepared to go to Kuala Lumpur as a Member of Parliament if Singapore became a state of the Federation, though he added "an impor-tant state". But he must show that the Chinese were not being sold out.'[12] Defeat in the Hong Lim poll, when it came at the end of April 1961, was a major blow to Lee's authority, and helped to open up the underlying splits within the PAP between its English-educated and moderate elements and the party's Chinese-educated and trade-union-based left wing.[13] In the week before the Hong Lim result, Lee travelled to Kuala Lumpur for talks with the Tunku and Tun Abdul Razak, the Malayan Deputy Prime Minister, where he argued that without the prospect of merger on the horizon, Singapore would become independent and Communist in the near future. By now Razak and other influential Malayan ministers had become converted, but the Tunku remained sceptical.[14] However, as re-actions to Hong Lim set in during May, the Malayan authorities be-gan to appreciate that neither the British nor the PAP government were prepared to employ coercive measures against left-wing activists in the colony pressing for abolition of the ISC and early independence, as long

[11] Tory to Sir Neil Pritchard (CRO), 18 April 1961, DO 169/10.
[12] Record of conversation between Lee Kuan Yew and Selkirk, 4 April 1961, FO 1091/104.
[13] See Lee Kuan Yew, *Singapore Story*, 351–4.
[14] The talks were on 23 April; see record of conversation between Lee Kuan Yew and Philip Moore, 28 April 1961, and Selkirk to Macleod, 4 May 1961, DO 169/25.

as their organizing and campaigning activities remained lawful. The only answer to the security dilemma posed to the Federation by the prospect of 'another Cuba' across the causeway, ready to spread subversion further north, appeared to be a merger. With Singapore coming under the jurisdiction of the federal authorities in Kuala Lumpur, effective measures of repression could be taken against radical and pro-Communist groups, in the way the white colonial power was no longer able or willing to do. The fundamental *quid pro quo* for Malaya's leaders was the inclusion of Sarawak, North Borneo and Brunei in such a scheme, as a way to ensure that Malay primacy in any new federation was not prejudiced by Chinese numbers (who would make up only 42 per cent of any Greater Malaysia that was formed).

The day before he was to deliver his speech before the Foreign Correspondents Association, the Tunku saw Tory to explain that he no longer felt that the Federation could insulate itself from developments in Singapore, and that some means had to be found to absorb the colony. Only Greater Malaysia offered such a route, and the Malayan Prime Minister indicated that he was now ready to take the lead with pressing for the scheme and would prepare a memorandum setting out his views for the British Government to consider. 'Given his violent prejudice hitherto', Tory reported, 'this represents almost miraculous change of heart. As suspected, now penny has dropped, he is perhaps moving ahead faster than we were prepared to go but we have more chance of steering him if we go along with him than if we try and restrain him at this juncture.' Despite Tory's anxiety to press on, British officials and ministers were more hesitant; Selkirk's (rather unhelpful) initial reaction to the Tunku's speech was to advise that 'we should neither (a) drag our feet nor (b) appear to be taking over the initiative'.[15]

British caution mainly derived from two aspects of the proposals for a Greater Malaysia. In the first place, the Governors of Sarawak and North Borneo, Sir Alexander Waddell and Sir William Goode, had strong reservations about any rapid moves to push their subjects into a wider federation, feeling that many more years of internal development would be needed before such plans could be contemplated. They were also concerned from Malayan attitudes that the intention was simply to absorb Sarawak and North Borneo, offering them no real degree of local autonomy to protect indigenous interests.[16] At the end of June, Selkirk convened a round-table conference of governors and officials in Singapore to discuss the Tunku's new position, where despite acknowledgement

---

[15] Kuala Lumpur to CRO, no. 382, 26 May 1961; Selkirk to Macleod, no. 183, 29 May 1961, DO 169/25.
[16] Waddell to Melville (CRO), 1 June 1961, *ibid.*

of the attractions of Greater Malaysia there were also strong doubts expressed over timing and the need for local consultation.[17] The British still held recent memories of the events of 1946–9, where the transfer of Sarawak to crown colony status had excited much local opposition, divided the Malay community, and culminated in the murder of the British governor. The Prime Minister was warned by Selkirk that similar unrest could again be expected if the scheme were rushed too quickly.[18] Matters were not helped by the Tunku's visit to the Borneo territories in July 1961, Goode reporting that the trip had been 'disastrously counter-productive... Tunku's public statements as reported have been tactless and he appears to be wilfully refusing to listen to local views.'[19] On 9 July, as if to underline the problems to come, A. M. Azahari, head of Brunei's main opposition Party Rakyat (People's Party), Ong Kee Hui, chairman of the Sarawak United People's Party (SUPP), representing a large part of the territory's Chinese population, and Donald Stephens, the leader of North Borneo's sizeable non-Muslim Kadazan community, issued a joint statement expressing their opposition to any merger of the Borneo territories with Malaya along the lines that the Tunku had begun to advocate.[20]

The second set of doubts about a Greater Malaysia revolved around the status of the British base facilities at Singapore. The free use of the base was an absolute requirement for London; without it British participation in SEATO and the commitments to Australia and New Zealand lacked all credibility, while the ongoing crisis in Laos demonstrated the immediate relevance of the issue. There had, it will be recalled, been problems over the operation of British forces from bases in Malaya when connected with SEATO exercises in Thailand (who technically had to route through Singapore before heading north). Any renegotiation of the Anglo-Malayan Defence Agreement of 1957 to cover Malaysia would need to accommodate Britain's SEATO role. That this would create problems was indicated when the Tunku despatched his formal ideas on the Malaysia scheme to London on 26 June 1961. These included the contention that after merger the Singapore bases 'would no longer be at the disposal of SEATO but could be maintained as bases for the defence of the Commonwealth'. The Tunku's memorandum also noted that Brunei, Sarawak and North Borneo could be brought quickly into the existing Malayan Federation as simply additional states, and before the

---

[17] See Selkirk to Macleod, no. 4, 27 June 1961, PREM 11/3418; it is interesting that at this early stage, Selkirk was warning that, 'The possibility cannot be ignored that developments on Grand Design may antagonise the Indonesian Government and might conceivably lead them to attempt an irredentist movement in the Borneo territories.'
[18] Mackie, *Konfrontasi*, 63; Selkirk to Macmillan, 27 June 1961, PREM 11/3737.
[19] Goode to Macleod, no. 141, 11 July 1961, CO 1030/980.
[20] Mackie, *Konfrontasi*, 78, n. 32.

federation was extended to Singapore, and requested that talks be held soon on all the issues raised by the proposals.[21] Conveying the Tunku's views to Macmillan, Selkirk pointed out both the drawbacks in his ideas over the Borneo territories and the defence position, and the advantages of the scheme overall, including the fact that Britain would be relieved of internal security responsibilities in Singapore and that with regard to Borneo, 'we should largely be freed from the anti-Colonial pressures of the United Nations and might well maintain our influence on a sounder long term basis. The parallel position of the Dutch in West Irian comes readily to mind.' Commending the idea of a Greater Malaysia, Selkirk warned that, 'Considerable risks are involved which can compare with those taken in 1947 in India, although the number of people involved is, of course, much less ... Negotiating gambits are, however, not all on the side of the Federation.'[22] Others in London could also see the benefits offered by the scheme, the Prime Minister's Foreign Affairs Private Secretary, Philip de Zulueta, finding that: 'At first sight and in spite of the obvious snags, this looks like perhaps giving us a dignified way of reducing our Far East commitments.'[23]

The formal British response to the Tunku's proposals, delivered in early August, was guarded and cautious. Macmillan invited the Malayan leader to London for talks on the issues raised, but only some time in late October or November. With regard to the defence issue, the Prime Minister noted, '... the present difficult state of affairs in South-East Asia, and the need in all our interests to maintain confidence there, makes it very important that nothing should be said which might cast doubt on the maintenance of British defence capabilities in the area', and he went on to stress that 'in view of the doubts and hesitations which have been expressed publicly in the [Borneo] territories over what close political association would involve for the various races there ... we do not give the impression that we are deciding on their future without regard for their wishes'. In his memoirs Macmillan commented that he 'certainly did not want a shot-gun wedding'.[24]

Political developments in Singapore during the summer of 1961 made it impossible to maintain such an attitude of reserve, and acted once more

---

[21] Tunku Abdul Rahman to Macmillan, T.348A/61, 26 June 1961 and enclosed memorandum SR(050)304, PREM 11/3418. The memorandum also included the statement that, 'It would be better of course if Sarawak could be returned to Brunei, at least the northern part of Sarawak, where the population is mainly Malays and Dyaks.'
[22] Selkirk to Macmillan, 27 June 1961, *ibid.*
[23] De Zulueta to Macmillan, 29 June 1961, *ibid.*
[24] See Sandys to Macmillan, 31 July 1961; Sandys to Tunku Abdul Rahman, no. 1150, 28 June 1961; Macmillan to Tunku Abdul Rahman, 3 August 1961, PREM 11/3418, and Harold Macmillan, *At the End of the Day, 1961–1963* (London, 1973), 248–9.

to boost the impetus towards the creation of Malaysia. The narrow victory of David Marshall of the Workers' Party in the Anson by-election on 15 July brought the nascent split in the PAP to a head, as its factions vied with each other during the campaign. The left wing of the PAP eventually repudiated the official party candidate and endorsed Marshall, while backing a campaign calling for the abolition of the ISC and full internal self-government. Lee's Government managed to scrape through a vote of confidence in the Assembly, but the left wing of the PAP defected to form the Barisan Socialis (Socialist Front) and crossed into opposition, leaving the rump of the PAP with only 26 seats in the 51-seat chamber. Further defections would spell the end of the PAP's majority, and the government was left very vulnerable to future votes of no confidence. Most observers predicted that in the Singapore-wide elections due before June 1964, a Barisan Socialis majority would be returned; only the formation of Malaysia, with its new constitutional and electoral arrangements, and with Kuala Lumpur prepared to take more drastic steps over internal security, seemed to offer Lee and the PAP any chance of retaining local power.[25] For the Malayan authorities, the emergence of the Barisan in Singapore, and the possibility of the collapse of PAP rule, presented them with the necessary incentive to push the British harder over Greater Malaysia.

The public pace was quickened considerably when ten days after the Anson by-election the Tunku proposed talks on merger with Lee. At the same time, the Malayan leadership began to actively court the support of political figures from the Borneo territories, while Lee met with representatives from Sarawak and North Borneo at a gathering of the Commonwealth Parliamentary Association in Singapore. Following visits to Kuala Lumpur in August, Donald Stephens, as well as Datu Mustapha, the main Malay–Muslim leader in North Borneo, and Datu Bandar, the head of the Party Negara Sarawak (PANAS, the chief Malay rival to SUPP), came out with enthusiastic support for Malaysia. Sensing that the political tide was turning, these leaders undoubtedly judged that it was advisable to back the new federation, while pressing for the best possible terms for entry and any spoils that might be on offer from Kuala Lumpur. A federal structure might also provide some shelter from the possibility of Chinese domination, a powerful consideration in Sarawak given that SUPP still constituted the best-organized and -supported political party in the colony. The views of the pro-Malaysia parties in the Borneo territories were coordinated from the end of August by the Malaysia Solidarity Consultative Committee (MSCC), a body chaired by Stephens with

---

[25] These developments are covered in Lee Kuan Yew, *Singapore Story*, 368–84.

the aim of educating local opinion about the scheme and presenting a common view to the British and Malayan authorities on the terms and conditions that must accompany the creation of the new federation. The result of Lee's subsequent talks on merger with the Tunku in August was rapid agreement on the principle that federal jurisdiction in Malaysia would extend to the areas of defence, external affairs and internal security, while Singapore would retain autonomy in education and labour policy.[26] Although details still had to be finalized, including such questions as Singapore citizens' voting rights in federal elections and the level of Singapore's representation in the federal assembly in Kuala Lumpur, the successful talks were seen as a greatly encouraging sign for the future.

During August, British officials also began to appreciate that the political crisis in Singapore meant that the Malaysia scheme had to be pushed forward, and that the opportunity created by the immediate political imperatives of Lee and the Tunku might well be unique. Towards the end of the month, Selkirk wrote to the Colonial Secretary, noting that 'the time has come when it is necessary to consider how far a crash programme for the "Greater Malaysia" scheme is desirable and necessary'. By early September, the Commissioner General was predicting the fall of the Singapore Government in a few months if no progress towards merger were made, while if the Borneo territories were not brought into Malaysia, 'the long-term alternatives for them would be independence or absorption by Indonesia or China. The first of these alternatives is not likely to be maintained and would probably lead to the second.' Selkirk doubted that the elaborate process of preparing the Borneo territories for democratic self- government prior to a closer relationship with Kuala Lumpur would gain many benefits for Britain: '...we have ... to face up to the fact that "one man, one vote" has not been a wild success in South East Asia'.[27] Again, towards the end of September, Macleod was being advised that, 'Once merger is achieved, the extent of the damage which the Barisan Socialis can inflict is so greatly reduced that the situation need not be unduly disturbing.'[28]

More pressure for Whitehall to speedily consider the Greater Malaysia proposals was provided by the despatch at the start of September of another request by the Malayan Prime Minister to Macmillan for an early meeting in London, though again indicating that the British should give a prior undertaking that the Borneo territories would be included in any

---

[26] Sopiee, *Malayan Union to Singapore Separation*, 159, and see Kuala Lumpur to CRO, no. 632, 25 August 1961, PREM 11/3418.
[27] Selkirk to Macleod, 24 August 1961, DO 169/10; Selkirk to Macleod, 16 September 1961, PREM 11/3418.
[28] Singapore to CO, no. 44, 23 September 1961, PREM 11/3422.

prospective federation before the incorporation of Singapore. Indeed, although the August talks between the Tunku and Lee Kuan Yew had been harmonious, the former had been unwilling to give any public and definite commitment to merger with Singapore until he had secured from the British the necessary assurances regarding the Borneo territories.[29] Ghazali bin Shafie, the Permanent Secretary at the Malayan Ministry of External Affairs (and the official most intimately connected with the Malaysia scheme), had told Tory that

Tunku was not bluffing in expressing his belief that people of Borneo territories could be brought quickly to accept desirability of Greater Malaysia if British Government gave necessary lead. Malayans had given up any hope of strong action by Lee against Communists . . . Nor did they believe any longer that we would take such action ourselves, e.g. by suspending constitution. Unless therefore we could commit Borneo territories without reservation to Greater Malaysia . . . they could see no alternative to allowing Singapore to go Communist. If solution to Singapore problem could not be found through Greater Malaysia, Federation would have to abandon whole idea and leave Singapore to us.[30]

Jockeying between London and the Malayan Government continued throughout September, the Tunku growing steadily more annoyed at what he saw as the delays and prevarications coming from the British side. When British officials pointed out that local opinion in the Borneo territories would need to be consulted over the scheme, adequate constitutional safeguards provided, and time allowed before they could join the new federation, the Tunku was dismissive. The Malayan Prime Minister feared, above all, that the British were stalling, hoping that anxieties over the internal security situation in Singapore would drive him into accepting an early merger, with only the promise of the eventual accession of the Borneo territories.[31]

With matters apparently so precariously poised, Macmillan sent an emollient message to the Tunku on 4 October, assuring him that the British did indeed intend to bring the Borneo territories into any new Malaysian federation, and the important thing was simply to decide how this was to be done.[32] Three days later the Tunku replied in positive tones, mentioning that the transfer of sovereignty over the Borneo territories to the new federation must be accomplished simultaneously with

[29] See Acting UK High Commissioner Singapore to CO, no. 390, 19 September 1961, PREM 11/3418.
[30] Kuala Lumpur to CRO, no. 687, 21 September 1961, PREM 11/3422.
[31] See Selkirk to Macmillan, 3 October 1961; Tunku Abdul Rahman to Macmillan, 21 September 1961, in Kuala Lumpur to CRO, no. 688, 21 September 1961; Kuala Lumpur to CRO, no. 705, 26 September 1961, *ibid.*; Moore to Ian Wallace (CO), 18 October 1961, CO 1030/986.
[32] Macmillan to Tunku Abdul Rahman, T.559/61, 4 October 1961, *ibid.*

a merger with Singapore. Formal talks could now proceed in London during November, but the complications of the status and attitude of the Borneo territories continued to trouble the British as they tried to satisfy the Tunku without prejudicing their colonial responsibilities to the peoples concerned. Having been informed of the exchanges with the Tunku, the Australian Prime Minister, Sir Robert Menzies, cautioned Macmillan: 'Any suggestion that the UK and the Malayan Government is prepared to allow other considerations to override the principle of self-determination could... have most damaging effects, most immediately in Borneo.'[33] The Tunku also appeared to be prejudging important issues yet to be settled; in October 1961 he announced to the Malayan Parliament (in misleading fashion) that the British had already agreed in principle that Singapore would not be available for SEATO use under the new defence arrangements for Malaysia, and that sovereignty over the Borneo territories would be passed directly to the federal authorities in Kuala Lumpur when Malaysia was brought into being.[34] This public statement on the defence issue was undoubtedly a bargaining ploy (suggested to the Tunku, some versions claimed, by Lee Kuan Yew), making clear that London could not expect satisfaction on the issue of free use of Singapore if it continued to procrastinate over the Borneo territories.[35]

Meanwhile, during late September and October, an inter-departmental group of Whitehall officials, the Greater Malaysia (Official) Committee, had been exploring the whole scheme with the aim of furnishing advice to ministers.[36] Its final report was full of caution over the treatment of the Borneo territories and how they were to be reconciled to joining a new federal structure, reflecting the deep reservations of the Governors of Sarawak and North Borneo that the indigenous peoples were not yet ready for accession, and in many cases feared Malay discrimination. In the former case, Waddell's latest advice was that 'any attempt to force merger by 1963 or at all prematurely will most likely result in racial conflict and outright rebellion in Sarawak'.[37] Moreover, the Government was legally committed to the Nine Cardinal Principles of the Rule of the English Rajahs, which had been repeated in the Sarawak constitution introduced

[33] Menzies to Macmillan, no. 925, 18 October 1961, CO 1030/992. Having been consulted over the summer, the Australian Government gave its qualified approval to the Greater Malaysia scheme in August, see Canberra to CRO, no. 785, 29 August 1961, PREM 11/3418.
[34] See Mackie, *Konfrontasi*, 43.
[35] See acting UK High Commissioner Singapore to CO, no. 406, 2 October 1961, PREM 11/3422; Singapore to DOS, no. 130, 6 October 1961, NSF, countries file, Malaya and Singapore General, 1/61–10/61, JFKL.
[36] See Bligh to Macmillan, 12 September 1961; Macmillan to Sandys, 13 September 1961, PREM 11/3418.
[37] CO memorandum, GM(61)5, 25 September 1961, CAB 134/1949.

in 1946. The eighth of these, reaffirmed as recently as 1960, had pledged Britain not to relinquish responsibility over their subjects until they had been given the chance to play a full part in their own government, and also committed the British to uphold the best wishes and desires of the indigenous communities. The various Legislative Assemblies in the Borneo territories established in the late 1950s could not yet be taken to represent local opinion, as few members were selected by direct elections, the franchise for which was still restricted.

Nevertheless, the Committee's final report endorsed the aim of creating a new federation, certainly before the Singapore constitution came up for review in 1963:

> ... if a merger of Singapore with Malaya can be achieved we shall not only succeed in extricating ourselves from an increasingly menacing situation in the former, but do so in the one way likely to reinforce rather than undermine the security of South-East Asia in general and our own interests in particular.

Over the Borneo territories, it was noted that their inclusion in a Greater Malaysia offered them the best hope for the future in the long term. Each was vulnerable individually, and

> Moreover, China, Indonesia and the Philippines have, or could readily work up, interests of one kind or another in them: in particular Indonesian irredentism is likely to prove an increasingly grave threat to which there may well be no answer except perhaps Greater Malaysia.

Hence:

> ... our choice lies between guiding them now into a Greater Malaysia which we are satisfied is their most desirable destination, despite the fact that the peoples are not yet themselves really capable of exercising considered judgement on the matter and are not yet ready to stand on their own feet in this wider association, or waiting until they have become so capable and ready, when the opportunity of Greater Malaysia may well have been lost and the alternative prospect of separate independence will be parlous and brief.

At the same time, constitutional safeguards would need to be formulated that offered the territories some measure of self-government, though it was recognized that anything so sweeping as including a right of secession would be unacceptable to the Malayan authorities. Overall, in the forthcoming talks with the Tunku, the Committee's report hoped that a merger of Singapore and Malaya could be accomplished first, and only after several years' further preparation would Sarawak and North Borneo join a new federation. In any event a commission of enquiry would need to be appointed to make an official survey of opinion in the Borneo territories towards the idea of a Greater Malaysia.[38]

[38] GM(61)11(Final), *ibid.*, and see also D(61)62, 24 October 1961, CAB 131/26.

While the Committee's officials debated the various merits and problems inherent in the new federation, senior ministers were already engaged in discussions about long-term British overseas commitments that led to their support for the project. Following the Chancellor of the Exchequer's calls for deep cuts in defence spending in June 1961, officials had identified internal security duties at Singapore as one major area of possible saving in the Far East, while some thought had been given to redeploying forces to Australia (though the prohibitive costs involved helped to make this an unpalatable option). In early October, ministers met to discuss the likely trends of defence spending into the 1960s. Even if a Greater Malaysia were established, it was considered unlikely that unrestricted use of the Singapore base could be relied upon; nevertheless, the scheme was endorsed as offering the best protection of future British interests. Moreover, over the longer haul, the Prime Minister looked towards the time when a land-force commitment to SEATO might have to be renounced, and when air and sea forces were moved from Singapore to new base facilities in Australia.[39]

The Greater Malaysia (Official) Committee's final report was in turn addressed by ministers at the Cabinet's Defence Committee on 25 October 1961, along with the pattern of the forthcoming negotiations with the Tunku. Leading the proceedings throughout, Duncan Sandys explained that the whole scheme of merger between Singapore and Malaya was dependent on the Tunku's need to incorporate the Borneo territories in order to counterbalance the weight of Chinese numbers:

This presented the British Government with a difficult problem of timing as the Borneo Territories were far from ready for such an association: *in the last analysis we must do what we thought right about that and not simply abide by local opinion in Borneo, but it would be important to carry local opinion with us and the Tunku must be made to understand the need to do so* [emphasis added]. At present he over-rated the strength of Malaya's attraction in the Borneo Territories. More difficult still was the problem of our bases in Singapore. The Tunku clearly aimed at getting all the military and economic advantages of a major British military presence in Malaya and Singapore while subjecting to his veto our operational use of our bases and other facilities.

The Commonwealth Secretary wholly commended the creation of a new Malaysian federation but was acutely aware that the path ahead was far from straightforward; the Tunku himself was felt to be desperately anxious to secure a merger and this could be employed against him. The Defence Committee went on to reject the arguments of Julian Amery, the Secretary of State for Air, who opposed the scheme and preferred to retain a grip

---

[39] See FP(61)1st mtg, 6 October 1961, and the Prime Minister's memorandum 'Our Foreign and Defence Policy for the Future,' 29 September 1961, CAB 134/1929.

on Singapore under existing treaty rights, concluding it would be much easier for the Tunku to 'take and sustain repressive measures' than the British, and the burden of carrying out internal security tasks on the island could be lifted. 'Moreover', the Committee noted with disarming understatement,

if Greater Malaysia was not in sight before the review of the Singapore Constitution due in 1963 we were likely to encounter trouble there (as we could even earlier if Mr Lee and his Government fell). In that case we should probably have to suspend the Constitution, perhaps for an indefinite period. Whether or not we suspended the Constitution we should be very ill-placed in Singapore (or Malaya) if we had to maintain our position in circumstances of local hostility.[40]

Duncan Sandys was to play a key role in the series of negotiations that led to the formation of Malaysia. He had already established a formidable reputation during his time at the Ministry of Defence in the late 1950s where he pushed through the controversial Defence White Paper of 1957 that brought an end to national service. He worked his officials mercilessly, while his physical stamina, if not his sharpness of mind, was often remarked upon by those unfortunate enough to be locked in argument with him. Nigel Fisher, who served on Sandys's ministerial team between 1962 and 1964, recalled the formidable demands he made of his officials, his long working hours and ruthless methods, where stamina in negotiation was a key asset. Major London venues of constitutional conferences were often bugged by the security service with his eager approval, while Sandys tended to by-pass his colleagues and to avoid taking matters to Cabinet or to use the Cabinet committee system, preferring to discuss matters privately with the Prime Minister.[41] Macmillan undoubtedly had great confidence in a minister he judged was loyal, reliable and, though occasionally ponderous, immensely hard-working. Writing in his diary in June 1961, Macmillan noted: 'Sandys is a great contrast to Macleod. As cool as a cucumber; methodical; very strong in character . . . tremendously hard-working; not easily shaken from his course – ambitious, and rather cruel . . .'[42]

The Anglo-Malayan talks on forming a Greater Malaysia finally got under way in London on 20 November 1961. Referring to the Borneo

---

[40] D(61)14th mtg, 25 October 1961, CAB 131/25; for Amery's arguments see D(61)66, Note by the Secretary of State for Air, 24 October 1961, CAB 131/26.

[41] Nigel Fisher Oral History. Note also the recollections of Sandys's character and negotiating technique contained in Lee Kuan Yew, *Singapore Story*, 364, 480.

[42] Diary entry, 4 June 1961, MSS. Macmillan dep. d. 42. The relationship between the Commonwealth Secretary and Prime Minister had certainly been reinforced during 1961 as they both tried to rein in the Colonial Office and Macleod, and then his successor as Colonial Secretary, Reginald Maudling, over the future of the Central African Federation.

territories, the Prime Minister indicated that some consultation would be required so their consent to join Malaysia could be demonstrated. The Tunku accepted this, but could foresee little difficulty: 'They would enter the proposed new association on the same basis as the existing States of the Federation with broadly the same limited amount of local autonomy.' Sandys reemphasized that 'the questions of consultation and timing were crucial since we must not only do what we thought right, but also ensure that what we did could properly be represented as meeting the broad wishes of the Borneo peoples'.[43] Ultimately, British ministers and officials were surprised and pleased with the course and outcome of the discussions. Although the Malayans at first mentioned the idea of a secret agreement to cover the use of the Singapore bases for SEATO purposes, they eventually acceded to the British view that a public declaration, preserving the deterrent effect of the British forces, would need to be issued.[44] One can speculate about the implicit linkage that seems central to the November talks. The British were privately assured by the Malayans of their continued freedom to use the Singapore base, though the arrangement would have to be carefully cloaked in language acceptable to the domestic Malayan audience. What is more difficult to judge on the available evidence is whether the Malayans were in turn assured that the Borneo territories would be incorporated within a new Greater Malaysia, with the procedure of a commission of enquiry merely an expedient to show that the requirements of self-determination were being met. It is certainly apparent that the Tunku (with help from Lee) had played up the possibility of a serious disagreement over the defence issue in order to produce a more forthcoming attitude in London over the Borneo territories, where real Malayan concerns lay.[45]

The two days of discussions resulted in a statement issued on 23 November where the British and Malayan Governments professed that the setting-up of a new Malaysian federation was 'a desirable aim' while the Malayans agreed to an extension of the 1957 Anglo-Malayan Defence Agreement. A joint commission of enquiry to ascertain the views of the peoples of Sarawak and North Borneo and make appropriate recommendations was also announced. The form of words used in explaining the extension of the defence agreement was, as we have seen, crucial, for while no explicit reference was made to the SEATO alliance, it was formally acknowledged that the UK would be allowed to retain its base facilities at Singapore 'for the purpose of assisting in the Defence of Malaysia and for

[43] Minutes GMD(B)(61) 1st mtg, 20 November 1961, CAB 134/1953.

[44] GMD(B)(61) 3rd mtg, 21 November 1961, *ibid.* GMD(61)5, 22 November 1961; GMD(61)6, 22 November 1961, CAB 134/1952.

[45] See e.g. Singapore to CO, no. 528, 2 December 1961, PREM 11/3866.

Commonwealth Defence and for the preservation of peace in Southeast Asia'.[46] The vagueness of the final phrase allowed the British to maintain that their use of the Singapore base would be unrestricted. When presenting the successful outcome of the talks to the Cabinet, Sandys reassured ministers: 'It was clearly understood that this right would enable us to use Singapore to fulfil our obligations under the South-East Asia Treaty.' Such open-ended interpretations were to be the subject of many later heated disputes, taken as they were as an infringement of the future Malaysia's sovereignty and independence, while the Prime Minister showed concern that his colleagues not embarrass the Tunku by over-emphasizing their own interpretation of the meaning of the new defence arrangements.[47]

With the British and Malayan Governments having reached initial agreement over how to carry the Malaysia scheme forward, the next few months would see the spotlight turned to the Borneo territories, as opinions were moulded and formed, surveys conducted and new political parties created by groups determined that they should not lose out with the imminent end of British colonial rule. At the same time, there was no reduction in the political tensions that gripped Singapore. In November 1961, Lee had presented the formal terms for merger with Malaya to the Singapore Assembly in the form of a White Paper. The terms had immediately sparked controversy in that by allocating Singapore 15 seats out of 159 in the new projected federal assembly, they did not provide for proportionate representation. They also described all 624,000 Singapore citizens as becoming 'nationals' of the new Malaysian federation, leaving ambiguity over whether they would be accorded the same rights (including voting powers) as other 'federal' citizens; a residence requirement and Malay language test would be needed before many of the foreign-born Chinese in Singapore could be classed as full Malaysian citizens. On 6 December, the Assembly voted 33–0 in favour of the White Paper terms, but the Barisan walked out of the debate and took no part in the vote. Lee had already committed himself to putting the merger proposals to the Singapore electorate in a referendum, and the Barisan was soon

---

[46] See Sandys statement to House of Commons, 27 November 1961, Nicholas Mansergh (ed.), *Documents and Speeches on Commonwealth Affairs, 1952–1962* (London, 1963), 211.
[47] CC(61)65th, 23 November 1961, CAB 128/35. In fact, British ministers were soon after put on guard by public statements from both the Tunku and Lee Kuan Yew suggesting that a future Malaysian Government would have a veto over use of the Singapore base. At the same time, in the House of Commons, Sandys was subjected to some uncomfortable questions from the Opposition benches about the differing interpretations being put on the agreement; see record of Watkinson–Razak talks, 27 November 1961, PREM 11/3866, and *Hansard, Parliamentary Debates*, 5th series, vol. 650, cols. 242–8, 28 November 1961.

directing its attacks against the citizenship clauses of the White Paper terms.[48] When the referendum bill was introduced into the Singapore Assembly in March 1962, the revelation that it gave voters only a choice between three different forms of merger, rather than including any option to reject merger completely, provoked yet more controversy, as did Lee's announcement that blank ballots would be counted as votes in favour of the White Paper terms. British officials felt that the referendum was clearly being organized in an unscrupulous manner so that Lee could not lose.[49]

Nevertheless, with the Barisan apparently gaining ground against the PAP Government, pressure from Kuala Lumpur for more extreme action to be taken against those groups and individuals identified with pro-Communist views was stepped up. Much to the annoyance of the Malayans, however, the local British authorities, with Selkirk most prominent as chair of the ISC, were loath to take repressive action as long as left-wing political activity remained legal and there was little firm evidence of a threat to the security situation.[50] Meanwhile, Lee's referendum bill was finally forced through the Assembly, but its clause on blank ballots triggered the resignation of another PAP backbencher, finally depriving the Singapore Government of a majority and making it reliant on minor-party support for survival.[51] By the middle of July 1962, Philip Moore, Selkirk's deputy in Singapore, was reporting that the bill had 'excited more popular feeling than the Merger issue itself did when it was debated last November, and everyone realises that the undemocratic features of the Bill are a reflection of the Government's inability to get a genuine popular vote in favour of its White Paper proposals'.[52] Only rapid progress in the formation of Malaysia, it was becoming more and more apparent, would give the PAP its crucial safety net. Such progress was now dependent on whether Britain and Malaya could devise a way to bring the Borneo territories into Malaysia, and the crucial factor here was the work of the commission of enquiry into attitudes towards joining a new federation that began its work in earnest in February 1962.

---

[48] Lee Kuan Yew, *Singapore Story*, 406–9; Milton E. Osborne, *Singapore and Malaysia* (Ithaca, 1964), 19–23.
[49] See e.g. Moore to Ian Wallace (CO), 21 June 1962, PREM 11/3867.
[50] See e.g. Singapore to CO, no. 243, 4 May 1962, and Brook notes for Macmillan 15 May 1962, PREM 11/3866.
[51] Moore to CO, no. 318, 3 July 1962, *ibid.*
[52] Moore to CO, 11 July 1962, CAB 134/1950.

3   The Greater Malaysia scheme II:
      the Cobbold Commission and
      the Borneo territories

By the early 1960s the days of formal European empires appeared to
be numbered. As nationalist movements began to move into power in
Asia and Africa, and as independence was granted by, or wrested from,
the departing Europeans, the principle of self-determination became
firmly established once more in the value-system of international affairs.
The dominant anti-colonial mood was most prominently reflected in the
changing make-up and atmosphere of the United Nations. In 1960 the
General Assembly had passed a resolution (without dissent) that, 'All
peoples have the right of self-determination . . . Inadequacy of political,
economic, social or educational preparedness should never serve as a
pretext for delaying independence.'[1] The British could be sure that their
handling of the Malaysia issue would be subject to a degree of international scrutiny, and they were determined that the veneer of legitimacy
should be attached to the whole process. Among some officials, it must
also be recognized, there was a genuine sense of responsibility and a desire
to chart the best course for peoples about to be released into a potentially
hostile local environment. There was, in addition, a practical need to ensure the widest degree of support for the idea of joining Malaysia from
the populations of Sarawak and North Borneo. As ministers were only
too aware, there was the unhappy precedent of the Central African Federation to consider, established against the wishes of the African majority
in the early 1950s, and which by 1961 was in the final stages of collapse.
The central African experience was also pertinent in that it highlighted
the dangers of Whitehall disunity as Britain readjusted its imperial responsibilities, with strong divisions between the Colonial and Commonwealth Relations Offices amid ministerial rancour. This too was relevant
to Malaysia, as Colonial Office reservations about the project and its impact in the Borneo territories were steadily overruled by a determined
Prime Minister and Commonwealth Secretary.[2]

[1] See J. P. D. Dunbabin, *The Post-Imperial Age: The Great Powers and the Wider World*
   (London, 1994), 6.
[2] See e.g. Darwin, *Britain and Decolonisation*, 269–78.

79

In the original suggestions for a Greater Malaysia that the Malayan Prime Minister presented to Macmillan in June 1961, the Tunku had himself put forward the notion of forming an independent commission for the Borneo territories which would work out the constitutional details by which they would join a new federation; the Tunku did not envisage in his message that a commission should actually investigate whether popular opinion was in favour of Malaysia in the first place.[3] From the British point of view, a commission of enquiry, as the Anglo-Malayan talks of November 1961 had settled, was required to survey popular wishes and produce a finding on the state of opinion. It would then be up to the British and Malayan Governments to consider its recommendations and chart a way forward. Matters did not begin very auspiciously, when it proved almost comically difficult for the two governments to agree on a chair for the Commission (early candidates included Malcolm MacDonald and Alan Lennox-Boyd), though finally chosen was Lord Cobbold, the former Governor of the Bank of England.[4] Joining Cobbold on the Commission were two British figures with abundant local experience, Sir Anthony Abell, a former Governor of Sarawak and High Commissioner in Brunei, and Sir David Watherston, the Chief Secretary of the Malayan Federation until his retirement in 1957, while from the Malayan side came Datu Wong Pow Nee, the Chief Minister of the state of Penang, and the authoritative voice of Ghazali.

It was immediately apparent to several British observers that the Commission would have anything but a straightforward job. One senior Colonial Office official reported in January 1962 that 'apart from Malays in Sarawak great majority of population of both colonies is at present opposed to acceptance of Malaysia now ... What is said by hospitably entertained delegates in Kuala Lumpur is no safe indication of opinion in these territories and I fear that some of these spokesmen have little claim to be regarded as representative leaders.'[5] Selkirk confessed to the Prime Minister that Cobbold was 'going to have a very delicate task. Opinion is still hanging on a knife-edge and it will need a great deal of gentle and tactful persuasion to bring it the right way.'[6] Goode and Waddell, the Governors of North Borneo and Sarawak, complained to the Colonial Secretary that they were being asked to present the advantages of the scheme to the local population, yet no details of any final constitutional arrangements had been put forward, making consultation 'a farce' (in the

---

[3] See Tunku Abdul Rahman to Macmillan, T.348A/61, 26 June 1961, and enclosed memorandum, SR(050)304, PREM 11/3418.
[4] See material in DO 169/297.
[5] Martin to Perth, 31 January 1962, box 2, file 1, Goode papers.
[6] Selkirk to Macmillan, 24 January 1962, PREM 11/4188.

former's words).[7] Nevertheless, as we shall see, objections from the local colonial service were not going to be allowed to interfere with the priorities that had already been established in London and Kuala Lumpur.

Flying into Kuching on 19 February 1962, the Cobbold Commission began its survey work immediately by receiving letters and memoranda, and undertaking extensive tours of Sarawak and North Borneo where private hearings were held at district centres, allowing (in theory) individuals and interested groups to come forward with their views.[8] Yet behind the facade of official receptions and orderly administrative procedures, within a month of the Commission's arrival the whole enterprise appeared in jeopardy. Part of the problem was that more critical opinions of the Malaysia scheme as envisaged by the Malayan Government were being registered than was comfortable, but there were also tensions between the Malayan members of the commission and local British officials, whom the former suspected of not doing enough to 'educate' local opinion, and even of stirring up opposition. After Ghazali and Wong Pow Nee had complained of being snubbed at an official reception in North Borneo, the Tunku began to let his criticisms of the local British colonial service appear in the Malayan press. Cobbold warned Macmillan and Maudling that the Commission's project might have to be abandoned if Malayan attitudes continued. As for the Tunku's comments to the press, these might 'be a fit of temper because the Tunku is beginning to appreciate the real position. Ghazali has doubtless reported wide opposition to the Tunku's blue print of the plan for Malaysia. He had previously been led up the garden path by sycophantic Borneo politicians.'[9]

The impediments raised to the Commission producing a favourable report and the views of local British officials were not welcome to the Commonwealth Secretary, or indeed to the Prime Minister himself. Relations between the Colonial and the Commonwealth Relations Offices had reached a low ebb by early 1962. The future disposition of the Central African Federation had generated conflicts, with the Colonial Office being more responsive to the demands of the overwhelming African majorities in Nyasaland and Northern Rhodesia, while the CRO tended to look to the interests of the white minority government in Southern Rhodesia. The fact that responsibilities for the territories making up the Federation were divided between the two departments contributed to

[7] See Goode to CO, no. 250, 12 December 1961; Maudling reply to Goode and Waddell, no. 388, 22 December 1961, CO 1030/986; Goode and Waddell's original complaint has been withheld from the file.
[8] By the time it had completed its work in April 1962, fifty hearings had been held at thirty-five different centres, while over 4,000 people appeared before the Commission in some 690 groups, see *Cobbold Report*, 3.
[9] Cobbold to Macmillan and Maudling, no. 668, 16 March 1962, PREM 11/3866.

confusion, muddle and distrust. Differences over future constitutional arrangements had led to major arguments in Cabinet between Sandys and Maudling, with the latter and his whole ministerial team threatening resignation. It was certainly felt within the Colonial Office that Sandys was intent on absorbing its remaining responsibilities under his ambit at the CRO. The Greater Malaysia project carried the same kind of potential conflicts and problems, with the CRO reflecting the perspective and voice of Kuala Lumpur, while the CO passed on the views of the Borneo territories. Furthermore, responsibility for the new Malaysia would eventually, of course, fall to the CRO, as the CO relinquished its hold in the area. It was felt that the alleged snubs delivered to the Malayan members of the Cobbold Commission while in North Borneo during March were indicative of such divisions of responsibility, de Zulueta noting to Macmillan that, 'The Colonial Office seems very hostile to Greater Malaysia.'[10]

The Cabinet's ministerial committee on Greater Malaysia, GEN 754, came together on 21 March to discuss the issue, but before its meeting Sandys saw a receptive Macmillan to argue that he should take sole charge of the negotiations that would be required to bring the federation into existence, leaving Maudling only a subsidiary role. The Commonwealth Secretary, as one official noted, thought 'it would be wrong to repeat the pattern of the Federation of Rhodesia and Nyasaland by having two Ministers with an interest and responsibility'. The Prime Minister and the Cabinet Secretary concurred, and agreed that a decision over areas of demarcation could be taken when the Cabinet came to consider Cobbold's final report.[11] Macmillan later wrote in his diary: 'Greater Malaysia is in trouble. I foresee a situation like that in Central Africa. The two departments will quarrel and we shall get nowhere. I am considering putting Borneo, Brunei etc under the CW Secy. But I must await the report of the Cobbold Ctee.'[12] In its subsequent discussion of the snubbing incidents, the Cabinet Committee noted (with what were surely Sandys's views) that the

episode pointed to the possibility of a serious danger, namely that the Tunku's advisers in Kuala Lumpur and the British Colonial Service officials in North Borneo might be suspicious of each other's aims and motives, to the point of generating an atmosphere of mistrust, such as had developed in the Central African Federation. If the Government, having considered the report of the Commission of Enquiry, should conclude that Greater Malaysia would be in the best interests of the peoples of North Borneo and Sarawak, it might be necessary to take

[10] De Zulueta note for Macmillan, 16 March 1962, *ibid.*
[11] Bligh note for record, 21 March 1962, *ibid.*
[12] Diary entry for 24 March 1962, MSS. Macmillan dep d.45.

special steps to ensure that the British Colonial Service officials in the territories fully appreciated the convictions underlying the Government's policy and could conscientiously devote themselves to its fulfilment.[13]

The stage was clearly set for the downgrading of Colonial Office perspectives on Malaysia as the Government moved ahead with its chosen policy.

Cobbold himself was having major difficulties in reconciling views within the Commission, its British members sharing some of the reservations put to them about the need for constitutional safeguards for the Borneo territories. By the end of March, Cobbold was writing to the Colonial Secretary regarding Sarawak, 'It is quite clear that, apart from the Malays, who think Malaysia would make life easier for them, and the younger nationalist and/or communist Chinese, who are shouting "independence in 1963", the bulk of the population would prefer to see continuation of British rule.' Cobbold felt that a majority might be brought round to the scheme if they believed that Malaysia 'is a partnership in a joint enterprise and does not mean Sarawak being handed over to rule by Malays', but he was not optimistic over the chances: 'Unfortunately almost every utterance from Malaya tends to confirm suspicions here that the Malayan Government intends to gobble up Sarawak quickly and on their own terms, and that HMG have agreed, or are about to agree, to this process.'[14] As the Commission came together to draft its report, British colonial officials could draw little comfort from the flow of telegrams that they saw from Kuala Lumpur back to the CRO, indicating the Tunku's unwillingness to make any major concessions on the terms for admittance of the Borneo territories. Most depressing was the news at the beginning of June that the Tunku had instructed the Malayan members of the Commission to withdraw if the British members insisted on including in the final report a recommendation that there should be division of responsibility between London and Kuala Lumpur during a transitional period, and hence dual sovereignty, after the formal creation of the new federation.[15]

Although his preferred solution would also be for London to continue to exercise powers over all matters other than external affairs, defence and some aspects of internal security during a transitional period

---

[13] GEN 754/3rd mtg, 21 March 1962, CAB 130/179; see Maudling's minute to Macmillan defending the behaviour of colonial officers in North Borneo, PM(62)22, 19 March 1962, CO 1030/987; also for the Prime Minister's anxieties over waiting for the necessary changes, see Macmillan minute, 5 April 1962; Brook note to Macmillan, 10 April 1962, PREM 11/3866.

[14] Cobbold to Maudling, 31 March 1962, *ibid.*

[15] Kuala Lumpur to CRO, no. 171, 3 June 1962, box 2, file 1, Goode papers.

of three to seven years, Cobbold considered that a tolerable compromise would instead involve the state governments of Sarawak and North Borneo exercising full self-government in such a phase, but headed by British governors with a large number of contracted expatriate colonial officials. As Cobbold argued in a private letter to Macmillan:

I think Kuala Lumpur already has enough on its hands: they have done well in Malaya, but they are fully stretched and I think they might make a mess of the Borneo territories in the early years. One has to remember three things: there is a lot of personal ambition and empire building in Kuala Lumpur; the Malayans have promised top jobs to several quite unripe Borneo politicians in order to get their support for Malaysia; and last, but not least, many of the local head-hunting tribes are backward and fearless and would revert with pleasure to their former pastimes.[16]

However, any dilution in the principle of a complete transfer of power to the Malayans was likely to be unacceptable in Kuala Lumpur, as Tory was quick to emphasize, and would open up Malaysia to powerful accusations that it was merely perpetuating the old colonial regime in a different guise.[17]

The CRO suggested that the British members of the Commission might exclude from the report their recommendations over a division of responsibility (and hence implicitly sovereignty) during a transitional period, leaving the matter for the British and Malayan Governments to decide. Instead, Cobbold and the other British members might send a confidential letter to both Macmillan and the Tunku stating their full misgivings and the belief that certain powers should still be exercised by London for some years after the formal transfer of controls.[18] With Ghazali on the point of returning to Kuala Lumpur for further consultations, agreement on the final form of the report was reached on 15 June, the British members conceding that there would be no reference to the idea of British governors continuing to exercise local powers after the formal transfer of sovereignty. Strong protests followed from Goode in North Borneo, arguing that the suppression of some of the findings of the survey 'just because the Tunku finds them disagreeable' put at stake the principle of self-determination, while other colonial service officers reported 'considerable dismay here at the way in which the Tunku's pressure, via the CRO, on the Cobbold Commission seems to be paying off...'[19] Rather than eliciting a sympathetic response in London, the Governor's views

[16] Cobbold to Macmillan (draft), 6 June 1962, PREM 11/3866.
[17] Kuala Lumpur to CRO, no. 349, 13 June 1962, PREM 11/3867.
[18] CRO to Kuala Lumpur, no. 184, 13 June 1962, box 2, file 1, Goode papers.
[19] See Goode to Maudling, 17 June 1962, and Goode to CO, no. 104, 19 June 1962, *ibid.*; Hall to Wallace, 19 June 1962, PREM 11/3867.

were derided as representative of a cast of mind that did not recognize the realities of Britain's emerging post-imperial position; the Prime Minister's irritation was almost palpable when he noted on one of Goode's protests to Maudling:

I am rather shocked by this telegram and the attitude it reveals. Does he realise, a) our weakness in Singapore, b) our *urgent* need to hand over the security problem there. The whole mood is based on a false assessment of our power. If this is CO point of view, we shall fail. What are we to do?[20]

Lord Cobbold delivered his final report to the British and Malayan Prime Ministers on 21 June 1962. All members of the Commission were united in the opinion that federation with Malaya offered Sarawak and North Borneo the best prospects for the future. The report also returned the verdict that about one third of the population of each of the territories strongly favoured an early Malaysia, with no great concern over the terms, one third, while favourable to the idea, wanted various conditions and safeguards, and the remaining third were generally opposed, though on varying grounds. Divergences between the British and Malayan members of the Commission over the issue of transitional arrangements were acknowledged, and 'whether the Federation should be formed in one stage or in two'.[21] In the separate recommendations of the British members, Abell and Watherston put across their view that 'the Malaysia project offers Sarawak and North Borneo better prospects of security and prosperity than any other solution in view', and that an early decision in principle to move forward be taken by the British and Malayan Governments with a view to a new Federation being established within the next year. However, the lack of political development in the Borneo territories, a legacy of British treaty obligations, and the 'overriding importance' of the 'maintenance of efficient administration and law and order', influenced the British members to favour a transitional period of from three to seven (with five the optimum) years during which 'there would be as little change as possible' with the state governments retaining most of their old powers under a Governorship system with many expatriate officers remaining in post. With regard to the new Federal constitution, although it would be based on the existing Malayan constitution, joint working parties would have to agree on the incorporation of safeguards for the Borneo territories, and also determine the way earmarked state powers should finally be passed to the federal authorities in Kuala Lumpur.[22]

---

[20] Macmillan note to Brook, 21 June 1962, (commenting on no. 104 above), *ibid.*
[21] *Cobbold Report*, para. 145.
[22] *Ibid.*, paras. 148(e), 150–4.

The Malayan members of the Commission also delivered a separate set of recommendations. In these it was recognized that among those who were undecided over Malaysia there existed a feeling that

they are being rushed into some adventure, of whose outcome they are uncertain. Fear is the dominating factor among them – fear of Malay domination, fear of Muslim subjugation . . . fear of being swamped by people from Malaya and Singapore who would deprive them of the land and opportunities in Government and other enterprises, fear of the threat to their languages and cultures and so on.[23]

Assurances and explanations would have to be given and, moreover, their reservations could be eased 'if the colonial administration could unequivocally commend the Malaysia proposals to them'.[24] Ghazali and Wong Pow Nee did not subscribe to the view that native political leadership in the Borneo territories was absent or underdeveloped and felt that 'relative inexperience in working a system of government within the framework of the Federation should not . . . be an insurmountable factor'.[25] The imperative need was to remove uncertainty before civil and racial strife was allowed to crystallize around the issue, and hence the Malayan members strongly recommended that a transfer of sovereignty must take place within the next twelve months.[26] They also emphatically stated that the only suitable way to bring the new federation into existence would be through a full and immediate legal transfer of sovereignty and powers to the central government. The federal authorities could then, in practice, delegate to the Chief Minister of a state 'as many executive functions as may be necessary for the maintenance of good administration for a transitional period'.[27]

Cobbold himself, in his own personal comments, underlined the degree of unity that there had been in the Commission over many basic issues, but he went on to signal his agreement with the position of the British members on the question of transitional arrangements. While maintaining that such matters should be settled between governments, the arrangements 'should provide for continuity of administration in the Borneo territories and should not result in any weakening, either real or apparent, of authority in Kuching and Jesselton'.[28] Moreover, the report was accompanied, as had been agreed, by two confidential letters containing the deeper worries of the British members, and their preference for a scheme of dual sovereignty. As Abell and Watherston put it in their separate memorandum: '. . . we have yielded a number of points of the first

---

[23] *Ibid.*, para. 178.   [24] *Ibid.*, para. 179.   [25] *Ibid.*, para. 184.
[26] *Ibid.*, para. 188.
[27] *Ibid.*, paras. 197–200, 202–5.   [28] *Ibid.*, para. 238.

importance under pressure. We were greatly concerned by the reluctance of our Malayan colleagues, apparently supported by their Government, to make any concessions in favour of non-Muslim susceptibilities and national pride.' Macmillan was also informed that the path of the Commission through the Borneo territories had not been as smooth or assured as was generally portrayed and was warned of the potential for unrest that Malaysia contained. Cobbold spoke for the other British members when he wrote:

> We wish to lay stress on the dangerous position which we believe exists in Sarawak and which might easily spread to North Borneo. The happy relationship between different races which was recently a notable feature of both territories has largely disappeared in recent months in Sarawak, and is under strain in North Borneo, mainly because of strong feelings about the Malaysia proposals. Sarawak has become divided on racial lines, and communal feelings are being whipped up by well organised Communist cells. Feelings were running high in Sarawak at the time of our visit, and but for the obvious presence of strong police and field force detachments, there might well have been incidents at several places.[29]

Indeed it was during the period from March to July 1962 that Special Branch in Sarawak were beginning to detect more activity from the so-called Clandestine Communist Organization (CCO), as opposition to Malaysia began to be mustered among the Chinese population.

While the British and Malayan Governments digested the contents of the Report, the Tunku made known his doubts and hesitations about taking the scheme forward through another set of formal negotiations in London. The Malayan Prime Minister was said by Tory to be wary of mounting domestic opposition to merger with Singapore, feared being talked into unwise compromises by the British, and wanted some prior assurance that the talks would have a positive outcome.[30] More substantially, as well as the separate recommendations in the Report itself, the Tunku had regarded the submission of confidential letters by its British members as evidence that coming to an agreement would be impossible (such statements of pessimism from Kuala Lumpur were also, of course, designed to establish an advantageous climate in advance of negotiations). In early July, the Tunku despatched a letter to Macmillan which rejected the British members' recommendations in the Cobbold Report, declined the Prime Minister's invitation to London, and suggested that the British should simply continue to administer the Borneo territories until such time in the future as they were ready to join Malaysia.[31]

---

[29] Memorandum by Abell and Watherston, 21 June 1962, and Cobbold to Macmillan, 21 June 1962, box 2, file 1, Goode papers.
[30] Kuala Lumpur to CRO, no. 398, 2 July 1962, PREM 11/3865.
[31] Tunku Abdul Rahman to Macmillan, 4 July 1962, PREM 11/3867.

The Cabinet's Oversea Policy Committee met the same day as the
Tunku's letter arrived, giving Macmillan the chance to tell his ministerial
colleagues that

the Tunku's message appeared to be based on a misunderstanding... The Tunku
had clearly made the mistake of assuming that the views of Lord Cobbold and of
the British members of his Commission were in fact the views of the British Government. This was not of course the case; the main disadvantage of independent
commissions was that they were independent.

A reply would be sent to the Tunku, highlighting the fact that the British
Government had no desire to retain any authority in the Borneo territories
in a transitional phase after Malaysia's formation, that they were not
committed in any way to Cobbold's views and that they would be prepared
to discuss with an open mind any proposals the Tunku might care to
make.[32] The following day the full Cabinet discussed future policy over
Greater Malaysia in the light of the Cobbold Report, with Macmillan
again arguing that only the establishment of a new federation 'offered
a reasonable prospect of maintaining stability in the area'. The Prime
Minister indicated his own feeling that if a new federation was established,
responsibility for the Borneo territories should be immediately handed to
Kuala Lumpur, otherwise, 'We should then be answerable for events in
those territories without having effective control in them.' The minutes
recorded, in what may have been a meek and final argument from the
Colonial Secretary, that

In discussion it was pointed out that it would be difficult to overlook the specific commitments into which we had entered to safeguard the interests of the
population of the Borneo territories, particularly Sarawak. It was hoped that any
arrangements eventually agreed for the transitional period could be presented as
being consistent with these undertakings.[33]

Nevertheless, the Cabinet endorsed the general policy of pressing for
an agreement on Greater Malaysia with the Tunku. Having received his
soothing reassurances over the transfer of sovereignty from Macmillan,
the Malayan Prime Minister at last consented to begin formal talks.[34]
The domestic political events of 12–13 July 1962, the Prime Minister's
infamous 'night of the long knives', served as a prelude to the Tunku's
subsequent arrival in London, where amid a dramatic culling of Cabinet

[32] OP(62) 2nd mtg, 4 July 1962, CAB 134/2370.
[33] CC 44th(62)7, 5 July 1962, CAB 128/36.
[34] See Macmillan to Tunku Abdul Rahman, in CRO to Kuala Lumpur, no. 642, 4 July
1962, PREM 11/3867; and Tunku Abdul Rahman to Macmillan, in Kuala Lumpur to
CRO, no. 410, 5 July 1962, PREM 11/3868.

members Maudling was made Chancellor of the Exchequer, providing Sandys the opportunity to take over the job of Colonial Secretary, while retaining his existing duties at the CRO.[35] With this important change, the divisions of ministerial responsibility so recently witnessed over central African affairs could now be avoided, with Sandys ready to push on with Greater Malaysia irrespective of the cries of discontent coming from the colonial service.

The talks in London held in July 1962 over the Cobbold Report were crucial to the successful implementation of the Malaysia scheme. Their ostensible purpose was to deal with questions concerning the Borneo territories, but they would also turn on issues that bore directly on Singapore, including the Tunku's wish to see an arrest programme carried out before merger, and Lee Kuan Yew's desire for concessions over the status of Singapore citizens within Malaysia if his referendum campaign were to receive a much needed boost. Somewhat unrealistically, the British still hoped that the Tunku would accept merger with Singapore before taking the Borneo territories, but their pressing requirement was to secure a deal that gave the territories some constitutional safeguards; Macmillan was advised by the Cabinet Secretary of the 'need to avoid giving any public impression that the UK and Malayan Governments intend to force North Borneo and Sarawak into the Federation willy-nilly'.[36] The possibility of linking the various issues had, in fact, already been raised by Selkirk with the Prime Minister in mid-May 1962, where the former had mentioned that to secure agreement on the practical aspects of Malaysia, 'we might have to be prepared to exercise some pressure'. The problems produced by the differences of opinion among members of the Cobbold Commission could be overcome: 'The Tunku might indeed offer to accept the Cobbold report if he were allowed to lock up all the extremist opposition in Singapore. Lord Selkirk hoped that this bargain would not be put to us as it would be a difficult one.'[37] The outlines of a deal were already apparent: if the British could satisfy the Tunku with an ISC-sanctioned arrest programme before merger then the Tunku might be prepared to be more forthcoming over the terms of federation with the Borneo territories.

That Singapore questions would assume great importance during the London talks was shown by the preliminary meetings held at Admiralty House between the Tunku and Macmillan immediately after the former's arrival on 17 July 1962. As had been anticipated, the Tunku began by

[35] For these events see Richard Lamb, *The Macmillan Years, 1957–1963: The Emerging Truth* (London, 1995), 444–51.
[36] Brook to Macmillan, 12 July 1962, PREM 11/3868.
[37] Record of meeting between Macmillan and Selkirk, 16 May 1962, PREM 11/3737.

pressing the British to 'clean up' the Communists in the colony before the new federation was formed, arguing that, 'In order to get a good result in the referendum [Lee Kuan Yew] needed a good press and the suppression of the communists. By speaking to the newspaper editors he had secured the first and now only the communist difficulty remained.' Macmillan's response was noncommittal, and he instead enquired about the future citizenship status of Singapore residents, to be told 'that because the majority of Singapore residents might not be loyal to the Federation they could not be given Malaysian citizenship but a Singapore citizenship. [The Tunku] was quite prepared to allow citizenship rights to the electors of Borneo but not to those of Singapore.' Singapore residents could, however, acquire voting rights at a federal level by fulfilling a five-year residence requirement.[38] This was the Malayan stance that was doing so much to harm Lee's attempt to secure a clear endorsement of the Malaysia proposals in the upcoming referendum.

During their first sessions together, Sandys argued with the Malayans that an early merger between the Federation and Singapore should be concluded, while the Borneo territories were prepared for later accession. These ideas were quickly rejected by the Tunku as impossible to sell to Malay domestic opinion, as was any suggestion that British governors might remain in the Borneo territories during a transitional phase.[39] Putting forward their own requirements on 18 July, the Malayans called for unanimity on the ISC over plans to detain Communists and their sympathizers (starting with 25 members of the Barisan) after the Singapore referendum, but before merger: 'The Malayan Government want HMG to be associated with the action so that action against Communists after merger, possibly more severe, can be presented as a continuation of policies initiated under HMG auspices.'[40] Lunching alone with the Tunku on 20 July, Sandys appeared to have made a breakthrough when the former, though continuing to oppose British governors in Borneo, conceded that Singapore might be incorporated before the Borneo territories if Lee's position deteriorated dramatically. For his part, Sandys proposed moving from the British recommendations of the Cobbold Report regarding a long transitional period, with the idea that Britain and Malaya might announce that the new Federation of Malaysia should be

---

[38] See de Zulueta note for Macmillan, 11 July 1962; de Zulueta note of Tunku Abdul Rahman–Macmillan meeting, 17 July 1962 PREM 11/3868; record of Admiralty House meeting, 17 July 1962, CO 1030/1024.

[39] See record of meeting at CRO, 17 July 1962, PREM 11/3865. At their first detailed session it was agreed by the participants that no full minutes of their talks would be taken, but it is still possible to piece together the substance of the negotiations from the available record.

[40] Record of meeting in Mr Sandys's room, 18 July 1962, DO 169/273.

established by 31 December 1963, with a total transfer of sovereignty of the Borneo territories by that date. Moreover, a secret agreement could be concluded providing that in the interim if Lee's Government should be on the verge of collapse, Singapore and Brunei would be incorporated very rapidly and ahead of the Borneo territories.

However, having consulted Razak soon after, the Tunku changed tack and refused any agreement to take in Singapore before the Borneo territories; moreover, he proclaimed on 26 July his intention to return to Malaya if the latest Malayan proposals were not accepted.[41] These proposals involved the transfer of sovereignty over the Borneo territories, Singapore and Brunei to the federation of Malaya by 8 February 1963 (the Tunku's birthday), with the new federation of Malaysia to be established by 31 August 1963, and with British governors staying in Borneo only to that date to help with transitional arrangements. Finally, there would be no new Malaysian constitution as such; the existing Malayan constitution would simply have to be amended to incorporate any safeguards that were felt necessary for the Borneo territories. The accelerated timescale favoured by the Malayans was greeted with alarm by Colonial Office officials and the Borneo Governors, but Sandys had little time for such objections when negotiations were so delicately poised.[42] Furthermore, with the British needing every bargaining instrument that they could find to move the talks forward, it began to look increasingly likely that acquiescence in a round-up of the opposition in Singapore would be forthcoming.

Strenuous opposition to any such concession came from the local British officials who would have to implement such as measure, Philip Moore maintaining, 'It seems to us plain foolishness to decide upon repressive action in Singapore.'[43] Doubting that the leading figures in the Barisan were actually engaged in subversion or were the 'compliant tool of Peking or Moscow', Moore wanted to 'stress again that in Singapore today we have a political and not a security problem. We know who most of the potential subversives are and they could easily be gathered in at any time they seemed to threaten the security of the state.' Moore's main concern was that 'to arrest leading members of the main Opposition party without adequate cause' would merely help to intensify anti-Malaysia feeling and unite opponents of the PAP.[44] In a similar

---

[41] Sandys note for Lansdowne, 20 July 1962, CO 1030/1024; Tunku Abdul Rahman to Sandys, 26 July 1962, and report on progress of talks for de Zulueta by William McIndoe (CRO), 26 July 1962, PREM 11/3868.
[42] See Joint note from Governors of North Borneo and Sarawak, 26 July 1962, DO 169/271; also Martin to Sandys, n.d. [but late July 1962], PREM 11/3868.
[43] Moore to CO, 11 July 1962, CAB 134/1950.
[44] Moore to Wallace, no. 363, 18 July 1962, CO 1030/1160.

fashion, Selkirk informed Sandys on 27 July that an arrest programme would be a dangerous move and was only likely to provoke more trouble: 'It would become abundantly clear that Malaysia was being imposed by the British, regardless of the will of the people concerned. It will then be presented as our plan for preserving our bases with the Tunku allowing himself to be used as our stooge.'[45] On the same day that Selkirk delivered his warning, the Prime Minister was briefed by de Zulueta on the stalled condition of the talks, and Lee Kuan Yew arrived in London to discuss citizenship and internal security questions with the Tunku and the British. Macmillan was advised that the differences over the dates for the establishment of Malaysia (between 8 February and 31 December 1963) were comparatively minor obstacles. However, de Zulueta reported the widely held view that Lee's position would become untenable without movement from the Tunku on the citizenship issue. The Prime Minister was encouraged to meet the Tunku halfway over dates, but to persuade him that concessions over citizenship should be made, with the British offering to go ahead with the Singapore arrests in order to clinch the whole deal.[46]

Macmillan was confident of his personal sway over the Tunku, and the latter was consequently invited to Chequers for lunch and more talks for 28 July. In this congenial setting, a provisional outline agreement was reached. Macmillan suggested that 31 August 1963 be taken as the date of full transfer of sovereignty to the new federal authorities, to be complemented by a confidential understanding that a merger could take place earlier if Lee's Government was about to fall, with British governors remaining in place until the original agreed date. There would need to be some safeguards for the Borneo territories, to be written into an amended version of the Malayan constitution, as well as a short transitional period where the state governments would retain some powers, but the Prime Minister gave the impression that these would be mere technical niceties, required for British domestic political purposes, as parliamentary approval for any Greater Malaysia bill might be complicated by the 'traditional British tenderness for minority groups . . . It would be a great help in the passage of any Bill if a clear declaration of intent had been made to cover the interests of the inhabitants of the Borneo territories.' In an oblique reference, Macmillan was also recorded as saying, 'It would also be helpful if the question of dangerous Communists in Singapore would be deferred until after the [UK] Parliamentary discussions.'[47] The meaning of this remark was soon to become apparent.

[45] Selkirk minute for Sandys, 27 July 1962, PREM 11/3868.
[46] De Zulueta note for Macmillan, 27 July 1962, *ibid.*
[47] Record of Chequers meeting, 28 July 1962, *ibid.* and DO 169/273.

On the following day, talks were held at the CRO between Sandys, Razak and Lee Kuan Yew, where Razak agreed to the principle of common citizenship. The Tunku subsequently endorsed this position at a meeting with Lee at the Ritz Hotel on 30 July, allowing for the amendment of the White Paper terms that had been approved by the Singapore Assembly the previous December. Although the change in nomenclature was important for presentational purposes, the Malayan position remained that Singapore citizens would still only be entitled to vote within Singapore itself, and that only five years' residence in another part of Malaysia would confer full federal voting rights.[48] With Lee then putting forward proposals for a post-referendum arrest programme, Sandys duly indicated that previous British resistance on the ISC to such action would be lifted, though when he saw Lee and the Tunku again on 31 July, he carefully phrased his comments to suggest that this could not be considered a formal commitment and that individual cases would need to be considered on their merits.[49]

The agreement made by the Tunku in London over the citizenship question, for which the British had assented to an arrest programme, paved the way for the staging of the referendum on merger in Singapore. Returning to Singapore on 14 August, Lee announced that residents would now be classed as Malaysian citizens under his scheme for merger, while he also set the date of 1 September for the referendum itself, allowing only a minimum of time for an effective opposition campaign. With the PAP's holding key advantages in a supportive media, and superior organization and funding, opportunities for the Barisan Socialis to put the case against merger were limited, while the form of the referendum, with merely three different types of merger being offered as alternatives, made it difficult to advocate the best course of action to voters. Eventually, the Barisan advised its supporters to cast blank ballots, despite the fact that the referendum bill stipulated that such votes would be taken as endorsement of the Legislative Assembly's earlier vote in favour of merger on White Paper terms. The whole resigned manner of the Barisan's approach probably helped to convince many voters that merger was inevitable and so at least should be secured on the best terms possible, while few would positively seek to defy the law and disenfranchise themselves by refusing to go to the polls. In the event, turn-out was in the order of 90 per cent, with 71 per cent of voters (397,000) opting for the PAP-supported White Paper-style merger, and only 3 per cent for

---

[48] See de Zulueta minute for Macmillan, 30 July 1962, PREM 11/3868, and the account in Lee Kuan Yew, *Singapore Story*, 437–8.
[49] Meeting between Sandys, Tunku Abdul Rahman and Lee Kuan Yew, 31 July 1962, CO 1030/1025. A few days later, Razak was maintaining that there had been agreement in London to work for a unanimous decision on the ISC over the arrests, see Kuala Lumpur to CRO, no. 526, 6 August 1962, DO 169/272.

the other two alternatives, while 25 per cent of ballots (144,000) were left blank. Even with the controversial methods by which the poll had been conducted, Lee could now claim widespread popular endorsement for the course his Government had been following.[50] Having suffered a heavy blow to its morale, the Barisan struggled to regroup from the setback, but Lee's skilful manoeuvring was still far from over.

On 1 August 1962, Sandys came to the House of Commons to announce the results of the Greater Malaysia negotiations and the publication of the report of the Cobbold Commission. As well as the 31 August 1963 target date for the new Federation, Sandys indicated that the British and Malayan Governments would seek to reach formal agreements covering such matters as transfers of sovereignty and new defence arrangements (as set out in their joint statement of November 1961), but also providing for 'detailed constitutional arrangements, including safeguards for the special interests of North Borneo and Sarawak, to be drawn up after consultation with the Legislatures of the two territories'. The safeguards would deal with religious freedom, education, federal representation, rights of indigenous peoples, and controls over immigration, citizenship and the state constitutions. Moreover, a transitional period after the formal transfer of sovereignty would allow certain federal powers to be delegated to the state governments. Lord Lansdowne, the Minister of State at the Colonial Office, was named as the chairman of an intergovernmental committee, where representatives from Britain, Malaya, Sarawak and North Borneo would work on the details of the safeguards that would need to be incorporated in the amended Malayan federal constitution.[51] The formal published aspects to the agreements reached at the London talks were also supplemented by an unpublished exchange of letters between the British and Malayan Governments, where they agreed that the new federation could come into existence before its 31 August 1963 target date if the PAP Government in Singapore was about to or had actually collapsed (with British governors staying on for the interim period).

The clock was now ticking down to 'Malaysia Day', leaving administrators and officials the frantic job of preparing the way for a rapid transfer of power in the Borneo territories. In view of the earlier expressions of doubts and reservations over Malaysia, the successful work of the Lansdowne Intergovernmental Committee, which held meetings with leading political figures from the Borneo territories during October–December 1962, and culminated in the production of a report in February 1963

---

[50] See Lee Kuan Yew, *Singapore Story*, 444–52; Osborne, *Singapore and Malaysia*, 27–8.
[51] Mansergh (ed.), *Commonwealth Affairs, 1952–62*, 211–12.

containing a set of agreed constitutional provisions, seems surprising in retrospect.[52] Yet once it was clear to the political leaders from Sarawak (with the important exception of SUPP) and North Borneo that the creation of the new federation was a foregone conclusion, attention rapidly turned to making the scheme work and currying favour in Kuala Lumpur. By the end of September 1962, the Legislative Councils (still largely nominated, rather than elected, bodies) in both territories had voted without dissent to welcome the establishment of Malaysia, on the understanding their interests would be protected by constitutional safeguards. The Tunku was slow to accept that a serious attempt had to be made to reassure opinion in Sarawak and North Borneo that Malaysia would not entail Malay domination; in early August, while still in London, he had told Goode that 'the people of the territories are good, simple people. They will be easy to handle if ideas are not put in their heads.'[53] He may also have suspected that the production of a 20-point agreed submission to the Lansdowne Committee by the political parties of North Borneo in mid-September was contrived and encouraged by still-disgruntled British colonial officials.

Nevertheless, with the more-diplomatic Razak serving as Lansdowne's deputy, it was possible to find compromises and create a greater atmosphere of goodwill and flexibility.[54] One factor helping to explain the changing attitude of several of the indigenous leaders from Sarawak was some of the promises made by the Malayans regarding the promotion of rural development programmes during trips to Kuala Lumpur in October.[55] Perhaps of even more importance, in terms of its symbolic value, was the Tunku's announcement the following month, just prior to a visit to the territories, that 40 seats in the new 159-seat Malaysian federal assembly were to be allocated to Sarawak (24) and North Borneo (16).[56] This level of representation was more generous than that suggested by the territories' proportion of population in the federation, and helped to indicate that their status would not be overlooked. During his talks with Lansdowne in Kuching, some of the Tunku's real views began to show through once again, however, where he 'at once raised the question of repressive measures against SUPP by HMG. He said that of course after Malaysia "we will clear things up, but something ought to be done

---

[52] See *Malaysia, Report of the Inter-Governmental Committee, 1962*, Cmnd 1954 (London, 1963).
[53] Note by Goode of conversation at the Ritz Hotel, 2 August 1962, box 3, file 1, Goode papers.
[54] See e.g. Martin to Tory, 27 November 1962, CO 1030/1032.
[55] Officer Administering government of Sarawak to CO, no. 509, 5 October 1962, CO 1030/1036.
[56] See material in CO 1030/1066.

now. These people only respect power and if a few of the leading political agitators are suspended, this would have a very beneficial effect."[57] Alongside all the constitutional niceties of the Lansdowne Committee's deliberations, what finally sealed agreement between all parties was the outbreak of the Brunei revolt in December 1962. Revelations soon after that Indonesia had provided some measure of support to the rebels in Brunei from camps over the border in Kalimantan convinced many observers that the only secure future for the Borneo territories lay under the protective wing of the new federation, with British military forces the ultimate guarantee against a predatory neighbour.

While unexpected events in Brunei helped to consolidate a degree of local support for Malaysia, they also presented the most significant challenge that the overall project had yet had to face. The prime focus of London and Kuala Lumpur over the previous eighteen months had been on Sarawak, North Borneo and Singapore, and consideration of the attitude of the sultanate of Brunei had been neglected. One reason was that the British did not hold direct administrative responsibility for Brunei, the territory being classed as a protectorate rather than a colony, though the advice delivered to the Sultan by the British resident was supreme in most important matters of state and the Shell oil company dominated local economic life. In 1959, Brunei was granted a new constitution, which gave full executive powers to the Sultan, but reserved defence and external affairs to a British High Commissioner. When the Malaysia scheme was first announced in 1961, many observers tended to assume that the small, predominantly Malay and Muslim population of Brunei would see little objection to joining the federation, but within a short space of time, A. M. Azahari, leader of the sultanate's most significant political force, the Party Rakyat, was signalling his strong opposition.

Born in 1928 in Brunei, Azahari had gone to Java in 1943 to study veterinary medicine, where he witnessed and took some part in the Indonesian nationalist revolution during the late 1940s. Returning to the sultanate in 1952, he divided his time between a chequered career in business and political activism, founding the Party Rakyat in 1956 on a strong anti-colonialist message.[58] Calling for greater measures of democracy within Brunei, he also favoured a merger of the three Borneo territories, and tried to secure the Sultan's backing for such a grouping. By contrast, Malaysia was seen primarily as a way of perpetuating British neo-colonialism through the device of the Sultan, the Malayan authorities in Kuala Lumpur, or perhaps both. The 1959 constitution had promised

---

[57] Lansdowne note on talks with the Tunku and Ghazali, 20 November 1962, CO 1030/1036.
[58] See CO note on Azahari, 27 September 1961, CO 1030/1013.

elections to the Legislative Council, and when these were held in August 1962, the Party Rakyat underlined the great strides it had made by scoring a resounding victory, winning all sixteen available elected seats in a chamber of thirty-three. Nevertheless, the Sultan still exercised complete control over the executive organs of the state and the route to effective power remained a long way off.

Meanwhile, progress towards Malaysia prejudiced Azahari's hopes for a purely North Borneo federation with Brunei at its head, while he would probably have little future in the new political structures accompanying the formation of a wider federation directed from Kuala Lumpur. During 1962, the Sultan finally, and rather cautiously, came out in support of joining Malaysia, but by the end of the year Brunei was in a state of revolutionary ferment, and the Party Rakyat stood ready to lead an insurrection against British political and economic influence, and the plans to take Brunei into Malaysia. Most worryingly for wider British policy was Indonesia's eventual support for the rebellion, and the initiation of a belligerent new tone from Jakarta attacking the plans for Malaysia, and in particular the role of Malaya as the main instigator and benefactor of the territorial and jurisdictional adjustments that were set to take place in the summer of 1963. To appreciate how Jakarta came into conflict with its close neighbour, it is now necessary to look at the ambivalent state of relations between Indonesia and Malaya from the time of the latter's independence, and the deep suspicions of British neo-colonial influence that were a recurrent feature of the Indonesian world view.

4   Britain, Indonesia and Malaya: from West Irian to the Brunei revolt

That strong Indonesian opposition to the new Malaysian federation should emerge was not generally anticipated by either British or American officials, and little attention seems to have been devoted to likely Indonesian reactions, at least up to the autumn of 1962. Indeed, to some Western observers the settlement of the West Irian dispute in August 1962 was seen as a potential watershed, marking a turn away from the more assertive and unpredictable trends of Indonesian foreign policy that had been witnessed since Sukarno's introduction of Guided Democracy in the summer of 1959. Washington's efforts at mediation, and the rapid transfer of West Irian by the Dutch to UN Administration in preparation for the final handover to Indonesia in May 1963, had helped to remove one of the main irritants to US–Indonesian relations, along with an immediate source of regional tension and instability. Howard Jones, the US Ambassador in Jakarta, informed President Kennedy directly in October 1962 that 'we had an opportunity today we had not had since 1950 to cement relations between the United States and Indonesia'.[1] Certainly, many Administration officials were anxious that they should exploit the capital that the American role in resolving the dispute had supposedly accumulated in Jakarta, and as we have seen, Kennedy's National Security Action Memorandum 179 aimed to focus the bureaucracy on the goal of improving ties with Indonesia and working up aid programmes that could influence the regime in a pro-Western direction. It seems especially ironic then, that just as the Dutch–Indonesian talks on West Irian were approaching their climax during the summer of 1962, the delicate negotiations over the Cobbold Report and the future of Malaysia were also being concluded in London. There seemed little to connect the two events in contemporary Western appraisals. The general feeling was that Indonesia was unlikely to embark on fresh adventures, at least in the short term, when it had West Irian to absorb and formidable economic problems at home to overcome.

---

[1] Memorandum of conversation, 11 October 1962, *FRUS, 1961–1963, XXIII*, 645.

Perhaps of even more importance, however, was that for almost a year virtually all the signals coming from Jakarta regarding the formation of Malaysia had been benign. In early August 1961, Selkirk had visited Jakarta for brief talks with Dr Subandrio, the Indonesian Foreign Minister, who had indicated that Indonesia was indifferent to the ideas then current for the scheme of a Greater Malaysia. When subsequently asked by the press what he felt about the concept, Subandrio merely commented that it was really a matter for the peoples concerned. This was followed on 13 November 1961 by a letter from Subandrio to *The New York Times*, where he cited the Indonesian attitude of goodwill to the proposals for Malaysia, 'As an example of our honesty and lack of expansionist intent . . .' A week later, during a UN plenary session on colonialism, Subandrio again stated that Indonesia had no objections to the new federation and wished the scheme success.[2]

One cloud on this favourable horizon was the response of the PKI to the London talks of November 1961 and the extension of the Anglo-Malayan Defence Agreement to cover Malaysia. In late December, the PKI's Central Committee passed a resolution condemning Malaysia as 'a form of neo-colonialism' which would 'suppress the democratic and patriotic movements of the peoples in [the Borneo territories] which aim at the attainment of national independence and freedom from imperialism', while with its British bases Malaysia would be 'smuggled into SEATO'. Moreover it observed, with some accuracy, that British interest in a new federation was 'because their position in Singapore is becoming weaker and weaker with the growth of [the] democratic movement and the influence of patriotic political parties', and 'the main point is that the British colonialists no longer dare to beat the people's movement with their own hands and they therefore borrow native hands for this'.[3] Throughout 1962 the PKI would build on this critique of Malaysia in its polemical literature, but the paramount concern of informed Indonesian opinion was directed elsewhere during these months as the West Irian campaign reached a conclusion. Bearing in mind Jakarta's current concerns, the CRO felt ready to advise in February 1962:

The Indonesian attitude towards Greater Malaysia is . . . likely to continue to be one of cautious welcome. Provided Greater Malaysia is clearly seen to be independent and provided that its rulers show no disposition to meddle in Indonesia's internal affairs (Sumatra, for instance), there is no obvious reason why Indonesia

---

[2] *Malaya/Indonesia Relations, 31st August 1957 to 15th September 1963* (Kuala Lumpur, 1963), 11–12.
[3] *Ibid.*, 42–3.

and Greater Malaysia should not be on good terms. In the long run, however, the Indonesians are bound to feel tempted by the idea of incorporating Greater Malaysia.[4]

British ministers and officials were undoubtedly happy to see the Americans take the initiative in defusing the prospect of Dutch–Indonesian hostilities over West Irian. In fact, by 1960–1 London was hoping that some of the earlier tensions present in its relationship with Jakarta would be replaced by a profitable realization of shared interests. These tensions had included long-simmering resentment on the Indonesian side at the British role in helping to restore Dutch rule during the reoccupation of 1945–6 (and where Indonesian fighters had clashed violently with British and Indian forces, most notably at Surabaya in November 1945), and more recently had included British participation in covert efforts to aid the Outer Island rebels in 1958. Now, however, there was a considerable British commercial stake in Indonesia (including the oil operations of Shell and large rubber estates), while arms sales to the regime by private contractors had been approved. Many British military planners recognized the key strategic position occupied by the Indonesian archipelago, and its significance for security and access to Singapore. Maintaining cordial relations with Jakarta, as with the Americans, began to seem more important than supporting Dutch retention of an obscure colonial foothold.[5] A potential source of disruption to British desires to keep out of the dispute, however, was the private undertaking extended to the Netherlands Government in 1959 that logistical support would be offered to Dutch military and naval operations if Jakarta's forces carried out a clear-cut aggression against West Irian (the offer was made partly to offset heavy criticisms from The Hague about British arms sales to Indonesia). By 1961, with the rapid Indonesian military build-up, this began to seem a rash promise. As we have seen, when the Prime Minister met Kennedy on Bermuda towards the end of December 1961, the President made clear that the Dutch could not expect any help from Washington if hostilities over West Irian should occur. Macmillan, in turn, explained the prior British commitment to assist the Dutch, but continued that 'we should be sorry to have to do this, as it would have the effect of increasing tension between Indonesia on the one hand and, on the other, Malaya and Singapore'. The Prime Minister had gone on to agree with Kennedy that 'it would be preferable that the Western Powers should refrain from offering to support the Dutch in resisting any Indonesian attack on [West

[4] CRO brief on Indonesian attitudes to proposed Federation of Malaysia, submitted to the Cobbold Commission, February 1962, DO 169/237.
[5] See e.g. CRO to Canberra, no. 2939, 21 December 1961, PREM 11/4309.

Irian]'.[6] By March 1962, the armed clashes occurring in and around West Irian led the Cabinet to consider the whole question of the 1959 undertaking. A decision was taken to rescind the commitment to the Dutch, the Cabinet minutes noting that, 'In view of the large British investments in Indonesia, which would be jeopardised by any overt action hostile to the interests of the Indonesian government, it would be preferable that in present circumstances any Dutch request for assistance should be turned aside with the suggestion that their requirements could be more expeditiously met by the US Government.'[7] In this stark example of *Realpolitik*, ministers already knew that the Americans would reject any such Dutch request, leaving their NATO ally shorn of all significant Western backing. Even the knowledge of Dutch support for British entry to the institutions of the European Economic Community was not enough, on this occasion, to outweigh the immediate threat to British interests in South East Asia that a regional conflict involving Indonesia might present.

Within some sections of the Foreign Office, there was a feeling that the US performance during the final stages of the West Irian dispute was evidence of a 'wet' approach towards Indonesia. Such attitudes roused Fred Warner, the head of the South East Asia Department, to explain that with 8,000 US military personnel deployed in South Vietnam, and another 10,000 having been temporarily despatched to Thailand in response to the renewal of fighting in Laos during May 1962, American policy was entirely understandable. Laos and Vietnam had to be considered front-line states in the containment struggle in South East Asia, and any trouble in the rear areas needed to be defused as smartly as possible. Edward Peck, the Deputy Under Secretary superintending the South East Asia Department, agreed with Warner, and went on to suggest that it was important to distinguish between forms of Communist aggression, which the Americans were committed to opposing, and 'aggression aimed at liquidating Colonial remnants, which may at times be more open and unashamed than some clandestine Communist subversive movement'. The positions in Laos and Vietnam were examples of the former, while Goa and West Irian fell into the latter category. Appeasement in the face of Communist threats was evidently to be discouraged, but threats to use force against former colonial powers excited powerful anti-colonial sentiments and affected British and US 'standing with the forces of nationalism, which can still be tactfully harnessed by the West but if spurned will succumb to the Communists'. The debate was soon joined by Sir Harold Caccia, the Permanent Under Secretary. Caccia

---

[6] Record of mtg at Government House, Bermuda, 22 December 1961, PREM 11/3782.
[7] CC(62) 25th mtg, 30 March 1962, CAB 128/36.

differed from his subordinates, and instead offered a warning of where such attitudes might lead:

> Even if Laos and Vietnam are different from Goa and West Irian, it is not good that these or other colonial remnants should be seized by force and for it to be demonstrated that this is a safe method of territorial aggrandisement... if strong arm methods are seen to succeed, there is the danger that they will not only be applied to colonial remnants. The occupation of the Rhineland was different from the Anschluss; that in turn was different from Czechoslovakia acts (1) and (2); so was that from Danzig. But the end was foreseeable and the original 'success' full of omen.
>
> We should try to avoid a repetition and persuade the Americans that this disapproval of aggression is nearly as important as twisting the arms of the Dutch to negotiate while there is yet time.[8]

Caccia's stance, that it was for the Americans publicly to oppose any Indonesian use of force, conveniently ignored the corresponding unwillingness of Britain to offer any kind of backing to the Dutch in their pressing time of need. It is also worth noting Warner and Peck's distinctions about forms of aggression against 'colonial remnants' in the context of the events to come in 1963, when their attitudes would have to be modified as the British found themselves in an analogous and uncomfortable position.

Following from this, there was evidently some nervousness about the future course of Indonesian policy among some British officials as a West Irian settlement drew nearer. In this regard, Malaysia began to be seen as the best and most viable long-term defence of the Borneo territories against Indonesian irredentism. One Foreign Office brief prepared in July 1962 argued:

> In the long run the most likely alternative to Greater Malaysia is Greater Indonesia. No Asian Government would consider that either independence or continued colonial rule could offer a lasting third choice for the Borneo territories in their present form. If these are not absorbed by Malaysia, they are likely to be swallowed up, sooner or later, by Indonesia or the Philippines or, just possibly, to be turned into outposts of Communist China.[9]

To some, such as Caccia, whose views have already been noted, the end of the West Irian chapter of appeasement was merely the harbinger of more serious conflicts to come; the response of the British Embassy in The

---

[8] Warner minute, 28 May 1962, Peck minute, 28 May 1962, Caccia minute, 29 May 1962, DJ103145/2, FO 371/166553.
[9] South East Asia Department brief on Indonesian and Philippine claims to Borneo territories, with CO additions, 4 July 1962, D1061/9, FO 371/166361. Similar arguments had been used by the Greater Malaysia (Official) Committee in its advice to ministers in October 1961.

Hague to the end of the crisis was notably downbeat, with the Ambassador warning London that, 'We may yet sail into stormy waters in South East Asia, with the Dutch at our shoulder to say: "We told you so." '[10] Yet the prevailing view was that fresh trouble from Indonesia was still some way off, and that the regime would need to consolidate before embarking upon any further overseas gambles, giving some opportunity for a regular pattern of friendly relations to be reestablished, not least through the revival of arms sales (in January 1962 an embargo had reluctantly been placed on arms exports to Indonesia, but was lifted in December, with Macmillan at the forefront of those keen that commercial opportunities not be lost for this lucrative trade, particularly to the Americans).[11] In early September 1962, the British Embassy in Jakarta was reporting that Indonesian denials of any claim to the Borneo territories and to the eastern part of New Guinea could probably be taken at immediate face value. Nevertheless, the Embassy went on to sound a cautionary note, by warning that though the Western powers might now find it slightly easier with the West Irian issue resolved, and could even gain ground with the regime,

it will not be easy. The struggle has lasted too long and has produced a set of slogans from which it will be difficult to free this slogan-ridden land. Indonesian leaders have too long proclaimed that Indonesia is anti-imperialist, anti-capitalist, anti-liberal, anti-'l'exploitation de l'homme par l'homme' and anti the old-established forces who believe in these things.

British commercial enterprises, especially those with Dutch connections such as Shell and Unilever, were seen by the Indonesian ruling elite as 'capitalist relics of a colonialist era. Few of them are counting with any confidence on more than another five or six years' operations in this country. Some think that they will be lucky even to get that.'[12]

The first external challenge to Malaysia arose from an unexpected source. In February 1962, attorneys for the heirs to the Sultan of Sulu, who had held sway in the northern part of Borneo before the arrival of the Brooke dynasty in the nineteenth century, began to put forward a claim of proprietary rights over the territory in an effort to see it incorporated into the Philippines. The legal arguments were convoluted. In 1878, the Sultan of Sulu had agreed to cede his sovereign rights over North Borneo to a British syndicate headed by Alfred Dent and Baron de Overbeck in return for an annual payment. From 1881 to 1946, the British North Borneo Company duly administered the territory, until it acquired crown

---

[10] The Hague to FO, no. 80, 17 August 1962, DO 169/237.
[11] See e.g. Samuel to Bligh, 15 October 1962, and Macmillan minute for de Zulueta, 17 October 1962, PREM 11/4870.
[12] Jakarta to FO, no. 77, 5 September 1962, 'Observations on West New Guinea settlement', DJ1016/343, DO 169/237, and in PREM 11/4870.

colony status. The heirs to the Sultan maintained that the original treaty wording was vague and implied a lease of the territory, rather than outright secession, while many Filipinos questioned the legal standing of the Sultan in carrying out the transfer.[13] There was some domestic debate over the issue within the Philippines following independence, and in April 1950 a resolution was introduced into the House of Representatives by Diosado Macapagal calling for the government to negotiate with the British on the return of North Borneo to Philippine sovereignty, only for the measure to fail in the Senate. The House of Representatives tried again in April 1962, and this time received Senate support for the so-called Ramos resolution urging the President to take 'necessary steps' within international law to recover a portion of North Borneo and adjacent islands. More crucially, Macapagal was now President, following his election victory in December 1961, and with the enthusiastic backing of his Under Secretary for Foreign Affairs, Salvador Lopez, began to raise the dispute at an official level with the British Government in June 1962. Macapagal, while professing no hostility to the idea of Malaysia, provided the North Borneo issue was resolved, also began to put forward the notion of a wider Malayan Confederation, embracing the Malay states, Borneo territories, Singapore and the Philippines.[14] At this stage, all the Philippine Government was calling for were talks with the British to settle the dispute; with no pressure on their position, and plans for Malaysia progressing in the wake of the Cobbold Commission's report, London felt no need to enter into any such speculative discussions. At one meeting with Averell Harriman in July 1962, Warner explained (to American approval) the British 'tactics of delay and prevarication until responsibility for the territory [of North Borneo] could be handed over to Greater Malaysia'.[15] Certainly, as long as Indonesia remained a disinterested party in the Malaysia project, then the Philippine claim was of little concern to policy-makers in London.

While the British hoped that their detachment from the West Irian dispute had not done irreparable damage to Anglo-Indonesian relations, Malaya had found its own relations with Jakarta put under considerable strain by the crisis. Concerned with the prospect of a major conflict breaking out in such close proximity, in September 1960 Tunku Abdul

[13] A summary can be found in John M. Gullick (ed.), *Malaysia and its Neighbours* (New York, 1967), 148–51.
[14] See especially Michael Leifer, *The Philippine Claim to Sabah* (London, 1967); *Malaya/Philippine Relations, 31st August 1957 to 15th September 1963* (Kuala Lumpur, 1964); for the original Philippine note opening the dispute, Manila to FO, no. 113, 22 June 1962, CO 1030/989.
[15] Warner notes of conversation with Harriman and Sullivan, 22 July 1962, D1015/25, FO 371/166354.

Rahman had intervened to offer Malayan mediation, and put forward a proposal that involved transfer of West Irian to UN trusteeship, in preparation for eventual accession to Indonesia. With Sukarno away on an overseas tour, Djuanda, the acting Indonesian President, responded positively to the Tunku's ideas. The British had been kept informed of the Malayan initiative and, along with the Australian Government, were strongly opposed to its contents.[16] The Tunku travelled to Washington in November, to discuss the matter with the outgoing Eisenhower Administration, and returned via London and The Hague. In London, Macmillan put strong pressure on the Tunku to retract his idea of trusteeship leading to Indonesian control, arguing that, 'if an agreement could be reached which really faced the facts and allowed for a trusteeship leading to eventual self-determination this might be acceptable. But if the trusteeship was only to last for a year and after that the territory was to go to Indonesia then such an arrangement would seem to put a premium on aggression.' The Tunku agreed to retract the notion of a trusteeship automatically leading to Indonesian control, and after visiting The Hague, began to advocate the introduction of a UN inspection commission for West Irian, a proposal the Dutch were prepared to consider.[17] Any intrusive involvement by the UN in the final disposition of West Irian was greeted with great suspicion in Indonesia, however, and Subandrio was soon launching a strong attack on the Tunku's mediation effort, which lapsed soon after amid bitterly critical comment in the Indonesian press. Although Malaya was later scrupulous in refusing the Dutch any transit rights for shipping and troops whose origin or destination was West Irian, and even allowed for Indonesian recruitment of Malayan volunteers to fight against the Dutch, active assistance to the Indonesian cause was not forthcoming. In February 1962, Sukarno had written to the Tunku asking for use of Malayan bases in the event of war with the Dutch, and the latter had refused.[18] The mutual recriminations that followed the Tunku's intervention over West Irian marked a new low in Malay–Indonesian relations, already under some strain due to the obvious contrast between Malaya's strong anti-Communism and ties with the West, and Sukarno's readiness to court the PKI and develop links with the Soviet Union and PRC. As Tory highlighted in one despatch of December 1958, 'To a Malaya newly emerged into independence Indonesia can pose as the sophisticated elder

[16] See Tunku Abdul Rahman to Macmillan, 19 October 1960; Canberra to CRO, no. 1071, 7 November 1960; Menzies to Macmillan, T.678/60, 7 November 1960 (for Australian opposition to the Tunku's intervention); Macmillan to Menzies, T.691/60, 14 November 1960, PREM 11/4309.
[17] Record of conversation at Admiralty House, 16 November 1960, *ibid.*
[18] See Kuala Lumpur to CRO, no. 59, 27 February 1962, CO 1030/1013.

brother, pointing out how far Malaya is still tied to Western apron-strings and offering the adult pleasures of Afro-Asian politics.'[19]

Animosity between the two states was, moreover, still being engendered by the continuing presence within Malaya of political refugees from the Indonesian Outer Island rebellion of 1958, the failure of Jakarta and Kuala Lumpur to agree an extradition treaty to cover such individuals, and the Indonesian belief that Malaya had exhibited considerable sympathy for the rebel cause. In this connection, there were strong suspicions by the Indonesians that Kuala Lumpur had its own irredentist designs in the region, was not averse to the idea of an eventual break-up of Indonesia and had fixed covetous eyes on Sumatra. The notion of Malaya (with British connivance) harbouring plans to foment unrest on Sumatra, perhaps through use of the remaining dissidents, was an element in the world view of Indonesian leaders and formed part of the background to confrontation and later Indonesian hostility to the Malaysia scheme. In talks at the State Department in April 1961 between Home and Rusk, the US Secretary of State enquired whether the British saw any connection between Indonesian claims to West Irian and the remaining British colonial possessions in South East Asia. Home replied that, 'the Tunku was convinced that if and when the Indonesian Government grew stronger they would go for Borneo. This would help to isolate Malaya and for this reason the Tunku had toyed from time to time with the idea of stirring up trouble in Sumatra.'[20] In early 1962, the Tunku reported a conversation with Dr Mohammad Hatta, who had served as Indonesian Vice-President under Sukarno until 1956, where Hatta had 'told him Indonesians were becoming very afraid of gravitational attraction of Federation of Malaya upon Sumatran Malays... One of main reasons why Indonesian Government were not opposing Malaysia openly was because they feared this would alienate Sumatran Malays still further from Djakarta.'[21] In July 1962, James Cable, handling Indonesian matters in the Foreign Office's South East Asia Department, responded to an Australian query over Indonesian intentions after West Irian with the view that a campaign against East Timor was a possibility, but over Malaysia suggested that 'the Indonesians would tread warily for fear that the Sumatrans might find Kuala Lumpur almost as attractive as Djakarta if it came to a direct tug of war'. Cable continued that he felt that the Indonesians 'had no genuine territorial ambitions at all. Their real problem was economic chaos and popular disillusionment at home. It was to distract from this

---

[19] Kuala Lumpur to CRO, Despatch no. 19, 19 December 1958, D10362/3, FO 371/143729.

[20] Record of conversation at State Department, 6 April 1961, PREM 11/4309.

[21] Kuala Lumpur to CRO, no. 103, 12 April 1962, CO 1030/1013.

that they worked up claims abroad...Dutch New Guinea had been an obvious objective for this purpose.'[22]

In fact, by September 1962 the Joint Intelligence Committee (JIC) in London was compiling its own assessment of future Indonesian intentions now that the West Irian campaign had been successfully completed, and their Australian counterparts were conducting a similar exercise, animated by anxieties over whether Jakarta would turn its attentions to the eastern portion of New Guinea.[23] The Foreign Office contribution to the JIC study noted that the Indonesians were likely in the long term to seek more external distractions from internal problems, but again mentioned East Timor as the most probable priority. A further claim might be launched in late 1963 or in 1964, though could come earlier with economic breakdown or domestic political crisis. By that stage it was conjectured that Greater Malaysia would already have come into being, while only a Communist government was likely to lay claim to the Borneo territories once they were safely in Malaysia. The idea was raised that tensions within Indonesia could lead to the breakaway of Sumatra and other of the Outer Islands, and that this could contribute to Indonesian hostility to the Greater Malaysia scheme as a rival attraction: 'A possible Indonesian intention could thus emerge of undermining and subverting Greater Malaysia before the Malayans could, as the Javanese would see it, do the same to Indonesia.'[24]

Simmering tensions between Indonesia and Malaya came to the surface once again in the autumn of 1962, with the outbreak of a revealing polemical exchange. The beginnings of the war of words that developed between Jakarta and Kuala Lumpur can be traced to the Tunku's reactions to a statement from Ali Sastroamidjojo, the chairman of the Indonesian Nationalist Party, and a former Prime Minister of Indonesia in the 1950s. Speaking at a party conference in central Java, Sastroamidjojo had maintained that Indonesia needed to be 'vigilant' at the prospect of neighbouring territories being used as foreign military bases, and hence could not remain indifferent to the formation of Malaysia. In a widely reported speech delivered to UMNO information officers on 24 September, the Tunku angrily stated that he failed 'to understand in what manner Malaysia can be of advantage or disadvantage to Indonesia...We have existed as an entity for many years. We have had no quarrel

[22] Cable minute, 27 July 1962, DH1022/2, FO 371/166510.
[23] See E. N. Larmour (UK High Commission, Canberra) to A. A. Golds (CRO), 27 August 1962, DO 169/67.
[24] Foreign Office contribution to JIC report on future Indonesian intentions, n.d. (but c. 6 October 1962); the eventual report, JIC(62)58, was not finalized until January 1963, in the wake of the Brunei revolt, and has yet to be released, see material in *ibid.*

with Indonesia nor have we attempted in any way to interfere with their affairs...Keep your hands out of our affairs.' Passing through Kuala Lumpur airport a day later, Subandrio told reporters that the exchange was an 'imaginary conflict', and said that since Indonesia would share a common frontier with Malaysia it was only natural that Indonesia could not be 'indifferent' to its formation.[25] More worrying were Subandrio's further comments to reporters in Singapore on 26 September, where he responded to a question over what Indonesia would do if a foreign base was established in the Borneo territories with the sharp (though improbable) answer that Indonesia would have to arrange for a Soviet base in Kalimantan.[26]

There was some bemusement among British officials at the tone and content of the Tunku's remarks in the so-called 'hands off Malaysia' speech. The Embassy in Jakarta commented that the Tunku must have known that Sastroamidjojo 'cut little political ice' in present-day Indonesia and his views could hardly be taken as official opinion, while in themselves they seemed moderate enough. Sastroamidjojo had himself seen the British Ambassador on 30 September to express his surprise at the reaction, saying he had meant nothing threatening. The feeling was that the Malayan Prime Minister was acting to preempt any more robust and real Indonesian opposition to come.[27] Within a few days, Subandrio was expressing dismay over the Tunku's outburst, claiming that Indonesia had no designs on any other territory, was not prepared to support the Philippine claim over North Borneo and wished Malaysia well; the British Ambassador was not sure that Subandrio could be taken at his word, 'but at least Indonesia appears to be putting no spoke in Malaysia's wheel for the time being'.[28] From Kuala Lumpur there was a slightly different interpretation of the Tunku's reactions; one official in the High Commission found the speech 'rather provocative' and asserted:

There seems little doubt that privately the Tunku does not like the Indonesians, and from time to time this feeling manifests itself publicly despite the fact that a sizeable portion of the Tunku's own political supporters think in terms of their blood ties with Indonesia, and generally are inclined to be pro-Indonesian. Federation officials seem to resent strongly the big brother/little brother attitude which they say they find in their dealings with the Indonesians.[29]

Nevertheless, from early October to early December 1962, there were few further outward signs that strained relations between Jakarta and

[25] See Kuala Lumpur to CRO, no. 710, 25 September 1962, DO 169/237.
[26] See Mackie, *Konfrontasi*, 106.
[27] Peterson to Cable, 3 October 1962, DO 169/237.
[28] Jakarta to FO, 9 October 1962, DH1022/4, FO 371/166510.
[29] Jenkins (Kuala Lumpur) to Bentliff (CRO), 1 October 1962, DO 169/237.

Kuala Lumpur would have a substantive impact on the plans for Malaysia. At the end of November, the Jakarta Embassy was still advising the Foreign Office, 'Our own guess is that Dr Subandrio will recognise his relative powerlessness to prevent the formation of Malaysia but that he will do his best to ensure that Indonesia's thunder is not stolen by branding Malaysia from the outset as a slave of neo-colonialism and a "lackey of the old-established forces".'[30] Yet during October reports had begun to emerge of heightened interest by Indonesian military intelligence in the Borneo territories, and a rise in the numbers of Indonesians visiting Sarawak.[31] Of particular concern were the activities of the Tentara Nasional Kalimantan Utara (TNKU – North Borneo Liberation Army). The TNKU was effectively the militant wing of Azahari's Party Rakyat, and since early 1962 had begun to assemble a guerrilla infrastructure of armed volunteers, supplies and training camps; before long there were indications that active assistance to the TNKU was being provided by the local Indonesian military authorities in Kalimantan. Although we have no access to British intelligence assessments of the Indonesian threat, there were other indications of impending trouble. One CIA source recorded Subandrio's 'off-the-record' comments that augmented his remarks to the press in Singapore about a Soviet base in Kalimantan. The Indonesian Foreign Minister was reported to have said:

In five years Communist China would be the chief enemy of Indonesia. The continuing buildup of Indonesia's military capability is designed specifically to face that threat. Indonesia–Malaya relations, from Indonesia's viewpoint, have reached a serious stage. Further public criticisms from Malaya may prompt Indonesia to . . . break off diplomatic relations and to actively support Indonesian agents and sympathisers in Malaya and the Borneo territories to fight against the Malayan Government . . . Indonesia has no territorial designs on the Borneo territories nor on Portuguese Timor, but Indonesia can not remain indifferent if the peoples of these territories request Indonesian assistance.[32]

On the British side, Lord Home, for one, was suspicious, as in the past, of Indonesian intentions. Towards the end of October, he had written to Lansdowne at the Colonial Office: 'I do not believe the Indonesians favour a Greater Malaysia any more than the Filipinos. They too have probably got designs on the Borneo territories though they have been careful never to put them forward.'[33] Nevertheless, and despite the growing evidence of TNKU activity in Kalimantan, it was not until November that

---

[30] Peterson to Cable, 28 November 1962, *ibid.*
[31] See Sarawak monthly intelligence report for October 1962, *ibid.*
[32] CIA Information Report, 13 October 1962, TDCS DB–3/651,725, NSF, countries series, Indonesia, 9/62–10/62, JFKL.
[33] Home to Lansdowne, 26 October 1962, DO 169/237.

serious concerns began to be raised about imminent danger. Rumours of an impending uprising among Brunei Malays began to be received by the British Resident in Sarawak's Fifth Division, resulting in the despatch of Special Branch officers to Limbang, and eventually a visit from Claude Fenner, the Inspector-General of the Malayan Police. No clear evidence was uncovered by Fenner, but the C-in-C Far East, Admiral Sir David Luce, updated his contingency plans for the deployment of forces to Brunei (no British troops were then present in any of the Borneo territories). On 25 November, ten TNKU members were arrested at Lawas, close to the Brunei border; uniforms, documents and badges were discovered along with a plan to attack the local police station. Three days later Special Branch officers from the Borneo territories met at Lawas to discuss the threat, but no disturbance was considered likely before 19 December.[34] Indications of unrest in Brunei were the cause of alarm in Kuala Lumpur, and on 1 December the Tunku sent for Tory to warn that there were clear signs of insurrection by the Party Rakyat, prompting Macmillan to comment: 'If this is true, it is serious.'[35] Selkirk also saw the Malayan Prime Minister and flew to Brunei and North Borneo on 2 December to look at the situation himself. There he found a disturbing picture, and what he called a 'general air of complacency', which he tried to dispel by reminding local officials that intelligence reports indicated perhaps 1,000 TNKU members on Brunei soil (there may have been, in fact, something like 4,000). Selkirk felt that Brunei 'is potentially in a dangerously revolutionary condition'.[36] However, although local police were put on alert, no troops were on immediate standby in Singapore for despatch to Brunei, much to the Tunku's later annoyance.

In the early hours of the morning of 8 December the rebellion in Brunei began. Police stations throughout the territory were attacked, along with the Sultan's palace and the power station in the capital itself. Limbang and Lawas (both actually in Sarawak) fell to TNKU forces and the oilfields at Seria, along with several Shell employees, were also soon in rebel hands. The tactical surprise achieved by the TNKU was certainly an embarrassment to the British authorities, while the initial military response was hampered by inadequate preparation and some bureaucratic muddle. At an emergency meeting of the Malayan Cabinet, the Tunku

[34] See memorandum for North Borneo Executive Council on Brunei rebellion, DEF 5945, box 1, file 4, Goode papers; Tom Pocock, *Fighting General: The Public and Private Campaigns of General Sir Walter Walker* (London, 1973), 130.
[35] Kuala Lumpur to CRO, no. 900, 1 December 1962, and Macmillan note, 2 December 1962, PREM 11/3869.
[36] Selkirk to FO, no. 320, 7 December 1962, *ibid.*

and other ministers strongly criticized the failure of the British authorities to act on the indications that had been received of impending trouble, with parallels drawn with the warnings that had been given prior to the outbreak of the Emergency in 1948.[37] The British High Commissioner for Brunei, Sir Dennis White, in London for his annual medical check-up when the revolt broke out, was soon in receipt of a provocative questionnaire from the Tunku regarding his alleged complacency. White offered his resignation to Sandys, but he was retained in post until late March 1963, when a suitable replacement was found in the form of Angus MacKintosh.[38]

Despite the initial confusion of events in the territory, two companies of the 1/2nd Gurkha Rifles from Singapore were hastily flown direct to Brunei town airfield, which was still (inexplicably) unoccupied on the first evening of the revolt. The Gurkhas consolidated their position around the airfield and quickly moved on the capital, finding the Sultan unharmed at his palace. Lightly armed and badly organized TNKU volunteers had little staying power once engaged by serious opposition and resistance began to crumble almost immediately. The arrival of 1st battalion The Queen's Own Highlanders in Brunei on 10 December signalled the beginning of more offensive operations to recapture Seria and other towns and villages taken by the TNKU, while Royal Marines from 42 Commando drove rebel forces from Limbang and freed the Resident of the Fifth Division among other British hostages. As mopping-up operations began in and around Brunei, with scattered remnants of the TNKU taking to the jungle, and some heading for the Kalimantan border, fears were raised about the internal security position in Sarawak, prompting the rapid despatch of a Royal Artillery battery (without its heavy guns) to Kuching, soon joined by 40 Commando.[39] By 16 December most major towns and centres were back firmly under government control and thousands of TNKU irregulars had been captured, allowing the authorities to announce that the revolt was over.

In some ways it had, as one commentator later put it, been 'a trivial, almost Gilbertian, little uprising' which had been quelled with relative ease by the security forces.[40] Selkirk's own appraisal of the revolt was that only good fortune prevented a far more serious outcome for the British; as he put it, 'the revolution came within an inch of being completely successful'. The arrests at Lawas in late November were felt to have forced

---

[37] Kuala Lumpur to Selkirk, no. 929, 11 December 1962, CO 1030/1160.
[38] See White to Sandys, 31 December 1962, and material in CO 1030/1493; the Tunku's questionnaire has been withheld from this file.
[39] See Pocock, *Fighting General*, 131–7.
[40] Mackie, *Konfrontasi*, 111.

the TNKU's hand into staging their uprising prematurely, and the prior
warning given to the local police was crucial,

otherwise airfields would have been taken, the Sultan captured and we would have
had to fight our way ashore from landing craft on an open coast in the north-
east monsoon. Although association with the revolt was widespread throughout
the entire population, there was not much fire and most rebels were ready to
surrender as soon as the police appeared.[41]

Despite the swift and efficient restoration of order, and the relative significance of Brunei compared to the other two Borneo territories involved
in the Malaysia scheme, the revolt had wide and serious repercussions
for British policy in the region.

For one, as Selkirk had highlighted, this was no armed rising by a discontented and unrepresentative minority, but a manifestation of predominant opinion within the territory. Azahari's Party Rakyat had been at the
forefront of opposition to Malaysia, and its position as the sole vehicle for
popular political expression in Brunei had been confirmed by its resounding success in the August 1962 Legislative Council elections. The Sultan's intention of joining Malaysia had become known in the summer of
1962, and planning for an uprising must have begun at some similar time,
though this, as with much else about the revolt, is ambiguous. Azahari
was away from Brunei in Manila on 8 December, and cannot realistically
have had much control over the TNKU's day-to-day activities, but as the
standard-bearer of Brunei political opinion he made known that the revolt
was actually directed against British colonialism and the Malaysia scheme
and aimed to forge a Unitary State of North Borneo with the Sultan as
head of state.[42] The latter denied any association with Azahari, but the
British were not so sure and doubted the Sultan's veracity, suspecting him
at the very least of having had notice of the uprising and being prepared to
procrastinate on where to swing until it became clear that the revolt would
fail.[43] From neighbouring Sarawak, Waddell offered the view that the revolt was backed by the great majority of the Brunei population, that the
Sultan's Government commanded no confidence at all, and that 'Brunei
is now without an effective civil administration and is kept going by British
troops.' Britain would have to avoid being seen to push the territory into
a 'shotgun marriage with Malaysia'.[44] The Sultan himself told Selkirk,
when they met on 18 December, that he was not yet convinced of the advantages of joining Malaysia 'but if he was so convinced he said he would

[41] Selkirk to Macmillan, 20 December 1962, PREM 11/4146.
[42] There is a useful discussion of the political background in Mackie, *Konfrontasi*, 115–17.
[43] See White to Sandys, no. 25, 20 December 1962, PREM 11/4346.
[44] Waddell to Sandys, C.308, 24 December 1962, *ibid.*

go in whether his people wanted it or not'.[45] Selkirk confessed he was 'somewhat at a loss to know how to handle the political future of Brunei', and that having faced 'a revolution inspired by the militant wing of a political organisation extending to almost the whole population', the Sultan's Government was evidently 'incompetent, unpopular and despised'.[46]

For a while the British toyed with the idea of persuading Azahari to change sides, by coopting his support for Brunei's accession to Malaysia in return for a legitimate role within the state, a notion which intrigued (and perhaps amused) the Prime Minister himself, while de Zulueta felt 'there might well be something to be said for getting Azahari committed to joining Malaysia and then letting him overthrow the Sultan who has evidently not been conspicuously loyal'.[47] Two developments seem to have precluded any further discussion of such nefarious schemes. The Sultan, probably realizing the precariousness of his position, soon agreed to talks with the Tunku on the terms for Brunei's entry to Malaysia, and Azahari turned up in Jakarta in early January 1963 and began to align himself with Indonesian propaganda efforts. With both the Sultan and the Tunku refusing to have any dealings with Azahari, by mid-January Selkirk was voicing his opposition to any deal with the rebel leader.[48] During March 1963, furthermore, the British launched a new initiative by encouraging imprisoned members of the Party Rakyat in Brunei to form a new political party supportive of Malaysia, and the High Commissioner was soon helping to lay the foundations for the Brunei Alliance Party.[49]

As well as the consequences of the revolt for the way Brunei would fit into the Malaysia scheme, of even greater concern to the British authorities was their strong belief that Indonesia had assisted with preparations for the TNKU's rising. From the beginning, this was a subject on which the Prime Minister was particularly anxious. On 9 December 1962, Macmillan recorded in his diary that he had

always feared that once the West New Guinea question was settled, and the Dutch 'ousted' [Sukarno] wd start in Borneo... I think we are sending enough

---

[45] Commissioner General's meeting, 19 December 1962, D1015/1, FO 371/169678.

[46] Selkirk to Sandys, no. 86, 23 December 1962, PREM 11/4346.

[47] See Jakarta to FO, no. 808, 25 December 1962; Macmillan to de Zulueta, 26 December 1962; de Zulueta minute for Macmillan, 27 December 1962, *ibid.*; background opinions on Azahari's essential moderation can be found in a note by White, 27 September 1961, CO 1030/1013.

[48] See Selkirk to CO, no. 96, 28 December 1962, PREM 11/4346; Selkirk to FO, no. 23, 14 January 1963, D1071/5, FO 371/169694; see also Fry to Peck, 21 January 1963, DH1071/8G, FO 371/169908, which suggests an abortive British contact with Azahari while in Jakarta.

[49] Commissioner General's meeting, 11 March 1963, D1015/6, FO 371/169678; White to Selkirk, 8 March 1963, PREM 11/4347.

reinforcements to get military control of Brunei. But I fear there will be a lot of political reaction. It will be represented as against 'Greater Malaysia', when it is really an Indonesian expansionist plot. (The Shell Company's oil installations in Brunei are of very great value.)[50]

About to depart for the conference at Nassau with President Kennedy, Macmillan wanted daily situation reports sent on to him in the Bahamas from the Colonial Office and Ministry of Defence, and was particularly concerned that evidence of Indonesian assistance to the TNKU should be amassed.[51] By the end of December, de Zulueta was informing the Prime Minister, 'There is no doubt that the Indonesians were considerably involved in [the Brunei revolt]. Dr Subandrio . . . has been personally directing operations and the Indonesian Intelligence have been training substantial numbers of infiltrators over the past 8 months. The Indonesians mean to have Brunei by one means or another.'[52]

Meanwhile, tension between Malaya and Indonesia had reached boiling-point. On 10 December, the Tunku accused the TNKU of trying to hand over the Borneo territories to Indonesia, while the following day in the Malayan Parliament he claimed that groups in Indonesia had financed, armed and trained the TNKU, naming Malinau in Kalimantan as a training base and going on to say that Malaya's 'feelings were hurt' and 'patience exhausted'. Subandrio hit back on 15 December, declaring that if the Tunku was determined to use any opportunity to be hostile to Indonesia, Jakarta would accept the challenge; soon after Sukarno was announcing that the Indonesian people sympathized with the people of North Kalimantan and mass rallies in solidarity with their struggle became more commonplace. Concurrently, the press in both Indonesia and Malaya were busy stoking the flames of the dispute, with the Tunku pictured as a lackey of the British with his support for their suppression of the Brunei 'freedom fighters', a charge given added potency with the revelation that Malayan police were assisting the security forces in Brunei with translation and interrogation of TNKU suspects, and Sukarno and the PKI (increasingly seen as synonymous in Malayan eyes) attacked for their efforts to incite rebellion and frustrate Malaysia.[53]

The most alarmed figure on the British side at this time appears to have been Selkirk, who was quickly convinced that Indonesia was 'set on trying to break our concept of Malaysia'.[54] With Sukarno's announcement

[50] Diary entry, 9 December 1962, Macmillan MSS. dep. d.48.
[51] De Zulueta to Huijsman, 14 December 1962, PREM 11/4346.
[52] De Zulueta minute for Macmillan, 27 December 1962, *ibid.*
[53] 'Chronology – War of Words between Indonesia and Malaya', NSF, countries, Indonesia, 3/63–4/63, JFKL; Mackie, *Konfrontasi*, 122–5.
[54] Selkirk to FO, no. 364, 17 December 1962, PREM 11/4346.

of support for the cause of the Brunei rebels, the Commissioner General
advised the Foreign Office that he thought 'our SEATO allies should realise that the Indonesians are playing with fire. We are up against a man
with much of the instability and lust for power of Hitler and military
forces, if not so efficient, at least comparable in size for the area... the
longer we appease him the more extensive the war will be which will
ensue.' Beside this alarmist message, the Prime Minister scrawled: 'We
must study *political* as much as military situation.'[55] The Commissioner
General followed this up with a personal letter to Macmillan, expressing the hope that some protest could be made to the UN while again
comparing Sukarno's rhetoric and performances to those of Hitler in the
1930s, and warning that 'if Soekarno wants to start guerrilla warfare in
the jungles of Borneo, I can see no end to it so long as he supports it'. At
the same time, Selkirk was concerned that the Malayans (especially the
Tunku) were themselves becoming over-provocative in their reactions.[56]
Opposition to any notion of raising Indonesian conduct in SEATO or
the UN came from Home and the Foreign Office, who pointed out that
'reference to SEATO would be extremely provocative to the Indonesians
and we could not count on full support of the Asian members, least of all
the Philippines. Similarly, Dutch experience over the West Irian dispute
suggests that the Security Council would be a broken reed.' Moreover,
airing the issue at the UN would probably induce an appearance from
Azahari, embarrassing questions about colonialism, and Manila's claim
to North Borneo. The Foreign Office's aversion to taking the issue to
any wider international forum was also endorsed by the Prime Minister, underlining the limited diplomatic options available if Indonesia kept
its activities in the Borneo territories at a low key.[57] With anti-colonial
sentiment in the ascendant at the UN, as British officials recognized, any
attempt to censure Indonesian behaviour might open up discussion of
the establishment of Malaysia and the attitudes of the Borneo peoples
themselves. The Indonesians were losing few opportunities to portray
the dispute as one where a popular rising was being directed against the
neo-colonial aspects of the new federation, and one which deserved the
support of the 'New Emerging Forces'.

The impetus behind Indonesia's adventurism in the Borneo territories
has been assigned to a number of different causes. With the arrival of
Malaysia due in August 1963, this was probably the last opportunity to
frustrate the new federation by challenging its legitimacy in the eyes of

[55] Selkirk to FO, no. 374, 19 December 1962, and Macmillan note n.d., *ibid.*
[56] Selkirk to Macmillan, 20 December 1962, *ibid.*
[57] See FO to Jakarta, no. 1092, 21 December 1962; de Zulueta minute for Macmillan and
    Macmillan note, 26 December 1962, *ibid.*

local and regional opinion. Several prominent Indonesians would later mention their concerns that Malaysia might become the springboard for enhanced Chinese influence close to their borders, while the existence of long-standing irredentist convictions among elite and governing circles was also a factor. From the PKI's point of view, Malaysia was clearly a way to preserve Western imperial influence and an important SEATO base adjacent to Indonesia. But the likeliest explanation is that confrontation emerged more in a hesitant and improvised way, a product of the political contradictions and tensions within Indonesian society, where Sukarno was still trying to play the role of charismatic nationalist leader and statesman, while also holding on to the allegiance of the PKI through the pursuit of an anti-imperialist line. In this sense, the most obvious feature of confrontation was its unpredictable nature, with Indonesian leaders ready to trim and alter their policies in reaction to fluctuating developments on both the international and domestic political stages.

By the end of 1962, the British had quickly come round to the view that Indonesia was not merely keen to give help to groups within the Borneo territories ready to frustrate plans for Malaysia, but was also embarked upon a campaign which aimed to absorb those territories through forcing their separate independence, making them even more vulnerable to internal subversion or external attack, or by encouraging alignment with Indonesia in the face of British repression. The JIC began a study of the extent of Indonesian involvement in Brunei and to update the paper it had worked on during the previous autumn on future Indonesian intentions. At the Foreign Office, Peck had already reached his own conclusion: 'The effective threat from Indonesia comes not from a possible direct attack in Singapore or the Borneo territories (in which their potential superiority in manpower and Soviet-supplied armaments would probably be seriously reduced by inept handling and planning) but from Indonesian covert support of a long, drawn out guerrilla war on the [Borneo] border.'[58] In Sarawak, fears over unrest developing in the wake of the Brunei revolt were reflected in the measures taken to restrict the activities of SUPP. Within the territory, Special Branch had long been preoccupied with the penetration of SUPP and the Chinese-dominated Trade Union Congress by members of the CCO. By the spring of 1962, the CCO was estimated to have about 800 cadres, controlling cells of between ten and thirty people. Of forty members of SUPP's Central Executive Committee, ten were considered CCO members.[59] Adding to

[58] Peck note on international implications of the Brunei revolt, 28 December 1962, D1016/15, FO 371/169680.
[59] 'Communist penetration of the Labour Unions and SUPP', 12 March 1962, paper prepared in the Governor's Secretariat, Kuching, box 2, file 7, Waddell papers.

concerns was the fact that SUPP itself had joined with Azahari in issuing an anti-Malaysia statement in July 1962, and a SUPP delegation had been due to meet Azahari in Manila on 8 December, before going on to New York to present a joint case against Malaysia to the UN General Assembly. The outbreak of the Brunei revolt prompted the authorities in Sarawak to declare a state of emergency, while an ordinance was introduced which allowed suspects to be held in preventive detention for up to two years without a court appearance; several key members of SUPP were subsequently arrested, and the three leading pro-SUPP Chinese newspapers banned.[60] These measures may, in fact, have driven many young Sarawak Chinese into more overt opposition to British rule and made them more susceptible to later Indonesian entreaties for them to take up arms.

The Brunei revolt was also regarded by Lee Kuan Yew, and by the Malayan Government, as convenient cover for the implementation of the arrest programme in Singapore that had been devised by Special Branch officers in the spring of 1962, and discussed with British ministers during the London talks in July. Events in Brunei had done little to inspire Malayan confidence in British willingness to act decisively to forestall an imminent threat, but they now expected firm measures to be taken against the political opposition in Singapore.[61] When it became clear that Azahari had met with Lim Chin Siong, the Barisan chairman, in Singapore just prior to the revolt on 3 December, Lee considered it a 'heaven-sent opportunity of justifying action'.[62] Nevertheless, the key local officials on the British side, Selkirk and Moore, were deeply reluctant to authorize any large-scale round-up of Barisan leaders and other alleged subversives, despite the tacit understanding previously reached by the Tunku, Lee and Sandys in London.[63]

The Malayan Government had by now come to regard an arrest programme as an essential pre-condition for merger with Singapore, hoping that responsibility for unpopular and tough measures would be taken by Lee and the British rather than themselves once Malaysia was formed.[64] With the Singapore Special Branch able to present new evidence of Communist penetration and control of the Barisan, combined with the

[60] See Chin Ung-Ho, *Chinese Politics in Sarawak: A Study of the Sarawak United People's Party* (Oxford, 1996), 72.
[61] See Kuala Lumpur to Singapore, no. 929, 11 December 1962, CO 1030/1160.
[62] Singapore to CO, no. 572, 10 December 1962, *ibid.*
[63] See the Tunku's criticisms of Selkirk in Lansdowne's notes of discussions with the Malayan Prime Minister and Ghazali, 20 and 21 November 1962, CO 1030/1036.
[64] The bargaining over the arrests is dealt with at greater length in the present author's 'Creating Malaysia: Singapore Security, the Borneo Territories and the Contours of British Policy, 1961–63,' *Journal of Imperial and Commonwealth History*, 2, 28, 2000.

alarming events in Brunei, Selkirk faced heavy pressure to drop his previous resistance on the ISC to carrying out arrests.[65] In a telegram of
12 December given personal approval by the Prime Minister, Sandys
informed Selkirk: 'As you know I have all along been reluctant to give
blanket approval in advance for arrests of subversive elements in Singapore. But if we are to avoid a dangerous disagreement with the Malayan
Government we shall have to take some action of this kind before merger.'
Sandys felt that 'we should move at once' with the Brunei revolt providing
the 'best possible background against which to take this action'.[66] The
following day the ISC met, and with Selkirk's agreement given the new
evidence produced on the links between Azahari and the Barisan leaders,
decided on a series of arrests to begin on 16 December. However, the
operation collapsed at the very last minute, when Lee Kuan Yew added
several names to the arrest list (including those of anti-Malaysia members of the Malayan Federal Assembly in Kuala Lumpur) prompting the
Federation's representative on the ISC to withdraw amid protests and
recriminations.[67]

Another meeting of the ISC was scheduled for 1 February 1963, and
frantic efforts were made by the British to remount Operation Cold Store,
as the arrest programme was dubbed. Despite Selkirk's fresh reservations
over the names that now appeared on the lists agreed to by Lee and Federation ministers, Sandys issued a terse instruction to the British Commissioner that there was no alternative but to accept majority opinion on
the ISC and vote for a unanimous decision. Selkirk acquiesced, and on
2 February, 111 suspects in Singapore and Malaya (including 24 members of the Barisan) were taken into detention.[68] With their defeat in the
referendum on Malaysia staged the previous September, and with the
heart of their leadership now forcibly removed from the political scene
in Singapore, the Barisan could offer little effective opposition (either
legal or extra-legal) during the remainder of 1963 to Lee's policies and
the plans for Malaysia.[69] As for the British, they had fulfilled their implicit bargain with the Tunku, and could expect that he too would follow
through on his prior intentions regarding Malaysia, despite the troubled
seas that might lie ahead.

[65] Singapore to CO, no. 572, 10 December 1962, CO 1030/1160.
[66] CO to Singapore, no. 546, 12 December 1962, *ibid.*
[67] See Singapore to CO, no. 582, 14 December 1962; Singapore to CO, no. 590, 17
December 1962, PREM 11/4346.
[68] CO to Singapore, no. 68, 1 February 1963; Singapore to CO, no. 71, 1 February 1963,
ibid.; Sandys minute for Macmillan, M.3/63, 1 February 1963; Selkirk to Macmillan,
no. 86, 4 February 1963, PREM 11/4184.
[69] See Osborne, *Singapore and Malaysia*, 30-4, where Lee's futile attempt to distance himself
from responsibility for the arrests is also examined.

The Brunei revolt meant that 1963 would hold a new degree of uncertainty for British policy-makers concerned with South East Asia. The high hopes of the summer of 1962, with the Laotian settlement at Geneva, the resolution of the West Irian crisis and the successful outcome to the London talks on Greater Malaysia were being steadily undermined from a number of different sources. By the end of 1962, the Geneva accords on Laos were looking somewhat threadbare, with Souvanna Phouma's coalition government resting on a precarious basis, considerable numbers of North Vietnamese forces still present in the country, and Washington beginning to revive its covert support to the Meo tribespeople of northern Laos.[70] With regard to West Irian, by late 1962 the Dutch had been quietly replaced by UN administrators, but instead of heralding a new phase of peaceful Indonesian internal development, the resolution of the crisis now appeared (at least in London) to be merely the prelude to a concerted campaign to remove Western influence from the region altogether. Finally, the plans for a Greater Malaysia were coming under heavy strain. Brunei had been considered the least troublesome territory to bring into the new federation, but now its future was far from clear. Admittedly, the threat of Indonesian subversion that the revolt had highlighted was solidifying support in Sarawak and North Borneo for the security that might be offered through joining Malaysia, and hence easing the work of the Lansdowne Intergovernmental Committee, but a hostile neighbourhood now awaited those territories as they prepared for the end of formal British rule. Moreover, as the differences over the implementation of Operation Cold Store had shown very clearly, there were continuing signs of distrust between the Tunku and Lee Kuan Yew as each manoeuvred for the position of maximum advantage in the Malaysia endgame.

It was soon apparent that the focus of attention for British policy-makers in early 1963 would be to solicit the support of friends and allies against the growing belligerence of Indonesia. The most important requirement here was to secure the active support of the Administration in Washington for British policies in the region, something the Dutch had manifestly failed to achieve over West Irian. In this context, then, one must note that Anglo-American relations in general were going through a difficult phase in the winter of 1962–3. By early December 1962 it had become apparent that the Americans intended to cancel further work on the air-to-surface Skybolt missile system, when Britain was reliant on this programme to update its V-bomber-based nuclear deterrent. Suspicions were reinforced in London that State Department opposition to

[70] See e.g. William Colby and Peter Forbath, *Honourable Men: My Life in the CIA* (London, 1978), 191–5.

proliferation, and the sensitivities of America's other NATO allies, were combining to drive the Kennedy Administration into putting Britain out of the nuclear business altogether.[71] Although the President and McNamara were actually strongly inclined to supply the British with the submarine-based Polaris system as a replacement, there was indeed pressure from within the State Department (voiced at most senior level by George Ball) to tie the British deterrent into a wider scheme for a Multilateral Nuclear Force under joint European control.[72] The fudged outcome of the subsequent Nassau conference, where Macmillan secured Polaris but with a vague British commitment to look more seriously at the Multilateral Force, could not conceal the damage that had been done to Anglo-American relations by this very public episode and underlined Britain's dependence on the United States for the national deterrent (with all the attendant consequences for Macmillan's European policies).

There had already been critical press reaction in Britain to the assertion of Dean Acheson in a speech of 5 December 1962 that the British had lost an empire but had not yet found a role, and news of the cancellation of Skybolt, and uncertainty over the nature of its replacement, added to the furore. From the official American point of view there was some displeasure at Macmillan's determination at Nassau to secure Polaris, while Kennedy himself saw the problem mainly in political terms: a substitute for Skybolt would need to be offered to Macmillan if he was to avoid a major political crisis at home (with David Ormsby Gore, the British Ambassador in Washington, raising the unlikely spectre of a Labour Government coming to power if the Prime Minister returned empty-handed from the Bahamas). At Nassau, Kennedy had certainly done the Prime Minister a favour, even if he did feel partly obligated through the prior arrangements surrounding Skybolt, but he later considered it to have been a mistake. As it entered its final year of sad decline, the Macmillan Government's efforts to rely on sentiment in dealing with the Americans would fall on deaf ears as Washington treated each issue on its own merits, and in the light of US interests.

When it came to the aftermath of the Brunei revolt and problems in South East Asia, the alarmist views of Indonesian intentions increasingly being circulated by British officials did not sit easily with the impressions and hopes for Indonesia held by several key American officials in late

---

[71] The best account can be found in Ian Clark, *Nuclear Diplomacy and the Special Relationship: America and Britain's Deterrent, 1957–1962* (Oxford, 1994).

[72] See the revealing memorandum of conversation in the Oval Room of the White House, 16 December 1962, NSF, Meetings and Memoranda, Meetings with the President, box 317, JFKL; and George W. Ball, *The Past Has Another Pattern* (New York, 1982), 262–8.

1962 and early 1963. More importantly, from Washington's perspective, a tussle over 'colonial remnants' in South East Asia was beginning to threaten their larger goals for the region, especially in the way the plans for Malaysia seemed to bring discord and instability in their wake. With the potential for the PKI to seize on the issue and turn it to their domestic advantage, the Kennedy Administration did not find itself in automatic sympathy with the problems now confronting their Western ally.

Part II

Outbreak

5   The emergence of confrontation:
January–May 1963

At the beginning of 1963, the British Government received another of the body blows that came to characterize the final years of Macmillan's premiership. With negotiations to admit Britain into the European Economic Community at an advanced stage, de Gaulle convened a press conference on 14 January where he announced in unabashed fashion that he was vetoing British entry. The whole thrust of the government's international policies, formulated in the summer of 1961, had been disposed of in a matter of minutes. 'It is the end – or at least the temporary bar – to everything for which I have worked for many years', Macmillan sadly noted in his diary. 'All our policies at home and abroad are in ruins.'[1] In parallel with the turn to Europe, the discussions in the Future Policy Committee in 1961 had shown that senior ministers had been thinking of significant reductions in South East Asia commitments. A Laotian settlement (drawing the teeth from plans for SEATO intervention in Indochina) and the creation of Malaysia, allowing the relinquishment of residual colonial responsibilities and a transfer of internal security duties at Singapore to Kuala Lumpur, appeared well on track by the summer of 1962.

The emergence of Indonesian hostility to the plans for Malaysia, however, constituted another setback to the notion of reducing commitments. Indeed, from this period onwards in British overseas policy, there was a tendency to shift attention away from the European stage to a renewed focus on the east of Suez role. This was hardly by choice, but came through the challenges to perceived British interests in the Middle East and South East Asia presented by such phenomena as the spread of Nasser-inspired Arab nationalism in South Arabia, Sukarno's adventurism, and the rising force of revolutionary Communism in Indochina, all at a time when the final process of decolonization was under way. In mid-January 1963, Selkirk wrote to warn the Prime Minister that recent developments in South East Asia underscored the 'importance of attaining Malaysia if we are to hope to maintain any stability in the area where, to the north we

[1] Diary entry, 22 January 1963, Macmillan MSS. dep. d.48.

have a desperate war in Vietnam and in the south there is Indonesia, well armed and highly unstable'. Rather than there being a margin for savings in defence costs, Britain's military role in the area would have to be increased beyond levels previously contemplated.[2]

In the immediate aftermath of the Brunei revolt, the Government's priority had been to assume a low-key response to signs of Indonesian involvement. The Foreign Office held that: 'Our policy towards Indonesia at the present juncture can be summed up as "firm but friendly".' Although the Indonesians would need to be reminded that Britain would resist all efforts at infiltration of the Borneo territories, 'this can be done in a tactful manner without waving a big stick'.[3] On 11 January 1963, the Foreign Secretary summoned the Indonesian Ambassador, and emphasized Britain's desire for friendly relations, though making evident his disquiet at Indonesian support for the Brunei rebels, asserting that there would be no toleration of 'interference of any kind in Her Majesty's territories or any attempts to stir up trouble'.[4] Undoubtedly lying at the back of British official minds at this time was the analogy that might be drawn with the Dutch experience over West Irian; there was no desire to stoke up a crisis atmosphere over Indonesian behaviour that might trigger calls for international intervention (in what were, essentially, internal colonial matters) or a postponement of Malaysia. The main concern here was in restraining the Malayan Prime Minister from fuelling the polemical exchange that had erupted between Jakarta and Kuala Lumpur in the wake of the revolt.

Following some less than temperate language from the Tunku, on 20 January Subandrio delivered a speech in Jojakarta where he announced that Indonesia would have to adopt a policy of 'confrontation' towards Malaya as that country was acting as 'the henchman of neo-Imperialism and neo-Colonialism pursuing a policy hostile to Indonesia'.[5] One of the reactions of London to this increase in tension was quietly to put elements of the UK strategic reserve on short notice to move to Malaya, relieving units there for service in Borneo.[6] Yet JIC estimates, agreed with Malayan officials following talks in Kuala Lumpur, suggested that there was little indication that the Indonesians were about to launch organized forays into the Borneo territories from across the border in Kalimantan

---

[2] Selkirk to Macmillan, 17 January 1963, PREM 11/4346.
[3] 'International implications of the Brunei revolt', 28 December 1962, D1016/15, FO 371/169680.
[4] Note of interview between Foreign Secretary and Indonesian Ambassador, 11 January 1963, DH1022/5, FO 371/169882.
[5] Jakarta to FO, no. 54, 21 January 1963, DO 169/237, and see Mackie, *Konfrontasi*, 125.
[6] Chief of the Defence Staff to C-in-C Far East, T.251924Z, 25 January 1963, DO 169/237.

(though significant numbers of TNKU guerrillas were still receiving training there), at least for the next two or three months.[7] One local factor that
had a bearing on such matters were the unusually severe monsoon storms
and consequent flood damage that afflicted Borneo from the middle of
January. The local British military commander, Major General Walter
Walker, gave priority to flood relief work over operations against the remaining Brunei rebels, beginning the battle for the 'hearts and minds' of
the local population that had been such a feature of the earlier counter-
insurgency campaign in Malaya.[8] Consequently alert status for forces in
the Far East was relaxed, and most of the UK-based forces stood down.[9]
Nevertheless, the Tunku felt compelled to announce to a press conference that 2,000 British troops were on their way to the Far East to meet
the current emergency. An alarmed Sandys instructed Tory to tell the
Malayan Prime Minister to desist from making such statements as 'we
should prefer to play the hand our own way at present and avoid giving the Indonesians a handle for charges that we are openly threatening
them... Until we have discussed with the Americans our future policies
towards Indonesia we do not want the Tunku to rock the boat.'[10]

Another way in which the Malayans might be tempted to 'rock the boat'
was in hatching schemes to foment unrest within Indonesia. Several dissident leaders from the 1958 Outer Island rebellion were still receiving
sanctuary in Malaya, while some could see attractions in drawing Sumatra
into a closer association with their relatively prosperous neighbour across
the straits of Malacca. In early January, Lansdowne was asking Selkirk
to impress on the Tunku the 'importance of not making public statements which might tend to reinforce Indonesia's suspicions of Malaysia
as a potentially hostile neighbour', the Minister of State remarking that
he was 'anxious about the Tunku's foreign policy. We should know all
about it and guard against him embarking upon adventures prejudicial
to the peace of SEA, adventures in which we would almost certainly become involved.'[11] British officials in Kuala Lumpur, however, saw little
prospect of restraining the Malayan Prime Minister, and had just about
managed to persuade him not to sever diplomatic relations with Indonesia
following Subandrio's announcement on confrontation.[12] Indeed, Tory

---

[7] A formal JIC assessment of future Indonesian aims and intentions was finally produced (after talks with senior Malayan officials) on 28 January 1963; references to
JIC(62)58(Final) can be found in DO 169/67.
[8] See Pocock, *Fighting General*, 145.
[9] COS 10th mtg/63, 5 February 1963, D1195/5G, FO 371/169735.
[10] Kuala Lumpur to CRO, no. 136, 29 January 1963; CRO to Kuala Lumpur, no. 220,
30 January 1963, DO 169/238.
[11] Lansdowne to Selkirk, no. 5, 3 January 1963, DO 169/237; Lansdowne minute, 6 January
1963, CO 1030/1493.
[12] See Kuala Lumpur to CRO, no. 97, 23 January 1963, DO 169/237.

was predicting that the Tunku's mood was only likely to worsen, as the opposition in Malaya might respond to appeals for support from their 'Malay cousins in Indonesia ... ':

Tunku and others are quite capable of seeking to appeal over heads of Soekarno and Javanese to Indonesian opinion elsewhere. They seem confident that if they really set out to do so they could make trouble for Soekarno at home. We understand already from MEA [Ministry of External Affairs] that they have received messages from Sumatra in favour of Malaysia and they are clearly much tempted to follow up leads of this kind into Indonesia. Feeling here therefore is anything but defensive and it will be useless to appeal for patience as such.[13]

By mid-February, Selkirk was complaining to the Prime Minister about

the very clumsy way in which the Tunku handles foreign affairs. He is in fact quite out of his depth and may well become an added menace to an already difficult situation ... his own contribution to the situation is not wholly negligible and it is therefore vitally important that we should be in a position to put over our view forcefully in Kuala Lumpur so as to restrain him from irresponsible talk and, if possible, clandestine intrigue.[14]

Yet the British themselves were also attracted by the possibilities of stirring up internal opposition to Sukarno. After the Brunei revolt, de Zulueta suggested to Macmillan that 'the best solution from the purely military point of view would be to encourage a subversive movement inside Indonesia–Borneo', though, '... even if this did seem a suitable operation politically, it would take some time to organise'.[15] This was also a notion that had attracted the active interest of the Foreign Secretary; on 1 February 1963 Home can be found eagerly minuting, 'I want to see the appreciation of the possibilities in Sumatra as soon as it is ready. It should be pretty easy to stir up revolt against Sukarno there.'[16] It appears that at this stage British ministers and officials felt that a counter-subversion programme would undermine their stance of non-provocation, and would be too unpredictable in its consequences. It could even hasten the very kind of conflict that Britain wanted to avoid, while memories of 1958 would suggest that such an effort might even solidify support for Sukarno, and prove embarrassing if outside interference were substantiated. By the spring of 1963 it seems that the Malayans were pressing the British for a promised JIC update of future Indonesian aims and intentions, which would also contain ideas on covert action. In mid-May, Tory was reporting from Kuala Lumpur that once the assessment had been completed it could be passed on to Ghazali and

[13] Kuala Lumpur to CRO, no. 105, 24 January 1963, *ibid*.
[14] Selkirk to Macmillan, 18 February 1963, PREM 11/4146.
[15] De Zulueta minute for Macmillan, 27 December 1962, PREM 11/4346.
[16] Home minute, 1 February 1963, DH1071/12G, FO 371/169908.

way would be clear for discussion with Tunku, Razak and Ghazali on possibility for special political action [a standard phrase to cover a covert operation by the intelligence services] ... Ghazali has now asked several times about progress and I fear that unless I can send him British paper very soon he may initiate separate contingency planning with Tunku without us. There is some reason to suspect that he may indeed already be doing so. This could be very dangerous.[17]

In the absence of access to intelligence-related materials it is difficult to see how British and Malayan thinking developed on this issue, but in early May the Tunku had enthusiastically told Tory about the potential for an uprising in Sulawesi, and while

he gave no indication that he was giving moral or physical assistance to the rebel movements ... he made it obvious as he had for that matter during the civil war [of 1958 in Indonesia] that he thought the only salvation for Indonesia and the only future security for Malaya lay in the overthrow of Soekarno's regime by anti-Communist forces strongly backed by the Muslims.[18]

This was a theme the Tunku was to return to with even greater vehemence in the autumn, and it appears safe to infer that the British indulged in joint planning with the Malayans partly in an attempt to keep a close watch on their activities and to hold them in check.

Another line of policy followed by British officials in early 1963 was to work to frustrate the development of any concerted front between Indonesia and the Philippines in their opposition to Malaysia. This was to be achieved by the offer of talks with Manila on what was regarded as the 'rather tiresome' Philippine claim to North Borneo.[19] The Prime Minister was told by Home that he and Sandys had become convinced that talks should be held with the Filipinos:

Their claim to North Borneo is ridiculous and we have told them that we will not negotiate about it. On the other hand we are concerned at the co-operation between the Filipinos and the Indonesians in opposing Malaysia. Some of the Filipinos are now realising that they are being made Sukarno's dupes and I think we have a good chance of separating them from the Indonesians.[20]

A Philippine delegation was duly invited to London to discuss questions and problems of mutual interest, but on 28 January, on the eve of the beginning of the talks, President Macapagal delivered an address to a joint session of Congress in Manila where he attacked the Malaysia scheme as

---

[17] See Kuala Lumpur to CRO, no. 842, 15 May 1963, and Kuala Lumpur to CRO, no. 877, 21 May 1963, DO 169/67. Internal evidence from this file shows that the revised intelligence assessment, JIC(63)41, was produced on 7 June 1963.
[18] Kuala Lumpur to CRO, no. 764, 2 May 1963, DO 169/240.
[19] De Zulueta minute for Macmillan, 27 December 1962, PREM 11/4346.
[20] Home minute for Macmillan, 28 December 1962, PM/62/160, *ibid.*

a violation of the principle of self-determination, and as a continuation of colonialism. Disputing the right of Malaya to take over North Borneo, the Philippine President put forward the suggestion of a referendum, possibly under UN auspices, to determine the final disposition of the territory, though only after it had been 'restored' to Manila's control.[21] The Anglo-Philippine talks themselves produced only a polite agreement to exchange further notes putting forward the legal basis on which claims to North Borneo were made; the British rebuffed Filipino notions that there might be an early referral of the dispute to the International Court of Justice in The Hague. It would appear, then, that rather than dividing the Philippines from Indonesia, the British offer of talks at this point had actually encouraged Manila's determination to express opposition to Malaysia.

The verbal fireworks of January between Malayan and Indonesian spokesmen continued into the following month, but there was little to show that Jakarta had a clearly formulated plan of how it would translate the rhetoric of confrontation into further action on the ground that would serve to undermine the new federation. Subandrio was visiting India at the end of January and in early February, and the British High Commissioner took the opportunity to see him in New Delhi. Having railed against the Tunku's perpetual hostility and after claiming that he 'clearly wished to annex Sumatra', the Indonesian Foreign Minister maintained that he wanted Lord Home to know that Indonesia had no quarrel with Britain, had no designs on the Borneo territories and did not object to the idea of Malaysia. This was a line that Subandrio repeated to Selkirk a few days later when passing through Singapore on his return to Jakarta, the latter reporting that he was 'friendly but evasive throughout and concentrated most of the time on personal attacks on the Tunku'. To Lee Kuan Yew, however, Subandrio was prepared to speak against Malaysia, and to threaten that 'unless the Tunku climbed down the Indonesians would "fix him", to which he added reference to the presence of refugee Sumitro [a leader of the 1958 rebellion] in Kuala Lumpur, and the Tunku's activities in Sumatra'.[22] Indeed, the tendency of Indonesian officials was to emphasize the threat that they felt Malaysia would present to their national security, and to refer back to the outside support offered to the rebellion of 1958.[23]

The uncertainties of Indonesian policy reflected the intentional ambivalence and flexibility that lay at the heart of confrontation itself. The

[21] See *Malaya/Philippine Relations*, appdx IV.
[22] See UK High Commission Delhi to CRO, no. 335, 31 January 1963, DO 169/238; Selkirk to FO, no. 71, 5 February 1963, DH1062/12, FO 371/169902.
[23] See e.g. Jakarta to DOS, no. 1303, 22 February 1963, NSF, countries, Indonesia, 1/63–2/63, JFKL.

posture involved a 'combination of threats, brinkmanship and play-acting, which could be modulated at will to a pitch of fierce hostility at one extreme or, at the other, of patient acquiescence while waiting for favourable opportunities to resume the long-term struggle, whatever its objectives may be'.[24] It was clear that many of those objectives lay not just in terms of intimidating and undermining an external opponent, but in manipulating forces and symbols on the domestic political scene. Hence while one of its tactics was undoubtedly to provoke a reaction that might lead to the isolation of an antagonist, it also constituted 'an attempt to intimidate to gain political ends by skirting the brink of hostilities in a context where enemy retaliation would only assist the cause of internal political solidarity'.[25] In all probability, Sukarno had yet to decide to commit Indonesia to a course of outright conflict with Malaysia, hoping rather to upset the plans for its inception, while he may have been using the campaign to forestall internal critics as he weighed up the consequences of accepting major amounts of international (and American) aid.

The overriding British priority at this nebulous stage of the dispute was, and would remain, securing the support of the United States in adopting a firm response to Indonesian demands and threats. The great fear in London was that they would experience the same kind of diplomatic isolation that had befallen the Dutch over West Irian. In Lansdowne's view,

The Indonesian mood of aggressive confidence was largely engendered by UK and US reluctance to give genuine support to their NATO ally over West Irian. I accept that we and the US were realistic if somewhat ambivalent over that issue. Sukarno's foreign policy will be decided by whether he thinks he can risk further adventures of that sort. Our object should be to put the danger of expansionist policies beyond any doubt whatsoever. If we do not, our effort to create Malaysia will not be worth a row of beans.[26]

Hence the Foreign Secretary was soon requesting official-level talks in Washington, which would also involve the Australians and New Zealanders, in order to exchange views and assessments of Indonesian aims and intentions. Delays in convening these were frustrating; Fred Warner, the head of the Foreign Office's South East Asia Department, noted: 'Hardly a day goes by without the Foreign Secretary asking "when are we going to start these talks?"' The need to come to an agreed position with the Americans had

---

[24] Mackie, *Konfrontasi*, 126.
[25] Michael Leifer, *The Foreign Relations of New States* (Camberwell, 1974), 56.
[26] Lansdowne minute, 23 January 1963, PREM 11/4182.

become a kind of linch-pin [sic] in our future planning. It is not that we are going to ask for military assistance . . . We have, however, come to the conclusion that a 'confrontation' with the Indonesians is necessary and that they will have to be told that if they continue their present course the Western world will be united against them. We do not want this to develop like the West Irian dispute with Sukarno knowing perfectly well that the West will not stand together.[27]

To strengthen their case, the British prepared a 'hard hitting brief' for the meetings in Washington, in order to 'dislodge the Howard P [Jones] policy of the State Department'.[28] 'Sukarno wishes to turn the Malayan seas into an Indonesian ocean, just as Mussolini set out to turn the Mediterranean into the "Mare Nostrum" ', one of these drafts ran. 'Mussolini, too, had no cut-and-dried plan, but seized each opportunity as events presented it.' Indonesian actions were opening a 'second front' to join the push initiated by North Vietnam, and 'it looks as though the authors of the southward and the northward push will make common cause so as each to achieve his own designs'.[29]

Having expended such energy and effort in coaxing Sukarno's regime towards a path of moderate and peaceful economic development, and wary of fostering a hostility to the West that could improve the fortunes of the PKI, officials in Washington were unlikely to accept the British thesis. Indeed, what was more discernible was a considerable degree of frustration that British late colonial plans seemed to be bringing a fresh degree of instability to South East Asia. The evolution of the Greater Malaysia scheme had been monitored by the State Department since 1961, but the British had not formally consulted the Americans on their views or sought their approval. The chief concern in Washington was with the degree of Communist influence in Singapore, and the vulnerability of the Borneo territories to Chinese subversion. Hence the initial tendency of US officials was to see Malaysia as a necessary, if artificial construct, which would help forestall some of the more worrying side-effects of the end of formal empire in the region. By January 1963, fears had begun to emerge within the State Department that Indonesia's support for the Brunei rebels and its professed intention to frustrate the formation of Malaysia indicated that the acquisition of West Irian had not satisfied Jakarta's territorial ambitions. Michael Forrestal of the NSC staff was on a South East Asian tour at this time, and Harriman took the chance of his presence in Jakarta to suggest that Forrestal and Howard Jones emphasize to Sukarno the joint threat to US and Indonesian interests posed by an

[27] Warner to Washington, 29 January 1963, DH1071/4, FO 371/169908.
[28] Peck minute, 29 January 1963, DH1071/15, *ibid.*
[29] Steering brief no. 1, 29 January 1963, DH1071/12G, *ibid.*

aggressive Communist China. Malaysia, it was argued, would act as a buffer to the north, while the United States was

convinced that only feasible way to build [a] strong opposition to ChiComs [sic] and their expansionist tendencies is through development of a Greater Malaysia. We have no doubt that British are sincere in wishing to liquidate this vestige of colonialism [in Borneo] in a manner which in long run will prove of greater benefit to the Indonesians. For these reasons we believe he [Sukarno] should not attempt to block Malaysia which we intend to support vigorously.[30]

The Indonesians proved only too ready to agree with the American argument concerning a Chinese Communist threat, but asserted instead that Malaysia offered an outlet for subversion to be spread through the region. General Nasution told Forrestal that 'just as [the Americans] were concerned about red menace, Indonesia was concerned about yellow peril. [The] Chinese . . . would remain [an] indigestible element in Southeast Asian countries, their loyalty primarily to motherland.' When it came to Malaysia, the Singapore Chinese 'would continue to dominate economics of area which meant they would exert political power even though perhaps from behind [the] scenes and ultimately, as Chinese began southward expansion, would constitute [a] military fifth column'. As it was not based on the true nationalist feelings of the area, Malaysia was 'an artificial solution that could not last', and while Indonesia had no territorial claims in North Kalimantan, it would feel bound to give moral and political support to the 'independence movement' based there.[31] Sukarno was also willing to reassure Jones and Forrestal that he was now determined to achieve Indonesia's remaining national goal of economic stability and growth, and was keen to attract American assistance.

When the British Ambassador in Washington, David Ormsby Gore, saw Harriman for a preliminary discussion about the Indonesian situation, the latter noted that it was 'too early to say that [Sukarno] was sold completely on new adventures', and there were still signs that the Indonesians would begin to focus attention on their economic problems. The Americans were still inclined, with international support, to provide financial aid to Indonesia: ' . . . the choice is whether we help genuine [Indonesian] efforts to improve the economy or throw it entirely to the USSR'. With regard to Brunei, Harriman did not agree with the British line that Indonesia had either 'created' the revolt or provided arms and personnel, though he did believe that training had been given to some of the rebels. Underlining US support for Malaysia as the only practical

[30] DOS to Jakarta, 16 January 1963, *FRUS, 1961–1963, XXIII*, 658–9.
[31] Jakarta to DOS, no. 1110, 18 January 1963, NSF, countries, Indonesia, 1/63–2/63, JFKL.

answer to the problem of the Borneo territories, Harriman was, however, at pains to highlight the notion that the Indonesian government 'regarded Communist China as its real enemy and [he] expected that Sukarno would continue to make every effort to avoid becoming a communist satellite'. Ormsby Gore could merely counter that Soviet aid to Indonesia could bring with it obligations, while speculating that PKI members might eventually find their way into the Cabinet.[32]

These were far from encouraging signs for British officials intent on securing wholehearted US support. They would have been even more concerned had they known that on the same day that Ormsby Gore was seeing Harriman, Robert Komer of the NSC staff was expressing his concern to McGeorge Bundy over what was described as 'all the anti-Sukarno emotionalism rampant these days...' Komer was pleased to find Harriman 'thoroughly statesmanlike' on the issues:

He says we're just going to have to 'sweat out Sukarno', alternately using the carrot and stick, but essentially living with this guy and trying to box him in. He agrees that we must turn Sukarno off Malaysia by (1) working harder to get the Phils to stop serving as a horse for Indos in Borneo; and (2) making more of a political demonstration of our interest in Malaysia...

The approach to avoid, in Harriman's opinion, was one which indicated US hostility through an aid cut-off, or tried to force Sukarno into alignment with the West; as Komer put it,

All these guys who advocate 'tough' policies towards neutralists like Nasser and Sukarno blink at the fact that it was precisely such policies which helped influence these countries to accept Moscow offers in the first place. The best way to keep Nasser or Sukarno from becoming prisoners of the USSR is to compete for them, not thrust them into Soviet hands. I can see we're going to have a tough time defending our Indo[nesian] policy for the next few months (especially with the Brits taking a 'head-in-sand' attitude).[33]

Warnings about too close an alignment with British plans for Malaysia were also coming from the US Embassy in Jakarta, with Jones informing the State Department in early February that though he had initially backed the concept, the 'real causes of the Brunei revolt, and...the broader implications of proceeding in the face of both Indonesian and Philippine opposition' had given him cause for concern. He now felt it prudent for the United States to maintain a detached position as far as possible. Given the recent arrests in Singapore, the Ambassador was

---

[32] See Washington to FO, no. 28 Saving, 17 January 1963, DH1071/3G, FO 371/169908; memorandum of conversation, 16 January 1963, 798.000/1–1663, RG 59.
[33] Komer memorandum for Bundy, 16 January 1963, *FRUS, 1961–1963, XXIII*, 656–7.

more inclined to doubt the long-term viability of the new Malaysian federation, and had received the impression that the British had not fully realized the military implications of resisting an Indonesian-backed guerrilla
movement in Borneo. For the United States to be dragged into military
responsibility for Malaysia, with the likelihood that this would result in
a direct clash with Indonesia, would be disastrous: 'It is quite clear to
me that our position in Asia, whether we like it or not, must be based
on India, Indonesia and Japan. Caught between the pincers of an aggressive Indonesia lost to Free World and an expansionist Communist China,
the rest of Southeast Asia would, I am afraid, ultimately be doomed.'[34]
A few days later Jones was writing to Forrestal about the need for caution
'against getting too far out on that particular limb, lest it be suddenly
sawed off. Between you and me, our support for Malaysia may well have
been another example of our following the British lead without examin-
ing sufficiently into the contents of the package. Whitehall's record for
satisfactory architecture of this kind has not been outstanding.'[35]

From Washington's perspective anything which might turn Indonesia
onto a path of unpredictable bellicosity was to be avoided, particularly
as its efforts to bring stability to the north of the region were beginning
to unravel with worrying rapidity. By early 1963, some members of the
Kennedy Administration had begun to appreciate that the enhanced efforts set in train in late 1961 to halt the rising tide of insurgency in South
Vietnam were inadequate. The provision of more US advisers and new
military equipment, combined with the initiation of the strategic hamlets
programme in 1962, had given some American analysts cause for optimism. However, the revealing engagement at Ap Bac in early January
1963, where well-armed and supported South Vietnamese troops had
been repulsed with heavy loss by a Viet Cong battalion in a set-piece battle, was an ominous indication of the deficiencies of Saigon's forces and of
Communist resilience.[36] Already some were anticipating the time when
the Americans would have to face up to the crucial choice of whether to
cut their losses or assume a more direct involvement with a consequent
escalation of the conflict. By May 1963, with the onset of the Buddhist
crisis in South Vietnam, the Diem regime was displaying in ever more
conspicuous fashion its repressive and unrepresentative character. As it
became more and more evident that the existing government in Saigon

---

[34] Jakarta to DOS, no. 1196, 5 February 1963, POL 3 MALAYSIA, RG 59.
[35] Jones to Forrestal, 8 February 1963, Forrestal file, box 461, Harriman papers; even
stronger objections to British plans for Malaysia were to follow, see Jakarta to DOS
no. 1242, 12 February 1963, NSF, countries, Indonesia, 1/63–2/63, JFKL.
[36] A subject covered in great detail by Neil Sheehan, *A Bright Shining Lie: John Paul Vann
and America in Vietnam* (London, 1988), 201 and *passim*.

was not prepared to undertake the necessary reforms to boost the par-
lous level of its domestic popularity, some officials in Washington began to consider the possibility of supplanting the Diem regime entirely.
Foremost among these was Roger Hilsman, who in early April 1963 was
moved from his job as head of the Bureau of Intelligence and Research at
the State Department to take Harriman's place as Assistant Secretary for
Far Eastern Affairs. Harriman himself, who had been promoted to the
position of Under Secretary for Political Affairs, came to share Hilsman's
conviction that Diem's inertia was a major impediment to the successful
prosecution of the war against the Viet Cong. Likewise, Harriman and
Hilsman agreed on the need to persuade and encourage Indonesia on
a stable path of economic development; keeping Indonesia 'quiet' and
denying the PKI any chance of enhancing their domestic position was a
vital adjunct to the State Department's Vietnam policies.[37]

When quadripartite talks were finally held in Washington from 10–12
February, the British found their State Department counterparts in a
sceptical mood when their strictures on Indonesia were delivered. Even
before the talks were convened, over dinner Harriman and his assistants were telling Warner of their 'gravest doubts about the future of
Malaysia', and their uncertainty over British resolve to assume the burden of Malaysia's defence after its formation: 'They fear that in the end
they may be asked to take over a guerrilla war in Borneo which could become little less formidable than that in South Vietnam. They also think
that Western relations with Indonesia . . . will be ruined and their own
position in the Philippines affected.'[38] The British had approached the
talks with the aim of extracting agreement on a joint warning to the Indonesians while getting the Americans to terminate their offers of future
economic aid as an inducement for Sukarno to behave.[39]

In the event, little impression was made by the British on their American
hosts. Harriman was adamant in maintaining that the defence of Malaysia
against subversion was the exclusive responsibility of Britain, with any
help that the Commonwealth might be ready to contribute. Ideas for a
non-aggression pact among the involved parties, coupled with territorial guarantees and a warning to Indonesia, were quickly rejected, the
Americans feeling that this would offer the impression of an 'imperialist'
line-up. The Australians complained that the susceptibilities of Indonesia
and the Philippines had not been taken sufficiently into account in the
plans for Malaysia, and together with the Americans and New Zealanders

[37] See e.g. Hilsman, *To Move a Nation*, 361 and *passim*, 471.
[38] Washington to FO, no. 448, 9 February 1963, D1071/18, FO 371/169694.
[39] See FO to Washington, no. 1258, 30 January 1963, PREM 11/4182.

stressed the long-term need to preserve good relations with Jakarta. Indeed, there were calls for restraint on the Tunku's part in the war of words with Sukarno, and concerns 'about the lack of evidence, for easy consumption by public opinion in the countries concerned and by the UN Delegations, of the extent to which the population of the Borneo territories had been and would be consulted about their future'.[40] This last comment was a sign that the Brunei revolt had done serious damage to British claims that popular opinion in the Borneo territories approved of Malaysia, and that proper mechanisms of consultation had been used.

Ormsby Gore's verdict on the talks was that

> our allies are fearful of impending trouble. The Australians and New Zealanders see themselves as gradually being drawn into any fighting necessary to keep the Indonesians out. They would be less anxious about this if they were sure that the Americans would be involved also, but the United States Government is determined to try and get the Commonwealth countries to shoulder this burden alone while they themselves concentrate on Viet Nam.[41]

Furthermore, the private soundings of American opinion taken by Warner confirmed the widespread view that the British were trying to 'dodge out of our commitments to Malaysia'. Over drinks, Paul Nitze, the Assistant Secretary of Defense for International Security Affairs, told Warner that 'the Pentagon . . . did not believe that the British would back Malaysia for long in face of Indonesian pressure'. The newly installed head of the CIA's Far Eastern Division, William Colby, was also 'most surprised to hear of our intention to continue to fight against the Indonesians after the formation of Malaysia'. Warner went on to warn that, 'we are taking on quite a responsibility here which may grow heavier and heavier as the months go by, and we must be quite clear that if we try to put it down again in one year or two years' time the Americans will feel that we have behaved very badly'.[42] By early March, Sir Edward Peck, the superintending Under Secretary of the South East Asia Department, was noting that,

> There are too many signs of cold feet over Malaysia, both in the US Administration and among Australians, for us to be complacent about US support in the event of big trouble with Indonesia. However, we must not waver in our determination to press on with Malaysia, particularly as the omens for the *internal*

---

[40] Washington to FO, no. 481, 12 February 1963, D1071/23, FO 371/169695; Washington to FO, no. 482, 13 February 1963, PREM 11/4182; Ormsby Gore to Home, no. 35, 15 February 1963, DH1071/18, FO 371/169908.
[41] Washington to FO, no. 482, 13 February 1963, PREM 11/4182.
[42] Warner to Peck, 11 February 1963, D1071/25G, FO 371/169695.

(inter territorial) arrangements are favourable. Our major objective is to terminate Colonial status by Aug. 31: after that the Malaysian/Indonesian dispute goes to a different forum and the Afro-Asian line-up will be different. We must not let our Allies' vacillations or pusillanimity deter us from this.[43]

Revealed here was the belief that the end of formal colonial control would defuse the criticism that could be levelled against a continued British presence in Malaysia. However, this analysis overlooked the extent to which ideas of indirect, British neo-colonial influence on the new federation were now the driving force behind much of the local opposition to the Malaysia scheme.

The British could, nevertheless, draw some comfort from the public declarations of support for the idea of Malaysia that emanated from the Kennedy Administration in mid-February. The most significant of these were the comments of the President himself at a press conference on 14 February, when he remarked to a questioner: 'We have supported the Malaysia Confederation, and it's under pressure from several areas. But I'm hopeful it will sustain itself, because it's the best hope of security for that very vital part of the world.'[44] Although Kennedy's remarks on Malaysia were widely perceived as backing for British policy, they did not meet with wholehearted approval from many Americans concerned with South East Asian affairs. In early March, Chester Cooper, then an Assistant Deputy Director of the CIA, and soon to be a senior NSC staff member, wrote to Harriman from the Far East that,

There is a great concern on the part of US officials out here that the President's recent statement re Malaysia indicates the issue is now closed, that as a consequence we have lost our flexibility and that it is now all over but [for] the shooting (and they do expect some shooting). I tried to point out that the President had no other choice but to give public support to the UK, but that I was sure we were still looking at Malaysia very carefully and were ready to examine all practical alternatives – *But* time was running out.[45]

A few days after the President's press conference, Forrestal delivered a memorandum to Kennedy on current US policy towards Malaysia with the comment that it represented a 'slight retreat' from the public declarations of support for British policy issued earlier. 'The US may find itself caught again between the incompatible policies of its friends', Forrestal advised. 'While we obviously cannot withdraw completely from the situation, we probably should take a small step out of it and try to use our influence to lever both sides into policies which run parallel rather

[43] Peck minute, 8 March 1963, D103145/3G, FO 371/169686.
[44] News conference of 14 February 1963, *The Public Papers of the Presidents, John F. Kennedy, 1963* (Washington, 1964), 180.
[45] Cooper to Harriman, 8 March 1963, box 451, Harriman papers.

than diverge.'[46] The memorandum itself had been drafted by Harriman and reflected the American stance adopted at the quadripartite talks. Though prepared to keep privately telling the Indonesians and Filipinos that Malaysia was considered the best solution to the problems of the area, the United States would take no responsibility for the new federation, and had warned the British that they had a 'serious problem' in assuring the UN and the world that the populations concerned had been adequately consulted.[47]

The need to satisfy international opinion that Malaysia was based on a wide degree of popular support was indeed beginning to enter the calculations of British policy-makers. Macapagal's assertion that a plebiscite in North Borneo was needed to satisfy the Philippine claim helped to prompt such thinking, and a further push was given in early February by the fact-finding tour to the territories involved in confrontation by the UN's Under Secretary for Special Political Affairs, C. V. Narasimhan. Ostensibly visiting Jakarta to discuss the final arrangements for the hand-over of West Irian by UN administrators to Indonesian sovereignty, Narasimhan took the opportunity to float ideas that could form the basis for a resolution of the differences between the parties to the dispute. Coming from a background in the Indian Civil Service, Narasimhan had been made the Secretary General's *chef du cabinet* in 1958. Following Hammerskjold's death in September 1961, Narasimhan had been touted as a possible successor, and the Foreign Office thought him still to be highly ambitious, though his views were sometimes regarded with suspicion due to the

subtlety and deviousness of manner with which they are presented. Nevertheless, he is prepared to play a hard and vigorous game for proposals which he has been persuaded to support. Although well-concealed, he has a certain distaste for Malays, whether of Malayan or Indonesian nationality. He is inclined to think they are unprincipled without having the compensating features of calmness and efficiency.[48]

From the first, Narasimhan was seen by the British as sympathetic to the idea of Malaysia. Selkirk and Sir Leslie Fry, the British Ambassador to Indonesia, met him as he passed through Singapore on 5 February, the latter describing him as 'the best type of British-trained Indian Civil Servant. I do not doubt for a moment that, from our point of view,

---

[46] Memorandum from Forrestal to Kennedy, 18 February 1963, NSF, countries, Borneo, General 2/63, JFKL.
[47] See memorandum from Rusk to Kennedy, 17 February 1963, *FRUS, 1961–1963, XXIII*, 710–11.
[48] Brief B, 22 February 1963, D1051/11, FO 371/169687.

Narasimhan's heart is in the right place.' After giving Fry the impression of 'being very pro-Tunku and pro-Malaysia generally', the UN official went on the assure Fry that 'anything which U Thant might decide to do about improving relations between Malaya and Indonesia should not be allowed to interfere with the time-table for Malaysia'. Narasimhan, Selkirk and Fry discussed the idea of an offer of a West Irian-style plebiscite in North Borneo, to be held after the creation of Malaysia (Fry admitting that, as with the Indonesian commitment to hold such an exercise in 1969, it might never actually be fulfilled). In turn, Selkirk recommended such a scheme to London as a way to reduce Philippine opposition to Malaysia.[49] The High Commission in Kuala Lumpur was quick to tell Sandys that the Malayans would oppose any such concession as it was likely to result in demands for similar exercises to be held in Brunei and Sarawak, where opinion on Malaysia was much more divided than in North Borneo.[50] Strong objections also soon followed from the Colonial Office, where officials in the Borneo territories worried about the impact such a concession might make on local confidence (and the constitutional validity of a plebiscite, which would create, in effect, the right to secede from the federation), as well as the unfortunate comparisons that might be drawn with Indonesian manipulation of any plebiscite held in West Irian.[51]

In the face of such concerted views, Foreign Office discussion was curtailed, the British choosing to rest their claims that self-determination had been granted to the peoples of the Borneo territories on the Cobbold Commission's work, the Lansdowne Intergovernmental Committee's consultations and the elections to, and votes of, the Legislative Assemblies in Sarawak and North Borneo. When Narasimhan stopped over in London on his return from South East Asia, he was presented with the reasons why the British could not contemplate any notion of a plebiscite prior to the formation of Malaysia. The British were once again reminded by Narasimhan of the nature of Indonesian fears, and that he had found them 'very distrustful not so much of the concept of Malaysia, as of Malayan intentions, either of annexing Sumatra or of allowing a Chinese Communist danger to develop in the Borneo Territories'.[52] By

[49] See Singapore to FO, no. 72, 8 February 1963, D1071/16, FO 371/169694; Fry to Peck, 9 February 1963, D1071/30, FO 371/169695; Singapore to FO, no. 81, 15 February 1963, CO 1030/1498.

[50] Kuala Lumpur to CRO, no. 284, 18 February 1963, *ibid.*

[51] Though Goode, in North Borneo, was at first supportive of the idea; see Sandys to Goode, Waddell and White, nos. 161, 122, 77, 19 February 1963; Goode to Sandys, no. 100, 20 February 1963; Waddell to Sandys, no. C82, 20 February 1963; White to Sandys, no. 29, 20 February 1963; Goode to Sandys, no. 102, 21 February 1963, CO 1030/1498.

[52] Peck record of talks of 25 February 1963, D1051/15, FO 371/169687.

mid-March, the plebiscite issue was moribund, one senior Foreign Office official arguing, 'Consultation of the popular will has gone through about as many forms as these unsophisticated people can stand: I doubt for instance if the British electorate could really have stood being asked five times in eight months whether they wished to join the Common Market without having doubts cast on the Government's determination!'[53]

Other efforts to promote regional dialogue were in any event already under way, as a result of Filipino suggestions (first made by Vice President Pelaez on his return from the talks with British officials in London) for a heads of state summit between the Asian parties to the dispute, with Thailand acting as a neutral convener. On 17 February, the Tunku told an interviewer that he would welcome such a gathering as a way to learn of the reasons for Indonesian hostility to Malaysia, though any conference could not be allowed to delay the formation of the federation.[54] There was immediate concern on the part of British officials in London at what might result from such a meeting, and whether it constituted any wavering on the part of the Malayan Prime Minister over the timetable for Malaysia. The Tunku was quick to reassure Tory that he had no intention of attending a conference before the creation of Malaysia, and that he had expressed his interest in a summit involving the Philippines and Indonesia, 'with [the] deliberate intention of "playing them along"'.[55] But despite this disclaimer, the Tunku was probably beginning to appreciate the gravity of the problems that concerted opposition to Malaysia presented, and could sense some of the doubt and uncertainty that was entering British minds over their commitment to defend the new federation.

It was in Manila that the first significant breakthrough in the diplomatic process arose. Early March saw a regional economic conference in the Philippine capital, which attracted the attendance of both Razak and Subandrio, and though they did not meet directly, Macapagal had separate talks with both, and on 11 March came forward with a proposal for ministerial-level talks to seek a solution to the problems raised by Malaysia, to be followed by a full summit meeting. Public responses were cautious, with Subandrio indicating his willingness to attend initial talks but only after relations between Malaya and Indonesia had been 'clarified' and Malaya had proved that Malaysia would not be used to subvert Indonesia. Razak asserted that before the process could begin

---

[53] See Peck to Dean, 18 February 1963, D1071/35; Peck to J. A. Pilcher (Manila), 13 March 1963, D1071/65G, FO 371/169695.
[54] See Mackie, *Konfrontasi*, 128-9; Kuala Lumpur to CRO, no. 292, 18 February 1963, DO 169/274.
[55] See CRO to Kuala Lumpur, no. 456, 19 February 1963; Kuala Lumpur to CRO, no. 313, 21 February 1963, *ibid.*

'the ground must be cleared first', with Indonesia's active policy of confrontation the major stumbling block. While the Tunku also welcomed
Macapagal's initiative, and said he would accept Subandrio's conditions,
he privately told British officials that he would stall any progress at least
until early April, when he was due in Manila to attend an Association of
South East Asian States meeting. Soon after, the Malayan Prime Minister
was publicly explaining that any talks would merely deal with the reasons
for Malaysia's formation rather than involve any consideration of how,
whether and when it should be formed, souring the atmosphere once
more.

The problem from the British point of view was their fear that a negotiated solution would involve them in some form of concession which could
fatally undermine the overall scheme for Malaysia that had been delicately
fashioned over the previous two years. Any departure from the already
agreed and finalized plans, or admission that the methods employed in
determining the popular will in the territories affected, was to be avoided.
Likewise, the time-tabling was crucial to the constitutional preparations
that were being made in the Borneo territories; any indication that there
were doubts in British or Malayan minds about the project as a result
of Indonesian disapproval could have a serious impact in the territories
themselves, and fuel opposition to Malaysia. Local council elections were
ongoing in North Borneo (from which the Electoral College to decide
on the composition of the Legislative Council would be drawn), but of
greater importance were the elections due for May–June 1963 in Sarawak,
where SUPP, with its doubts and hesitations over Malaysia, stood as a
significant challenge. Moreover, North Borneo and Sarawak were still
crown colonies, and the very idea that their future disposition might be
discussed (let alone decided) by a meeting between Malaya, Indonesia
and the Philippines was hardly a prospect likely to endear itself to British
officials and ministers, and set a potentially dangerous precedent for other
territories still within the empire.

In any event, the Malayans and Indonesians were proceeding very
cautiously, and talks between officials to prepare the way for a foreign
ministers meeting only got under way on 9 April, and made very slow
progress on establishing an agenda. The very broad and vague list of
shared concerns that resulted was accompanied by tentative agreement
for a meeting to go forward in Manila before the middle of May.[56] Some
impetus to a flagging process was given by Narasimhan's second tour
of the region which began towards the end of April, as the UN sought
to reduce tensions. Having visited the Borneo territories, Narasimhan

[56] See Mackie, *Konfrontasi*, 131.

went on to Manila where he discussed with Macapagal the idea of a post-Malaysia plebiscite in North Borneo as a possible agenda item for the proposed ministerial-level talks, and as a method of resolving the issue of the Philippine claim. Foreign Office disapproval of any such notion was heightened when it also emerged that Narasimhan's ideas involved delaying any outright transfer of sovereignty over the Borneo territories until a plebiscite could be arranged (with a UN or Malayan administration in the interim), while he had also been telling the Malayans that the British would not help Malaysia defend the territories. The Foreign Secretary noted his rejection of the plebiscite option with a sharp minute: 'We are too nice. These clever fellows always lead us into trouble. I shall be very firm.'[57] Having overseen the ceremony that transferred West Irian from UN administration to Indonesian sovereignty on 1 May 1963, Narasimhan returned to New York with a stop-off in London on 7 May where he was told by Home of the British position. Narasimhan accepted this with equanimity, and relayed his doubts over whether the Indonesians were sincere in their desire for a compromise settlement, and said he had been 'shocked by the instances of Dr Subandrio and President Sukarno mocking the Malayan national anthem by singing obscene lyrics to its tune'.[58]

Nevertheless, it was difficult for the British to bury the idea of a self-determination exercise. The Americans, for one, felt that this option could help to deflect regional accusations of neo-colonialism over Malaysia and 'effectively spike Indonesia's guns', and at the time of Narasimhan's visit, US embassy officials in London were urging the British to keep an open mind on the issue, and at least not to stake out any public position.[59] Another reason for British concern was the capacity of their Malayan allies for independent and unpredictable action. The chances of the talks process between the parties to the dispute gaining some impetus appear to have increased towards the end of April. According to the Tunku's account, Sukarno sent a secret emissary to meet him in Penang with the suggestion for a bilateral meeting in the third week in May to be held either in Phnom Penh or Tokyo. As a result, Ghazali had been despatched by the Tunku to pass on the news to Macapagal in Manila

---

[57] Warner minute, 3 May 1963; Home minute (n.d. but c. 4 May 1963), D1071/107; see also Manila to FO, no. 414, 1 May 1963, D1071/112, FO 371/169699.

[58] Record of conversation between Mr Narasimhan and the Foreign Secretary, 7 May 1963, D1193/18, FO 371/169734; see also material in DO 169/100. Macmillan is said to have agreed with the objections raised to any concession over a plebiscite, see Wright to de Zulueta, 13 May 1963, and de Zulueta to Wright, 18 May 1963, D1071/133, FO 371/169700.

[59] See Washington to FO, no. 1378, 8 May 1963, D1071/126; Oliver Foster to Cable, 11 May 1963, D1071/134G, *ibid.*

(so that no wedge might be driven between the Philippines and Malaya by Sukarno's offer).[60] By the end of May, after some squabbles over who should actually take the initiative, these tentative steps culminated with Sukarno's public invitation for the Tunku to join him for talks in Tokyo, which the latter made clear he was happy to attend.[61]

That the Indonesians meant to build up the pressure on the Malayans and British, at the same time as engaging in the diplomatic process, had been underscored on 12 April 1963 when about 60 TNKU uniformed irregulars launched a cross-border raid on the Tebedu police station in Sarawak's First Division, an event which seemed to mark a significant escalation in confrontation. Although the security forces reacted quickly to the incursion, with 40 Royal Marine Commando, 2/10th Gurkha Rifles, and a company of 42 Royal Marine Commando active in operations, the real fear of the authorities was that dormant elements of the CCO in Sarawak (with 1,400 members and upwards of 10,000 local Chinese sympathizers) were readying themselves for an insurrection along Brunei lines, and that the Indonesians were prepared actively to assist them.[62] Only sporadic raids followed the Tebedu incident, however, and British and Gurkha infantry units resumed their familiar routine of patrolling and reconnaissance of the long and exposed borders of Sarawak and North Borneo. In this sense then, the Tebedu raid can be seen as a way of illustrating Indonesian capabilities in the build-up to a negotiation that it was hoped would produce Malayan concessions.

The Tebedu raid also made it even more apparent to the Government in London that the Greater Malaysia scheme, rather than allowing a reduction in defence burdens in the Far East, was threatening to increase the commitment that would be necessary in the region. During the first half of 1963 efforts had again been made to address the increasing burdens placed on the economy by high levels of defence spending. In early February 1963, the Cabinet's Defence Committee had met at Chequers to consider the position. The Chancellor of the Exchequer, Reginald Maudling, presented the argument that defence had to be looked at in the wider economic and financial context. Forecast expenditures for 1963–4, up 10 per cent from the previous year, were described as 'an unprecedented rise in time of peace'. The UK was spending more on defence than any other European country, with the exception of France and Portugal, while the 'failure of the Brussels negotiations was a

---

[60] See Kuala Lumpur to CRO, no. 766, 2 May 1963, DO 169/274.
[61] See Mackie, *Konfrontasi*, 132, 148.
[62] See Ministry of Defence Sitrep no. 15 on the Borneo territories, 17 April 1963, and Waddell to Sandys, no. 141, 14 April 1963 (with Macmillan's comment: 'Remember Brunei'), PREM 11/4347. See also the concerns about the impact on British prestige in Sarawak (Governor's Deputy) to Sandys, no. C.182, 6 May 1963, DO 169/240.

serious set-back to our hopes of strengthening our international economic
position. Moreover, in many parts of the world we were now carrying, in
effect, the burden of defending the economic interests of our European
competitors.' Maudling felt that sustaining such levels of spending threatened the whole health and vitality of the economy and that savings must
be found. The Committee hoped that the Americans and Britain's
European allies would see that cut-backs in British contributions to
NATO were preferable to any reductions east of Suez.

In the Far East, British forces based at Singapore were seen as having
four key commitments: to provide for the external defence of a future
Malaysia, to deter Indonesian aggression, to meet SEATO obligations,
and to act as reinforcements for Hong Kong.

With the possible exception of Hong Kong, it did not appear that any of these
roles could be abandoned without a fundamental change in our policy. Moreover,
apart from their military value our forces in the Far East had political and prestige
significance. Their withdrawal would be regarded as a major political defeat and,
quite apart from its serious effect on Australia, New Zealand and the United
States, would encourage the spread of Communism.

Any reduction in British forces in the Far East '—could not be secured
except by a reduction in our political commitments. This in turn would
involve the abandonment of our support of Malaysia; and it would make
little sense to maintain our commitment to SEATO once we had abandoned Malaysia.' There was a call to 'consider realistically the economic
and political consequences of withdrawal. In the last resort the defence
of Australia and New Zealand might be the only commitment to which
it would be essential that we should contribute; and that by itself might
require a military posture wholly different from that which we now
maintained.'[63]

With the Prime Minister's express endorsement, another review was
undertaken of the implications of a major reduction or withdrawal of
forces from Hong Kong and Singapore, presaging some of the hard
choices that the Labour Government was later to confront. When the
Committee came together once again at the beginning of April, the
Defence Secretary had to admit to his colleagues that he could see no
possibility of achieving economies in European defence efforts, leading
Maudling to repeat his contention that savings must therefore be found in
the Middle and Far East. Immediately after this meeting, the Cabinet Secretary suggested to the Prime Minister that it was now time to look closely
at the liabilities that had been amassed in South East Asia over the previous few years. The Indonesian threat to Malaysia seemed to rule out any
reduction of British forces, while the quadripartite talks in Washington

[63] D(63)3rd mtg, 9 February 1963, CAB 131/28.

had revealed worrying differences with the Americans and Australians; as Burke Trend put it, '. . . I have an uneasy feeling that events in [South East Asia] may soon crystallize quite rapidly into a position in which we shall find ourselves committed – perhaps against our better political judgment and certainly to our financial disadvantage – to carrying, single-handed, a greater burden than we have clearly contemplated hitherto.'[64]

The Prime Minister in turn despatched a minute (drafted by Trend) to the Foreign Secretary, which summarized concerns over the future defence of Malaysia. Here, it was argued that the hesitation of the United States, Australia and New Zealand about offering help was because

they are not sure that it really makes sense to think simply in terms of defending Malaysia; and they suspect that we are not giving sufficient consideration to the logically prior problem of keeping Indonesia and the Philippines neutral. If they are right, we are indeed taking on a formidable liability, as becomes clear if you look at the map and see how Malaysia will be more or less encircled by Indonesia on the west and south, by the Philippines to the east and by the dubiously neutral structure in Indo-China to the north. I doubt whether this is a situation which, if it really got out of control, we could deal with single handed; nor do I see why we should be expected to do so.

As well as calling for another memorandum on the problem, Macmillan felt that more pressure would have to be placed on Australia and New Zealand for active contributions.[65] Home responded on 16 April with a paper that had been produced through joint consultation between the Foreign Office, Ministry of Defence and CRO. This asserted that Indonesian behaviour since 1961 amounted to the opening of a second front in South East Asia to add to the challenge posed by North Vietnam and Communist China. The Indonesians were pictured as harbouring expansionist aims in Borneo, and were said to envy and dislike prosperous Malaya: 'Sukarno has had much difficulty in holding together his island empire; he feels that Malaya is a rival attraction for Sumatrans, and that its economic and political stability shows up his own failures.' The military threat from the Philippines was discounted, and the COS considered that there were sufficient forces in the Far East to meet Indonesian-sponsored infiltration of the Borneo territories. An overt attack, however, would require UK reinforcements, including the provision of V-bombers to suppress the Indonesian air force.[66] This was a confident assessment, but it held out little prospect of either an early end to the conflict or any lessening of existing burdens.

Bearing these conclusions in mind, Trend was anxious to stress to the Prime Minister that 'so long as we are committed to defend Malaysia

[64] Trend minute for Macmillan, 2 April 1963, PREM 11/4189.
[65] Macmillan minute for Home, M.131/63, 3 April 1963, D1193/13G, FO 371/169734.
[66] 'The Future Defence of Malaysia,' 16 April 1963, *ibid.*

against attack, we shall be unable – even if attack is limited to infiltration – to make any significant reduction in our forces in South East Asia'. There was also no hope of making cuts in British forces in West Germany, and 'Little by little, the defence "economies", which the Chequers meeting undertook to secure, are being shown to be impossible as a result of our overseas obligations.' It would be necessary to consider if the commitment to Malaysia had to be considered 'indefinite' and if the burden could be more evenly shared with Australia and New Zealand.[67] The Oversea Policy Committee considered the Foreign Secretary's paper on 24 April, and concluded that while forces would have to be committed in the short term (and indeed might have to be increased after the formation of Malaysia), there should be no express long-term commitments regarding force levels. Moreover, approaches would have to be made to Australia and New Zealand for more assistance.[68] In fact, there were few signs in the summer of 1963 that either Canberra or Wellington was prepared to provide much help; indeed, though Menzies did force through his Cabinet an increase in defence spending during May, the Australians were still hesitant about associating themselves with the new Anglo-Malaysian Defence Agreement.[69] British concerns also focussed on the Department of External Affairs, which was considered far too ready to adopt an Indonesian perspective over Malaysia and was alert for signs that the British were looking for a way to withdraw altogether from South East Asia. As one brief put it,

There is still a feeling in some Australian circles that we have dreamed up Malaysia as a rather transparent, intrinsically flimsy and probably impermanent device to solve our colonial problems in Singapore and the Borneo territories. They suspect that in the long term we will withdraw from South East Asia and leave them, with New Zealand, to hold the baby.[70]

Meanwhile, Whitehall had been conducting a fairly lacklustre review of the consequences of a withdrawal from both the Middle and Far East, and had been attempting to come to some agreement on the cost of the commitments involved.[71] Its negative conclusions fed into a paper from the Cabinet Secretary that was deliberated by the Defence Committee in mid-June, and which affirmed the necessity of retaining a 'politico-military

---

[67] Trend minute for Macmillan, 23 April 1963, PREM 11/4347.
[68] OP(63)4th mtg, 24 April 1963, CAB 134/2371.
[69] See Edwards, *Crises and Commitments*, 262-4.
[70] See brief for visit of Australian Minister of External Affairs, n.d. (but c. 27 March 1963), DO 169/102.
[71] The papers of the Official Oversea Coordinating Committee, GEN 796, which conducted the review, can be found at CAB 130/190; see GEN 796/2, 7 May 1963, which contains the Treasury estimate of £375 million a year spent on forces in the Far East.

position based on Singapore', despite the lack of overriding commercial interests in the area and the likelihood that the cost of deployments in the Far East would rise to £400 million by 1970.[72] The Prime Minister still wondered if there was 'room for argument': 'It might... be that in the Far East, apart from the possibility of an increased contribution from Australia and New Zealand, the security of Malaysia would be more effectively safeguarded in the long term by the negotiation of a political understanding with Indonesia than by the maintenance of British forces in Singapore.' Nevertheless, the Committee as a whole could see no opportunity for an early or major withdrawal from Singapore. In summing up, the Defence Secretary highlighted the Government's dilemma in that though the economic arguments in favour of reductions were powerful, so too were the 'political difficulties and dangers', therefore no major decisions of policy could yet be taken.[73] In the short term, there seemed little option but to continue with the existing list of commitments and responsibilities, irrespective of the liabilities that confrontation and the unpredictable situation in Indochina might produce.

The Prime Minister's interventions in the debates over defence spending in the spring and summer of 1963 illustrated his awareness of this fundamental difficulty, and the desirability of finding a way out from an indefinite commitment to the defence of Malaysia. From one perspective, this would seem to indicate that attempts to negotiate with the Indonesians should be encouraged rather than avoided. But readiness to see talks go ahead contained the double problem of defining what ground they should cover and what concessions could possibly appease Malaysia's hostile neighbours, and the uncomfortable fact that British interests during any negotiation involving the Asian parties could well be prejudiced by the unpredictable nature of the Tunku, and the increasing tendency of the Malayans to take an independent line from their former colonial rulers. Abandoning the Malaysia project at this stage was clearly impossible, while Britain still had formal responsibilities as the sovereign power in Sarawak and North Borneo, at least until 31 August 1963. Towards the end of May 1963, Britain's senior political and military representatives in South East Asia came together for their annual conference at Eden Hall in Singapore. Selkirk reported to Macmillan that it was clear to all present that

---

[72] See D(63)19, 14 June 1963, CAB 131/28. This paper highlighted the fact that overall defence spending for 1965–6, which had been set at £1,850 million by the Defence Committee in April 1962, was set to exceed that figure by about £170 million.
[73] D(63)8th mtg, 19 June 1963, *ibid.*

the next three to six months will be fundamental, not only to our future position in South East Asia and all that involves in our relations with the United States, Australia and New Zealand, but to the whole evolution of this part of the world. From a purely material angle we have greater investment in Malaysia than we have in India. Moreover towards the Borneo people in particular we have by any standards a high moral obligation. They have put complete confidence in us, they do not really want us to go and they have, albeit a bit reluctantly, accepted our advice that their true interest lies in joining Malaysia. The Malayans themselves have discovered the complete inadequacy of their own defence without British support. To let them down now would be to change their whole relationship with the United Kingdom and quite probably allow in forms of government which are wholly alien to the present leaders in Malaya.[74]

A British withdrawal it was reckoned, therefore, would merely generate further instability, with the chief beneficiaries being anti-Western forces in Malaysia, and an expansionist Indonesia.

The first few months of 1963 had seen the left-wing opposition to Lee Kuan Yew effectively dealt with in Singapore, while most of the leaders of political opinion in the Borneo territories had become reconciled to the formation of Malaysia through the work of the Lansdowne Intergovernmental Committee. In addition, following the upheaval and confusion surrounding the Brunei revolt, the Sultan now appeared to be negotiating seriously on entry to the federation. The internal omens for Malaysia had never seemed better. It seems doubly ironic, therefore, that just as the inner dimensions of British plans were coming to fruition, the external environment should now seem especially perilous and filled with uncertainty. British ministers and officials were compelled to contemplate their limited options, but so many of the variable factors were out of their hands. Most importantly, the leaders of Malaya, Indonesia and the Philippines were themselves taking the initiative in resolving their differences; the most obvious manifestation of this was the meeting scheduled between the Tunku and Sukarno in Tokyo. During the summer months of 1963, the British found themselves nervous onlookers as the three Asian states tried to remove the sources of tension between them, and establish a new basis for cooperation through the idea of a Malay Confederation, or Maphilindo, a process that culminated in the high point of the frenetic diplomatic activity preceding the creation of Malaysia: the Manila summit of August 1963.

[74] Selkirk to Macmillan, 14 June 1963, PREM 11/4188.

6   The path to the Manila summit,
      May–July 1963

The idea of a negotiated resolution to the tensions produced by the formation of Malaysia was certainly welcome to the architects of the Kennedy Administration's accommodating approach to Indonesia. There would be little likelihood of assembling international backing for a package of financial assistance for the Indonesian economy when the leadership in Jakarta was promoting insurgency against its Western-orientated Malayan neighbour and indulging in virulent anti-imperialist rhetoric. Moreover, the Indonesian Government was responding only slowly to the IMF's conditions that a stabilization plan, involving a real effort to reduce expenditures and balance the budget, should be put in place before large-scale Western financial help to ease chronic shortages of foreign exchange could be authorized. Compounding this difficulty was the fact that strong criticisms within the United States were now being directed at the Administration's handling of relations with Indonesia, and in particular, its readiness to extend further aid to Sukarno's regime.

Much to the consternation of US officials, in March 1963 the Clay Committee had delivered its comprehensive and critical report on the foreign aid programme. This investigation had been instigated by President Kennedy after the congressional mauling inflicted on the 1962 aid bill, and widespread dissatisfaction with the work of the Agency for International Development. The expectation had been that a specially selected panel, including several business-minded and conservative members, under the respected guidance of General Lucius Clay, would look over existing programmes with a faintly critical eye, and then reach the considered verdict that they were necessary to national security. This in turn would help to assuage the Administration's congressional critics, and ease the passage of the 1963 aid bill. Instead, Clay's report contained sharp comment on the need to set stronger standards and conditions for aid and attacked the programme's inefficient and over-bureaucratic aspects, while even recommending that the Administration's request for an appropriation of $4.9 billion in the 1963 bill could be cut by $500 million.[1]

During the spring and early summer the congressional opponents of what they alleged was a profligate aid policy seized on the Clay report and decimated the aid bill. The state which received the heaviest degree of criticism from Clay was Indonesia, the report finding: '... we do not see how external assistance can be granted to this nation by free world countries unless it puts its internal house in order, provides fair treatment to foreign creditors and enterprises and refrains from international adventures'.[2] When aid to Indonesia under the 1963 bill came up for hearings before the House Committee on Foreign Affairs there occurred what one study has described as 'tantamount to a revolt', with Administration officials (including Hilsman) being subjected to sceptical cross-examination throughout April and May 1963.[3] The leader of the revolt was the senior Republican member of the Committee, Representative William S. Broomfield of Michigan. In one address to the House on 13 May, Broomfield talked about the West Irian transfer as amounting to an 'Asian "anschluss" ', pointed out that Indonesia had been a massive recipient of Soviet arms over the previous two years and labelled the Clay report's comments a 'masterpiece of understatement'.[4] Broomfield's calls for the suspension of all further economic and military support for Indonesia were echoed by other members of Congress, who pointed to the recent visit to Jakarta of Liu Shaoqi, the Chairman of the PRC, as showing where Sukarno's true allegiance lay.[5]

As pressures in Congress on the Administration's aid programme to Indonesia steadily mounted, Jakarta contributed to the pessimistic mood among Administration officials by bringing to a head the long-simmering issue of the operation of foreign oil companies in Indonesia. The three principal oil companies working there, Shell, Stanvac (Standard Oil of New Jersey and Socony Mobil) and Caltex (Standard Oil of California and Texaco), produced 90 per cent of the country's petroleum, and their exports brought in $250 million of foreign exchange a year for the government in Jakarta under a formula providing for a 50/50 split in foreign receipts. Since early 1961 all three companies had been engaged in protracted negotiations for new contracts, with the Indonesians aiming to secure a new 60/40 split, and the eventual transfer of all domestic

---

[1] See Schlesinger, *Thousand Days*, 518–22.
[2] See Washington to FO, no. 125, 25 March 1963, DH103145/1, FO 371/169888.
[3] See Bunnell, 'Kennedy Initiatives,' 317–21.
[4] *Congressional Record, 1963, vol. 109, part 6* (Washington, 1963), 8362–3.
[5] See *ibid.*, 8097.

marketing, refining and processing facilities to state ownership. The companies had stalled, concerned about the departure from the 50/50 principle (which also applied in the Middle East), and the way costings would be calculated under the new ratios. Additional problems had arisen over the amount of compensation payable for the transfer of facilities and their maintenance once in Indonesian hands; by the spring of 1963 the American companies were said to be 'hardly on speaking terms' with the Indonesian negotiators. On 26 April 1963, the Indonesians decided to force the issue by introducing Regulation 18, which would allow the authorities in Jakarta to draw up unilateral conditions for the operation of the companies if a successful conclusion to negotiations was not reached by 15 June. The companies reacted to this dramatic turn by telling the US Government that they would consider such action effective expropriation and would refuse to continue their operations under such circumstances. Stanvac and Caltex proceeded to make preparations to withdraw key personnel and dependants from Indonesia. Company executives also approached Harriman and Hilsman, asking that the State Department intervene to protect their interests.[6]

Harriman and other Administration officials, acutely aware of congressional displeasure, saw the potential for Indonesian actions leaving the United States with little choice but to suspend any further consideration of aid to Jakarta, while the Indonesians turned to the Communist bloc for technical assistance.[7] One particular worry was that the PRC was interested in supplies of Indonesian oil as a way to cut their dependence on Soviet sources. An intelligence report passed to the British in March 1963 by a US Embassy official in Jakarta maintained that on a recent visit a group of Chinese doctors had carried with them an inch-thick blueprint of a scheme whereby the oilfields would be taken over and operated by Chinese and other oil experts, and the whole production sold to the PRC for hard currency.[8] Despite the British belief that such stories were being circulated in order to pressure the oil companies into concessions, they undoubtedly fed into American fears over 'losing' Indonesia, along with the $340 million of investments held by Stanvac and Caltex. Furthermore, it was believed that if the Indonesians went ahead with expropriation, the resulting loss of foreign exchange (amounting to

[6] See Brubeck memorandum for Bundy on 'Status of American Oil Companies' Negotiations in Indonesia', 21 May 1963, NSF, countries, Indonesia, 5/63, JFKL; Forrestal memorandum for Kennedy, 10 June 1963, Indonesia, 6/63–8/63, *ibid.*
[7] The Hickenlooper Amendment, passed in early 1963, compelled the US Government to suspend aid to any state which expropriated American private property without compensation.
[8] Jakarta to FO, no. 192, 12 March 1963, DH1532/1G, FO 371/169944; see the concerns raised by Hilsman, *To Move a Nation*, 389.

30 per cent of annual receipts) would plunge the economy into yet more turmoil and scupper the chance of economic reform; only the PKI, it was believed, could benefit from such an outcome.

On 17 May 1963, Harriman and George Ball decided on a plan of action that involved sending a special presidential envoy to Sukarno who would provide 'good offices' and facilitate final negotiations between the oil companies and the Indonesian Government. Wilson Wyatt, the smooth-talking Lieutenant Governor of Kentucky, was selected for this delicate mission. To give expert advice, Harriman turned to Walter Levy, an independent oil consultant who had worked with Harriman during the oil negotiations with the Iranian government in 1951. Harriman spoke to Levy by telephone to ask for his help on Wyatt's team, explaining, 'Things are going to hell here on the account of the Indonesians', adding that, 'due to the stupidity of the Indonesian Government and the rigidity perhaps of the oil companies, ... they have about four weeks to negotiate or else the whole thing collapses and Indonesia falls into the hands of the Chinese and the Russians'.[9] While Wyatt was being prepared for his mission, a cable was despatched to Jones telling him to make strong representations to Sukarno about the serious impact that a failure to conclude new contracts with the US companies would have on relations with the United States. 'We believe that with [the] publication [of] Regulation 18 US–Indonesian relations have reached [their] most serious turn since Indonesian independence', the Ambassador was informed, 'We are dangerously close to the end of the road.'

Showing a copy of the telegram to the President, Forrestal's covering note emphasized the concern felt about 'the effect of complete breakdown [of the oil negotiations] on Congress. There is already sentiment for barring all aid to Indonesia and news of this might pull down the house of cards.' In a reflection of the prevailing doubts over the Ambassador's ability to deliver clear and tough messages to Sukarno, Forrestal also advised that, 'The cable is somewhat over-written because experience has shown that it is difficult to convince Howard Jones that he must start using his goodwill in Indonesia to save this situation.'[10] Harriman also wrote to Jones on 25 May in an attempt, as he put it, 'to convey to you the atmosphere that exists in Washington ... These oil negotiations are a crossroads in our relations with Indonesia, either to achieve a sound basis for moving forward, or a disastrous breakdown. I feel that this is not a question of whether a contract is achieved ... but how. An agreement must

---

[9] Harriman–Levy telephone conversation, 17 May 1963, box 581, Harriman papers.
[10] State Department to Jakarta, no. 1037, 18 May 1963; Forrestal memorandum for Kennedy, n.d. (but 18 May 1963), NSF, countries, Indonesia, 5/63, JFKL.

be reached.'[11] In the event, the Ambassador had only a limited opportunity to pass American concerns to Sukarno before the latter's departing for one of his frequent trips to Tokyo on 22 May, but the Indonesian President agreed to hold a special round of talks in the Japanese capital which would involve both Kennedy's personal emissary and the oil companies.

The British initially observed the discomforting effects of Regulation 18 on the Americans with some satisfaction, hoping that it would worsen US relations with Jakarta. 'As long as there is a chance of getting the Americans out in front', one official opined, 'I believe we should sit tight and keep our traps shut.'[12] Notwithstanding this desire to let the Indonesian and American negotiators scrap things out in Tokyo, the involvement of Shell gave the British a substantial commercial stake in the outcome and made it virtually impossible to stay aloof. In his characteristically pessimistic tone, Macmillan noted in his diary, 'The Indonesians are going to seize Shell – £50 million gone in a day. There is, it seems, no remedy, except war. The Americans don't mind. American Administration cannot face a "Suez" and American (local) oil companies will be quit [sic] pleased. What will happen when Venezuela goes Communist and seizes all the American plants and concessions?'[13] In Washington on 24 May, Ormsby Gore rang Harriman, hoping to coordinate a united approach with the Americans in the upcoming Tokyo negotiations. 'I don't think we can agree to consult', Harriman asserted to the Ambassador, 'it is going to be difficult enough negotiating...I don't think we can go into this as a joint enterprise...you can be sure...that they are not going to make any proposals which affect any of Shell's vital interests. But we cannot agree to consult...because it may be a very rapid transaction.'[14]

This response did not go down well in London, and though Roger Hilsman had earlier assured British officials in Washington that the Americans would not cut a separate deal without Shell, and that they would refuse to link the oil talks in any way with the Malaysia issue, the Foreign Secretary was far from convinced.[15] On 27 May, and following a request from Home, the Prime Minister sent a personal message to Sukarno in Tokyo, telling him of the grave concern felt about the state of the oil negotiations and asking that Shell be accorded fair treatment.[16] This

---

[11] Harriman to Jones, 25 May 1963, box 472, Harriman papers.
[12] Cable minute, 20 May 1963, DH1051/19, FO 371/169890.
[13] Diary entry, 20 May 1963, Macmillan MSS. dep. d.49.
[14] Harriman–Ormsby Gore telephone conversation, 24 May 1963, box 581, Harriman papers.
[15] See the assurance given in Washington to FO, no. 1543, 20 May 1963, PREM 11/4308.
[16] See Home minute for Macmillan, 'British Oil in Indonesia', PM/63/78, 27 May 1963, and Macmillan telegram for Sukarno, T.241/63, 27 May 1963, contained in FO to Tokyo, no. 415, 27 May 1963, PREM 11/4308.

intervention, coming just a day before the oil talks in Tokyo were due to open, was seen as a serious blunder by the Americans, with Wyatt particularly annoyed.[17] Some in Washington even felt the message had been deliberately contrived by British officials as a way to de-rail the negotiations and precipitate a complete break in US–Indonesian relations. Harriman called Ormsby Gore to complain in strong terms: 'Why it should have been sent the day before the start of the talks, I can't understand. I thought we had an agreement that we were to carry the ball. It changes the whole atmosphere of our emissary's approach . . . I can't imagine the value of it – the timing. It looks as if you had no confidence in us. It makes us extremely unhappy.' When the Ambassador tried to explain that the British were worried that Shell might be left out, and that the Indonesians 'might well think it a quite clever tactic to reach an agreement with you . . . ', Harriman cut him off quickly by saying, 'I thought there was an agreement you would stay in the background. If the task fails, I am afraid we will have to blame you for it.'[18]

Despite such signs of displeasure from the Americans, there were few regrets in London. The Prime Minister was advised by de Zulueta: '. . . whatever Mr Harriman may say it is difficult to feel that we are entirely safe to leave oil negotiations in the hands of representatives of American companies when such considerable British interests are involved'.[19] One difficulty was that the British seemed incapable of understanding that Wyatt was not in Tokyo to fight purely for the interests of Stanvac and Caltex, but was officially acting as Kennedy's personal representative with the aim of facilitating an agreement between the companies and the Indonesians. The notion of Wyatt standing at arm's length from the companies was one that Harriman was keen to promote, and the association with Shell did not help with this idea. Despite Harriman's assurances, the British were given fresh cause for concern when they were told from Tokyo that Wyatt did not mention Shell in his first round of talks with the Indonesians, and that the initial negotiations would proceed with Stanvac and Caltex alone.[20]

When the commercial counsellor of the British Embassy in Tokyo subsequently tried to arrange for Shell representatives to take part in the talks, Wyatt demurred. During their sessions together, the Indonesians were friendly and accommodating with the Americans, but told Wyatt

---

[17] See Tokyo to DOS, no. 2845, 28 May 1963, NSF, countries, Indonesia, 5/63, JFKL.

[18] Harriman–Ormsby Gore telephone conversation, 28 May 1963, box 581, Harriman papers; see also Ormsby Gore's report in Washington to FO, no. 1643, 28 May 1963, PREM 11/4308.

[19] De Zulueta minute for Macmillan, 29 May 1963, *ibid.*

[20] See the concerns raised in Home minute for Macmillan, PM/63/80, 30 May 1963, *ibid.*

that whether Shell was finally included in any final agreement would depend on a successful outcome of the impending talks between Malaya and Indonesia. With some flexibility on both sides, and aided by a tough but fair-minded Wyatt, on 2 June a Heads of Agreement was signed, setting out the terms to govern new contracts based on a 60/40 split of profits. In the event, Shell was only included in this arrangement after Harriman had reminded Wyatt that this was indeed necessary, and the Indonesians acceded to the American request.[21]

Officials in Washington were greatly encouraged by the outcome of Wyatt's mission. Forrestal told the President that he thought it would 'prove to be one of the smoothest and most efficient bits of preventive diplomacy which the United States has undertaken in some time'.[22] Equally gratifying was the fact that on 26 May, the Indonesian Government introduced new regulations designed to curb inflation as part of the stabilization programme stipulated by the IMF. Under the direction of First Minister Djuanda, these new measures had at their heart the aim of balancing the budget and promoting private productive enterprise. Although the dismantling of price regulation in some public services and cuts in public expenditure had a generally deflationary effect, the changes were soon subject to widespread criticism in Indonesia, with the PKI leading the denunciations of this rightward swing in economic policy. Many ordinary Indonesians felt the effects of sharp rises in the charges of state-owned utilities and transport systems, and by the late summer the price of rice was once again on the increase. However, Djuanda's painful stabilization programme was a clear sign to the Kennedy Administration that their Indonesian strategy was working, and that Sukarno was turning to more responsible, and Western-orientated, paths of national development.

Indeed, some commentators have referred to a 'right turn' in Indonesian politics during this period, indicated by the economic reforms, but seen most dramatically by Sukarno's willingness to pursue a dialogue with Malaya and his invitation for the Tunku to meet him in Tokyo. It is certainly the case that in early 1963 Jakarta continued to value its relations with the West, and particularly the United States, and hoped to attract the international confidence necessary to secure the financial stabilization package still being considered by the OECD and IMF. At the same time, the evident unpopularity of Djuanda's reforms, and the criticism they attracted from the PKI, made it just as necessary for the regime to pursue the external struggle against neo-colonialism and imperialism. The Indonesians may also have been trying to test the resolve of

[21] See de Zulueta minute for Macmillan, 4 June 1963, PREM 11/4308.
[22] Forrestal memorandum for Kennedy, 10 June 1963, NSF, countries, Indonesia, 6/63–8/63, JFKL.

Kuala Lumpur, as the Malayan leadership was made increasingly aware of Malaysia's vulnerability to subversion aided from outside. Certainly, the British were clear that the new signs of conciliation coming from Jakarta were nothing more than a temporary swing away from the path that was closest to Sukarno's heart.

What transpired when the Tunku and Sukarno met privately on 31 May and 1 June in Tokyo is still far from clear. The Indonesian President later asserted that the Tunku agreed to an investigation into whether the peoples of the Borneo territories wanted to join Malaysia, but at the time the Malayan Prime Minister informed the press that he had not discussed any conditions that would precede the formation of Malaysia or any delay in the timetable. The concrete result of the talks was a communique that avowed that each government would 'refrain from making acrimonious attacks and disparaging references to each other', and to resolve their differences 'in a spirit of friendliness and goodwill'. The way was now clear for a foreign ministers' meeting to be convened in Manila on 7 June, which would address the dispute between Malaya, Indonesia and the Philippines, and make recommendations to be subject to further endorsement by another summit.[23] After his return to Kuala Lumpur, the Tunku informed the British that in Tokyo he had tried to explain to Sukarno that the purpose of Malaysia was to contain the threat posed by the political radicalism of Chinese-dominated Singapore, and reported that the Indonesians had been friendly and seemed resigned to the establishment of the federation. Relating his pleasure at the results, the Malayan Prime Minister felt that Sukarno 'had clearly called off his confrontation without having had to be given anything in return'.[24]

At the subsequent foreign ministers' meeting in Manila, Subandrio and Pelaez tried without success in protracted discussions to convince Razak that Malaysia should be delayed while some form of assessment of opinion in the Borneo territories could be completed. Refusing to concede any need to postpone Malaysia's formation, Razak argued that Narasimhan had been satisfied that popular opinion was favourable during his brief tour of North Borneo and Sarawak in April. Subandrio was keen to let it be known that all Indonesia wanted was some gesture towards the principle of self-determination involving the further visit of a UN representative.[25] On 11 June, over an indistinct telephone line to Manila, the Tunku gave Razak his assent to the idea of an 'assessor' being called in to the Borneo territories, subject to the agreement of the British Government. The final 'Manila Accord' reached by the foreign ministers

---

[23] See Mackie, *Konfrontasi*, 148–9.
[24] Kuala Lumpur to CRO, no. 977, 7 June 1963, DO 169/240.
[25] See Kuala Lumpur to CRO, no. 1068, 18 June 1963, DO 169/275.

contained references to the Philippine idea of Maphilindo, a loose Malay confederation with the aim of strengthening cooperation and understanding between the three states through a series of regular meetings, while the Malayans were prepared to concede that the Filipinos had a right to pursue their claim to North Borneo once Malaysia came into existence. The crucial substance of the Accord, however, was contained in the two clauses that affirmed the adherence of all three countries to the principle of self-determination, and where Indonesia and the Philippines agreed to 'welcome' the formation of Malaysia if the UN Secretary General or his representative ascertained that the peoples of the Borneo territories supported the scheme. The Malayans undertook to consult the British Government to permit the conduct of such an assessment. Informing Tory about the course of the negotiations in Manila, the Tunku made clear that he considered the use of a UN ascertainment 'a patently shallow device designed to make it possible for the Summit Conference to give its blessing to Malaysia on the basis of investigations which it had itself approved. [He] was contemptuous about this face-saving device but said he was prepared to play along with it.'[26]

Razak was also eager to reassure the British that there would be no question of a referendum in the Borneo territories, or any delay in the creation of Malaysia. At the same time, the Malayans hoped that London would agree quickly (and publicly) to the idea of a UN ascertainment mission, believing that (as the British were told) no more than a return visit by Narasimhan would be involved.[27] According to Razak, in Manila Subandrio had himself categorically stated 'he would have no objection to this [UN] representative being Narasimhan, and he emphasised his interest in obtaining the right answer from this enquiry'. The Indonesian Foreign Minister was also ready to affirm that 'Indonesians definitely do not under any circumstances want Northern Borneo territory themselves, nor do they want any weak independent State there', while he 'welcomed Malaysia and says that he only requires a further confirmation that the peoples of the territories support Malaysia, in order to come out in public in favour of it'.[28] Although the CRO felt that Razak had played a good hand at Manila, there were immediate concerns raised in the Borneo territories about any fresh visit by a UN assessor, with local political leaders afraid that it would only unsettle the people and encourage opposition.[29] Within a few days, however, British officials were

[26] Kuala Lumpur to CRO, no. 1011, 12 June 1963, DO 169/274.
[27] Manila to FO, no. 491, 12 June 1963, D1074/21, FO 371/169722.
[28] Manila to FO, no. 497, 13 June 1963, D1074/22, *ibid.*
[29] On the strong reservations of Donald Stephens and the Datu Bandar, see Goode to Sandys, no. 313 Ocular, 17 June 1963, DO 169/275.

receiving reports that the Indonesians were putting a very different interpretation on the agreements reached at Manila. Selkirk had encountered
Subandrio while passing through Singapore airport on 14 June, and the
latter had claimed that he had secured a commitment to a referendum,
while at the UN there were indications from the Indonesians that they
would oppose any attempt to nominate Narasimhan for a return visit to
Borneo.[30]

Although the Foreign Office was initially keen to press on with the
idea of a Narasimhan-led ascertainment mission, the Colonial Office was
far more reserved about its readiness to make any such advance commitment, a view also held by Sandys, the responsible minister. When
the Malayan High Commissioner in London went to see Sandys on 25
June to discern his official response to the results of the Manila meeting,
Sandys expressed his surprise at the absence of advance consultation with
the British over the whole process, and stated that a formal reply to the
idea of a UN enquiry was not necessary until a full-scale summit between
Malaya, Indonesia and the Philippines had endorsed the Manila Accord.
Only then would the British make their public response.[31] Another effort
to elicit British opinions was made by Narasimhan himself, who passed
through London once more on 10 July and took the chance to see the
Lord Privy Seal, Edward Heath. With the Foreign Office pressing the
case for the British not to appear intransigent, and despite the reluctance
of the local governors, Heath informed Narasimhan that a return visit
to the Borneo territories by him would be acceptable, though no final
decision would be taken until after the summit; no other representative
but Narasimhan would be considered.[32]

While, on the surface at least, relations between Indonesia and Malaya
showed distinct signs of improvement in the summer of 1963, and as
hopes began to be raised that Jakarta was prepared to reconcile itself to
the creation of Malaysia, the final stages of the tortuous negotiations over
the terms on which the new federation would be established were moving to a climax. Their intricate path can only be presented in outline, but
they served to illustrate the deep and fundamental tensions present in the
relationship between Malaya and Singapore, and would eventually make
a contribution to the precipitate departure of the latter from Malaysia in
1965. Disputes over the economic and financial arrangements that were

---

[30] See Commissioner General's meeting, 15 June 1963, D1015/14, FO 371/169678; New
York to FO, no. 955, 2 July 1963, DO 169/275.
[31] See note of a meeting between the Malayan High Commissioner and Sandys, 25 June
1963, D1071/184, FO 371/169703.
[32] See Cable minute, 'Mr Narasimhan's visit to London', 9 July 1963, and record of conversation between Heath and Narasimhan, 10 July 1963, DO 169/275.

to accompany Singapore's membership of Malaysia were also conducted against the backdrop of mounting distrust and suspicion between the Tunku and Lee Kuan Yew, following the relative harmony that had featured in relations during 1962. The disagreements over the execution of Operation Cold Store had certainly helped to sour the atmosphere, and Lee had not helped matters when he claimed, in response to questions from reporters, that if the Singapore Government had been left to make the decision alone, no arrests would have been carried out. In view of Lee's private enthusiasm for ISC action, this was hardly a statement likely to endear itself to British or Malayan officials, and he was soon forced to clarify his comments, and to say that the PAP Government stood by the ISC's decision.[33]

For his part, one must also note Lee's insecurity over whether the Tunku would see through the merger now that the leading left-wing elements in Singapore were in detention.[34] Suspicions about the future intentions of the authorities in Kuala Lumpur were also being raised in Lee's mind by signs that the Tunku was cultivating contacts with the former Chief Minister, Lim Yew Hock, and was working to boost the political fortunes of the Singapore Alliance as a counter-weight to the PAP. A further worry was the efforts of Tan Siew Sin, the Federation Minister of Finance, to establish an electoral base in Singapore for the MCA.[35] Fundamentally, Lee feared (with some justification) that the Malayan leadership wanted to replace him with an alternative government in Singapore once Malaysia was established, centred around the moderate coalition of the Singapore Alliance, and possibly led by Lim Yew Hock.[36] British officials tried in vain to dispel any such notions from the minds of Federation ministers in the first part of 1963, but Lee was already tempted by the idea of calling a snap general election in Singapore before the formation of Malaysia, in order to consolidate his own position in the Assembly, wrong-foot his opponents in Kuala Lumpur and take advantage of the disruption in Barisan ranks caused by the results of the referendum and the effect on morale and organization of the Cold Store detentions.[37]

It was against this kind of political background that negotiations between Malaya and Singapore on the final conditions for the creation of Malaysia had got under way at the end of February 1963. They quickly

---

[33] Osborne, *Singapore and Malaysia*, 31.
[34] See Selkirk to Sandys, no. 87, 4 February 1963; Selkirk to Sandys, no. 108, 13 February 1963, DO 169/248.
[35] Osborne, *Singapore and Malaysia*, 44–5.
[36] These points are very well covered in Albert Lau, *A Moment of Anguish: Singapore in Malaysia and the Politics of Disengagement* (Singapore, 1998), 21–4; see also Lee Kuan Yew, *Singapore Story*, 460–6.
[37] See e.g. Moore minute for Selkirk, POL/7691, 22 November 1962, DO 169/248.

foundered over two issues. Ever since talks with Malaya on merger had begun in the summer of 1961, the Singapore authorities had stressed that agreement on the arrangements for a common market with the territories of the new federation had to precede the formation of Malaysia. The Malayans, although agreeing in principle to a common market, felt that the details could be finalized at a later stage. This difference was hardly surprising in view of Singapore's pressing need for expanding markets for its industries (and its unemployment problem rising in the early 1960s), clashing with Kuala Lumpur's uncertainty over how the Malayan economy would fare in unbridled competition with the lower labour costs of Singapore. There were also serious disagreements over Singapore's financial contribution to the revenues of the new federation, with the Singapore authorities anxious to retain control over their local taxes and excise duties, and to continue to devote a higher share to provision of social services than was then common in Malaya.[38] By the end of April, deadlock had been reached, and the Malayans began to raise the idea of going ahead with Malaysia without Singapore. The stakes were also increased by the concurrent acrimony in relations between the Federation and Brunei, as the Tunku and the Sultan could not come to agreement over who would dispose of Brunei's considerable oil revenues and what place in order of precedence among the Conference of Malay Rulers would be assumed by the latter once Malaysia had been formed.

Tensions between Malaya and Singapore over the common market and control of revenue issues reached a peak on 19 June 1963 with the announcement by the Tunku that the Malayan Cabinet had agreed the final terms on which the entry of both Singapore and Brunei to Malaysia would be acceptable. These were conveyed to Lee and the Sultan in the form of an ultimatum; there would be no more negotiations and a reply was required within forty-eight hours.[39] Seeing the Malayan Prime Minister after the Cabinet meeting, Selkirk reported that the former had explained it had been 'resolved with firm determination to bring to a close the prolonged and irritating negotiations with Lee Kuan Yew and the Sultan of Brunei whom Tunku described respectively as a snake and an old woman'. Although he hinted that he might have to request that Malaysia be formed without Singapore and Brunei, the Tunku conveyed his basic feeling that both territories would eventually 'come to heel'.[40]

---

[38] For a succinct summary of the complex issues involved, see Osborne, *Singapore and Malaysia*, 50–4.
[39] Kuala Lumpur to CRO, no. 1094, 19 June 1963, DO 169/221.
[40] Kuala Lumpur to CRO, no. 1095, 19 June 1963, *ibid.* and Garner minute for Sandys, 10 June 1963, DO 169/265.

With the passing of the deadline, the British were forced to issue a series
of invitations for last-ditch talks in London.

The whole rationale for Malaysia had been built around the core of
a merger between Malaya and Singapore, to allow the authorities in
Kuala Lumpur to take control of internal security in the colony, contain political radicalism and permit the British to make continuing use of
their base facilities. Now the Malayans appeared ready to discard the
concept altogether, and merely to take under their wing the Borneo
territories (possibly without the troublesome Brunei). With the PAP's
merger policy in tatters, Lee was likely to find his position untenable,
and the British might then have to face a radical left-wing government
in Singapore insisting they leave the base in the near future. In addition, the extended Anglo-Malayan Defence Agreement saddled the
British with a commitment to external Malaysian defence. The justification for these onerous defence obligations began to look very thin
when they bore no relationship to the maintenance of the Singapore
base, the key to Britain's overall position in South East Asia. Compounding these dilemmas was the delicate state of Malaya's relations
with its regional neighbours. The crisis talks in London on the final
terms for merger would have to be conducted against the backdrop of
the recent Manila Accord and the upcoming heads of state summit; too
much pressure on the authorities in Kuala Lumpur could have repercussions in the negotiating stance taken by the Tunku with Sukarno and
Macapagal.

One final point that must be noted, and that added to the pressure on
ministers, was the domestic political crisis that blew over the Macmillan
Government during the summer of 1963. The immediate cause for this
was the resignation on 4 June of John Profumo, the Secretary of State for
War, following revelations that he had lied to Parliament over his illicit
relationship with Christine Keeler. As the full scale of the Profumo affair,
along with its security implications, was divulged with great relish by the
press, Macmillan desperately tried to restore the battered reputation of
the government through the appointment of Lord Denning to head a full
judicial enquiry into the scandal. However, the Prime Minister's generally
ineffectual response, epitomized by his display in the Commons debate on
17 June, only added to the public impression of a leader out of touch with
the times. Macmillan was not the only figure in the Government under
great stress during this period. Unfounded rumours were also circulating
that Sandys was in some way caught up in the sexual scandal, and at
Cabinet on 19 June he confessed to some discomfort with the current allegations. Having discussed the possibility of resignation with Macmillan,
he instead requested that Denning also deal with any allegations levelled

against him (Denning's report, published in September 1963, cleared Sandys of any involvement).[41] While ministers in London digested the latest salacious headlines, the Foreign Office contemplated the consequences of Lee and the Tunku failing to agree on the final terms for merger. In an interesting observation in view of what ultimately transpired, one senior official in the South East Asia Department conjectured that if Singapore did not join Malaysia, then the British would have to consider reducing their defence commitments to the Borneo territories,

by ensuring that these territories develop in a manner acceptable to their Indonesian and Philippine neighbours. This would probably mean not federation with Malaysia, but independence on their own. If such independence led to absorption by Indonesia and the Philippines, this would be less damaging to British interests than the obligation to fight an interminable war with Indonesia to keep the Borneo territories out of her hands.

Separate independence for Singapore and the Borneo territories would probably also mean that only Malaya would be available for British base facilities, and hence the government in Kuala Lumpur would have to be more liberal in its approach to their use by British forces than hitherto, at least until an amphibious capability could be developed based in Australia. Such an eventuality would necessarily have a serious impact on Britain's commitments under SEATO.[42] In all such thinking there was a realization that a pull-back to Australia should have been considered earlier, also entailing a major reappraisal of what tasks British forces were expected to accomplish in South East Asia. After all, since the late 1950s, when planning and force assignments for SEATO finally gained some degree of substance, there had been a supposition that the Commonwealth Brigade Group in Malaya, backed up by air and naval units based on Singapore, would rapidly be committed alongside the Americans to resisting an overt North Vietnamese or Chinese aggression in the Treaty area. This scenario looked increasingly tenuous if British forces were deployed in northern Australia. Moreover, it was Britain's contribution to SEATO, many British officials felt, that still gave them some weight with the Americans in discussions over resisting Communist pressures in South East Asia and other aspects of overall Western policies in the region.

All these considerations made the Foreign Office and Home very resistant to any notion of settling for a Malaysia that did not include

---

[41] See Lamb, *Macmillan Years*, 456–88.
[42] Cable minute, 13 June 1963, and Peck minute, 20 June 1963, offering substantial agreement with such reasoning, D1071/178, FO 371/169702.

Singapore.[43] Sandys himself was well aware of such concerns about departing from the original scheme, noting: 'Ministers would clearly wish to think very carefully before agreeing to accept an extension of their commitments under the present Malaya Defence Agreement to cover a "Little Malaysia".'[44] He was also in receipt of strong views from the Borneo territories that Singapore's exclusion would play into the hands of Malaysia's opponents, and strengthen the perception that the scheme was merely a cloak for Malayan aggrandizement.[45] Privately, the British had much sympathy for Lee's position in the dispute, believing that his detailed proposals for common market arrangements were sound and logical, and that only Malayan fears over Singapore's economic prowess were holding them back from agreement. It was also felt that the Tunku should be given a sharp reminder of his own stake in the Malaysia scheme, and the fact that he relied on British forces for his current defence against a predatory Indonesian neighbour. Following one meeting at the CRO, an official minuted that Sandys 'thought it would probably be necessary to threaten the Tunku with separate independence for Singapore and it was agreed that this might force the Tunku to reach agreement with Singapore since without her the Malaya Defence Agreement would not continue for long and our free use of the Singapore base would soon be put in jeopardy'.[46] Yet Malayan ministers would have been well aware that such threats carried little credibility when the British had so much riding on the formation of a Malaysia that included Singapore. With all sides having much to lose, and the Tunku's patience wearing precariously thin, the Malayans would have to be treated with great delicacy and tact if they were to be won over to a conciliatory approach.

The last-gasp negotiations, involving Lee, Razak and British officials, began on 24 June. Many days of hard bargaining followed in London, with the Singapore side giving most ground, aided and abetted by Sandys. Agreement on final terms was finally achieved on 5 July following a gruelling thirteen-hour overnight session, and after Lee had forced last-minute concessions from the British over the disposition of service lands when the crown finally renounced its hold over Singapore.[47] In the final deal, the Malayans were prepared to have the provisions for a common

[43] Home minute for Sandys, FS/63/58, 24 June 1963, D1071/181, FO 371/169703, and in DO 169/221.
[44] Sandys to Goode and Waddell, nos. 518 and 579, 21 June 1963, *ibid.*
[45] Waddell to Sandys, no. 301, 24 June 1963, *ibid.*
[46] Milton minute for Golds, 21 June 1963, *ibid.*
[47] See Moore to Selkirk, no. 455, 4 July 1963; minutes of mtg held in Commonwealth Secretary's room, 5 July 1963; Moore to Selkirk, no. 466, 8 July 1963, CO 1030/1515.

market written into the new Malaysia constitution, though it was not of the ideal form hoped for by the Singapore Government. For its part, Singapore agreed that 40 per cent of its income revenue would go towards pan-Malaysia expenditures, subject to periodic review. Furthermore, Singapore would provide a loan of $150 million to the Borneo territories on very generous terms, though 50 per cent of the labour force used on projects financed from the loan should come from Singapore.[48] This last provision, along with several other details, was worked out between Lee and the Tunku during a private meeting on 7 July at the Ritz Hotel. In rather unconventional fashion, the brief notes covering these points were scribbled out on the back of an envelope and signed by the Tunku, and later confirmed by letter from Lee Kuan Yew.[49]

In the early hours of 9 July 1963 the Malaysia Agreement was signed between the representatives of the United Kingdom, the Federation of Malaya, Singapore, North Borneo and Sarawak. The British Government committed itself to relinquishing sovereignty in Singapore, North Borneo and Sarawak to a new federal Malaysian government in Kuala Lumpur on 31 August 1963. The Anglo-Malayan Defence Agreement of 1957 would be extended to cover all the territories of Malaysia, though the British could retain and use their base facilities in Singapore. The safeguards for the Borneo territories mentioned in the report of the Lansdowne Intergovernmental Committee were to be incorporated in the Malaysian constitution, and the common market and financial terms between Malaya and Singapore were formalized.[50] The most glaring omission from the Agreement was the signature of the Sultan of Brunei. Taking great umbrage at the whole Malayan approach to the negotiations, the Sultan had had to be gently coaxed into coming to London for a final round of talks, but had refused to give way on either the question of oil revenues or his place in the Conference of Rulers.[51]

Despite the tensions between Malaya and Singapore, and the disappointment of Brunei's exclusion from Malaysia, the British could feel relief that the main parties had come together behind an agreed document. Further satisfaction came when the Singapore Assembly debated and approved the Malaysia Agreement by a comfortable margin

[48] Osborne, *Singapore and Malaysia*, 55–61; Lau, *Moment of Anguish*, 16.
[49] See the 'Ritz Hotel Agreement,' 7 July 1963, and Lee Kuan Yew to Tunku Abdul Rahman, 10 July 1963, PREM 11/4349; see also Lee Kuan Yew, *Singapore Story*, 482.
[50] *Malaysia: Agreement concluded between the United Kingdom of Great Britain and Northern Ireland, the Federation of Malaya, North Borneo, Sarawak and Singapore*, Cmnd 2094 (London, 1963).
[51] See e.g. Brunei to CO, no. 182 Ocular, 25 June 1963, PREM 11/4904.

(25 to 17) on 1 August.[52] With the security situation in the Borneo
territories relatively quiet, the signs for Malaysia in Sarawak, where opposition was most anticipated, were even better than expected. The process
of indirect elections (staged from April to June) culminated in the middle
of July with the formation of a new Legislative Council, where a clear
majority of seats was held by the pro-Malaysia parties of the Sarawak
Alliance, and Stephen Ningkan was made Chief Minister.[53] Even within
SUPP, the radical elements of the party's Chinese rank and file membership tended to be counteracted by the more moderate stance of its
leading figures, Ong Kee Hui and Stephen Yong. Both men were concerned about Indonesian designs on the Borneo territories, moved to
condemn the Brunei revolt, and by early 1963, though favouring separate independence for Sarawak, had struck up an ambiguous stance on
Malaysia, calling for UN involvement and a plebiscite rather than for the
abandonment of the whole scheme. The Brunei revolt had already given
the authorities in Sarawak the pretext to invoke emergency regulations,
while SUPP's opponents had lost little chance in linking the party with
the new subversive threat from Indonesia.[54]

What is perhaps most noticeable is that British officials, aware that the
party leadership had kept its options on Malaysia open, were not unduly
concerned by the idea of a SUPP victory in the state-wide elections.[55]
Having toured Sarawak in May 1963, Sir Saville Garner, the Permanent Secretary at the CRO, reported to Sandys that no-one could predict the results of the elections, and it was 'quite possible that SUPP
might be in the lead, but I am not sure that we need altogether despair even if they were to win; provided that their leader can rely on
moderate support and could avoid being run by the Communist
minority'. Another official accompanying Garner concurred, finding the
Governor and Chief Secretary far from pessimistic about working with
SUPP, while 'it was possible that the prospect of forming a state government within Malaysia (when the Federal Government would be ruthless with SUPP extremists) might prove too tempting for Ong Kee Hui
to resist'.[56] As it transpired the complicated three-tier electoral system
devised by the British helped to deny SUPP a decisive role in the
Legislative Council, leaving the Sarawak Alliance, with much support

[52] Lau, *Moment of Anguish*, 26.
[53] Gordon P. Means, *Malaysian Politics* (London, 1970), 303.
[54] See Chin Ung-Ho, *Chinese Politics in Sarawak*, 72.
[55] See F. D. Jakeway (Chief Secretary, Sarawak) to J. Higham, 14 June 1963, CO
1030/1621.
[56] Garner minute for Sandys, 10 June 1963; D. G. R. Bentliff note, n.d. (but c. early June
1963), DO 169/265.

from the many independent candidates standing, to form the state's first elected government.[57]

For the moment, at least, the internal components of Malaysia were lining up well, but the external environment remained uncertain, and paramount here were the attitudes and policies of the United States. The British would have taken some heart from the reports they had received of Averell Harriman's stance at the ANZUS Council meeting held in Wellington in early June, when the organization had also publicly welcomed the establishment of Malaysia. Harriman had met Australian and New Zealand enquiries over the extent of American assistance in the event of Indonesian aggression drawing in their forces to the defence of Malaysia, with an assurance that US obligations would come into play if an overt attack on Australian or New Zealand forces was carried out in the Treaty area. He repeated such assurances to the Australian Cabinet in Canberra on 7 June and maintained that the United States would wish Australia to extend to Malaysia its existing commitment to Malayan defence.[58] Questioned over American attitudes towards organized subversion from Indonesia into Malaysia, Harriman replied that this would be 'much affected by the seriousness with which Australia itself was taking the situation. The United States had assumed extensive obligations abroad and had not yet turned away an appeal by its friends. If there were a commitment on Australia's part... he did not think that the United States would let Australia down but he could make no commitment', adding that 'this was a grey area between the two countries'. The wide press reporting of some of Harriman's remarks in Wellington and Canberra, and the implication that they represented a firm warning from the United States to Indonesia, prompted President Kennedy to contact Hilsman to ask whether Harriman had actually gone a little too far.[59] Indeed, when Menzies visited Washington in early July he tried to elicit a repeat of Harriman's assurances from Kennedy, but all the latter would offer was further State Department study of whether the ANZUS Treaty would apply, and if it did, consultations in advance of possible Australian troop deployments to Malaysia.[60] Nevertheless, Harriman's statements did much to boost Australian confidence that the Americans would

[57] Of 429 district council seats available, 138 went to the Alliance, 116 to SUPP, 116 to independents and 59 to PANAS; this eventually translated into 19 Alliance seats in the Council Negri, 9 independent (7 of whom came into a coalition with the Alliance), 5 SUPP and 3 PANAS; see Means, *Malaysian Politics*, 304, and Robert O. Tilman, 'Elections in Sarawak', *Asian Survey*, 3, 10, 1963, 507–18.
[58] See Edwards, *Crises and Commitments*, 265–6.
[59] See Hilsman, *To Move a Nation*, 392.
[60] See memorandum for the Australian Ambassador in Washington, Sir Howard Beale, 4 October 1963, *FRUS, 1961–1963, XXIII*, 734–6.

ultimately come to their aid if serious fighting developed with their
Indonesian neighbour, and helped to dispel some of the earlier coolness
that had been displayed by officials in Canberra towards Malaysia.[61]

From an American point of view, the economic reforms initiated in
Indonesia in May, the Tokyo oil agreement, the Manila Accord and the
enunciation of the principles of Maphilindo appeared to herald an end
to their headaches over how to handle the Sukarno regime. In mid-June
1963, Robert W. Barnett, the US Deputy Assistant Secretary of State for
Far Eastern Affairs, visited Indonesia for more talks about the potential
for an enhanced programme of American and international financial aid.
Barnett's trip through the region before his arrival in Jakarta had convinced him that Sukarno realized Indonesia's economic problems and
was now determined to take action, and that Indonesia was deserving
of Western support.[62] In Jakarta, the British Ambassador was told by
Barnett that 'in the stabilization of Indonesia and in the withholding of
this enormous strategic asset from Communist domination lay America's
overriding interest in the area', the Ambassador ruefully noting, 'The implication was "overriding Malaysia" if the two interests should diverge.'[63]
However, Sukarno's apparent interest in a diplomatic solution to the dispute with Kuala Lumpur made it seem possible that good relations with
Jakarta and support for Malaysia might, in fact, be compatible. On 8
July 1963, Hilsman was even confident enough to despatch a memorandum to Forrestal calling for a presidential trip to the Far East in the
coming autumn which included Indonesia on the itinerary. The reasoning was clear to Hilsman: a turning point had been reached in South East
Asian history, and 'Indonesia, from all the evidence, has made a fundamental decision to turn away from the Communist bloc and towards
the West.... The President's trip will go far towards making the decision stick.'[64] Yet the optimists within the State Department and on the
NSC staff were overlooking both the momentum within Indonesia that
had been built up behind a policy of confrontation, and the opponents
within the United States of an accommodating approach to Sukarno's
regime.

[61] The Australian Prime Minister relayed this encouraging news directly to Macmillan;
see de Zulueta record of conversation between Menzies and Macmillan, 24 June 1963,
PREM 11/4096.
[62] See Barnett memorandum for Harriman, 'Aid to Indonesia: Assessment of Indonesia's
own intentions', 2 July 1963, POF, countries, Indonesia, general, 1961–3, box 119,
JFKL. Barnett was heavily influenced by the accounts given by Macapagal of Sukarno's
developing views.
[63] Jakarta to FO, no. 608, 13 June 1963, DH103145/4, FO 371/169888.
[64] Hilsman memorandum for Forrestal, 'Presidential Visit to the Far East', 8 July 1963,
Presidential Far East Trip Plans, 1963, box 5–6, Hilsman papers.

The announcement of the London Agreement on Malaysia was greeted with anger by the Indonesians. The PKI argued that the agreement invalidated the whole talks process. On 10 July, Sukarno delivered a speech where he accused the Tunku of breaking his word (allegedly given at their Tokyo meeting) that Malaysia would be delayed to allow a UN referendum to be held in the Borneo territories, and went on to threaten cancellation of his attendance at the Manila summit.[65] The London Agreement had made no mention of the provisions of the Manila Accord of early June, and envisaged the creation of Malaysia on 31 August with no room for compromise.[66] Malayan attempts to assure the Indonesians that they were not violating articles 10 and 11 of the Manila Accord (outlining the UN ascertainment exercise) were reinforced by the determined efforts of Howard Jones in Jakarta, who saw Sukarno on 16 July to press the case for the summit meeting with the Tunku. American suspicions that the British had no serious interest in furthering the Manila process were fuelled at this time by the expulsion from North Borneo of two Indonesian consular officials suspected of being intelligence officers, despite appeals by US officials to show restraint over the matter.[67]

The adoption of a harder Indonesian line in the build-up to the summit could be explained by several factors. Simple negotiating tactics may have played a role, with the Malayans being sent a clear signal that serious concessions would need to be forthcoming, and that a mere face-saving formula would not be enough; Sukarno may have felt that the Tunku was still looking for a way out of his predicament and would be susceptible to pressure. Internal opposition was also building from the PKI against the swing in Indonesian diplomacy marked by the Manila Accord and the economic measures associated with the stabilization programme. The Indonesians may also have been disappointed at the turn of events in July, with SUPP unable to secure power in Sarawak by electoral means, and the Tunku's and Lee's apparently successful attempts to agree the final terms for Malaysia. It was also possible that the last-minute decision of Brunei not to join the new federation may have given the Indonesians encouragement to pursue a tougher line in the hope of triggering further defections. After several more hesitations and outbursts, on 27 July Sukarno finally announced that he would go to Manila, but that the meeting would represent merely another facet of the overall policy of confrontation.[68]

---

[65] Jones, *Indonesia*, 278.
[66] Mackie, *Konfrontasi*, 154.
[67] See Goode to Sandys, no. 375, 19 July 1963, PREM 11/4342, and DOS to London, no. 375, 16 July 1963, POL 3 MALAYSIA, RG 59.
[68] Mackie, *Konfrontasi*, 155–7.

With the summit still on track, if precariously poised, American policy-makers continued to have cause for optimism, but two further developments towards the end of July signalled that Washington's Indonesian policy had run into serious trouble. Following the conclusion of a survey of the new Indonesian economic measures carried out by an IMF evaluation team, on 24 July the IMF Board of Directors approved a stand-by arrangement that from 1 August allowed Indonesia to borrow $50 million, though subject to further conditions on budgetary prudence. Two days later, a hurried meeting in Paris of the Development Assistance Committee of the OECD listened to IMF and American officials argue in favour of the projected $250 million package of financial assistance that the Kennedy Administration had earlier anticipated.[69] However, unimpressed with Indonesian economic performance, the Committee failed to approve such a large commitment.[70] This was a major setback to those Americans who hoped that the prospect of large-scale Western financial backing would serve to moderate Indonesian behaviour on the international stage. On 26 July, another blow to American policy was inflicted with passage through the House Foreign Affairs Committee of an amendment to the 1963 foreign aid bill, put forward by Broomfield, that prohibited further economic and military assistance to Indonesia unless the President made a public determination that such aid was in the national interest of the United States.[71] The Broomfield amendment was only one chapter in the disastrous saga of the 1963 aid bill, which eventually emerged from Congress authorizing only $3.6 billion of expenditure, but it was immensely frustrating for State Department and White House proponents of an accommodating approach to Sukarno's regime. Far more presidential credibility would have to be staked on the policy if it was to be carried forward into 1964, and Sukarno's critics given yet more ammunition if his volatile actions were to lead Indonesia into more open conflict with America's friends and allies.

To many observers of the South East Asia scene in the summer of 1963, Indonesian policy seemed poised at a crossroads between confrontation with her Malayan neighbour, backed by Britain, and a path of moderate economic reform conditioned by Western financial aid. As has been argued, this was probably a misleading way to interpret the Indonesian domestic scene. Moves towards better relations with the West only served to underline how at variance with the radicalism of the PKI

---

[69] See Komer memorandum for Kennedy, and attached State Department memorandum 'Indonesian Stabilization Program', 23 July 1963, NSF, countries, Indonesia, 6/63–8/63, JFKL.
[70] Bunnell, 'Kennedy Initiatives,' 384–90.
[71] Hilsman, *To Move a Nation*, 395.

were governing circles in Jakarta; the internal dynamic of competition between the various groups within Indonesian society may well have required some form of confrontation with Indonesia's perceived enemies to be expressed. It was more than likely that Sukarno was engaged in a series of tactical shifts and manoeuvres rather than a carefully constructed plan of campaign, though the eventual aspiration of removing British influence from the region and enhancing Indonesian freedom to intimidate the Borneo territories lay at the back of his thinking. It was against this unpredictable backdrop that the main Asian protagonists in confrontation came together for their summit meeting in Manila, and through the subsequent discussions, agreements and misunderstandings set the stage for the later emergence of full-blown hostility and conflict.

7 From the Manila summit to the creation of Malaysia: August–September 1963

The Manila summit constituted the high point of the diplomacy that accompanied the formation of Malaysia. During this crucial phase of the unfolding crisis, the principal protagonists appeared to have made significant moves to reconcile their differences and agree a procedure by which the new federation might be accepted. The rancour, accusation and mutual recrimination that followed was based largely around conflicting interpretations of the nature of the agreements made and the circumstances that accompanied their implementation. Another important background factor was behind-the-scenes efforts on the part of the British to offer advice, frequently delivered in the form of instructions, to the Malayans over the conduct of the negotiations, and the contrasting concern of the United States that maximum flexibility should be given to the Tunku in how he dealt with his neighbours and the issue of Malaysia. Indeed, perceptions of London's interference with the talks between the Asian states were to lend a degree of credibility to later Indonesian claims of neo-colonial influence circumscribing the autonomy of Kuala Lumpur. By September, the dispute between Malaya and Indonesia erupted once more into full-blown animosity, and the British were now also targeted by Jakarta as the interlopers who had forestalled an inter-Asian settlement. At the same time, the British had come to believe that after the lull of the summer, the Indonesians were now reverting to type and displaying their true character as aggressive expansionists, bent on destroying Malaysia, and absorbing the Borneo territories in the process. Finally, the British were also developing a personal fixation with the bellicose Indonesian President, whom they regarded as the source of all their troubles; one American official was told by Fred Warner, the head of the Foreign Office's South East Asia Department, that 'it was difficult for [the] British to take [a] moderate attitude towards Sukarno whom they looked upon as [a] special enemy in [the] same way [the] US regards Castro'.[1]

[1] London to DOS, no. 778, 15 August 1963, POL 3 MALAYSIA, RG 59.

172

The initial signs from the summit were that rapid agreement could be reached over how to accomplish the ascertainment of opinion in the Borneo territories mentioned in the foreign ministers' accord made in June. A day after he arrived in Manila, on 31 July 1963, the Tunku appeared ready to leave the whole procedure to the discretion of the UN Secretary General, U Thant. The UN's representative at the summit conference, Alfred Mackenzie (a Canadian), was therefore asked to despatch a request to U Thant in New York for him to carry out a survey mission as outlined by article 10 of the Manila Accord. The ascertainment was to be conducted in line with the terms of UN General Assembly Resolution 1541, and in accordance with the principle of self-determination; the resolution in question, passed in December 1960, strongly implied that a supervised referendum was required to assess the will of the people of any territory achieving self-government through integration with an existing independent state.[2]

Such an arrangement was clearly unacceptable to the British, who must have been particularly aggrieved that the prior understanding over a return visit by Narasimhan to the Borneo territories had been quickly by-passed as a way to satisfy the terms of the Manila Accord. Not only would preparation and conduct of a referendum inevitably delay the formation of Malaysia, with all kinds of implications for confidence in the whole scheme within the Borneo territories, but the results of such a test of opinion could not be predicted with absolute confidence, while new opportunities for Indonesian subversion would be presented. The British position was that the work of the Cobbold Commission and the Lansdowne Intergovernmental Committee, followed by the results of the Legislative Council elections in Sarawak and North Borneo, fulfilled the requirements of self-determination. Any acceptance of a referendum would undermine all past British arguments that popular opinion had been adequately consulted. An obviously worried Duncan Sandys cabled the British Embassy in Manila, and asked that the Tunku be approached on the morning of 1 August, where the Malayan Prime Minister was to be reminded that he was bound by multilateral agreement to bring about Malaysia on 31 August, and that while a visit to the Borneo territories by the UN Secretary General or his representative would be acceptable, a referendum or plebiscite was out of the question. Sandys expected prior consultation with London before any agreement was reached that could prejudice these British requirements.[3] Whitehall's concern intensified,

[2] See Mackie, *Konfrontasi*, 157–8.
[3] FO (Sandys) to Manila (for Tunku Abdul Rahman), no. 988, 1 August 1963, PREM 11/4349.

however, after it became clear that the Tunku had already requested Malayan Cabinet approval for leaving the method of ascertainment to U Thant, and to allow for some postponement in Malaysia if the Secretary General found it impossible to complete his task before 31 August; the Tunku hoped that Sandys would agree to give him this small measure of flexibility.[4] Later the same day, Sandys informed the Cabinet in London that the Tunku had been persuaded to ask for the UN investigation and was prepared to accept a short delay in setting up Malaysia. Ministers agreed that any shift of Malaysia Day away from 31 August was 'more likely to lead to an indefinite postponement of the project than to promote an early resolution of the current differences between Malaya and Indonesia'; the Malayan Prime Minister would need to be warned of the dangers of delay and the importance of adhering to the original target date.[5]

With news soon leaking in Manila of British opposition to any delay with Malaysia, concern quickly spread among American officials that London's pressure on the Malayans should not prejudice the chance of a successful outcome to the summit. The US Ambassador in the Philippines, William E. Stevenson, voiced the widely held view that British actions tended to confirm 'charges [that] Malaysia [is] merely [a] neo-colonialist device to allow [the] British [to] continue hegemony. As I understand US policy, we want newly independent nations [to] seek their own solutions to regional problems without outside interference.' It was hoped that the State Department could persuade the British 'to allow [the] Tunku [to] handle this problem in his own way' otherwise 'we are likely to see most of the gains achieved in recent months go down [the] drain'.[6] Hilsman coordinated a response to these worrying signs, informing the US Embassy in London that the Department was 'deeply disturbed by reported British signal-calling for Tunku in Summit discussions . . . This British interference could have disastrous effect on prospects [of] Summit success, giving [the] Indonesians and Philippines [an] unparalleled opportunity [to] write off [the] Tunku as "neo-colonialist tool".' Furthermore, Hilsman noted that

Whatever [the] Tunku is up to, we find it hard [to] believe British [are] unwilling [to] permit him [to] make own decisions. If he has become convinced that future relations with Indonesians and Philippines necessitate [a] risk to internal position inherent in postponement, we can see no justification for blunt attempt by outsiders to override him. If he [is] simply exercising tactical flexibility, [it] would be [a] major blunder [to] ruin his tactics. Tunku, after all, is [the] man who will have to live with decisions.

[4] Manila to FO, no. 586, 1 August 1963, PREM 11/4349, containing the text of the Tunku's telegram to Razak explaining his line to the Malayan Cabinet.
[5] CC(63) 51st mtg, 1 August 1963, CAB 128/37.
[6] Manila to DOS, no. 152, 1 August 1963, POL 7 PHIL, RG 59.

It was vitally important, in American estimations, that the Asian states themselves should resolve the dispute, while British efforts to dictate the Tunku's position would merely serve to destroy any chances of a settlement.[7] Instructing that representations be made at the highest levels, Hilsman asserted that the British 'must see that in adopting intransigent position they are gambling not only with [the] future [of] Malaysia, but also with [the] future of Indo[nesian] orientation, and whole US strategic investment in Far East. Purpose is [to] seek only [a] few days delay to provide Sukarno [with a] figleaf.'[8] American views were reinforced by Harriman in a telephone call to the Minister at the British Embassy in Washington, Denis Greenhill, who was told that interference with the Tunku 'would look very much like a colonial effort', and that if Sukarno returned to Jakarta and 'starts the guerrilla war, we don't know where it will end'. Greenhill's response was to argue that a delay in Malaysia was 'a pretty slippery slope to start on', to which Harriman retorted that the 'slippery slope would be if Sukarno goes back and starts his guerrilla war'.[9] The reaction of British officials in London was to argue that any concession to the Indonesian view could lead to a referendum in which dissidents from Kalimantan would be allowed to spread their message in the Borneo territories, the local colonial authorities were excluded from any role in supervising the polling, and votes given to resident Indonesians (about 70,000 Indonesian migrant workers were then present in North Borneo).[10] Warner himself was adamant that if the 'crux of US view was that [the] Tunku should be given [a] free hand to work out [a] solution . . . this [was] impossible in light of UK responsibilities . . . "if Malaysia should collapse UK will have to pick up pieces"'.[11]

Meanwhile, in Manila the Tunku was having to manoeuvre between his desire to reach an amicable settlement and his need to appease his British allies. The pressure on the Malayan delegation had been increased by the fact that late on 1 August a reply had been received from U Thant to Mackenzie's earlier request, anticipating that a General Assembly-approved referendum would meet the ascertainment requirement, with UN observers being deployed: it was unlikely that the operation could start before 15 October and the whole process might take until 30 November to complete. Full UK cooperation would be

[7] DOS to London, no. 767, 1 August 1963, POL 3 MALAYSIA, RG 59.
[8] DOS to London, no. 790, 1 August 1963, *ibid.*
[9] DOS to London, no. 773, 1 August 1963, *ibid.*; Harriman–Greenhill telephone conversation, 1 August 1963, box 581, Harriman papers.
[10] London to DOS, no. 578, 2 August 1963, POL 3 MALAYSIA, RG 59. An official in the State Department's Far East Bureau added the handwritten aside to a report of such arguments: 'In short UK–Malaya might well lose.'
[11] See London to DOS, no. 591, 2 August 1963, *ibid.*

needed and the estimated cost of $400,000 would have to be borne by the parties.[12] With another meeting between the principals due again on 2 August to sign a declaration confirming the vague generalities of regional cooperation through the idea of Maphilindo, the Tunku was given another message from Sandys which warned against any postponement or referendum, arguing that: 'No amount of plebiscites will alter Sukarno's basic hostility to Malaysia. His ultimate objective is clearly to round off his empire by absorbing into it the three North Borneo territories. He sees Malaysia as a serious obstacle to his ambitions and, whatever he may say, he will continue to try and undermine it.' The Tunku was told that he could count on the British in any conflict with Indonesia.[13] Sandys's own view was that a plebiscite 'would not only arouse political doubts in Borneo, but... we also cannot foresee what the result of it would be if it were conducted in this atmosphere'. The practical problems of such an exercise would be immense, and included deciding on the form of question to be asked, possible Indonesian interference with propaganda and subversion, and likely demands for the withdrawal of British troops during the voting: 'We should be involved in every sort of dispute and the result might conceivably be different from the recent free elections.'[14]

For his part, the Tunku informed the British that he would tell Sukarno and Macapagal that he could not accept a pre-Malaysia referendum in the face of British opposition, but would still be ready to refer the matter to the UN Secretary General if agreement could be reached on U Thant handling the ascertainment himself or through a personal representative within a month to six weeks (with the initial intention of meeting a 31 August deadline). If this proved unacceptable, the Tunku would be willing to agree to a post-Malaysia referendum, but under the same terms and conditions as the Indonesians had negotiated over West Irian.[15] Failure to agree any of these proposals, the Tunku claimed, would give him the pretext to walk out of the conference. In his formal reply to Sandys, the Tunku went on to assert: 'I realize only too well that any postponement of Malaysia would be tantamount to a surrender, which will be used to advantage by the Communists... You can rest assured that Malaysia will be announced on the 31st August as scheduled.'[16] The Tunku's change of tack was not only attributable to the British stance; the previous day Razak had informed the Tunku that the Malayan Cabinet was unhappy with any

[12] See New York to FO, no. 221, 1 August 1963, D1075/25, FO 371/169724; Manila to DOS, no. 157, 2 August 1963, POL 3 MALAYSIA, RG 59.
[13] FO to Manila, no. 1003, 2 August 1963, PREM 11/4349.
[14] FO (Sandys) to Manila, no. 1002, 2 August 1963, ibid.
[15] Manila to FO, no. 587, 2 August 1963, D1075/17, FO 371/169723.
[16] Manila to FO, no. 593, 3 August 1963, PREM 11/4349.

idea of postponement of Malaysia, which would be difficult to defend in the Borneo territories and with the Malayan public.[17] While the Tunku's new position may have helped to reassure his British critics, it was difficult to overlook the basic point, as one British official in Manila observed, that he 'had somewhat "mucked up" the negotiations by taking [a] position at [the] beginning which he knew UK could not accept and now finding it necessary backtrack and leave himself open to charge of reneging'.[18]

During the conference session that followed, the Malayan delegation consequently balked at U Thant's procedural suggestions, and it was announced that the closing of the summit would be delayed. The Americans were told by Macapagal that at the 2 August talks the Tunku had made no mention of the idea of the Secretary General conducting a personal ascertainment rather than a referendum, claiming that Malaya, Indonesia and the Philippines had initially all agreed to a UN-supervised plebiscite and a delay in Malaysia. The difficulty emphasized by the Malayans was this would require British concurrence; moreover the Philippine President reported that 'crux of present impasse was Sukarno's bitter feelings against the British and their manipulations of the conference. This came to head ... when Tunku read letter from British Embassy here instructing Tunku hold firm on 31 August date. Macapagal said Sukarno became incensed and blow-up was avoided by Macapagal adjourning meeting for lunch.' Sukarno would not agree to any proposals that he suspected came from a British source, making the Tunku's position very difficult, and Macapagal appealed to the Americans to help in overcoming British resistance.[19] Late on 2 August, Mackenzie telephoned U Thant to explain that deadlock had been reached and a fresh initiative would be needed from New York to avert a complete collapse; he maintained that a reversion to a brief and more limited type of survey of the recent elections, involving some minor delay to Malaysia, would be acceptable to the conference. Sir Patrick Dean, Britain's Ambassador to the UN, was assured by Narasimhan, who was closely following developments in Manila, that

if the proposal were accepted U Thant would almost certainly send him [to head the survey], but that if he did not he would send a thoroughly reliable man. The ascertainment of the views of the people would be done by polling the representatives already elected in North Borneo and Sarawak ... There is no question of attempting an independent qualitative assessment.[20]

---

[17] Kuala Lumpur to CRO, no. 1454, 2 August 1963, PREM 11/4349; Razak had been passing on to Tory copies of the cables from the Malayan delegation in Manila.
[18] Manila to DOS, no. 157, 2 August 1963, POL 3 MALAYSIA, RG 59.
[19] Manila to DOS, no. 161, 2 August 1963, POL 3 MALAYSIA, RG 59; Manila to DOS, no. 165, 3 August 1963, *ibid.*
[20] New York to FO, no. 1150, 2 August 1963, D1075/23, FO 371/169724.

British officials in Manila later confirmed that 'it was Mackenzie who really helped to get the plebiscite solution thrown out of court and who paved the way for the acceptance of the less objectionable inspection team compromise'.[21]

The Americans wanted the British to allow the Tunku as much negotiating space as possible to consider such a new formula. On 2 August in London, the Minister at the US Embassy had managed to see Home (the Prime Minister was unavailable), and emphasized the importance attached to allowing the Tunku flexibility over the date for Malaysia; the Foreign Secretary hinted that he would not be utterly opposed to a slight alteration if there was a 'clear and evident gain to be derived'.[22] Nevertheless, Sandys was in the process of further entrenching the British position by indicating in the House of Commons the government's unwillingness to countenance any change in the date for Malaysia. Having seen a (garbled) copy of Sandys's message of 2 August to the Tunku, Hilsman was initially angered by British reluctance to make concessions, telephoning Greenhill at home to complain that Sandys's cable was 'outrageous' and that the British were 'deliberately spoiling for a fight with Sukarno in which [they] would inevitably be unable to cope and would finally come to the Americans for help'.[23] When it was explained that Sandys had only registered his opposition to the plebiscite scheme, Hilsman was slightly pacified, but he still argued with Greenhill that the more limited form of ascertainment, then under consideration by U Thant, should be supported, as it 'would reveal the real intentions of Sukarno. It offered a face-saver if he wanted to take it.' Hilsman suggested that the British could count on Washington for support if they endorsed the new form of ascertainment proposed and if the Indonesian President refused acceptance, the American attitude would be 'to hell with him' and the British could stick to their prior position; anxious to mollify the Americans, British officials in Washington were inclined to favour a brief UN survey. However, London's view, with the Foreign Office deferring to the judgement of Sandys and CRO officials, was that no advance agreement could be offered to any deal that might be concocted in Manila: 'We have...made our views clear to the Tunku and understand him to be adopting an attitude that combines flexibility on points of detail with determination to resist concessions liable to damage Malaysia...We accordingly think it right to leave further negotiation to the Tunku.'[24]

[21] See Peters to Warner, 7 August 1963, D1075/58, FO 371/169725.
[22] FO to Washington, no. 7448, 3 August 1963, PREM 11/4349.
[23] Greenhill to Peck, 5 August 1963, D1075/59, FO 371/169725.
[24] Washington to FO, no. 2420, 2 August 1963; FO to Washington, no. 7440, 3 August 1963, D1075/22, FO 371/169724.

The American belief was that the intransigence of Sandys was the main obstacle to the successful outcome of the summit, while they also feared being faced with the prospect of bailing the British out if full-blown hostilities with Indonesia were to develop.[25] On 3 August, the President himself stepped in with a message to Macmillan:

I am quite concerned that hopefully successful Manila summit will be torpedoed unless 31 August date for Malaysia can be postponed briefly to give Sukarno a fig leaf. If in fact the Tunku is willing, and if there is a good chance Sukarno can be bought this cheaply, we would urge you give this an urgent look. I well realize that kowtowing to Sukarno is a risky enterprise, but a little give now may be worth the risk, especially if the likely alternative is a further step up of subversive pressures. This is your show, but I feel we ought to place our worries frankly before you.[26]

As British officials worked on a draft reply to Kennedy's message, de Zulueta commented to the Prime Minister that, 'The Americans are being very pro-Indonesian and seem to take the view that all Sukarno wants is "a fig leaf" but this seems rather an optimistic assessment... Of course we do not wish to be blamed for the breakdown of the Manila Conference but censure may be better than the collapse of Malaysia.'[27] While Sandys was firmly committed to the 31 August date, the Foreign Secretary was more reserved on the need to maintain a rigid stance, and argued from Moscow (where he was present, along with Rusk, for the signing of the Partial Test Ban Treaty) that,

Sukarno will cause us trouble after Malaysia, but if we agree to a small postponement to meet American wishes, we are more likely to obtain full American support afterwards. There is also the subsidiary point that we should not let the Tunku shuffle the blame on us for any possible failure to agree at the Manila Summit now for subsequent trouble with Indonesia.[28]

Nevertheless, Macmillan's reply to Kennedy held that any proposal put to the British as a result of the summit would be given 'careful consideration', but he 'did not believe Sukarno can be bought off with a fig leaf. He would need something much bigger to cover him effectively.' The Prime Minister warned that latest reports from Manila were that Sukarno was trying to obtain a veto on the use of foreign bases in the Maphilindo area and this was 'very dangerous for us all'. A delay would sow confusion and he suggested that the Tunku was 'battling hard' and should be allowed

[25] See e.g. DOS to Moscow (for Rusk), no. 6, 3 August 1963, POL 3 MALAYSIA, RG 59.
[26] Kennedy to Macmillan, T.430/63, 3 August 1963, in FO to Washington, no. 7462, 4 August 1963, PREM 11/4349.
[27] De Zulueta minute for Macmillan, 4 August 1963, *ibid.*
[28] Home to Macmillan, no. 1742, 4 August 1963, *ibid.*

to 'play his hand', concluding, 'There is an old French saying – what is postponed is lost.'[29]

As this transatlantic exchange was progressing, the UN Secretary General's new proposals had been cabled to the Manila talks. The inevitability of a postponement in Malaysia entailed by even a limited UN survey mission did not deter the Tunku from embracing the chance to reach agreement with the Indonesians and Filipinos. Hard bargaining over the precise wording of the final communique continued until the morning of 5 August. The text of the resulting Manila 'Joint Statement' has been called 'a masterpiece of evasion and compromise'.[30] Paragraph 4 of the statement made reference to the previous Manila Accord and called on the UN Secretary General or his representative to

ascertain prior to the establishment of the Federation of Malaysia the wishes of the people of Sabah (North Borneo) and Sarawak within the context of General Assembly resolution 1541 (XV), Principle 9 of the Annex, by a fresh approach, which in the opinion of the Secretary General is necessary to ensure complete compliance with the principle of self-determination within the requirements embodied in Principle 9, taking into consideration: The recent elections in Sabah and Sarawak...

The ascertainment process would consist of investigating the elections and determining whether Malaysia figured as a major issue, whether electoral registers were in order, and whether polling was conducted free from coercion and votes counted properly. The impact of the detention, imprisonment or absence of some electors in the Borneo territories was also to be assessed. Ambiguity surrounded the task laid out in the joint statement, while the reference to self-determination was blurred by the call for the UN Secretary General to concern himself merely with verifying the election results in the Borneo territories. The Malayan delegation also conceded to a provision in the joint statement for observers from the three Maphilindo countries to witness the work of the UN ascertainment mission, and agreed to endeavour to persuade the British to cooperate with this whole procedure. The wording of the Manila Accord and Joint Statement certainly gave considerable leeway to the Malayans on how seriously they would take the ascertainment process, which in any event could be argued was only to be carried out in order to allow Indonesia and the Philippines to 'welcome' the formation of Malaysia (a point Razak later claimed he had emphasized to the summit meeting). The Malayans were clearly confident that any UN ascertainment would find in favour of Malaysia.

[29] Macmillan to Kennedy, T.434/63, 4 August 1963, *ibid.*
[30] Mackie, *Konfrontasi*, 163.

Two other significant matters were addressed by the Manila Agreements. Indonesia's objections to the presence of British bases on Malaysian territory, and the freedom of action allowed them by the defence provisions of the London Agreement, were met in the Joint Statement by the agreement that 'foreign bases – temporary in nature – should not be allowed to be used directly or indirectly to subvert the national independence' of the Maphilindo countries, a formulation which was vague and noncommittal enough to satisfy everybody (including the Philippines with its large US bases). On the question of the Philippine claim to North Borneo, the earlier statement in the Manila Accord of June was reaffirmed, where it was agreed that the incorporation of North Borneo within Malaysia would not prejudice the claim itself, though no procedure was settled on to bring about a resolution of the outstanding issues. The form of the final Manila communique suggests that at this stage the Indonesians and Filipinos were happy to settle for a face-saving formula that would allow Malaysia to come into existence. But presented with the possible collapse of the summit, the Indonesians may have preferred to settle for the ambiguity of the procedure agreed upon, anticipating it would be enough to disrupt and cast doubt on Malaysia, divide the Malayans and the British, and unnerve the Borneo territories.

The feeling on the British side was that the Tunku had conceded more than was prudent at Manila (Sukarno, after all, had announced no end to the policy of confrontation). Reflecting on the reports from Manila, the Prime Minister noted on 5 August:

I fear that the Tunku may have had to yield to the Indonesians (which is what the Americans wanted). The President and the American machine are rather 'sold out' to the Indonesians, although their eyes have been opened a little by the recent Indonesian threat to the American as well as the British oil companies. However, I felt sure it was right to resist President Kennedy's attempt to make *us* propose a postponement. The Tunku would be quite ready, in that event, to shift the blame for failure on to us.[31]

To Kennedy, the Prime Minister had signalled, in somewhat disingenuous fashion:

...it looks as if you may have been right about Sukarno's fig leaf. However, it may have all have turned out for the best. The Tunku does seem to have made some concession, but I still feel it better that he should have done this on his own rather than at our instance. If anything had gone wrong he could certainly have put the blame on us: now we can hold his hand.[32]

[31] Diary entry, 5 August 1963, MSS. Macmillan dep. d.50.
[32] Macmillan to Kennedy, T.442/63, 6 August 1963, PREM 11/4349.

British concern that events were moving well beyond their control was heightened by the fact that on his return to Malaya on 6 August, the Tunku had publicly admitted that he was prepared to postpone Malaysia for a few days if the UN ascertainment mission could not finish its work before 31 August. Signalling to Tory in Kuala Lumpur, Sandys hoped that the Tunku could be more candid in explaining what was being asked of the British, 'to ensure that last act of this farce goes as successfully as can be expected'. The Commonwealth Secretary wanted no further talk of postponement, and furthermore was inclined to turn down the idea of allowing Indonesian and Philippine observers to accompany the UN survey in the Borneo territories.[33] Whitehall's interdepartmental view was that the government should accept the Manila proposals, on the assumptions that the Secretary General could complete his task in time to allow Malaysia Day to stand on 31 August and that his report was not subject to confirmation by the Indonesian and Philippines Governments. The overriding consideration in acceptance was the impact on American opinion; as Macmillan put it to Home: 'I do not think we should risk forfeiting future American support against Indonesia (which we shall certainly need notwithstanding this agreement) by adopting an intransigent attitude.'[34] The chances of the ascertainment being finished in time were known to be slim. Home had seen U Thant in Moscow on 6 August, who had explained that while General Assembly approval for the ascertainment procedure would not now be needed, he did not think an assessment and report could be completed before 14 September.[35]

The British moved quickly to reinforce their position and distance themselves from any commitment regarding the outcome of the UN survey of opinion. The Tunku was informed by Sandys that if the final UN report should prove to be unfavourable, the British Government would feel free to reject its conclusions, and to base their claim of self-determination on the Borneo election results.[36] Nevertheless, Sandys was further put out when on 8 August he received an appeal from the Malayan Prime Minister asking that U Thant be allowed a short period beyond 31 August to complete his survey.[37] Coming only a few days after the Tunku's assurances that no concession over postponement would be made, this constituted a blow to the British position, prompting Sandys to despatch another indignant cable to Tory in Kuala Lumpur: 'Before we can consider any

---

[33] Sandys to Tory, no. 1884, 6 August 1963, *ibid.*
[34] Peck minute, 5 August 1963; Macmillan to Home, T.443B/63, 6 August 1963, *ibid.*
[35] Home to FO, no. 1762, 6 August 1963, *ibid.*
[36] Sandys to Tunku Abdul Rahman (via UK High Commission Kuala Lumpur), no. 1893, 6 August 1963, *ibid.*
[37] Tunku Abdul Rahman to Sandys, no. 1493, 8 August 1963, DO 169/222.

question of postponement we require an absolutely firm undertaking from Tunku that he will go ahead with Malaysia on whatever later date may now be agreed between the signatories [to the London Agreement of July] irrespective of the nature of the Secretary General's report.' Sandys suggested that if the report was unfavourable, the Tunku could go ahead with Malaysia and then offer an after-the-event West Irian-style plebiscite in order to deflect some of the inevitable criticism. The Tunku would also have to be reminded that Britain still retained sovereignty and control in the Borneo territories, and that

> We cannot recognise that Manila Conference or anyone else has right to invite the Secretary General's representatives into territories for which we are still responsible... If we agree to receive teams it must be absolutely clear that we are doing so only at the special request which we have received from the Malayan Government in order to help them. This means that we do not wish ourselves to be associated with the request for an enquiry or with the eventual report. We do not wish the Secretary General's decision on the report to be addressed to us nor do we wish to be committed to recognising the validity of the findings.

Moreover, Sandys repeated his strong objections to any Indonesian and Philippine observers being allowed into the Borneo territories.[38] The Tunku's response to such pressure was to give a verbal undertaking to Tory that he would bring Malaysia into being whatever the final UN report might conclude, selecting 16 September as his new target date for the inauguration, saying he was 'prepared to face the consequences provided that [Britain] stood by him'. The presence of outside observers, the Tunku felt, was essential if Indonesian rejection of the Manila process was to be avoided.[39] For Sandys, this was not insurance enough, and he instructed Tory to return to the Tunku and obtain a written assurance of his intention to create Malaysia. On 10 August 1963 this assurance was given in a letter from the Tunku to Tory; presumably the British could, if necessary, threaten to make its contents public if there were more signs of wavering in the crucial days to come.[40] The arrangements being devised in New York by the UN Secretariat for the Borneo survey team gave the British some consolation for the frustrations that they had recently experienced. Although Narasimhan would not, in the event, lead the mission, the choice for the task of an American, Laurence Michelmore, the UN's Deputy Director of

---

[38] Sandys to Tory, no. 1926, 8 August 1963, *ibid.*
[39] Tory to Sandys, no. 1503, 9 August 1963, PREM 11/4349.
[40] Sandys to Tory, no. 1946, 10 August 1963; Tory to Sandys, no. 1514, 10 August 1963, *ibid.*

Personnel, was reassuring. Although George Janacek, a Czech, would act as Michelmore's deputy, he had been with the UN since 1946, and was felt to be impartial (though a heavy drinker), and would anyway be assigned to cover North Borneo, where opinion was more decisively clear-cut in favour of Malaysia. Narasimhan, for his part, would oversee the mission from the New York end, and was ready to assure the Americans, as Sir Patrick Dean put it, 'that the assessment teams will be hand picked to produce the right results from our point of view'.[41] Even on the question of observers, there was a belief now that they held little threat, and the Foreign Office appears to have been behind the suggestion to U Thant that two observer teams (one for Sarawak and one for North Borneo) could be allowed, with each team having one Indonesian, one Filipino and one Malayan member. The UN mission was to be shown every courtesy in the Borneo territories themselves. The Deputy Under Secretary at the Colonial Office cabled to Goode:

...we have good reason to think that [the] Secretary General's teams are being very carefully picked and I am quite sure that the right tactics for North Borneo and Sarawak will be to co-operate with them to the fullest and help them in every way. If this is done, I think the leaders of the teams themselves will help you to keep the observers in their place.[42]

The British, however, also wanted U Thant to agree that a new date for the creation of Malaysia of 14 September could now be stipulated, in accordance with his mission's timetable.[43] When British insistence that a new date for Malaysia be publicly named became clear, the Americans pressed that there should no such announcement, but British officials held firm.[44] On the part of U Thant there was great reluctance to commit himself in advance on the matter of timing, and he could offer no firm date to the British.

Reports of the Tunku's performance in Manila, and talk of a postponement in Malaysia, were not well received by the politicians in Singapore and the Borneo territories who had invested so much in the success of the scheme. The Legislative Council in North Borneo passed a motion rejecting any attempt to delay Malaysia and opposing the introduction of

[41] New York to FO, no. 1205, 8 August 1963, D1073/45, FO 371/169711.
[42] Martin to Goode, no. 802, 10 August 1963, DO 169/222.
[43] FO to New York, no. 2604, 9 August 1963, PREM 11/4349; the Foreign Office position on observers may have been due to American influence – on 6 August Hilsman had asked British officials in Washington that the introduction of observers should not be vetoed, see London to DOS, no. 653, 7 August 1963, POL 3 MALAYSIA, RG 59.
[44] Washington to FO, no. 2493, 10 August 1963; FO to Washington, no. 7767, 10 August 1963, PREM 11/4349.

any outside observers.[45] Lee Kuan Yew contacted Selkirk after the Manila meeting to express his indignation at both the incompetence of the Tunku and the weakness of the British in not standing firm with the Malayans.[46] One of Lee's provocative ideas was that Singapore, Sarawak and North Borneo should state their intention to proceed to separate independence on 31 August and wait for the Tunku to join them.[47] Donald Stephens had been receptive to such notions, but it appears at this stage that Ghazali, during a secret trip to Sarawak, managed to persuade Stephen Ningkan and the Sarawak Alliance to hold to the original plans.[48] On 14 August, Lee asserted publicly that Singapore would not be bound by the results of the Manila conference and that he would insist on independence on 31 August as provided by the London Agreement; within a few days he was visiting the Borneo territories in a fresh attempt to forge an arrangement on joint action. In Kuching, Lee gained the support of Ningkan and Stephens for his ideas on declaring independence, reportedly saying that the ball 'was at the feet of Sabah and Sarawak and it was up to them to kick it into goal'.[49] Already some of the internal tensions between the component parts of the future Malaysia were making themselves felt, with Lee Kuan Yew, above all, seeing the opportunity to line up non-Malay opposition to having affairs determined by the priorities of Kuala Lumpur.

The nine-man UN survey team finally arrived in Kuching on 16 August, with some of its members soon heading on to Jesselton.[50] It could not, however, begin its work of collecting evidence and convening meetings, as the observer issue had still to be settled, adding another layer of controversy to the already problematic nature of the mission. The Indonesians and Filipinos insisted that each Maphilindo country be allowed 20 officials and 10 assistants on the observer teams, numbers which the British regarded as suspiciously high, but which led them to counter with the proposal to raise their initial suggestion to permit four members, rather than two, from each country. There was also confusion over the status of the observers. U Thant had made clear that Michelmore's UN

---

[45] Goode to Sandys, no. 426, 8 August 1963, *ibid.*
[46] Singapore to DOS, no. 98, 6 August 1963; Singapore to DOS, no. 115, 12 August 1963, POL 3 MALAYSIA, RG 59.
[47] See Selkirk to Sandys, no. 554, 9 August 1963, DO 169/222. Selkirk was worried by the impression given by the Tunku of bowing to Sukarno at Manila and its impact on the Singapore Chinese, and could sympathize with Lee's attitude.
[48] See Singapore to DOS, no. 117, 12 August 1963; Singapore to DOS, no. 144, 19 August 1963, POL 3 MALAYSIA, RG 59.
[49] See Means, *Malaysian Politics*, 317; Osborne, *Malaysia and Singapore*, 67.
[50] Its members were Michelmore, Janacek, George Howard (Argentina), Neville Kanakateratne (Ceylon), Kenneth Dadzic (Ghana), Irshed Baqai (Pakistan), Abdel Dajani (Jordan), Jose Machado (Brazil), and Yasushi Akashi (Japan).

team was exclusively responsible to him, while its final report would not be subject to ratification or confirmation by any of the governments concerned. In contrast, the Indonesian and Philippine attitude seemed to be that their observers would consult with the UN team on its findings, while also keeping a watchful eye over the conduct of the British colonial authorities. On 23 August, the British accepted a compromise put forward by U Thant that involved allowing another four Indonesian and Filipino 'clerical assistants' to join the four official observers, provided that the observers were subject to the restrictions specified by the authorities in the Borneo territories. Indonesian and Filipino concurrence was forthcoming, and on 26 August Michelmore's mission was able to begin conducting interviews and hearings. The observers, though, had yet to arrive, as the British refused to grant the 17 visa requests made by the Indonesians for their members. The list supplied by the Indonesians had not only been too long, but contained several senior officials and known Indonesian intelligence officers; the Indonesians had also asked that they be allowed to use their own aircraft to transport their teams around the Borneo territories.[51]

British suspicions about the intentions and composition of the Indonesian observer teams were undoubtedly intensified by some of the intelligence reports they were receiving during this period. In the middle of August, the military attaché at the British Embassy in Jakarta was reporting that his Malayan counterpart had passed on what were purported to be the minutes of a meeting held on 14 August between Subandrio and Nasution. Here it was recorded that 'Operation A would continue' and that it was the aim of the Indonesians to send members of the Army intelligence staff, headed by Colonel Abdul Rachman, with the observers. The teams were to disrupt the work of the UN mission, organize anti-British and anti-Malayan propaganda, and make contact with the TNKU. The meeting concluded with the assertion that it was the Indonesian goal to end British influence in South East Asia.[52] Unsurprisingly, the British put in a request to know exactly who could be classed as 'clerical assistants' among the Indonesian and Filipino observers, and an impasse seems to have been reached.

From the Indonesian perspective, the British were doing all they could to sabotage the agreement concluded at Manila and were continuing to act in the manner of an arrogant colonial power, even in the final days of their formal rule. To the British, Indonesian behaviour suggested that

[51] Mackie, *Konfrontasi*, 170–3.
[52] Jakarta to FO, nos. 897 and 898, 16 August 1963, CO 1030/1529.

they were ready to wreck the UN ascertainment process, or at least allow them to denounce its results if the final report should confirm the desire for Malaysia, while the naming of intelligence officers among the observers was either another example of their subversive tendencies or a crude attempt at psychological warfare. Whatever the case, the omens did not appear good. On the day the Michelmore mission arrived in Kuching, Macmillan had seen Sandys and was noting dejectedly in his diary, 'The delay in "Malaysia" is *very* bad and there is a danger that the UN team may report unfavourably. What terrible troubles are caused by the UN. Yet, in some cases, I suppose it is useful. It is strongly *anti-white* in bias.' A few days later, the Prime Minister was complaining, 'Malaysia is going bad on us, owing to Tunku's weakness in giving in to Sukarno (the Americans, in spite of my strong telegram to President K [of 4 August], have been taking their usual line – support for enemies more than for friends. Cynics wd say that they learned this from the British!)'[53] Pessimism on the British side was also being increased by the fact that cross-border incidents in Sarawak had picked up during August. On 8 August an estimated seventy guerrillas had entered the Song district in the Third Division (leading to the deaths of one Gurkha officer and 15 Indonesians), while at Long Lopeng in the Fifth Division on 19 August another six Indonesians were captured 15 miles inside the border (with two security force casualties). Four days later five Indonesians were reported killed out of a party of thirty to forty in the Gumbang area of the First Division. One obvious inference was that recent incursions were designed to have some influence over the climate within which the UN ascertainment mission was carried out.

The most pressing need in such circumstances, from the British point of view, was to stiffen the Tunku's resolve. Therefore, the Commonwealth Secretary was despatched to Kuala Lumpur on 23 August, as he put it to Menzies, 'to hold the Tunku's hand. I am afraid he has rather lost his nerve just lately.'[54] The arrival of Sandys in Kuala Lumpur was an obvious and public sign of British hopes to stage manage the tricky reception of the UN mission's report and the announcement of a new date for Malaysia. The Tunku was described by Charles F. Baldwin, the US Ambassador to Malaya, as 'visibly unenthusiastic about visit of Sandys and colleagues...'[55] The tendency of the British to assume that he needed firm guidance and even instruction on appropriate action was

---

[53] Diary entries, 16 and 19 August 1963, MSS. Macmillan dep. d.50.
[54] Sandys to Menzies, no. 1571, 22 August 1963, PREM 11/4349.
[55] Kuala Lumpur to DOS, no. 162, 24 August 1963, POL 3 MALAYSIA, RG 59.

not appreciated by the Malayan Prime Minister; he confided to Baldwin that the British seemed

unable [to] agree with his own basic philosophy . . . which is that while it may be impossible [to] trust [the] Indos and possibly Phils every possible effort should be made to bring Malaysia into existence under peaceful conditions and fend off Indo hostility. While British may recognize [the] desirability [of] those objectives, their actions, Tunku said, seem primarily motivated at times by considerations of pride and prestige or by belief that Indos will misbehave regardless of what Malayans and British do.

The Tunku told the American Ambassador that he would be grateful for anything the Americans could do to 'persuade British to "have more confidence" in his ability [to] handle [the] situation'. Only a few hours earlier, Baldwin had heard Tory describe the Tunku as a 'foolish old man', while giving vent to his irritation over 'Malayan stubbornness'.[56] British attitudes, Roger Hilsman later recalled, helped to fuel perceptions of neo-colonialism, and 'they regarded the Tunku as a rather incompetent little brown brother who had to be protected from himself'.[57]

The first job faced by Sandys was to dissuade Ningkan and Stephens, who had flown to Kuala Lumpur with Lee Kuan Yew, from going ahead with their joint plans for the old Malaysia Day. The two Borneo leaders were pacified by the announcement on 23 August by Sir Alexander Waddell that Sarawak would attain full internal self-government on 31 August regardless of other developments, with the Governor saying he would automatically accept the advice of the new Chief Minister; this procedure would also be followed in North Borneo.[58] Having been given some assurances from Sandys that no more concessions would be forthcoming from the British side on the observer issue, Ningkan and Stephens indicated they would drop any ideas to coordinate action with Lee Kuan Yew by establishing a mini-Malaysia on 31 August.[59] Having met the Borneo politicians on 24 August, Sandys went on to see the Malayan Prime Minister to tell him, 'very frankly that we considered that we had not been properly consulted over the Manila Agreement and that this was the cause of most of the subsequent difficulties. I reminded him that we heartily disliked the idea of a UN enquiry in a British territory, which was without precedent.' The mistrust by now present between the

[56] Kuala Lumpur to DOS, no. 138, 16 August 1963, *ibid.* It should be noted that Tun Razak, in contrast to the Tunku, was widely seen by British officials as a steadfast, determined and reliable supporter of their position at this time.
[57] Hilsman, *To Move a Nation*, 399.
[58] Kuala Lumpur to DOS, no. 164, 24 August 1963, POL 3 MALAYSIA, RG 59. The grant of full self-government to Sarawak and North Borneo on 31 August prompted a protest from the Malayan Prime Minister, see Tunku Abdul Rahman to Macmillan, T.466/63, 2 September 1963, PREM 11/4350.
[59] Sandys to Tory, no. 1677, 24 August 1963, PREM 11/4349.

British minister and the Tunku was fully reflected in Sandys's account of the exchange which followed where the Malayan leader

reaffirmed that he intended to bring in Malaysia irrespective of what the Secretary General's report might say. I told him that I had been informed that he had told the Representatives from North Borneo and Sarawak [Stephens and Ningkan] only a few hours earlier that if the report was unfavourable Malaysia would have to be abandoned. He seemed a little embarrassed and said they must have misunderstood him. But I have no doubt that this is what he did say to them since they all told me that this had greatly disturbed them.

The Tunku went on to explain that the Malayan Government still wanted flexibility, hoping that the date for Malaysia could be any time before 30 September, but after Sandys had adamantly opposed any wavering on the issue, the Tunku committed himself to 16 September (though the Commonwealth Secretary evidently remained unconvinced).[60]

Two days later, Sandys and the Tunku clashed again, the former describing it as the 'most difficult meeting I [have] ever had with him', the Malayan Prime Minister being in a 'highly emotional and touchy state'. The Tunku informed Sandys and Tory that he proposed sending a telegram to Subandrio inviting him to Singapore to review the situation in direct talks. The Commonwealth Secretary objected to this move, arguing that it would seem to the peoples of the Borneo territories that he was appeasing Indonesia and abandoning Malaysia; the evidence given to Michelmore's UN team could even be influenced by such wavering. According to Sandys, the Tunku was

very intractable and said he must be allowed to conduct his relations with Indonesia in his own way. This was *his* 'cold war' which he must handle as he thought best. If things went wrong there would be a 'hot war' which *we* would have to deal with. He went so far as to say that it was no concern of the British what he said to Subandrio... all the anxiety in the Borneo territories merely showed the silliness of the local inhabitants who were very immature; and that they should trust him.

The Malayan Prime Minister concluded the meeting by saying: 'I have reached the end of my tether and I do not want to discuss anything further with anybody.' Both Sandys and Tory had 'got the impression that the Tunku realised that at Manila and since he had been guilty of failure to consult us as he should have and that he knew quite well that his efforts to appease Indonesia had lost him a good deal of respect inside and outside his country'.[61]

Despite this inauspicious encounter, the Malayan Cabinet meeting that followed later the same day produced agreement on a tougher line,

[60] Sandys to CRO, SOSLON no. 62, 27 August 1963, DO 169/216.
[61] *Ibid.*

probably due to the influence of Razak and Ghazali. Subandrio would be invited to Singapore, but to meet Razak rather than the Tunku, who would explain that no concessions could be expected on the observer issue and that a public announcement was to be made on 29 August that the federation of Malaysia would be established on 16 September. Subandrio turned down the invitation, but instead invited Razak to Jakarta, though in the event it was Ghazali who was sent, arriving in the Indonesian capital on 29 August. Subandrio's apparent indifference at receiving the news from Ghazali that Kuala Lumpur was about to announce that the formation of Malaysia was to be set for 16 September appears curious in retrospect. In fact, the Indonesian Foreign Minister suggested that the first of the regular high-level consultative meetings provided for under the Maphilindo agreement might take place in Kuala Lumpur in October. One reason for this muted initial response may have been that Subandrio had asked Ghazali that the Malayan Government should make its official announcement in a way that did not preempt the findings of the UN survey.

The official statement from Kuala Lumpur (released simultaneously by London) was hardly in accordance with such a wish, and as he left Jakarta, Ghazali reiterated to the assembled press that the formation of Malaysia was not conditional on the UN team's final report. The following day, Howard Jones saw Sukarno, the Ambassador recording that he was in a rage, crying that he had been 'duped and humiliated by the British... I will not take it!' It was not until 3 September that strong official protests were delivered from the Indonesian and Philippine Governments, the former calling the naming of a new Malaysia Day a 'reckless and premature decision' and alleging that the announcement violated the Manila Agreements (a later Indonesian claim, which the UN Secretary General, for one, felt contained some validity, was that the Tunku had extended a secret pledge in Manila to delay the formation of Malaysia to 30 September). Nevertheless, despite the protests, the Malayans continued to argue that their actions did not contravene the Manila Agreements, as the UN mission's only purpose was to allow Indonesia and the Philippines to 'welcome' Malaysia.[62] One substantive result to emerge from Ghazali's trip to Jakarta was a resolution of the observer issue. The Indonesians had put forward a revised list of observers, which excluded the two senior intelligence officers previously listed as 'clerical assistants' and acceded to the idea that they would have to use British-provided air

[62] See Mackie, *Konfrontasi*, 174–5; Jones, *Indonesia*, 288–9. For U Thant's views on the existence of a secret pledge, see New York to FO, no. 1432, 12 September 1963, PREM 11/4350.

transport. This was accepted by the British authorities, finally allowing the Indonesian and Filipino observer teams to arrive in Kuching and Jesselton on 1 September, in time to witness only the last few days of the UN mission's work (final hearings were held on 3 and 4 September).[63]

The announcement of a new Malaysia Day, and the reported views of Ghazali and Sandys that an unfavourable UN report would have no effect on this event, was greeted with despondency in Washington. Harriman protested once more in a 'roughly worded' letter to Sandys about the inflexibility of the British position, while US officials worried about the effect on the prestige of the UN and the Secretary General if one of its leading members brushed aside the results of a survey the British had themselves accepted.[64] Commenting on Sandys's performance, Hilsman would tell a senior British official, who was also a friend, that, 'I knew that some of the people I would have to deal with in this job were going to be emotional. But I never dreamed that among the most emotional of all would be some Anglo-Saxons.' The Briton replied that, 'John Bull is the national symbol ... but there are few Englishmen who are more like this one in the china shop.'[65]

Sandys's work in the 'china shop' of South East Asia was far from over. Indeed, over the two weeks preceding the new Malaysia Day, the British were faced with a bewildering array of problems and disputes that threatened to derail the whole federal edifice just before it came into precarious life. Most of the difficulty arose over the familiar issues of Singapore's position within the new structures and Lee Kuan Yew's desire to prove his own confident powers of leadership. On 31 August, he reneged on a promise given to Sandys only the day before by unilaterally announcing that he was transferring all reserve powers held by the British to himself.[66] Although the declaration had no legal validity and in practical terms had no real meaning, it was an open challenge to London's authority. Yet the British realized that they could hardly act decisively against Lee at such a critical moment, while suspending the constitution and assuming direct rule, which would mean, according to Selkirk, 'virtually a military reoccupation of Singapore', was hardly credible in the anti-colonial atmosphere of the day.[67]

---

[63] See material in D1073/165G, FO 371/169717.

[64] Harriman to Sandys, 28 August 1963; Harriman to Sandys, 29 August 1963, D103145/11, FO 371/169888; Warner to Trench, 2 September 1963, D1073/165G, FO 371/169717; DOS to London, no. 1369, 29 August 1963, POL 3 MALAYSIA, RG 59.

[65] Hilsman, *To Move a Nation*, 404.

[66] Sandys to CO, no. 130, 1 September 1963, PREM 11/4350.

[67] See Selkirk to Sandys, OCULAR no. 651, 5 September 1963; Sandys to Macmillan, SOSLON no. 109, 5 September 1963, *ibid.*

Lee followed up this announcement by dissolving the Singapore Assembly on 3 September, paving the way for fresh elections. Privately, Lee also threatened the British that he would declare separate independence for Singapore on 12 September unless aspects of the London Agreement on Malaysia were not revised or clarified to his satisfaction.[68] Macmillan gloomily noted in his diary: 'Telegrams rather bad from SE Asia. I have told Duncan Sandys to stay in Malaysia till the day. But (a) what will the UN say? (b) what will Singapore Chinese do. Once again, how much more difficult it is to get rid of an Empire than to win it.'[69] The British had to contemplate on one hand the prospect of a Barisan victory, with disastrous consequences for Malaysia and their bases, while on the other they had to contend with the assertive and restless figure of Lee, whose ambitions could also prejudice the new federation.[70] Worrying also was the idea of a physical confrontation between Lee and the Malayan authorities if they tried to assume federal powers in Singapore on 16 September after he had declared independence.[71]

British officials and ministers were quite clear that Lee's actions represented a bold and ruthless bid for power in the new Malaysia. The Singapore Prime Minister already believed he had the measure of the Tunku, and following the latter's apparent submission at Manila, Lee felt that by an uncompromising stand at this crucial juncture he could improve his own position and extract more concessions from the Malayans. In Sandys's opinion, Lee was

unashamedly exploiting the delay in the establishment of Malaysia to further his personal ambitions. Political blackmail or 'brinkmanship' (as he described it to me himself) is his normal method of achieving his ends. While expressing enthusiasm for Malaysia, his objective is to show up the Tunku as feeble and wooly [sic] minded and to build up his own reputation as a tough, clear sighted leader whose will it would be dangerous for anyone to oppose. He speaks freely about his wish to get rid of the Tunku within the next two or three years when his usefulness has been exhausted. Although he professes to believe that a Chinaman could not become Prime Minister of Malaysia, I have little doubt that is his goal.

However, given the circumstances in which the British found themselves, both the Commonwealth Secretary and Selkirk could advocate little else but that Lee's demands should be met (they were, in any case, reckoned to be relatively minor matters compared to the larger issues at

---

[68] K. J. Ratnam and R. S. Milne, *The Malayan Parliamentary Election of 1964* (Singapore, 1967), 322; and see Lee Kuan Yew, *Singapore Story*, 498–9.
[69] Macmillan diary, 7 September 1963, MSS. Macmillan dep. d.50.
[70] See e.g. de Zulueta minute for Macmillan, 3 September 1963, PREM 11/4350.
[71] See Sandys to Macmillan, SOSLON no. 109, 5 September 1963, *ibid.*

stake).[72] Several days' hard argument followed, but eventually, on 11 September, agreement was reached, with the Malayan side giving ground on the outstanding matters of contention.[73] On the following day, when election nominations for candidates closed in Singapore, Lee was able to announce the resolution of his remaining grievances and to set polling day for 21 September, allowing the minimum time in law for campaigning.

While last-minute arrangements were put in hand for the inauguration of Malaysia, and while Lee was manoeuvring for political supremacy in Singapore, Michelmore's UN ascertainment mission completed its task in Sarawak and North Borneo. Its arrival in Kuching had been greeted with crowds shouting anti-Malaysia slogans and carrying anti-Malaysia posters, and hostile street receptions accompanied it around Sarawak (with riots at Sibu and Miri), despite the fact that on 14 August the colonial authorities had banned all rallies and demonstrations during the mission's time in the territory.[74] The UN teams were reportedly unimpressed with such shows of popular feeling, the Ghanaian member noting at Kuching that the protesters were all Chinese and '90 per cent under 21 years of age'.[75] In what could only have been a rather cursory process, the UN team interviewed local politicians in the Borneo territories and spoke to recently elected members of the Legislative Councils. They received the general impression that the elections had been fair and that Malaysia had figured as a major issue. Of course, by the summer of 1963 the only organized party opposition to Malaysia came from some members of the Pasok Momogun in North Borneo and SUPP in Sarawak, while there was no consideration of the impact on the election results of the use of a complicated three-tier indirect voting system. Many wards in North Borneo had gone uncontested and only 74,633 of a registered electorate of 160,000 had actually cast votes. In a submission given to the survey team by SUPP, the idea that the 1963 Sarawak elections provided endorsement for Malaysia was challenged on the basis that they were

<hr/>

[72] See *ibid.*, and Selkirk to Sandys, OCULAR, no. 651, 5 September 1963; Macmillan to Sandys, LONSOS no. 171, 6 September 1963, PREM 11/4350. For the view of the key protagonist, see Lee Kuan Yew, *Singapore Story*, 498–503.
[73] See Sandys to Macmillan, SOSLON, no. 139, 11 September 1963, PREM 11/4350; Kuala Lumpur to DOS, no. 218, 9 September 1963, POL 3 MALAYSIA, RG 59; *Supplementary Agreement Relating to Malaysia*, 11 September 1963, supplement to Cmnd. 2094 (London, 1963).
[74] See Chin Ung-Ho, *Chinese Politics in Sarawak*, 79; the riots at Sibu were reported to have involved 3,000 demonstrators, see *The Times* (including photographs), 2 September 1963.
[75] Singapore to DOS, no. 144, 19 August 1963, NSF, countries, Malaya–Singapore, 12/62–8/63, JFKL.

local council elections, where local and racial issues had predominated, and that where Malaysia had figured, in the urban areas, SUPP had won heavy majorities; in some constituencies there had been no SUPP candidate and hence no way to register doubts about Malaysia. SUPP argued that a referendum was the only sure way to determine the state of local opinion, but to no avail.[76] The day after the UN team had attended its initial meeting, on 5 September the Council Negri in Sarawak endorsed the London Agreement on Malaysia by 31 votes in favour to 5 votes (all SUPP) against. Michelmore's mission also looked at the question of detainees and concluded the small numbers prevented from campaigning or voting would have had no impact on the final results.[77]

Indications that the Michelmore mission would report favourably on the desires of the peoples of North Borneo and Sarawak for Malaysia were received with some relief in London and Kuala Lumpur, and contrasted with a degree of disbelief at the likely outcome in Jakarta. Sandys had actually drafted the text of a statement rejecting the UN report if it should prove negative, standing by previous British assertions that opinion had been thoroughly investigated in the past, and that the Manila Agreement had not made Malaysia conditional on the UN ascertainment of opinion.[78] U Thant gave advance and confidential notice of the contents of the report to the concerned parties in New York on 11 September, and Sir Patrick Dean was soon telling the Foreign Office that it 'appears to be a solid piece of work and does not appear to contain much ammunition for the Indonesians even in the case of Sarawak'. As Sandys moved to issue a statement from Kuching welcoming the Secretary General's report, U Thant was berated by the Indonesian and Philippine representatives at the UN who doubted the impartiality of Michelmore and questioned the speed and superficial nature of the report, as well as the restrictions placed on their observers.[79] In an attempt to forestall any strong and public response from Indonesia and the Philippines, on 10 September Greenhill had seen Harriman to urge that the Americans make a public declaration of support and welcome for Malaysia assuming the UN report was favourable. The US officials present seemed to agree and suggested that advance private warning be given to Jakarta and Manila of the US declaration. Accordingly on 13 September, Kennedy sent personal messages to Sukarno and Macapagal, informing them of US intentions. Robert Komer had found the original State Department drafts of these 'utterly anodyne' and had added a stiffer tone to the effect

[76] Chin Ung-Ho, *Chinese Politics in Sarawak*, 80.
[77] See Mackie, *Konfrontasi*, 176.
[78] Sandys to CRO, SOSLON no. 136, 11 September 1963, PREM 11/4350.
[79] See FO to New York, no. 531, 13 September 1963, and New York to FO, no. 1431, 13 September 1963, *ibid.*

that 'if they went down the wrong Malaysia road we simply could *not* give them aid...', while also adding the prospect of a presidential visit in 1964 to sweeten the pill.[80] However, Howard Jones's efforts to moderate Indonesian behaviour only managed to produce a response from Sukarno that he could not consider an unfavourable UN report a fair test of opinion (and elicited the comment from Macmillan, when learning of such approaches: 'Are the Americans going on with their policy of unsuccessful bribery?').[81]

The Secretary General's report was made public on 14 September. U Thant's conclusions were that a sizeable majority of the peoples of Sabah (North Borneo) and Sarawak had given serious thought to the implications of their participation in Malaysia and favoured joining such an enlarged federation. There were also critical words for the Malayan and British Governments, with the Secretary General expressing some resentment over the tight deadlines for the ascertainment process, regret over the delay on the observer issue, and his unhappiness that the date for Malaysia Day had been fixed before his findings had been made known.[82] Nevertheless, the report represented a powerful endorsement of the British and Malayan arguments over opinion in the Borneo territories, and the onus was now on Jakarta and Manila to 'welcome' Malaysia into existence. Hopes that confrontation might now be brought to an amicable end were, however, to be comprehensively dashed in the days that followed.

On the morning of 15 September, Jones was summoned to meet Sukarno, the Ambassador making entreaties to the Indonesians to show restraint, accept Malaysia and work within the ideals of Maphilindo. The Indonesian President grew steadily more agitated and interrupted to say, '"I cannot accept it. It is true I joined in asking UN to ascertain public opinion in Kalimantan. But we specified certain procedures which were not carried out."' Sukarno specifically mentioned that the UN team had given insufficient attention to the issue of detainees, and had interviewed only four such individuals. The Ambassador's efforts to coax out of Sukarno other ways in which he considered the survey inadequate were met with an 'emotional outburst on subject of how colonial powers controlled elections. "I know this game...I have seen the Dutch play it. Interview head men of tribes. Interview local officials. Interview people while soldiers with bayonets stand by. What do you expect? No, no, no.

---

[80] See FO to Washington, no. 8981, 9 September 1963; Washington to FO, no. 2813, 10 September 1963, *ibid.*; memorandum of conversation, 10 September 1963, *FRUS, 1961–1963, XXIII*, 725–7; Komer memorandum for Bundy, 17 September 1963, NSF, countries, Indonesia, 9/63, JFKL.
[81] Macmillan's aside is on Jakarta to FO, no. 1097, 13 September 1963, PREM 11/4870.
[82] See Hilsman, *To Move a Nation*, 403.

I will not accept it. I will accept a real test but not this." '[83] The argument that the UN enquiry had deviated from the Manila Agreements in its procedures was reiterated by Subandrio on the same day in the official Indonesian statement on the report. Indonesia could not endorse the birth of Malaysia and would not recognize it, while only a 'corrected' UN enquiry based on the Manila Agreements could allow Indonesian acceptance of the formation of Malaysia.[84] The Philippines also refused to recognize Malaysia on the basis of the UN enquiry's findings.

Tempers were by now running high in both Jakarta and Kuala Lumpur. Mass meetings were held in the Indonesian capital on 15 September by the 'Central Youth Front', and the following day, when Malaysia was officially born, a crowd of 10,000 demonstrators marched to the Malayan Embassy to present resolutions which objected to the UN survey. Their representatives were received graciously by a senior Embassy official, who listened to their grievances and explained the Ambassador's absence (he was seeing Subandrio to be told that Indonesia did not recognize a 'Malaysian' Embassy in Jakarta). Some stones were thrown and windows broken, but the crowd soon headed off towards the British Embassy, which was under police guard, where a delegation demanded to see the British Ambassador, Sir Andrew Gilchrist. They arrived outside the brand-new building and began to unleash a barrage of stones at its tempting large plate glass windows, smashing, so the Ambassador meticulously noted, all 938 of them. The crowd were next treated to the spectacle of the uniformed assistant military attache, Major Roderick ('Red Rory') Walker, emerging from the building to march up and down the Embassy compound while playing the bagpipes, in a bizarre example of late imperial gusto.[85]

An argument then ensued between the demonstrators and an Embassy official over the number of delegates that might be admitted to present their protests to Gilchrist; frustrated members of the crowd then broke into the Embassy compound, managing to tear down the British flag, and tow away the Ambassador's car, both of which were burnt. (Beside Gilchrist's comment, 'The charred corpse of my poor old Princess is causing an elegant traffic jam', Macmillan noted: 'I hope the historian will not misunderstand this paragraph.')[86] Gilchrist finally agreed to see some of the protestors amid the broken glass of his Embassy, but their

---

[83] Jakarta to DOS, no. 530, 15 September 1963, NSF, countries, Indonesia 9/63, JFKL.
[84] Mackie, *Konfrontasi*, 183; see also Jones, *Indonesia*, 290–2.
[85] Jakarta to FO, nos. 1120 and 1122, 16 September 1963, PREM 11/4310. Walker was an ex-SAS man who earlier in his career had led his troops (again playing the pipes) against 8,000 tribesmen in Oman.
[86] Jakarta to FO, no. 1133, 17 September 1963, *ibid.*

exchange only added to the tension, and the combative Scot was not concerned to hide his disdain for the Indonesians. Having denounced the UN Secretary General, the delegation departed, crying 'Hidup [long live] Sukarno!', while the Ambassador shouted back 'Hidup U Thant.' All the while, British appeals for the Indonesian police present to intercede in a forceful manner fell on unresponsive ears; Gilchrist reported: 'At no point did the police use physical force against the mob: the most they did was to wave rifles at them in a meaningless way. Tear gas was available but was not used. It was clearly intended by the authorities that the mob should have a good run for its money.'[87] The Indonesians later claimed that Walker's bagpipe playing had preceded the stone throwing, and that British behaviour had been unnecessarily provocative. The Ambassador was keen to refute such charges, and his own diary notes read: 'Sitting at desk, stones through window. Very soon all gone, planned with care. Pipes/Walker 10 minutes later when Embassy already wrecked. After 30 minutes Princess dragged out and ruined, took pictures. Delegation allowed in. They complained of UN report, gave me opportunity to say Hidup U Thant. Glass thick, reporters present. Flag down.'[88] Nevertheless, the unfortunate impression soon spread of arrogant and overbearing British officials adopting a colonial attitude to the genuine feelings of ordinary Indonesians concerned over the future of their neighbours in Borneo.

The temperature was raised a few degrees the following day by events in Kuala Lumpur. With Indonesian officials putting out the ambiguous line that although they were refusing to recognize Malaysia this did not amount to a severance of relations with *Malaya*, Malaysia announced it was breaking relations with Indonesia and the Philippines, and ordered its diplomatic staff home. At midday, about 300 members of the self-styled 'Malayan Peoples Action Group' (drawn from UMNO's youth wing) marched on the Indonesian Embassy with banners calling Sukarno a tool of the PKI. The police presence did not deter the crowd from growing increasingly unruly; stones and firecrackers were thrown, Embassy windows broken and demonstrators entered the compound, where a small shed was set ablaze. Some reports actually had protestors entering the Embassy building itself; in any event, the Indonesian Garuda shield was removed from the front of the Embassy as the police pushed the mob back. Subsequent events are confused, but it seems the emblem was tied to the back of a car and towed through the streets followed by chanting

---

[87] Jakarta to FO, no. 1127, 16 September 1963, *ibid.*; Mackie, *Konfrontasi*, 185–6; Jones, *Indonesia*, 262. The British consulate at Medan on Sumatra was also completely destroyed on 16 September.
[88] Diary notes, 16 September 1963, file 13A, Gilchrist papers.

protestors. The procession eventually made its way to the Tunku's official residence, where he came to meet the mob at the entrance, who cheered 'Hidup Tunku', lifted him to their shoulders and lowered him to the ground, from where he stepped onto the crest. The Tunku was moved to tears by the crowd's gesture, but cautioned them to leave matters for the government to handle, while telling them 'You can take that (crest) away and bury it.' Despite the efforts to suppress the Tunku's remarks, the local Reuters correspondent filed a report containing them and stories (with many extra embellishments) were soon circulating of this episode.[89]

Inflamed Indonesian opinion spilled over on 18 September when several truckloads of young activists turned up outside the now windowless British Embassy in Jakarta in the early afternoon. They entered the building and watched by horrified Embassy staff began to set fire to its contents and tried to seize documents. Gilchrist returned from lunch with Walker to see a pillar of smoke rising from his Embassy, and ordering the latter to save the car they were driving, he joined the Embassy staff huddled in a corner of the compound. Here they remained for several hours, while their building was ransacked and gutted by fire and the mob threw the occasional bottle or stone their way, until the police finally arrived in force to begin ferrying away the British personnel to a safer area. That evening British-owned homes, businesses and cars in Jakarta were systematically attacked by groups equipped with accurate information of their whereabouts. British companies and offices were meanwhile beginning to be taken over by their Indonesian workers under the direction of PKI-aligned trade unions; over the next forty-eight hours reports arrived of further attacks on Shell installations on Sumatra and in Kalimantan, and of takeovers of the large British rubber estates in western Java. Amid PKI calls for the nationalization of all British firms, the government, probably alarmed by the process that had been set in train, officially took the seized properties into 'protective custody' and ended worker control, though ambiguity over the position of British investments continued into the following year. On 21 September, the Indonesian authorities announced that they were severing all trade links with Malaysia, including their crucial commercial ties to Singapore, giving a fresh economic dimension to confrontation.[90]

The role of the Indonesian Government in these episodes has been the subject of considerable speculation. The British were convinced that the organization and direction of the demonstrators was officially inspired,

[89] This reconstruction is based on Kuala Lumpur to DOS, no. 253, 17 September 1963, and Kuala Lumpur to DOS, no. 259, 18 September 1963, POL 25–3 MALAYSIA, RG 59.
[90] Mackie, *Konfrontasi*, 191–3.

and that the destruction of the British Embassy and the moves against British enterprises and property were a carefully calculated raising of the pressures of confrontation, and a warning of what the British could expect in the future. Certainly Sukarno is known to have been outraged at the Tunku's alleged insult to the symbol of Indonesia, and would probably have wanted to see some response stage-managed. Yet it is improbable that Sukarno or his ministers were in complete control of events, and more likely that they were nervous of the political and social tensions that their policies had unleashed. The stabilization programme introduced earlier in the year (largely to attract Western financial assistance) was the subject of bitter comment from the PKI, who were keen to break free of its requirements and launch a more concerted drive against the remaining neo-colonial influences afflicting Indonesia. In contrast, middle-class Indonesians, religious elites and the Army had no desire to see the country turned over to mob rule and were anxious that the PKI should not be allowed to dictate developments. Indonesians may have been steadfastly opposed to the creation of Malaysia, but the methods that were employed in the anti-Malaysia struggle, and the domestic consequences they could produce in the form of a radicalization of society, had to be carefully watched. As ever, Sukarno was caught in the middle of this conundrum, and lacking any strong organizational base, he had to tack his personal position according to the prevailing wind and attempt to maintain his grip on power as the ultimate arbiter in the factional disputes that beset Indonesian political life. In an effort to prevent the situation deteriorating completely, on 19 September Sukarno had issued a statement which conveyed disapproval and regret for the events of the previous day and warned against further unauthorized actions, while in London, the Indonesian Ambassador dissociated his Government from the mob violence and guaranteed that the lives and property of British subjects would be safeguarded.

From the British perspective, such assurances were not likely to assuage their firm belief that Sukarno was set on an expansionist course. Even before the Embassy incidents, Warner was noting that 'the removal of American and British forces from the whole Maphilindo and South East Asia area is now the principal aim of Indonesian policy'.[91] The events surrounding the birth of Malaysia confirmed that the 'phoney war' during the summer of Manila-centred diplomacy was over, and the immediate Indonesian challenge in the Borneo territories would have to be forcefully met. Most officials were now resigned to writing off the UK commercial stake in Indonesia (amounting to about £160 million). The

[91] Warner minute, 6 September 1963, DH103145/11, FO 371/169888.

very real nature of the Indonesian threat was underlined at the end of September, by the most serious border incursion experienced to date in Sarawak, when a group of 200 troops overwhelmed an outpost at Long Jawai, 50 miles inside the territory's Third Division.[92] The 1/2nd Gurkha Rifles were quickly deployed to the area, and engaged in a highly success-ful interception of the Indonesian raiders, but the action so deep within Sarawak was a graphic demonstration of Indonesia's capacity to continue to carry out harassing operations. Such incidents also added to fears over the stability of the Borneo territories and the viability of the whole Malaysian edifice. The security forces were concerned over the possi-bility that CCO strength in Sarawak might be significantly augmented by new recruits and training from Kalimantan, and the presence of so many Indonesian migrant workers on the estates around Tawau in North Borneo was also seen as a major subversive threat.

On the political front there was a recognition that the pro-Malaysia Borneo political leaders would need firm support from Kuala Lumpur in their efforts to reassure the local populations that they would be ade-quately defended and that they would not be 'sold out' to the Indonesians. The Tunku's performance during the summer of 1963 was hardly reas-suring in this regard, and more worrying still to British officials was the Malayan Prime Minister's feeling that the concessions made to Lee had been a step too far (while the Commonwealth Secretary was clearly not his favourite British minister). 'I understand unofficially that Mr Sandys' victory has been rather a Pyrrhic one,' de Zulueta minuted to the Prime Minister, continuing: 'The Tunku apparently indicated that he would do whatever the British wanted but that he washed his hands of the results. In other words, he no longer feels personally responsible for Malaysia and if he can do a deal with the Indonesians by himself, he will.'[93] This was almost certainly an exaggeration, but the discontent felt by the Borneo politicians regarding Malayan attitudes and performance was reflected in the interest they displayed in the various overtures made by Lee Kuan Yew for them to join with Singapore in creating a mini-Malaysia rather than waiting for a vacillating Malayan Government. Indeed, there were signs that Ningkan and Stephens considered Lee to be a potential na-tional leader.[94] All this had serious implications for the Tunku's political strategy within a future Malaysia, for continued UMNO Alliance domi-nation in the Federation depended on the Borneo political parties (who would hold almost a third of the seats in the Malaysian Parliamentary

[92] See Robert Jackson, *The Malayan Emergency: The Commonwealth's Wars, 1948–1966* (London, 1991), 124–5.
[93] De Zulueta minute for Macmillan, 11 September 1963, PREM 11/4350.
[94] See e.g. Singapore to DOS, no. 247, 9 September 1963, POL 3 MALAYSIA, RG 59.

Assembly) being relatively acquiescent and ready to respond, in the last resort, to claims and fears about the Chinese role in Malaysian national life. Instead, the Tunku's behaviour had done much to alienate local opinion in the Borneo territories (not least through a major dispute over the efforts of the Sarawak Alliance to select an Iban as Sarawak's first head of state, rather than accept Kuala Lumpur's choice of a Malay candidate), while the origins of Lee's later calls in 1964 for an inclusive and genuinely 'Malaysian Malaysia' can already be glimpsed in his handling of affairs in the lead-up to the launch of the new federation.[95]

Evident also was Lee's determination to move quickly to consolidate his position and embrace the new political configurations and possibilities for electoral realignments that Malaysia presented. Singapore's own state elections were carefully staged on 21 September, their snap timing allowing only the barest minimum period (just over four days) for the opposition Barisan to conduct their campaign. They were additionally handicapped by the fact that many of their key leaders were still in detention following Cold Store, or preparing their cases before coming to trial, while the party had great problems securing sites for rallies, conducting canvassing and printing election literature in view of the tight restrictions imposed by the authorities. Most crucially the government dominated the mass media outlets, and with the inauguration of Malaysia taking place five days before polling, could campaign on the fulfilment of their earlier goal of bringing about 'independence through merger'. The election gave the PAP 47 per cent of the vote and 37 seats in the Singapore Assembly, while the Barisan picked up 33 per cent and 13 seats. The Singapore Alliance, which included UMNO and MCA candidates (and would have expected to gain support from Singapore's Malay voters), failed to win a single seat. Immediately after the elections, the new federal authorities, who now, of course, had responsibility for internal security, began to make preventive arrests among Barisan supporters at Nanyang University, while a strike on 8 October by the Association of Trade Unions precipitated more action, including the arrest of three recently elected Assemblymen.[96] The days of political dissent in Singapore were clearly numbered, and having consolidated his base in Singapore, Lee looked forward to making inroads in the Tunku's parliamentary strength, by introducing PAP candidates into Malaya itself (and drawing off votes from the MCA) during the Malaysian federal elections that were due in 1964.

[95] See Waddell to Sandys, no. 490, 30 August 1963, PREM 11/4349; Sandys to Waddell, no. 1797, 1 September 1963, Sandys to CRO, SOSLON no. 152, 13 September 1963, PREM 11/4350.

[96] There are good appraisals of the 1963 Singapore elections in Osborne, *Singapore and Malaysia*, and Ratnam and Milne, *The Malayan Parliamentary Election of 1964*.

The complex internal political dynamics thrown up by the formation of Malaysia, and that were to make its future operation so problematic, were matched by the uncertainties surrounding its external environment. The Defence Agreement with Britain provided some assurance that Indonesian military confrontation would be met forcefully in the jungles of Borneo, but wider international support still had to be garnered. To decision-makers in London, as had been clear from the beginning of 1963, the key to this particular problem lay with the attitudes of the Kennedy Administration in Washington. Faced with the prospect of a prolonged confrontation against Malaysia, the British would need, once again, to persuade the Americans to use what leverage they had in Jakarta to put pressure on the Indonesians. A conciliatory response to Jakarta's threats and blandishments was only likely to encourage further demands and weaken the legitimacy of the federation in the eyes of international opinion and its own anxious populace. British officials knew, however, that in their attempts to convert the line adopted by the Americans towards Indonesia since 1961, they would be facing an uphill task.

While there was genuine American sympathy with the plight of British companies, dependants and diplomatic personnel in Indonesia, as well as an appropriate protest at lack of action to prevent the destruction of the British Embassy in Jakarta, senior State Department officials were not willing to step into an open clash with Sukarno at this stage, and were indeed annoyed that British plans, policies and actions had frustrated their own aspirations for what was still seen as the most significant country in the region.[97] In Washington itself it was Harriman who was regarded by British officials as the main obstacle to a change of American emphasis, someone who was 'surprisingly lenient towards Sukarno's political faults' and who regarded Malaysia 'as a scissors and paste job by Her Majesty's Government'.[98] From Jakarta, notwithstanding the doubts of some of his own staff, Howard Jones remained, as another British official put it, 'unalterably convinced that all Sukarno desired was to be treated as an important Asian leader and that, provided his vanity was continuously flattered, he would ultimately act in the interests of the West'.[99]

When David Ormsby Gore, the British Ambassador in Washington, saw Harriman and Hilsman immediately after the Embassy incidents to explain the 'impossibility of dealing rationally' with the Indonesians and the need to discontinue current US aid, he was rebuffed. Indeed, Harriman reacted very strongly against any notions the British might

[97] See e.g. Jones, *Indonesia*, 263.
[98] Greenhill to Warner, 16 August 1963, DH103145/9, FO 371/169888.
[99] Peterson to Cable, 14 August 1963, DH1022/28, FO 371/169883.

have of taking retaliatory action against the Indonesians (such as severing relations or making a public show of sending reinforcements to the Far East). Hilsman voiced the opinion that Subandrio had given Sukarno an entirely false impression of the probable outcome of the UN survey in the Borneo territories, hence the latter had been knocked off balance. Hilsman also believed that Sukarno was still undecided about his future course and that, 'Whatever one might think about the "spontaneous" attacks on the British and Malaysian [sic] Embassies and the pretence that they had got beyond the control of the police, they should not be taken as signs that Sukarno had definitely decided on a policy of outright hostility to Her Majesty's Government.'[100] To news of American assurances that they were in the process of drafting a personal letter from Kennedy to Sukarno for use if the situation should deteriorate again, the Foreign Office responded with some scorn: 'We note that it will be held in reserve for "any future emergency". It seems to us that the present situation already constitutes a very serious emergency, and indeed we can hardly see how it could be worse, short of an Indonesian invasion of Malaysia.'[101]

Although congressional outrage against Sukarno was mounting, and there was greater scepticism over Indonesian behaviour from the White House (and, significantly, from McGeorge Bundy), US State Department officials tended to apportion a fair degree of blame to the British for what had transpired over the previous two months. The Americans were, moreover, well aware that a large body of neutral and Asian opinion held that the real responsibility for the breakdown of the promising development of Maphilindo diplomacy in the summer of 1963 lay with the British (the villain of the piece being Duncan Sandys). It was British intervention at the Manila summit with the Tunku's negotiating stance that had excited fresh accusations of neo-colonial influence, while their attempt to manage the subsequent UN survey had been further tainted by the obstructions raised over the observer issue. Both Harriman and Hilsman believed that provocative British behaviour had served to make it impossible for the Indonesians to find a face-saving way out of their brash venture into confrontation; the British had been engaging, as the latter put it to the former the day after Malaysia's formation, in a 'self-fulfilling prophecy – they have been prophesying that the Indonesians would not come around and then behaving in such a way that they will not'.[102]

---

[100] See FO to Washington, no. 9245, 18 September 1963; Washington to FO, no. 2902, 18 September 1963; Trench to Warner, 19 September 1963, DH103145/13, FO 371/169888.
[101] FO to Washington, no. 9343, 20 September 1963, PREM 11/4308.
[102] Harriman–Hilsman telephone conversation, 17 September 1963, box 581, Harriman papers.

The consensus among the key policy-makers in the US Administration was that the only way forward was to reach a negotiated settlement to confrontation, and as quickly as possible. An accommodation between Indonesia, Malaysia and the Philippines would necessarily involve a return to the spirit of the Manila summit, while British entreaties for the USA to help isolate Sukarno would have to be turned aside, at least in the short term. Finally, and most importantly, American desires to settle confrontation were given added and urgent impetus by their own, more direct involvement further north in the conflict steadily engulfing Vietnam, where US credibility was now being firmly put at stake.

8 Avoiding escalation, September–December 1963

During the course of 1963, the Communist insurgency in South Vietnam had made striking gains, prompting alarm in the Kennedy Administration that the commitment of additional resources that had been made to the Diem regime in late 1961 would not be sufficient to avert a collapse of the entire position. In September, the President conducted interviews for television news that emphasized his belief in the domino theory, the threat to South East Asia from Communist China, and his opposition to any early withdrawal of US personnel from Vietnam. However, at the same time, he was also indicating disapproval for the current policies of the government in Saigon, and underlining the fact that the war was essentially one for the Vietnamese themselves to fight.[1] With 16,000 US advisers already working within South Vietnam, however, pressures were beginning to mount for a further escalation of American effort. It seemed likely that several critical decisions would have to be taken soon over the future level of commitment, and with an election due in November 1964, the domestic political calculations of the Administration were by no means clear-cut. There was evidently much to be said for doing everything to avoid any further disturbances off mainland South East Asia, where any instance of overt Indonesian aggression could present fresh dilemmas as to how the United States would respond.

Indeed, the consequences of a development of the dispute into an open war between Indonesia and Malaysia backed by Britain, and with the potential for Australian and New Zealand participation, would be disastrous for US policies in the region. Indonesia might well move closer towards Communist China in the battle with the 'Old Established Forces' of imperialism, the domestic position of the PKI would be immeasurably enhanced and anti-Communist elements within the Army put on the defensive. All the effort and capital that had been expended since 1961 in cultivating a friendly and constructive dialogue with Jakarta (and with the Army) would be lost. Pressures to offer more than diplomatic support to

---

[1] See Richard Reeves, *President Kennedy: Profile of Power* (New York, 1993), 586–9.

the British would certainly be strong, while the ANZUS Treaty entailed commitments to assist Australian and New Zealand forces that might well be invoked if they were deployed to assist Malaysia. At the beginning of December 1963, Robert Komer can be found warning McGeorge Bundy that 'Malaysia/Indo[nesia] could easily become more critical to our interests than [the] Vietnam war.'[2] The months between the creation of Malaysia and the abrupt end to Kennedy's presidency would see US officials striving to prevent an escalation of confrontation and pushing for new efforts at diplomacy and negotiation. This came, moreover, at the very time when a negotiated settlement was being eschewed by the Administration when it came to their own problems in Vietnam.[3]

The American involvement in Vietnam, and the divisions it produced, impinged on US policy towards Indonesia in other respects. The Diem regime's repression of Buddhist monks and student demonstrators throughout the summer of 1963, combined with its general character of ineptitude and corruption, had convinced significant elements in the State Department, led by Harriman, Hilsman and George Ball, that only a complete clear-out of the Saigon Government could prevent defeat and allow a proper counter-insurgency campaign to be conducted. On the NSC staff, Michael Forrestal, handling the Far East brief under Bundy's direction and personally close to Harriman, was another source of ideas that dramatic action was required to arrest the decline. In direct contrast, the US military authorities, with the staunch backing of McNamara at the Pentagon, wanted to press ahead with the war effort under the existing regime, while any notion of forcibly removing Diem was also opposed by the Vice President, Lyndon B. Johnson. This serious split in the Vietnam policy of the Kennedy Administration came to a head, in notorious fashion, in late August 1963 when Harriman, Hilsman and Ball managed to get partial (though just enough) clearance to despatch a cable to Saigon, which gave the Ambassador there, Henry Cabot Lodge Jr, authority to approach generals in the South Vietnamese Army regarding possible US support for a coup attempt against the Diem regime.[4]

While nothing immediate came from these overtures, the bitter recriminations which followed this episode served almost to paralyse Vietnam policy-making. Kennedy himself was rapidly running out of patience

[2] Komer memorandum for Bundy, 3 December 1963, Komer memos, box 6, NSF name file, LBJL.
[3] Some insight into this issue is provided by Fredrik Logevall, 'De Gaulle, Neutralization and American Involvement in Vietnam, 1963–1964', *Pacific Historical Review*, 41, 1992, 69–102.
[4] See Halberstam, *Best and the Brightest*, 262–5; Hilsman, *To Move a Nation*, 483–94; Ball, *Past Has Another Pattern*, 371–4.

with Diem, but was convinced that he needed to carry military opinion and McNamara with him, and was frustrated by the contradictory advice he continually received on progress in the war itself.[5] Nevertheless, the arguments in Washington seemed to be swinging behind the position of Harriman and Hilsman; when the coup finally took place on 1 November, bringing with it Diem's bloody demise, US recognition was swiftly extended to the new military *junta* that now held power in Saigon. The resolution of the issue could not, however, conceal the animosities that had by now been generated in the Administration. Above all McNamara, and increasingly Rusk, were determined to check the growth of a Harriman–Hilsman axis at the State Department. After Kennedy's assassination, the American advocates of Diem's overthrow would find their influence over Far Eastern policy in general dramatically reduced, as Johnson deferred to McNamara and displayed his disdain for Hilsman.[6] All this would have important implications for US relations with Indonesia during the first few months of 1964, as Diem's opponents in Washington also tended to be those who wanted to continue with a conciliatory path towards Sukarno's regime.

The subtleties of such Washington bureaucratic infighting were largely lost on the British, who were more concerned with the short-term issue of how to deal with the enhanced Indonesian threat. One immediate worry was that the final signing of contracts with the Western oil companies was due on 25 September, but the Shell representative in Jakarta was informed by the Indonesians that though Stanvac and Caltex would be included, his company would not. The Foreign Office instructed Ormsby Gore to approach Harriman in order to reaffirm the united front established during the earlier Tokyo negotiations, but Harriman proved unresponsive.[7] From Jakarta, Jones advised the State Department that if the US companies were faced with a decision on whether they should sign without Shell, US political and economic interests dictated that they answer in the affirmative.[8] Ormsby Gore reported back to London that the Americans were advising Stanvac and Caltex to sign separately if Shell could not be brought in, and suggested that the Prime Minister should now directly prompt Kennedy to send a personal message of protest to Sukarno at recent Indonesian behaviour.[9]

---

[5] A good survey of this period, and criticism of Kennedy's indecision, is provided by Geoffrey Warner, 'The United States and Vietnam: from Kennedy to Johnson', *International Affairs*, 73, 2, 1997, 333–49.

[6] See Halberstam, *Best and the Brightest*, 369–78.

[7] See the discussion in Cabinet, CC(63)53rd mtg, 19 September 1963, CAB 128/37; FO to Washington, no. 9311, 19 September 1963, PREM 11/4308.

[8] Jakarta to DOS, no. 652, 21 September 1963, PET 6 INDON, RG 59.

[9] Washington to FO, no. 2952, 23 September 1963, PREM 11/4308.

Relations between Kennedy and Macmillan were evidently put under strain by events in Indonesia, and the issue of the oil contracts brought matters to a head. The Prime Minister urged that the united front between the companies should be preserved:

... it is not only of commercial interests that I am thinking. As a result of Indonesian policies we are now faced with as dangerous a situation in South East Asia as we have seen since the end of the war. I feel sure you agree with me that President Sukarno is out to destroy Malaysia. If he were allowed to do that, he would then turn in other directions.[10]

Macmillan made clear that the British were committed to Malaysia and would stand by it. Despite its agitated tone, the appeal had no effect. In a reply that was terse and clinical, the President simply stated that the US oil companies should be left to make their own commercial judgement on signature. No salve was offered to soothe damaged British sensibilities.[11] Ormsby Gore took Bundy to task over Kennedy's message, saying it was 'pretty feeble in the circumstances', but Bundy merely replied that US sources indicated that the Indonesians would sign with Shell anyway.[12]

The oil issue subsided as quickly as it had arisen when, as Bundy had predicted, the Indonesians signed the Tokyo Agreement with all three Western companies, but British officials were justified in believing that Washington was concerned more for its overall relationship with Indonesia than for sentimental appeals to Anglo-American solidarity.[13] From the Foreign Office, Warner was keen to emphasize that:

The Americans must face up to the fact that Britain is engaged in a very serious conflict with Indonesia in which we have already lost our brand new Embassy and millions of pounds worth of investments. British troops are engaged in fighting in the jungle and we are deploying a bigger military effort in Borneo than anywhere else in the world. The press and the public are thoroughly aroused. [...]

It is a very difficult problem and the outlook is grim. We have to hold our end up if we are not to be squashed by the Americans into allowing our position to slide.[14]

Officials at the Washington Embassy were more inclined to note that while there were, 'in the State Department, and elsewhere "nigger lovers" who believe you can make a silk purse out of Sukarno's ear', there were also significant bodies of sceptical and hostile opinion towards Indonesia in Congress, the press and within the US Administration (including Bundy).

[10] Macmillan to Kennedy, T.492/63, 23 September 1963, *ibid.*
[11] Kennedy to Macmillan, T.494/63, 24 September 1963, *ibid.*
[12] Washington to FO, no. 2984, 25 September 1963, DH1532/10, FO 371/169944.
[13] Bligh to Macmillan, 25 September 1963, PREM 11/4308.
[14] Warner to Trench, 24 September 1963, DH103145/13, FO 371/169888.

Even Harriman was reported as saying of Sukarno that, ' "We have got to sweat through with this madman – after him we may be able to get something better." ' The Americans believed rather, that 'our judgement in regard to Indonesia is influenced too much by emotion, rather than reason. This leads them to fear that we might suddenly fly off the handle without any warning and take some step which might embroil them.' The despatch of Macmillan's precipitate message to Sukarno preceding the delicate Tokyo oil negotiations in late May had left a deep impression on Harriman. The creation of Malaysia had increasingly come to be seen as a hazardous project that was a source of instability, while the suspicion existed that British intentions were to reduce their defence commitments in the region, while handing over to Washington responsibility for the turmoil that was left behind. American views and opinions would need to be accorded greater respect if their support was to be solicited.[15]

Meanwhile, Jakarta's severance of her trading links with Malaysia on 21 September had effectively ended any prospect of Western financial support for a large-scale loan to Indonesia, and a few days later the US Government officially withdrew from the scheme. The American stance over aid was also hardened, as domestic criticisms of Indonesian behaviour gathered pace; consideration of future assistance to Jakarta was suspended, along with deliveries of arms and ammunition covered by existing contracts.[16] Important to the general atmosphere in Washington was the wide reporting given to a belligerent speech, delivered by Sukarno in Jojakarta on 25 September, where he had bitterly denounced Tunku Abdul Rahman and called for an intensified campaign of confrontation, taking up the uncompromising PKI slogan of 'ganjang (crush) Malaysia'. However, confirmation from Washington that consideration of future assistance was being suspended was mitigated, at least in British eyes, by the fact that existing non-military aid programmes to Indonesia, consisting largely of PL 480 food aid and civic action schemes with the army, totalling about $70 million for the fiscal year 1963–4, would continue. At the end of September, the Foreign Secretary was attending the opening sessions of the UN General Assembly in New York, and took the opportunity to discuss confrontation with a sympathetic Dean Rusk. The Secretary of State himself was not a great believer in the Harriman–Hilsman approach to Indonesia, and was more receptive to the mood in Congress. Moreover, Sukarno's Jojakarta speech had made a strong impression on Rusk. He told Home that he felt Sukarno's remarks amounted to 'virtually a declaration of war' and wondered, if the guerrilla fighting in Borneo

---

[15] Trench to Warner, 26 September 1963, DH103145/16, *ibid.*
[16] See DOS to Jakarta, 24 September 1963, *FRUS, 1961–1963, XXIII*, 688–9; Jones, *Indonesia*, 318, 324; Mackie, *Konfrontasi*, 193.

made no progress, the British could take counter-offensive action some-where else in Indonesia (he was surely thinking of Sumatra). Rusk was agreeable to Home's suggestion that quadripartite talks on the dispute, involving the Australians and New Zealanders, could be reconvened in Washington. Home was not shy in telling Rusk that 'it was clear that a pol-icy of appeasing Sukarno in the hope he would stop making trouble clearly did not pay'. Discussion of future actions led the Foreign Secretary to conclude that caution would be required in taking the dispute to the UN, because it was 'so unpredictable: we might end up with a resolution which included a call for the withdrawal of British bases in South East Asia'.[17]

With a shadow now hanging over the US aid programme to Indonesia, US officials considered that the only way forward was to promote negotia-tions between the parties to the dispute, before the inflammatory rhetoric now emanating from Jakarta and Kuala Lumpur developed into some-thing more serious. The essence of this negotiating effort, as Komer ex-plained to Bundy, was 'to work out some face-saving compromise to give Sukarno, [the] Tunku and Macapagal a way out', through a further sum-mit meeting.[18] An indication of such a possibility was given by Subandrio, arriving in New York for the UN General Assembly on 19 September, who had expressed interest in tentative Japanese offers to mediate, while also informing Rusk he wanted to find a peaceful solution.[19] Hopes for an early tripartite meeting were, however, put firmly in perspective by a radio broadcast delivered by the Tunku on 20 September, giving his response to the overtures that had been received from the Filipinos about the chance of another Manila-style summit. The Malaysian Prime Minister set out preconditions for any such meeting, including the restoration of diplo-matic relations between the parties to the dispute, the end of guerrilla ac-tivity and withdrawal of Indonesian irregular forces from the Sarawak bor-der region.[20] Having received a carefully worded message from President Kennedy on 26 September proposing a halt to any further provocative actions by all sides, Sukarno told Jones that he was prepared to order a 'temporary standstill' and attend another Manila-style summit without preconditions.[21]

Macmillan was in turn urged by Kennedy to press the Tunku to agree to the idea of such a standstill, maintaining that, 'our problem now is to ensure that no one else rocks the boat. Since the Tunku is still in

---

[17] New York to FO, no. 1553, 26 September 1963, PREM 11/4870.
[18] Komer memorandum, 25 September 1963, NSF, countries, Malaya and Singapore, 8/63–9/63, JFKL.
[19] The Japanese Prime Minister, Ikeda Hayato, was due to visit Jakarta and Manila and had offered to sound out local opinion.
[20] The Times, 21 September 1963.
[21] See DOS to Jakarta, no. 379, 26 September 1963, POL INDON–UK, RG 59.

a pugnacious mood, here is where we might both apply some balm...
Encouraging a summit can wait till later, but we are inclined to feel that
such a meeting and refurbishing of Maphilindo would help save face all
round, once tempers have been allowed to cool.'[22] Still in New York, the
Foreign Secretary advised Macmillan that he should back the approach
suggested by Kennedy:

> ...Maphilindo is probably the only way out. The action of the President...may
> have some influence on Sukarno temporarily but it probably won't last. The
> danger of Maphilindo is that the Tunku always seems to waver and leave room
> for doubt as to what he has said. This leads to misunderstandings later. But they
> have to live together or fight and as we are strongly in favour of the former I think,
> subject to what Duncan [Sandys] says, I would risk a Summit. How far you go
> with the Tunku is really a matter for Duncan.[23]

As over the outcome of the Manila summit, the Foreign Office was acutely
conscious of the need to attract American support and was ready to defer
to US initiatives, but on this occasion Home was prepared to follow the
wishes of the Commonwealth Secretary. Having acquiesced in the whole
Maphilindo process during the summer of 1963, and even finally agreed
to the UN survey, and for little apparent reward, Sandys was now in
no mood to compromise, and the Prime Minister appears to have been
ready to follow his preferences. In his reply to the President, Macmillan
refuted the assertion that the Tunku was in a 'pugnacious mood', but
agreed to ask the Malayan leader to continue to exercise restraint, though,
'After his experience of the value of Sukarno's assurances, the Tunku
can reasonably require conciliatory Indonesian words to be matched by
deeds.' As for a summit meeting, although it might help the process of
reconciliation, 'Sukarno is going too far in suggesting a meeting without
preconditions. The Prime Minister of Malaysia clearly could not attend
a meeting of other heads of Government so long as Sukarno refuses even
to recognise the existence of Malaysia...' Diplomatic recognition would
have to be the price for a summit. Macmillan also submitted that the
Tunku would probably insist that Sukarno publicly call off confrontation
completely before a meeting, 'But you and I should be able to persuade
him that [recognition] is a sufficient moral victory by itself and that other
matters could be reasonably left over for discussion with Sukarno at the
proposed meeting.'[24]

British officials, led by the Kuala Lumpur-centred concerns of the
CRO, were clearly of the opinion that the Malaysians could not afford to

---

[22] Kennedy to Macmillan, no. 3922, 28 September 1963, PREM 11/4350.
[23] Home to Macmillan, no. 1579, 28 September 1963, *ibid.*
[24] Macmillan to Kennedy, T.511/63, 30 September 1963, *ibid.*

212 Conflict and confrontation in South East Asia

make too many concessions. The Tunku's agreement to attend a summit without satisfying the precondition of diplomatic recognition was only likely to undermine his domestic credibility when his leadership was already under scrutiny for his performance throughout the summer. The British calculated Sukarno was likely to use a summit simply to raise further questions over Malaysia's legitimacy as a state, a problem which could be avoided if prior recognition was accorded. Moreover, there were real doubts that the Indonesian leader could draw back from confrontation at such an early stage, so bound up with the dispute had his credibility become.

The Foreign Secretary went on from New York to meet the President for talks at the White House on 4 October. Here Kennedy put forward an interesting proposition: 'Perhaps [the British] had some sort of fixation about President Sukarno, not unlike the one the United States had over Castro.' The Foreign Secretary declared that 'the last thing the British wanted was a conflict with the Indonesians', but while they were exercising restraint, they doubted 'whether Sukarno could be brought to see sense, since he had lived on excitement for so long. Unless he was squeezed, and United States economic aid seemed to be the most effective sanction, he might easily go for further expansion.' When Kennedy asked how the conflict might develop, Home answered that guerrilla warfare rather than open hostilities was more likely and, repeating the interest he had expressed back in February in counter-subversion, added: 'The Indonesians were vulnerable. For instance Sumatra could be pinched off quite easily.' Discussion of possible economic pressure led to the President confirming that while the food aid provided under PL 480 was continuing, the proposal for a stabilization loan had been suspended and the supply of 15,000 rifles halted. Kennedy was reluctant to cut all aid: 'This was a card that could only be played once. Sukarno quite obviously did not want to burn all of his bridges with the US. We should wait and see how the situation developed.' Mildly dissenting from this opinion, Home secured the President's agreement to the early staging of the quadripartite talks he had suggested to Rusk.[25]

The Foreign Secretary's mention to Kennedy of the potential to exploit Indonesia's internal tensions brings one to contemporary Indonesian accusations that the British intended to use subversive means in order to defend Malaysia, charges fuelled by claims made over the content of materials discovered in the gutted British Embassy in Jakarta. The issue of whether the Indonesians managed to gain possession of authentic British documents during this period is difficult to resolve: the British always

---

[25] Memorandum of conversation, 4 October 1963, *FRUS, 1961–1963, XXIII*, 737–8.

insisted that papers later circulated by the Indonesians were crude forgeries manufactured for propaganda purposes. When the mob had entered the Embassy building on 18 September there had been insufficient time to destroy or remove all sensitive cables, cyphers and codes (Gilchrist had actually decided against burning the Embassy's archive the day before).[26] The material that could be gathered was secured in the Embassy strongroom, although one of the two keys that operated the door was actually left in the lock. After the evacuation of Embassy personnel had taken place, American and Australian diplomatic staff arranged a rota to keep watch over the building, nevertheless, as Gilchrist noted, 'All this time, and for days to come, always nagging at my mind was the question of the strong-rooms. We knew from experience how long it takes to get through the concrete (about 7 hours), but failure of the generators would mean that a heavy cable would have to be laid: no sign.'[27] Over the next few days, it emerged from loose papers retrieved in the building that the out-telegram file had, in fact, been compromised, and on 23 September uniformed Indonesians were reported as trying to break into the strongroom. With the help of the French, American, Australian and Canadian Ambassadors, Gilchrist rushed into the Embassy building and remonstrated with the Indonesians present (one of whom was trying to conceal a large bag of tools). In the resulting confusion and commotion, several of the Embassy staff gained access to the strongroom, and unnoticed managed to retrieve the most sensitive material still kept on the site, which was taken to the safety of the US Embassy and then destroyed.[28]

Despite this apparent success, the Indonesians were soon claiming that they had discovered material in the Embassy pointing to British subversive intentions and activities in Sumatra. In the middle of October, Gilchrist was reporting that Howard Jones had been alarmed by a conversation (held in June) with Philip Moore, the Deputy Commissioner in Singapore, where the latter was said to have 'talked with some confidence about the possibility of a break up of Indonesia into its separate parts, with particular reference to Sumatra'. Gilchrist felt that Jones was making connections

with allegations about documents found in my embassy relating to plans for British action in Sumatra, allegations which I have consistently and truthfully denied to Mr Jones (my own view on Sumatra has always been that whatever we

[26] Diary notes 17, 18 September 1963, file 13A, Gilchrist papers.
[27] Diary notes, 19 September 1963, *ibid.*
[28] Diary notes 23 September 1963, *ibid.*; see Cable to Ramsbotham, 26 September 1963, D1023/1, FO 371/169683. See also Jakarta to DOS, no. 752, 27 September 1963, POL 2-1 INDON, RG 59.

plan on a contingency basis it would be highly unreal to rely on any possibilities there and that we should certainly not talk about them in any other vein).[29]

Moore denied completely the version of their conversation presented by Jones, but contemporary Indonesian suspicions of British and Malayan policy were built on their recent memory of the support extended to the Outer Island rebels in 1958 from across the straits of Malacca.

Certainly, the Tunku was making little secret of the way his mind was moving over the possibilities of confrontation leading to a break-up of Indonesia. On 5 October, the Malaysian Prime Minister delivered a speech where he called on the Indonesian people to overthrow Sukarno, while repeating his preconditions for a summit meeting. A few days later, the Deputy High Commissioner in Kuala Lumpur, James Bottomley, took the First Lord of the Admiralty, Lord Carrington, and the C-in-C Far East, Admiral Sir Varyl Begg, to see the Tunku, who 'delivered himself of some very strong views on the subjects of President Sukarno and the best things to do about Indonesia'. Carrington was not impressed with the lack of discretion shown, the Tunku making such comments as:

Sukarno is now a helpless sex maniac, and incapable of rational thought on politics . . . anti-Jakarta feeling is strong and the pressure is reaching the stage at which Indonesia could well explode . . . Anti-Jakarta elements should be encouraged and assisted to split Indonesia up – Action could be independent; the Sumatran Malay rulers could easily bring their states into Malaysia alongside their Malayan cousins; Indonesian Borneo together; Celebes another; and so on. There could be an all-embracing Federation of all the Malaysian countries. He was keeping in touch with Indonesian dissidents. They wanted money and other material assistance. This should be provided.

The Tunku wanted to use the powerful British transmitters in Singapore to beam anti-Sukarno propaganda into Sumatra. Bottomley came away unsure whether the Malaysian Prime Minister was serious in his assessment or just engaging in wishful thinking. Bottomley reflected:

One thing that struck me was how far he was clearly influenced by the experiences of and continuing appeals from those of his class in Sumatra – many of them his relations – who have suffered under the Soekarno regime. This seems rather like judging the prospects of a counter-revolution in Russia in the 1920s, by talking to emigre Grand Dukes in Monte Carlo.[30]

American annoyance with the lack of progress in the negotiating process was illustrated by a discussion in early October between Rusk and Dato Ong, the Malaysian Ambassador to the United States, dealing with

[29] Jakarta to FO, no. 1323, 15 October 1963, DH103145/16, FO 371/169888. See also Jones, *Indonesia*, 273–4, where the discussion with Moore is mentioned.
[30] Bottomley to Sir Neil Pritchard (CRO), 11 October 1963, DO 169/242.

the recent efforts of Thanat Khomen, the Thai Foreign Minister, to organize a ministerial-level conference of the Maphilindo powers.[31] The US Secretary of State had responded sharply to Ong's contention that normal diplomatic relations would need to be resumed before any such meeting, and over Malaysian complaints about lack of US support, by asking: 'How could the United States Government ask the farm boy from Kansas to go and be killed for Malaysia if Malaysia was, for reasons of prestige, unwilling to try negotiation?' Ong was reminded that 'we view diplomacy as first line [of] defense and that Malaysia should take care not to dissipate present strong assurances of support from her friends by imposing such rigid pre-conditions that it [is] impossible to bring parties together'. Rusk contended that an early tripartite meeting would in itself amount to a resumption of relations. Malaysian officials agreed with the Americans that early negotiations were highly desirable, and suggested that the Tunku's preconditions were meant for a formal heads of state summit, rather than for ministerial talks. Ong went on to refer to the Tunku's problems in avoiding internal dissension, especially from Lee Kuan Yew, if he should appear to show weakness.[32]

Neither of the propositions advanced by Rusk, that early talks were essential to a resolution of the dispute and that Malaysia would have to accept a meeting without preconditions, was well received in London.[33] Even more disconcerting then, was news the British received of an interview between Charles Baldwin and the Tunku on 9 October, where the US Ambassador (much against his personal will) carried out State Department instructions to press for a ministerial meeting without preconditions.[34] That same day, Ormsby Gore saw Rusk and Hilsman in Washington, in what the latter called a 'very unsatisfactory' meeting, to complain over the pressure being placed on the Malaysians, with particular reference to the meeting with Ong in New York. The Ambassador also asked when the US–UK–Australian–New Zealand quadripartite meetings might be held. Rusk explained US eagerness to see ministerial talks convened under Thanat's auspices, and expressed concern at the provocative speeches of the Tunku. When queried as to whether he had any alternative suggestion to talks between the Maphilindo powers, all Ormsby Gore could reply was that pressure was now on Sukarno and a go-slow approach would allow him to realize the general international disfavour his actions were generating. Hilsman was obviously

[31] New York to FO, no. 1676, 5 October 1963, D1075/72, FO 371/169726.
[32] Rusk (USUN) to DOS, no. 61, 4 October 1963, POL INDON–MALAYSIA, RG 59.
[33] FO to Washington, no. 1278, 10 October 1963, PREM 11/4905.
[34] Kuala Lumpur to DOS, no. 361, 9 October 1963, POL INDON–MALAYSIA, RG 59; New York to FO, no. 1702, 10 October 1963, PREM 11/4905.

unimpressed with this line and argued that efforts to achieve a cooling-off period were not working and only talks between the parties to the dispute could prevent a rapid escalation of the conflict, suggesting that Malaysia could eventually make the concession of a West Irian-style plebiscite. Finally, the Secretary of State suggested that the quadripartite meetings could be held in the middle of October, when Sir Garfield Barwick, the Australian Minister for External Affairs, was due for a scheduled visit to Washington. They were to be 'informal and held in the most inconspicuous manner possible', while Hilsman stressed that if the Indonesians learned of them, all US influence in Jakarta would be lost.[35]

The Americans were displeased with British attitudes. Harriman later complained to Komer that 'Ormsby Gore had the effrontery to tell the Secretary we shouldn't bear down on Ong so hard . . . this is a bit more of Sandys.'[36] The British were similarly troubled by the attitudes displayed by Rusk and Hilsman. Warner noted, 'It is clear . . . that we are going to have a difficult time with the Americans. They seem determined to force the Tunku into discussions under circumstances which are bound to make Sukarno think that he will get the sort of grudging support from the Americans which he got over the New Guinea problem.'[37] Warner was certainly accurate in that many of the American fears over confrontation mirrored those that had previously been apparent during the West Irian crisis, particularly regarding the domestic consequences of any escalation of the fighting. To Komer it was self-evident that although the USA would have to support Malaysia

if we let things drift to the point where Sukarno's continued subversive build-up forces us to enter the lists against him, we may practically push him into Communist hands . . . At a minimum we'd end up with a major anti-Indonesian effort on our hands, on top of Laos and Vietnam. At a maximum we'd lose Indonesia to the Bloc.[38]

Also on the minds of US officials in Washington at this time were the obligations implied under the terms of the ANZUS Treaty for the USA to provide assistance to Australian forces if they were subject to attack.

---

[35] DOS to London, no. 2323, 10 October 1963, POL INDON–MALAYSIA, RG 59; see Harriman–Hilsman telephone conversation, 9 October 1963, box 481, Harriman papers; Rusk later asserted to Ormby Gore, in a misleading manner, that he had been suggesting talks between officials, and not a ministerial-level meeting, Washington to FO, no. 3123, 10 October 1963, D1075/75, FO 371/169726.

[36] Harriman–Komer telephone conversation, 9 October 1963, box 481, Harriman papers.

[37] Warner minute, 10 October 1963, DH1071/21G, FO 371/169909.

[38] Komer memorandum for Bundy, 9 October 1963, *FRUS, 1961–1963, XXIII*, 742–3; see also Harriman–Komer telephone conversation, 9 October 1963, box 481, Harriman papers.

On 25 September, Menzies had told the Australian House of Representatives that military assistance would be offered to defend Malaysia against invasion or subversive activity given outside support or direction.[39] This was a strikingly firm guarantee, and although no Australian troops were yet deployed in the Borneo territories, the possibility raised some uncomfortable problems for the Americans. The ANZUS Treaty did not specify mutual assistance in the event of 'communist' aggression, but instead simply called for action if there was any attack on the forces of the signatories in the Pacific area. As we have seen, Harriman had assured the Australians in June 1963 that if there was an overt attack on Australian forces stationed in Malaysia, the Treaty would come into operation. Despite Kennedy's remark to Menzies in July that the situation would need to be clarified, no subsequent discussions were held between officials from the State Department and the Department of External Affairs. By the beginning of October, the President was clearly very uneasy over the whole prospect of being drawn directly into confrontation through ANZUS, telling the Australian Ambassador that, 'we must be clear where we are going and at what point we will get into a war. He agreed that the ultimate deterrent to Sukarno was probably the United States, but, if the United States got into a war over the Borneo Territories, it would take some explaining.'[40]

Such problems and concerns were given some consideration by Kennedy during a meeting on confrontation with Harriman, Hilsman, Ball and other senior representatives from the Defense Department and CIA on 9 October 1963. Harriman was unhappy with some of the papers on future action prepared for this meeting, particularly the way it was recommended that US obligations under ANZUS should be reasserted through a warning to Subandrio that an intensification of Indonesian covert action or an overt attack might invoke the Treaty. Harriman preferred to emphasize action through the UN, feeling that otherwise it looked like a 'white man's war all the way through'.[41] The meeting resulted in presidential approval for the final version of the diplomatic actions recommended by the State Department to prevent a further deterioration of the situation. These included encouragement of Thanat Khoman's efforts to bring about a tripartite ministerial meeting in Bangkok, and informing the Tunku of Washington's dismay at his recent belligerent statements and that repetition would prejudice future support, or as Harriman put it: 'We ought to tell the Tunku we can't

[39] Chin Kin Wah, *The Defence of Malaysia and Singapore: The Transformation of a Security System, 1957–1971* (Cambridge, 1983), 84.
[40] Memorandum of conversation, 2 October 1963, *FRUS, 1961–1963, XXIII*, 733.
[41] Harriman–Bell telephone conversation, 9 October 1963, box 481, Harriman papers.

be of much help unless he shuts his trap.'[42] Furthermore, a warning to Subandrio that an escalation of hostilities might involve the USA through its obligations under the UN Charter (not ANZUS) was also to be delivered by Jones, while attempts were to be made to detach the Philippines from alignment with Indonesia, and efforts continued to enlist British and Australian backing for moves to produce direct negotiations between the three parties to the dispute.[43]

Over the ANZUS Treaty, there was no question of it being triggered by subversion or guerrilla warfare on the scale then being witnessed in the Borneo territories, and although it was recognized that it would have to come into play if an overt Indonesian attack were delivered against Australian forces, the definition of such an attack would have to be jointly determined. Moreover, with State Department legal opinion highlighting that the terms of the Treaty merely called for 'action' to meet the common danger, the actual assistance that might be provided by the United States was to be highly selective, and could constitute such measures as diplomatic protests or appeals to the UN. In the forthcoming quadripartite talks involving the Australians, they would have to be informed of these conclusions, and reminded that primary responsibility for the defence of Malaysia must lie with the Commonwealth countries. Moreover, the Australians would have to be encouraged to avoid provocative behaviour, and use their influence to restrain the Tunku from further statements such as those of 5 October. A particular US concern was that the Australian parliamentary elections due in late November had contributed to a hardening of Canberra's position with regard to confrontation, and that Menzies's Conservative Government would employ even firmer language in the upcoming election campaign (the opposition Labour Party, and its leader Arthur Calwell, had been notably lukewarm in their approach to Malaysia). As the State Department argued: 'We cannot put ourselves in the position of being dragged into the military defense of Malaysia if our diplomatic efforts are undermined by others.'[44]

During the course of the quadripartite talks, convened in Washington in mid-October, a number of bilateral meetings were held between the Americans and Australians over the issue of obligations under the ANZUS Treaty (with the President himself displaying a close

[42] Harriman–Forrestal telephone conversation, 9 October 1963, *ibid.*
[43] See memorandum from Forrestal to Kennedy, 9 October 1963, box 488, Harriman papers; memorandum from DOS to the President: Malaysia Dispute, 9 October 1963, POL 32-1 INDON–MALAYSIA, RG 59, which incorporates Harriman's revisions, unlike the version printed in *FRUS, 1961–1963, XXIII*, 743–7.
[44] Memorandum from DOS to the President, Malaysia Dispute – Obligations and Actions under ANZUS, 9 October 1963, POL 32-1 INDON–MALAYSIA, RG 59.

personal interest). Barwick was presented with a carefully worded State Department memorandum, which called for close consultation between Washington and Canberra on statements and actions associated with confrontation, including the deployment of any Australian forces in the Borneo territories, and stressed the US desire to 'use all available diplomatic and political means to prevent any provocation, real or imagined, which could lead to an acceleration of hostilities'. In the event of an overt attack on Australian forces, the appropriate form of American action to be taken would again be subject to consultation and could involve merely diplomatic activity; in the most extreme case, US military commitments would be limited to air and sea forces and logistic support. Barwick indicated his assent to this formula in a meeting with the President on 17 October, adding that in the past 'he had tried to avoid antipathy with Indonesia, although this had caused him to be called an appeaser. Australia, however, was now going into an election and they must have a more robust criticism of Sukarno.' The Australian minister assured Kennedy that this 'would not be bellicose, only critical'. The President offered the view that 'Sukarno may try to "play the United States" in this situation', but this allowed for the exercise of leverage, and moreover, 'the time might come when the United States would have to change its policy towards Indonesia, and the President wanted to make sure that our position throughout had been reasonable. Our policy towards Indonesia had been deliberately ambivalent – not to face Sukarno with a white trio and to avoid a polemic between Sukarno and the United States.'[45] In such remarks, which echo Harriman's earlier comments over the appearance of 'a white man's war', one sees an awareness of the racial dimension to Western involvement in South East Asia, with fears that Indonesia could project itself to the wider international community as a state struggling against the pernicious forces of Western and white neo-colonialism, if publicly concerted policies were followed by London, Washington, Canberra and Wellington. Over the four-power talks themselves, Harriman had hoped that the discussions would be kept as low-key as possible, telling Ormsby Gore in one telephone call, 'We don't want it to get around; [it] will look like White Man's talks and we want to try to keep it Asian talks.'[46]

There was little appreciation for such an approach on the British side, who preferred to emphasize the threat to shared Western interests in the SEATO area as a whole now presented by Indonesian policy. 'The

[45] Memoranda of conversation and attached paper, 16 and 17 October 1963, *FRUS, 1961–1963, XXIII*, 747–53.
[46] Harriman–Ormsby Gore telephone conversation, 14 October 1963, box 481, Harriman papers.

Americans will argue that our effective presence in this area must depend on the good-will of the Indonesians', one Foreign Office brief noted.

Our reply will be that Indonesian acquiescence will never be given so long as the present regime continues. Moreover, if we allow Indonesia to dominate the Philippines and Malaysia, these countries will no longer be available for our purpose and our footholds in South East Asia will be limited to an increasingly isolated Thailand and shaky positions in Laos and South Vietnam.

There was a real need to persuade the Americans that the British bases in Malaysia and Singapore fulfilled a wider Western interest: 'Sometimes they even seem to think that they are a hangover from the colonial era and thus just a political irritant in the area which cannot be justified.' Recent American concerns over the escalation of confrontation had led them to

dash about, trying to fix up negotiations between Malaysia and Indonesia at almost any price. To justify this dangerous policy they seize upon every 'conciliatory' gesture or statement of the Indonesians, no matter how irrelevant or cynical. They accept that Indonesia is aggressive and its President's assurances totally invalid, but argue that there is a real chance of agreement if we stop provoking Sukarno by the insults of the Tunku and the bagpipes of the British.

Initiatives for ministerial-level talks or a revival of Maphilindo would have to be stifled. The bleak conclusion reached was that the Indonesian regime was 'necessarily hostile to the Western Powers and cannot be moderated for the time being, except by disastrous concessions...we cannot ride this tiger'.[47]

During the quadripartite talks, the Americans were subjected to concerted arguments that pressure on the Malaysians to attend early ministerial-level talks should be relaxed. Harriman adamantly refused to suspend current aid to Indonesia, and was not prepared to see corresponding US assistance extended to Malaysia. The Americans were accused by Barwick of 'encouraging Sukarno to demand one concession after another', while the New Zealanders saw US policy as 'leading to a Far Eastern Munich'. Faced with such opposition, Harriman and Hilsman were ready to concede that immediate substantive talks between Malaysia, Indonesia and the Philippines would not be possible, but they were still keen to secure endorsement of Thanat Khomen's efforts to bring about the conditions under which a tripartite ministerial meeting might be held.[48] By the second day of the talks, the Americans had agreed to consider making some limited gestures in support of Malaysia. For their part the British, Australians and New Zealanders reaffirmed that military and economic support for

[47] FO steering briefs, 16 October 1963, DH1071/24G, FO 371/169909.
[48] Ormsby Gore to FO, no. 3202, 16 October 1963, PREM 11/4905, and in DH1071/26G, FO 371/169909.

Malaysia was primarily a Commonwealth responsibility. They would also continue to encourage restraint in the Tunku's public statements and actions, while he could be informed of the quadripartite talks as long as they were presented as not prearranged or part of a regular procedure, Rusk being anxious that the Malaysian Prime Minister was not led 'to believe that he had a blank check'.[49]

Hence the most significant outcome of the meetings in Washington was agreement that 'the time was not yet ripe' for tripartite talks to end the dispute (though the Thais were still to be given support with their diplomatic efforts to break the impasse over preconditions). Ormsby Gore reported that Harriman was still mentioning 'our being involved in an interminable war unless some sort of meeting was arranged quite soon. This in spite of the fact that he had earlier said it would be necessary for Sukarno to give in 100 percent. It is therefore likely that they will start back-sliding before long.'[50] Some comfort could be drawn on the British side by a subsequent conversation between Bundy and Warner, where the former made clear that neither he nor the President shared the view of 'certain members' of the US Embassy in Jakarta or the State Department that Sukarno was eager to find a way out of confrontation. Nevertheless, Bundy explained that the Administration believed that maintaining some contact with Sukarno was essential, and so if a presidential tour of the Far East were to take place in early 1964, Indonesia and Malaysia would both have to feature on the itinerary. Bundy suggested that if acute problems over Indonesia were to develop in the future, then Ormsby Gore should take the issues up with him personally or even with the President direct.[51]

The quadripartite talks appear to mark the immediate end of intensive US efforts to promote an early negotiated settlement to confrontation through a high-level meeting between the major participants to the dispute. Having agreed not to press the Tunku to drop his preconditions for talks, there was little immediate likelihood of a revival of Maphilindo, a prospect which grew even dimmer with the expansion of Indonesian cross-border raids in Borneo from mid-October. During November, Thai efforts to encourage dialogue, principally around the annual Colombo Plan ministerial conference in Bangkok, came to nothing, and culminated at the end of the month with the Tunku's rejection of a fresh call from Macapagal to attend a new Maphilindo summit.[52] Some American

---

[49] See Ormsby Gore to FO, no. 3211, 17 October DH1071/27G, *ibid.*; memorandum of quadripartite talks, 18 October 1963, *FRUS, 1961–1963, XXIII*, 753–5.

[50] Ormsby Gore to FO, no. 3217, 17 October 1963, PREM 11/4905.

[51] Warner to FO, no. 3251, 19 October 1963, DH1071/29G, FO 371/169909.

[52] See Kuala Lumpur to CRO, no. 2585, 17 November 1963, PREM 11/4905; DOS to Manila, no. 584, 18 October 1963, POL 32-1 MALAYSIA–PHIL; DOS to Bangkok, no. 688, 30 October 1963, POL 16 MALAYSIA; Kuala Lumpur to DOS, no. 469, 20 November 1963, POL 17 MALAYSIA–PHIL, all RG 59.

officials were increasingly concerned with the lack of any progress in resolving the dispute, especially as signs grew that more serious military clashes, either across the Borneo border, or in the airspace around Kuching, were in the offing. Forrestal had regarded the results of the quadripartite talks as 'dismal' and by mid-November was pressing Bundy for a new American initiative, perhaps through the despatch of Harriman to the region. With Jones in Washington for consultations, Forrestal, Hilsman and the Ambassador worked up a package of measures to kick-start serious negotiations to end confrontation, and these were discussed with the President during a meeting on 19 November.[53]

Knowing the great store that Sukarno placed on the prospect of a presidential visit in 1964, Jones suggested telling the Indonesians that the current political climate ruled out any such event and only an easing of tensions in South East Asia could put it back on the agenda. Sukarno would be asked by Kennedy for assurances that he was ready to settle the dispute peacefully and engage in tripartite talks to that end, and to withdraw his support from the forces involved in cross-border raids or activity within the Borneo territories. For its part, the United States would use its influence to promote a tripartite meeting, and following a political settlement, reactivate proposals for a multilateral stabilization loan to help the Indonesian economy, provide 150,000 tons of rice, and plan for a presidential visit. Hilsman would follow up this initiative with a trip to Kuala Lumpur and Jakarta in December. When the President enquired about what terms Sukarno would accept for a settlement, Jones replied that this was far from clear and would depend on negotiation, but that he could envisage a possible answer in following the West Irian precedent, with Malaysia offering a plebiscite in Sarawak and Sabah in five or six years' time on whether they wanted to remain in the new federation. Kennedy indicated his approval for this approach, and said he would be willing to visit Indonesia in April or May 1964 if a political settlement were reached.[54] The optimism of Hilsman, Forrestal and Jones surrounding this new initiative proved premature; the President's assassination in Dallas three days later ended any immediate hopes in Washington of a diplomatic breakthrough and generated a fresh degree of uncertainty over US policies towards Indonesia.

An end to confrontation, though not on Indonesian terms, would certainly have been welcome to the British. During the final three months of 1963, estimates of the costs and burdens of sustaining a counter-insurgency campaign in Borneo were revised upwards. The increase of

---

[53] See memorandum from Forrestal to Bundy, 18 November 1963, *FRUS, 1961–1963, XXIII*, 759–60, Jones, *Indonesia*, 295–7; Hilsman, *To Move a Nation*, 407.
[54] Memorandum of conversation, 19 November 1963, *FRUS, 1961–1963, XXIII*, 694–6.

cross-border incursions during the autumn served to stretch existing British military resources in South East Asia to their limit.[55] The Minister of Defence, Peter Thorneycroft, had informed the Prime Minister in early October that countering the Indonesian threat in Borneo over the following six months would require the commitment of three brigade HQs, with eight major infantry units backed up with artillery, logistical and air support, as well as two SAS squadrons. Units would have to be found from elsewhere to replace those sent from Malaya/Singapore on to Borneo, and regular rotations arranged for those involved in protracted deployments. The most immediate problem was an acute shortage of helicopters. The new commitments were only the beginning, Thorneycroft warning, 'At worst, costs might well compare with those involved in the Malayan emergency', while he and the Chiefs of Staff were worried about the implications for Britain's ability to deploy forces to meet other emergencies, including potential SEATO operations to the north (the latter one of the key reasons, it will be recalled, why Malaysia had been established in the first place).[56] By the middle of October, taking the projected demands into account, the Defence and Oversea Policy (Official) Committee had concluded, as the Cabinet Secretary noted: 'If these operations [in Borneo] are protracted, our capacity to meet commitments in other parts of the world will be seriously impaired... our policy should be to work for a negotiated settlement while showing the Indonesians that we were prepared to maintain an effective military defence of Malaysian territory...'[57] It seems especially ironic that just as British officials at the Washington talks were arguing that early negotiations should not be encouraged, other officials in Whitehall had come to the conclusion that the likely costs of confrontation made the search for a political solution imperative.

It will be recalled that in April 1963 the Prime Minister had expressed doubts over whether enough thought had been given to the problems entailed in defending Malaysia from the Indonesian threat, and highlighted the chance it could become a 'formidable liability'.[58] In June, Macmillan had speculated in the Cabinet's Defence Committee whether 'the security of Malaysia would be more effectively safeguarded in the long term by the negotiation of a political understanding with Indonesia than by the maintenance of British forces in Singapore'.[59] But despite such occasional departures, the orthodox line held throughout the year had been that the British position at Singapore was essential to maintain

---

[55] For deployment of UK forces see annex to COS 329/63, 27 September 1963, CAB 148/16.

[56] Thorneycroft minute for Macmillan, Annex A to DOP(O)(63)3, 2 October 1963, *ibid.*

[57] Trend minute, 17 October 1963, PREM 11/4870.

[58] Macmillan minute for Home, M.131/63, 3 April 1963, PREM 11/4347 and in D1193/13G, FO 371/169734.

[59] D(63)8th mtg, 19 June 1963, CAB 131/28.

British interests as a whole in South East Asia, and that Malaysia was the key to retaining access and use of the base facilities there. Having gone to such elaborate lengths to secure the successful formation of the new federation, it was generally felt to be inconceivable that it should be left to defend itself in a hostile environment, or that its security should be compromised and its legitimacy questioned through the negotiation of a political agreement with an untrustworthy and unstable Indonesia. Yet as Macmillan departed from the premiership on 9 October, under the pressures of party feeling, the domestic scandals of the summer and ill-health, his anxieties over the direction of British policy and the costs of defending Malaysia, particularly with US attitudes in such an ambivalent state, were appearing uncannily accurate. Macmillan's eventual replacement as Prime Minister, following the Conservative Party's extraordinary fight over the succession (only finally resolved on 18 October), was the re-styled Sir Alec Douglas-Home, who as Foreign Secretary had been intimately acquainted with the dilemmas and difficulties generated by confrontation. Home's successor at the Foreign Office, R. A. Butler, had less immediate experience of the issues concerned, but would at least have to deal for the most part with a new American President less tolerant of Sukarno's misdeeds than his predecessor.[60]

In the days leading up to Kennedy's death, the most immediately troubling aspect of US policy towards Indonesia for British officials was the question of the ongoing aid and civic action programmes. On 12 November, the *Washington Post* had reported that Indonesian officers were continuing to receive counter-insurgency training from American instructors at Fort Bragg, the home of the US Special Forces in North Carolina. At the same time questions were being asked by Representative Frances P. Bolton in Congress, over reports that the State Department had given approval for the Lockheed aircraft company to renew a contract (worth $5.5 million) for servicing and supply of spare parts for the C-130 transports it had begun selling to Indonesia in 1959.[61] The fact that the C-130s were being used to ferry troops and equipment around Kalimantan added to the sensitivity of the issue. The story was soon taken up by the *Daily Telegraph* in outraged editorial comment, and was raised in the House of Lords, one questioner asking: 'What would the Americans say if we were to supply spare parts for aircraft to be used by the Vietcong in South Vietnam against American forces helping to defend that

---

[60] The two main concerns over Butler's appointment and performance as Foreign Secretary were the extent to which Home would encroach on his domain and his apparent deference to Sandys over Cyprus, Yemen and Malaysia, see Anthony Howard, *RAB: The Life of R. A. Butler* (London, 1987), 324–32.

[61] See Ormsby Gore to FO, no. 3512, 12 November 1963, PREM 11/4870.

territory?' The issue was put even more bluntly by Lord Boothby, who commented that if the report in the *Daily Telegraph* were correct, '... the US are in effect, if not in intention, waging war against us in the island of Borneo'. There were calls for strong protests to be made to Washington.[62]

The British were certainly worried by the cumulative impact of the Indonesian trainees, the C-130 spares, and the imminent visit to Washington of General Nasution, who had decided to take up a long-standing invitation from General Maxwell Taylor, the Chairman of the JCS. The Foreign Office also learned from Shell that the State Department was encouraging US oil companies to arrange for the import of kerosene into Indonesia to meet any shortfalls, while the Americans were known to be considering whether to increase their supplies of rice to make up for the poor Indonesian harvest for 1963. These were not the kind of signals that it was desired Washington should be sending to Jakarta, and were disappointing following the coordination in approach that had been the aim of the quadripartite talks in October.[63] Thorneycroft complained that

... the United States in their anxiety to preserve their bases in the Philippines and to avoid getting involved in a major struggle with Indonesia, have throughout tended to appease the Indonesians and to take steps which effectively have increased Indonesian determination to carry on with their present policy. This American attitude appears to be based on the mistaken view that their position in South East Asia would still be tenable if Indonesia achieved her objective of getting us out of Singapore and engulfing Malaysia.

It made no sense, the Minister of Defence argued, for the Americans to urge the British to maintain a military presence in South East Asia when their attitude towards Indonesia compromised that very presence.[64] However, American officials were quick to remind their British counterparts that the British had gone ahead with arms sales to Indonesia in the period 1959–61 (including Gannet naval patrol and torpedo aircraft), despite Dutch protests and the volatility of the West Irian issue; one diplomat at the Embassy in Washington concluded after 'glancing through the 1959 papers on the subject of Indonesian "defence" needs' that 'the story is even worse than I remembered it... we were apparently then longing to sell the Indonesians warships – the Admiralty thought that it would be fine to supply destroyers or cruisers although they would not have been quite so happy about selling an aircraft carrier!'[65]

[62] *Hansard, House of Lords Debates*, 5th series, vol. 253, 14 November 1963, cols. 127–8.
[63] See e.g. Warner minute, 8 November 1963, DH103145/23G, FO 371/169889.
[64] Thorneycroft minute for Butler, 4 November 1963; and see Butler minute for Thorneycroft, 8 November 1963, *ibid.*
[65] Trench to Cable, 19 November 1963, DH103145/25G, FO 371/169889.

Ormsby Gore's own representations about the C-130 spares had simply been parried by Rusk with the comment that it was a strictly commercial matter, while Lockheed were not expected to go ahead with new supplies until February 1964 at the earliest. 'When I saw [Rusk] later at a party', the Ambassador noted, 'he smiled and said that he hoped I had noted his restraint during my official visit in not referring to our sale of Viscounts to China or Gannets to Indonesia in spite of Dutch objections.' Australian protests over US rice sales to Indonesia had been met with similar rebuttals highlighting sales of Australian wheat to the PRC. Embassy officials preferred to maintain a low-key watchfulness over US policy rather than to irritate the Americans with a constant barrage of enquiries or complaints, while ensuring that British behaviour in the aid or arms-sales fields was above reproach; Ormsby Gore mentioned the 'danger that the Americans may come to feel that we are asking them to act towards Indonesia in a way that we ourselves have been most reluctant to do in other situations such as over Cuba'.[66] This was, though, not an attitude that found much support within the Foreign Office, with Caccia insisting that the British should not be reticent in putting their position to the Americans. The Permanent Under Secretary rejected Rusk's analogies in forthright terms: 'The Viscounts we sold to China are not being used to supply and reinforce Chinese soldiers against American soldiers. Indeed, so far as we know, no American servicemen have been killed by Chinese lately, whereas the Indonesians have inflicted 26 casualties on our own soldiers this year.'[67] Yet, as they were only too aware, the British were on weak ground when it came to such protests; the Decca company still had an ongoing contract to supply an early-warning radar system to Indonesia, while the Strategic Exports Committee only settled on discreet measures to restrict the sales of equipment with a military potential in mid-November, and a public announcement on future policy had yet to be made.[68]

The Nasution visit was another cause of friction between Washington and London. Nasution was, of course, seen by the Americans as one of the key personalities on the Indonesian scene, the leading source of anti-Communist pressure, and the most likely successor to Sukarno; as one State Department assessment put it, '...he is the closest thing we have to a friend in Sukarno's court...If Indonesian public order were to deteriorate sharply, he would control the power necessary to contain the communists and would use it.'[69] Although there was some

[66] Ormsby Gore to Caccia, 20 November 1963, DH103145/28G, *ibid.*
[67] Caccia to Ormsby Gore, 29 November 1963, *ibid.*
[68] See Butler to Home, PM/63/146, 19 November 1963, PREM 11/4870.
[69] See *FRUS, 1961–1963, XXIII*, 698.

embarrassment in Washington over the timing of the visit, Nasution was still to be treated with the greatest consideration (with a meeting with the President on his itinerary). In the event, Nasution arrived in Washington on 24 November, and acted as President Sukarno's representative at Kennedy's funeral, while it was with Lyndon B. Johnson and other senior Administration figures, including Harriman, Ball and McNamara (as well as CIA officials), that he held talks over the next few days. The new President avowed, in comments probably suggested by Harriman and Jones, that US policies towards Indonesia would remain unchanged, though he 'expressed the strong hope' that Indonesian guerrilla action 'would not go too far and made clear his disquiet at the situation', while stressing the need for a tripartite meeting to pave the way for an Asian political settlement.[70] In his talks with the Americans, Nasution was very frank with his description of the training the Indonesian Army in Kalimantan was giving to anti-Malaysia guerrillas, while even admitting that some of these trainees were Chinese, and that Indonesians had themselves participated in crossborder raids as 'volunteers'. The candid admission of the training of Chinese infiltrators can have done little to reassure his audience, and indeed made Nasution's earlier claims that Indonesian objections to Malaysia were rooted in its potential to allow Chinese Communist influence to spread in Borneo ring somewhat hollow.

The Prime Minister was also in Washington for Kennedy's funeral, where he held talks with Rusk. The Secretary of State was notably sympathetic to British concerns, even suggesting that 'it would be much better to avoid getting entangled in an area of Soekarno's own choosing such as Borneo. Why could not something be done in Sumatra?' To this Home replied that 'this had been an idea of his for two years but he had not been able to persuade others that it was a good one'.[71] Of even greater significance for detecting trends in US thinking were comments made by Bundy to de Zulueta at the end of November, where the latter described the situation over Malaysia as 'purely an Anglo-Saxon problem' and expressed the hope that a high-level Anglo-American meeting could soon be organized to discuss confrontation. When asked how he saw the position, Bundy replied that

President Sukarno was determined to expand and should be stopped. The difficult question was how to do it. Malaysia was important and good in itself but also a stabilising influence in the area. Maphilindo was a good conception but had no reality at least at the moment. He would not mind so much if President Sukarno

[70] Memorandum of conversation, 29 November 1963, *ibid.*, 699–701.
[71] Record of conversation between the Prime Minister and US Secretary of State, 26 November 1963, PREM 11/4790.

turned his attention to Portuguese Timor but in any case he had expansionist ambitions.[72]

The sceptical tone of the National Security Adviser was again evident, and it could be expected that President Johnson would rely heavily on Bundy, at least during the early days of the transition (indeed, despite being aware that Bundy had disparaged him when Vice President, Johnson did come to value his advice, largely because McNamara rated Bundy so highly).

As 1963 drew to a close, the main preoccupation of the British Government regarding confrontation was to ensure that Indonesia was starved of any outside support for its policies, while building up effective counter-measures in the Borneo territories against internal subversion and the cross-border raids from Kalimantan. On the former front, in mid-December at a meeting of the North Atlantic Council in Paris, Butler and Thorneycroft had appealed to Britain's NATO allies not to supply military equipment to Indonesia (a plea which must have been received with great irony by the Dutch). At the same time it was announced that Decca were being asked to cease work on the Indonesian radar system, and the Fairey aircraft company were told to end their servicing contract with the Gannets supplied in 1959–60. Rusk had been in Paris for the NATO meeting, and travelled on to London where he held talks with Butler and Sandys on 19 December. The Secretary of State had affirmed in reassuring manner that 'there was no doubt about US solidarity with the British in the face of attacks against Malaysia by the Indonesians'. Rusk went on to emphasize, however, that bearing in mind their existing commitments in Vietnam, Thailand, Laos and Cambodia, the United States 'wished to remain in the background in a supporting role in dealing with Indonesian confrontation'. He again expressed reluctance at the idea of cutting off all aid to Indonesia, though he would take another look at the aircraft spares issue and the training of Indonesian officers in counter-insurgency techniques. Rusk also recommended the fullest exchange of intelligence on confrontation, and a joint study of the possibilities of raising Indonesian behaviour at the UN. When the Secretary of State asked if the British had considered taking retaliatory action against Indonesia, Sandys replied that the guerrilla raids in Borneo were becoming more and more provocative and 'for the present we were concentrating on countering subversion in Malaysia. But he would like to consider some counter-subversion in Sumatra.'[73] That same day,

[72] De Zulueta to Ormsby Gore, 26 November 1963, DH103145/29, FO 371/169889.
[73] Two versions of this meeting are available: memorandum of conversation, 19 December 1963, *FRUS, 1961–1963, XXIII,* 762–3; record of a conversation at the Foreign Office between Foreign Secretary and US Secretary of State, 19 December 1963, PREM 11/4905.

Rusk saw the Prime Minister and made clear that the American attitude over confrontation would differ from that adopted during the West Irian crisis.[74]

By early December, British concerns over the demands being raised by confrontation were reflected in the first major despatch on the situation from Lord Head, who had replaced Tory as High Commissioner in Kuala Lumpur, and taken into his office several of the regional and advisory functions previously performed by Selkirk (whose own position of Commissioner General for South East Asia had been wound up, largely on grounds of economy, in September). Head's worrying prediction was that the present British commitment might last three or four years, and that 12–14 infantry battalions could eventually be needed in the Borneo territories.[75] One way to offset the costs of confrontation, as the Cabinet's Defence and Oversea Policy Committee was quick to underline, was to call on Australia and New Zealand for greater contributions to Malaysian defence. As well as assistance with air and naval support, there was a particular need for contingents in the Commonwealth Brigade to take their turn in the rotation of units for Borneo operations and for specialist SAS troops to be released for service in the border areas with Kalimantan. The general feeling was that Canberra and Wellington were underestimating the threat posed by Indonesia; as the Cabinet Secretary put it to Home, '…we have to face the fact that [the] situation is gradually growing worse, not better, and that the Australians and New Zealanders ought not to procrastinate much longer'.[76] However, Australia and New Zealand responded only partially to requests for more assistance, and exhibited great reluctance to commit ground troops while the situation was still being contained, Menzies arguing that his Government did not think that Indonesia wanted war or was yet committed to major military escalation (the Australians were also concerned that American reservations about support under ANZUS remained in place).[77]

Oliver Wright, who had replaced de Zulueta as the Prime Minister's Principal Private Secretary was not altogether sure that 'we have got our own policy fixed on the right lines yet. We have got the negative aspect all right: namely that we defend Malaysia and give the Indonesians a bloody nose if they attack. What is lacking is a positive aspect.' The

[74] Record of conversation at 10 Downing Street between the Prime Minister and US Secretary of State, 19 December 1963, PREM 11/4870.
[75] Kuala Lumpur to CRO, no. 11, 11 December 1963, D1051/6, FO 371/175065.
[76] DO(63)3rd mtg, 4 December 1963, CAB 148/15; Trend minute for Home, 18 December 1963, PREM 11/4905.
[77] Home to Holyoake, T.65H/63, 16 December 1963, and Home to Menzies, T.66H/63, 17 December 1963; Holyoake to Home, T.69H/63, 19 December 1963; Menzies to Home, T.75H/63, 24 December 1963, ibid.

problem came, Wright observed, from the fact that there was a dual character to the conflict with Indonesia. Britain was committed to the defence of Malaysia largely due to Commonwealth interests, but keeping Indonesia non-Communist was also overall a vital Western interest, and one emphasized more by Britain's allies and friends: 'It will help neither us nor Malaysia to drive Indonesia communist in the process of defending Malaysia . . . I cannot help feeling that, in military terms, Indonesia adds up really to a very small row of beans and that our present position could easily become one of taking a sledge hammer to crack a nut.'[78] The Prime Minister evidently agreed with Wright's analysis, suggesting to Butler that while the negative, military side of policy to Indonesia seemed to be adequate, a more positive, political policy appeared lacking: 'Ought we not, in addition to our military readiness, be actively promoting a political solution? Or, if that would make our position ambiguous, encouraging our friends to promote one? Experience shows that is the only one likely to stick.'[79] The Foreign Secretary was quick to reply that he had the imperative for a political settlement very much in mind, and was preparing a major paper for Cabinet outlining the various options open to the British in confrontation.[80]

There were other powerful incentives to find an acceptable diplomatic route to a settlement at this time, the most notable of which was the action fought between Malaysian and Indonesian troops at Kalabakan in Sabah on 29 December 1963. Two battalions of the Royal Malay Regiment had arrived in the Borneo territories during the autumn, the 5th being despatched to join British forces near Kuching, while the 3rd was sent to defend Tawau in Sabah. During 1963, most ventures by Indonesian guerrillas had been across the Sarawak border, and Sabah had been comparatively quiet. The Malay forces were inexperienced, while the Indonesian attack, when it came, was spearheaded by regulars, an increasing feature of such forays. Outlying Malay positions in the village of Kalabakan were taken by surprise, leaving eight Malay soldiers killed and nineteen wounded, and the successful Indonesian raiders went to ground in the local area. Gurkha reinforcements were quickly flown into Tawau and the Indonesians tracked down, but severe damage to Malaysian morale had been inflicted.[81] The Tunku immediately flew to Sabah to visit the wounded and was evidently rattled by the setback. Lee Kuan Yew saw the Tunku on 6 January 1964, the day after returning from his trip to the Borneo territories, and reported that he seemed 'like a man who had

---

[78] Wright minute for Home, 17 December 1963, *ibid.*
[79] Home minute for Butler, M.40H/63, 19 December 1963, *ibid.*
[80] Butler minute for Home, PM/63/158, 23 December 1963, *ibid.*
[81] A good account of Kalabakan can be found in Pocock, *Fighting General*, 175–9.

been punched below the belt.... He did not seem to know what to do next, but to be worried lest the verdict of history upon him should be that his earlier successes were over-shadowed by disaster in his declining years.'[82] Thorneycroft was also visiting Malaysia at this time, and had to persuade the Malaysian Prime Minister not to declare a state of emergency, the latter now maintaining that 'offensive measures must be mounted and they must be directed against the enemy within [a reference to the Indonesian community in Sabah]'. Thorneycroft tried to mollify the Tunku with the suggestion that the 'fomenting of difficulties within Indonesia might be one of the covert actions in the list of possible options'.[83]

These latest developments in confrontation raised difficult dilemmas for the British in how to offer support and guidance to their Malaysian allies. The heavy-handed advice and attitude of Sandys during the delicate period of August–September 1963 had created much resentment in Kuala Lumpur, resulting, the UK High Commission noted in November, in a 'certain soreness on the Malaysian side, among both officials and Ministers... just at present, constructive advice is unwelcome'.[84] In a similar vein, Head was also quick to point to the underlying doubts over how long the British would maintain their presence in the region: 'Our trouble in Malaysia is that there are too many people who think the British are broke, interested in their own standard-of-living and the next election, and if it is too difficult for them will duck from under and shirk their responsibilities in Malaysia.'[85] It was felt that the British would need to make their determination to resist the Indonesian threat unequivocal if Malaysian morale were to be sustained, even though mention of covert or more offensive operations against Indonesia could entail an expansion of a conflict that Britain was very anxious to contain. Similarly, a more positive political approach, looking to the conditions that could lead to a settlement, might well have to be pursued to reassure the Malaysians that confrontation would not prove to be interminable. But what kind of settlement was it possible to conceive of, that would bring an end to confrontation and provide some degree of satisfaction to Sukarno, without weakening the domestic position of the Tunku, who would have to face the first federal elections in Malaysia in April 1964?

[82] Note of meeting between Thorneycroft, Moore and Lee Kuan Yew, 7 January 1964, PREM 11/4905.

[83] Note of meeting between Tunku Abdul Rahman and Thorneycroft, 6 January 1964, *ibid.*

[84] Kuala Lumpur to CRO, 8 November 1963, DO 169/230.

[85] Head to Garner, 18 November 1963, DO 169/231; see also the comments of the US Ambassador to Malaysia in Kuala Lumpur to DOS, no. 452, 14 November 1963, POL INDON–MALAYSIA, RG 59.

To several officials in the Foreign Office, including it would seem the Permanent Under Secretary himself, the idea of offering some form of future plebiscite on Malaysia in the Borneo territories, following the West Irian precedent, began to appear once more as an option worth considering. The process would certainly be irritating, one member of the South East Asia Department noted, 'but it might save the Malaysians and ourselves a great deal of money and lives'. However, the adamant opposition of the CRO to any such notion, which they feared might lead to the break-up of Malaysia, stood as the chief obstacle in Whitehall to suggesting such a device.[86] It was also difficult to overcome the fact that many British officials simply did not trust Sukarno to honour any agreement he might temporarily reach with the Tunku, and would, at little prompting, be prepared to resume his guerrilla campaign. In this regard, the advice of the British Ambassador in Jakarta was important in blocking any moves to make concessions, Gilchrist noting in January 1964, for example, that Sukarno was 'nowhere near ready to abandon confrontation in earnest and the Tunku must settle for nothing less. The moment has not yet come to build a golden bridge.'[87]

At the same time, pressure from the United States to find a political solution to the conflict was still likely to be encountered. Indeed, the events of 1963 had demonstrated quite clearly that the Americans were prepared to tolerate Indonesian misdeeds for the sake of their wider goals and fears about the deteriorating situation in South East Asia. By preserving a reasonable and friendly dialogue with Jakarta, and maintaining a low level of aid (particularly to anti-Communist elements in the Army), US officials hoped to keep open Indonesian ties to the West and counter the internal threat from the PKI. As long as Roger Hilsman at the State Department's Bureau of Far Eastern Affairs, with the crucial support of Harriman, continued to pursue policies that reflected President Kennedy's desire to cultivate a positive US–Indonesian relationship, then the British could not easily anticipate forging a common approach with Washington. Over the succeeding few months a conjunction of factors, however, was to transform this picture so that by the time Home visited Washington in February 1964 for his first official and extensive discussions as Prime Minister with President Johnson, a new degree of harmony had spread over Anglo-American attitudes to confrontation. The origins of these important changes lie with the interaction between the evolving Vietnam policies of the United States and the changes in personnel and attitudes that accompanied Lyndon Johnson's arrival in the White House.

[86] See Pilcher minute, 7 January 1964, D1051/41, FO 371/175067.
[87] Jakarta to FO, no. 98, 11 January 1964, PREM 11/4905.

Part III

Denouement

9 The diplomacy of confrontation, Anglo-American relations and the Vietnam War, January–June 1964

During the first six months of 1964, the Malaysia–Indonesia confrontation assumed an increasingly steady pattern of low-intensity guerrilla warfare in the Borneo territories, nurtured by cross-border raiding parties from Kalimantan and defamatory exchanges of propaganda between Kuala Lumpur and Jakarta, all interspersed with flurries of diplomatic activity as intermediaries tried to bring the sides together and an inconclusive and ritualistic set of meetings was staged. By the end of the period, there was still no sign of a settlement in sight, while moves to resolve the conflict had often merely served to stoke up fresh tensions, accusations and intransigence. In the regional context, the war in Vietnam provided an ominous backdrop, as chronic governmental instability in Saigon engendered despair in US officials trying to shore up the deteriorating position. In both Washington and Hanoi, escalation of one form or another was under discussion. The Johnson Administration became increasingly convinced that direct action against the north would need to be taken both to restore morale in Saigon and to help stem the flow of supplies fuelling the insurgency, though not before the presidential election in November was safely out of the way. The North Vietnamese, meanwhile, began preparations in the spring of 1964 to despatch regular army units south to augment the guerrilla forces of the National Liberation Front.[1]

Regular troops also became more commonly employed by Indonesian commanders from early 1964 onwards, though the security forces in the Borneo territories repeatedly demonstrated their prowess over Indonesian intruders in successive engagements during this period and appeared to be well able to deal with the military pressures of confrontation. Yet, as we have seen, British ministers were concerned by the drain on resources that the conflict entailed, and there was a widespread awareness that the posture of their forces was essentially passive. As was evidenced in Washington over Vietnam at this time, strong arguments built up to take more proactive measures to counter the Indonesian threat. In April 1964,

[1] See e.g. Smith, *International History of the Vietnam War, vol. III*, 242–54, 345–7.

the Defence and Oversea Policy Committee decided to sanction counter-
battery fire against fixed Indonesian gun and mortar positions, and to
allow 'hot pursuit' of Indonesian raiding parties back across the border
up to a depth of 3,000 yards.[2] In June, authorization was extended for
the conduct of 'credibly deniable' offensive patrol operations, again up
to 3,000 yards into Kalimantan, so that ambushes could be laid and attacks conducted on Indonesian lateral communications. Nevertheless,
the British were extremely anxious that they and Malaysia appear as the
injured parties in the conflict, and the above steps were taken with some
degree of reluctance and hesitation, emphasized by the fact, for example,
that their implementation was linked to the outcome of ongoing diplomatic initiatives, while the Malaysians were encouraged to take their case
against Indonesia to the UN Security Council before the more offensive cross-border incursions were approved.[3] They had also no desire
to provoke a stronger Indonesian counter-escalation and an expansion
of the fighting in unpredictable directions. Another sign that London
was concerned about the stretching of its resources that the open-ended
commitment to confrontation involved was given in May 1964, when a
further request was made to Canberra regarding the use in the Borneo
territories of Australian combat troops, only for it to be turned down
once again by the Menzies Government (though they did at this time accede to a Malaysian request to provide an engineer squadron for Borneo,
prompting some public discussion over whether the United States might
be drawn more directly into the conflict through the ANZUS Treaty).[4]

Within Malaysia itself, the outcome of the first federal elections held on
25 April 1964 was a triumph for Tunku Abdul Rahman and the UMNO
Alliance, who had played on the themes of patriotic support for the government during a time of national emergency to great effect. Victory for
the Alliance, with its candidates winning 89 out of the 104 seats con-
tested in peninsula Malaya, and 59 per cent of the popular vote, was
made even sweeter by the rout that was suffered by the PAP in its attempt to extend its reach out of Singapore and appeal to voters in several
constituencies north of the causeway.[5] The decision by Lee Kuan Yew

[2] See DO(64)17th mtg, 8 April 1964, CAB 148/1; CRO to Kuala Lumpur, no. 1261, 24 April 1964, PREM 11/4908.
[3] See DO(64)28th mtg, 22 June 1964, CAB 148/1; and see also Home minute for Thorneycroft, M.46/64, 5 May 1964, PREM 11/4908, where attacks into Kalimantan were for the moment rejected, with the thought from the Prime Minister that, 'We have always recognized that the only real solution to this problem is a political one.'
[4] See Menzies to Home, T.202/64, 15 May 1964, PREM 11/4908, and Edwards, *Crises and Commitments*, 288–91.
[5] See Lau, *Moment of Anguish*, 91–124. The London Agreement of 1963 on Malaysia had prohibited Singapore citizens from standing as candidates in Malaya, and vice versa, but had not ruled out parties campaigning in different parts of Malaysia.

to intervene in mainland politics by fielding candidates in the election (so breaking a pledge that the Tunku alleged Lee had made earlier) put relations between Kuala Lumpur and Singapore under severe strain and set the stage for the eruption of deep-seated communal tensions while raising immediate questions among many Malays about the wisdom of merger. In a corresponding fashion, the strains of confrontation were also serving to polarize political conditions within Indonesia. After Djuanda's death in November 1963, a struggle ensued between Subandrio and his rivals within the Indonesian hierarchy to take over the position of First Deputy Prime Minister, and nominal successor to Sukarno. With little other basis of support, Subandrio drew closer to the PKI and its espousal of stronger ties with the PRC, and distanced himself from the Army. The PKI itself grew stronger and more assertive during 1964 as it sensed the opportunities for influencing domestic policy through the struggle against neo-colonialism on Indonesia's borders, and as popular mobilization behind the slogans and rhetoric of confrontation gathered pace. Important here was the adoption of the language of class struggle in the countryside as implementation of earlier land reform laws was pushed against the resistance of landlords, Moslem and conservative elites in the provincial bureaucracy, and among the Army's regional commands. Nonetheless, the PKI seems to have been making no preparations for any overt bid for power in the short term, being content to follow and nudge Sukarno in an anti-Western and pro-PRC direction.[6] The Army, for its part, found its attempts to check Communist influence frustrated by the need to demonstrate its militancy in the anti-Malaysia campaign and by its declining influence over Sukarno.

Western responses to the course that confrontation took after early 1964 were greatly conditioned by the change in tone and emphasis of US relations with Indonesia that was witnessed under the presidency of Lyndon Johnson, presenting a marked contrast with the attitudes of his predecessor. Some of this undoubtedly had much to do with Indonesian behaviour itself, which became yet more belligerent during 1964, and as the anti-imperialist rhetoric of Sukarno was increasingly directed towards the United States. This, in turn, had a significant impact on congressional and wider public attitudes to preserving ties with Jakarta. Nonetheless, it is also very important to recognize how changes in personnel affecting US Far Eastern policy in early 1964, combined with a predominating concern over the conflict in Vietnam, came to play an influential role in the development of views and policies towards Indonesia. A key part of this development, as has already been noted, was the rapid loss in

---

[6] See e.g. Rex Mortimer, *Indonesian Communism Under Sukarno: Ideology and Politics, 1959–1965* (Ithaca, 1974), 245–6, 295–320.

influence at the State Department of Hilsman and Harriman, who had previously enjoyed a degree of patronage and support from President Kennedy. Under the new dispensation, Johnson instead developed a liking for the quiet, steady and deferential nature of Rusk, relied heavily on McGeorge Bundy, and perhaps most importantly, admired the loyalties and abilities of McNamara. Indeed, the Secretary of Defense was soon operating over much wider areas of policy-making, a critical consideration when it came to the expansion of the war in Vietnam.[7]

Kennedy had valued Roger Hilsman's advice and questioning of military estimates of progress in Vietnam during 1962–3, as well as appreciating the Assistant Secretary's irreverence, but those same qualities had earned Hilsman many enemies in Washington. McNamara was intensely critical of his role in lobbying for Diem's removal in the bitter debates that took place in the summer of 1963, while Rusk felt uncomfortable with the fact he was being by-passed by an activist junior. Most importantly, Lyndon Johnson had also built up a strong dislike for Hilsman while Vice President, having sided with those who felt that the United States should have persevered with a Diem government in Saigon. In March 1964, it was made clear to Hilsman that his dismissal was imminent, and after turning down an ambassadorial posting to the Philippines, he resigned and moved back into academic life at Columbia University. On McNamara's recommendation, Hilsman was replaced by William Bundy, McGeorge's older brother, who was moved from his job as Assistant Secretary for International Security Affairs at the Defense Department.[8] Despite his best efforts, Harriman never succeeded in establishing a close relationship with the new President. Alongside Harriman's friendship with Robert Kennedy, the consequences of the Diem coup again played a role, with Johnson believing Harriman's lobbying had contributed to the Vietnamese leader's overthrow. Meanwhile, Rusk began to reestablish his prerogatives with the President, no doubt aided by Johnson's profound insecurity when it came to the realm of foreign affairs.[9] As Harriman's influence declined, Michael Forrestal, the NSC staffer who had pushed the Jones line with an often sceptical McGeorge Bundy, also found himself isolated. While Forrestal had enjoyed easy access to President Kennedy, under Johnson the White House aide found it more difficult to get his views across (handicapped no doubt also by his closeness to Harriman); in July 1964 he was moved from his NSC Far East brief, to a coordinating

[7] See Halberstam, *Best and Brightest*, 369–77, 459.
[8] *Ibid.*, 392–8; Roger Hilsman Oral History.
[9] For Johnson and his foreign policy advisers in the early months of the presidency, see Robert Dallek, *Flawed Giant: Lyndon Johnson and His Times, 1961–1973* (New York, 1998), 84–90.

job heading the State Department's Vietnam Task Force, and by the following January, he too had left government service.

Soon after assuming his new office, Johnson faced some important decisions regarding future policy towards Indonesia that reflected the ambiguities surrounding an American approach that combined opposition to Sukarno's course of confrontation with a desire to keep up a friendly dialogue with the regime and encourage those opposed to any growth in Communist influence. The Foreign Assistance Act of 1963 had been signed into law by the President on 16 December, but the Broomfield Amendment attached to the legislation required that a presidential determination be signed that assistance extended to Indonesia was 'essential to the national interest of the United States'. Such a public declaration could create some political embarrassment for the President, in both justifying the statement and taking the fall-out if Indonesia slipped into greater instability and even Communist control. Nevertheless, when the Administration came to debate the issue at the beginning of January 1964, Hilsman was adamant that US aid programmes had yielded benefits in 1963, and should be continued in the coming year if any American leverage on the local political scene was not to be lost and anti-Communist elements within the country weakened.[10] Johnson had, however, already indicated his reluctance to sign any determination on aid, asking McNamara to investigate the whole subject, including whether any items in the current programme had any military potential.[11]

Discussing the matter with McNamara on 2 January 1964, the President reported a conversation with Richard Russell, one of his oldest friends in the Senate, where deep scepticism over agreeing to further aid to Indonesia was expressed, asserting 'I just feel that I ought to be impeached if I approve it, that's just how deeply I feel.' Johnson went on to recall a speech he had made in 1947 regarding the Truman Doctrine, 'in which I said that when you let a bully come in . . . your front yard he'll run you out of your bedroom the next, and I don't think we ought to encourage this guy [Sukarno] to do what he's doing down there . . . I think any assistance just shows weakness on our part.' McNamara replied that he felt 'exactly that way', and that he would press such views on the State Department.[12] Later the same day an inter-agency meeting (involving

[10] See Hilsman memorandum for Rusk, 2 January 1964, and draft memorandum to the President, 'Aid to Indonesia', Indonesia, general, 1961–7, box 472, Harriman papers.
[11] Hilsman, *To Move a Nation*, 407.
[12] Johnson–McNamara telephone conversation, 2 January 1964, PN013, WH 6401.03, Johnson tapes, LBJL. Johnson was almost certainly referring to a speech he delivered on the floor of the House in May 1947, strongly supporting the Truman Administration's aid bill for Greece and Turkey, see Robert Dallek, *Lone Star Rising: Lyndon Johnson and His Times, 1908–1960* (New York, 1991), 292.

McNamara, McGeorge and William Bundy, Harriman and Hilsman) was held in Rusk's office to decide on the final recommendations over aid to make to the President. This resulted in a decision to oppose any further C-130 sales by Lockheed to Indonesia, and to indicate reluctance to authorize any new export licences for spares. It also seemed to signal the adoption of a more sceptical line on aid, with delays and reductions advocated in the 1964 programmes, but no complete cut-off for fear of Indonesian reprisals. The meeting recommended that a presidential determination to cover aid in the civic action and military assistance programmes be issued, but in the context of 'very tight control over all aspects of both aid and trade with Indonesia, with progressive cuts in our aid programs as the situation and Indonesian behaviour warrant'. Moreover, it was agreed, much to Forrestal's consternation, that McNamara would review the list of military assistance items still in the 'pipeline' for delivery under the schedule for 1963 (amounting to about $7.5 million of equipment), and suspend deliveries if they could be considered to significantly enhance Indonesian military capabilities, reporting to the President after the fact.[13]

The question of aid to Indonesia was addressed by the National Security Council at a meeting held on 7 January 1964. Both Rusk and McNamara put forward the view that some aid should be continued, the former pointing out: 'The stakes are very high. More is involved in Indonesia, with its 100 million people, than is at stake in Viet Nam.' Both also felt that Johnson should go ahead and sign a presidential determination, though Rusk wanted to see the determination limited in time and scope, and McNamara noted that all agencies would closely monitor aid in the pipeline and hold up consideration of any major new assistance. Agreeing that a determination should be signed, McGeorge Bundy suggested that the Attorney General should be sent to Jakarta to tell Sukarno that assistance would not be continued unless confrontation was halted; Jones, although a first-rate ambassador, 'was not the man to tell Sukarno the hard and brutal truth'.[14] At the mention of another mission along the lines of his West Irian experience of early 1962, Robert Kennedy 'demurred and said he did not look forward to a trip to Indonesia'. Kennedy himself was worried that the announcement of a presidential determination would give a major boost to Sukarno and send confusing signals to US

---

[13] Notes on meeting on Indonesia in the Secretary's Office, 2 January 1964, box 2, Malaysia–Indonesia 1963–4, Hilsman papers; Rusk memorandum for the President, 6 January 1964, Indonesia memos, 11/63–4/64, box 246, NSF country file, LBJL. For Forrestal's strong protests see his memorandum for Bundy, 6 January 1964, *ibid.*

[14] The case for a visit by a high-level American emissary had already been made by Robert Komer, see Komer memorandum for Bundy, 9 December 1963, *FRUS, 1961–1963, XXIII*, 760–1.

domestic opinion, and along with David Bell, the Director of the Agency for International Development, wondered if the decision could be delayed. Further discussion allowed Harriman the chance to argue that the President sign a determination unlimited in time, as otherwise the question would keep recurring; he 'favored continuing a limited program for keeping a foot in the door. If the Indonesians turn against us and seize US investments, the Chinese Communists might get the US oil companies, thereby altering the strategic balance in the area.' Rusk added that the 'question was whether we decide to stay at the table and play a little longer rather than leave the table now'.[15]

Despite the collective view of his senior foreign policy advisers that some form of determination be signed, Johnson preferred to defer a decision and for Rusk and McNamara to explain to congressional leaders that a delay was required to assess the outcome of recent diplomatic moves in the area and while the despatch of a presidential emissary to Sukarno was considered by the Administration. Johnson would not agree to sign a determination under present circumstances, and as he wished he was eventually provided with an opinion from the Attorney General that a determination to cover current aid was not actually required, and hence a delay of some weeks could be legally justified. Although Bundy advised the President that this was not an option favoured by his principal officers, the legal opinion gave the Administration a 'reasonable' time to review the situation under the new congressional policy, while existing programmes could continue.[16]

The reluctance of the President to sign even a limited determination on aid to Indonesia was a reflection of his innate scepticism over the whole subject, derived from his instinctive sense that the British and Malaysians were the injured victims of the aggressive designs of an expansionist and dictatorial leader whom he personally disliked. This was an obvious disappointment to those in the State Department who had worked throughout the previous year to preserve a degree of US influence in Indonesian affairs. Hilsman felt that President Kennedy would have signed the determination as a routine matter, while McNamara's new oversight role over the aid programme was not seen as a positive sign. Recollecting events at a later date, Hilsman remembered that Johnson 'put the responsibility in the hands of McNamara, and that's not where it belonged... that was

[15] Summary record of NSC meeting, 7 January 1964, box 1, NSF, NSC meetings file, LBJL; Notes on NSC meeting, 7 January 1964, box 2, Malaysia–Indonesia 1963–4, Hilsman papers.
[16] See Forrestal memorandum for Bundy, 10 January 1964; Bundy memorandum for Johnson, 12 January 1964, Indonesia memos, 11/63–4/64, box 246, NSF country file, LBJL.

another element in my feeling that he was just not going to listen to the Harriman–Forrestal–Hilsman–Ball group'.[17] The discussions over US aid to Indonesia in early 1964 were, moreover, couched in a very defensive tone, compared to those of only a few months before. Whereas the justification of the programmes had tended to be seen in terms of the potential leverage that they could exert over Indonesian policies and actions, an argument that now figured just as prominently was the adverse repercussions on direct US commercial and strategic interests that could result from any decision to terminate aid. As Bundy argued to the President, '. . . a cut-off today could trigger a violent reaction from Sukarno and block efforts to settle dispute by Filipinos and Thais. It could also cost us half a billion of private investment. It could hand Indonesia's future to the Communists. Aswan Dam case should remind us that neutrals are ready to seize on *our* acts to justify *their* outrages – and to some extent they get away with it.'[18]

The despatch of Robert Kennedy to meet Sukarno in an attempt to defuse tensions in the region and bring about the conditions whereby some kind of negotiated solution to confrontation might be reached obviously provided good political cover for the President's difficulties over aid to Indonesia. Kennedy was the preferred choice of Bundy and his NSC staff for the mission to the Far East, and had actually been initially suggested by Harriman; according to Bundy, 'Johnson felt that he had been sort of manoeuvred into approving by staff people who weren't thinking about the Johnson interest.'[19] Johnson talked with Richard Russell on 10 January, saying he was 'going to send Bobby Kennedy to Indonesia and just let him put it right in his [Sukarno's] lap'. Russell hoped Johnson would 'Tell him to be tough too', to which the President responded, 'I think he will . . . Well, he wasn't so tough last time he saw Sukarno. He took away from the Dutch and gave it to Sukarno, didn't he?' Johnson continued, '. . . let him go out there and let him have whatever row it is with Sukarno'. After a short sanitization on the tape recording of this conversation, the President finished, '. . . if we're going to have a break just let him [Sukarno?] break it'.[20] There was certainly a high degree of pessimism over the trip, and Kennedy was evidently reluctant to go. Having talked to Komer, Forrestal told Harriman in a telephone conversation that Kennedy's mission was 'going to be our last shot', maintaining 'the

---

[17] Roger Hilsman Oral History.
[18] Bundy memorandum for Johnson, 7 January 1964, Indonesia memos, 11/63–4/64, box 246, NSF country file, LBJL.
[19] See Arthur M. Schlesinger Jr, *Robert Kennedy and His Times* (London, 1978), 633.
[20] Johnson–Russell telephone conversation, 10 January 1964, PN02, WH 6401.11, Johnson tapes, LBJL.

point of someone going out is to tell Sukarno that we are on the verge
of having to do something beyond our control – to cut our assistance
to Indonesia', to which Harriman responded, '. . . that wouldn't do. It
would force us to close out. . . if he went out there he has to stop all of
this [guerrilla?] activity'.[21]

Kennedy's Far Eastern tour encompassed a meeting with Sukarno in
Tokyo, followed by stops in Manila, Kuala Lumpur and Jakarta, before returning via London. His outline brief, prepared by Forrestal and
Hilsman, presented his goal as being to persuade Sukarno to agree to a
cease-fire in confrontation so that talks putting an 'Asian solution' to the
conflict could be arranged. The Malaysians would also need to drop their
precondition of diplomatic recognition if formal negotiations were to proceed. The British, described as 'fast losing both patience and objectivity',
had to be persuaded 'to let the Tunku be independent' and determine
his own approach to negotiations with Jakarta.[22] Although the Americans would express no preference for the kind of eventual settlement that
might be reached, it was considered that the offer of a plebiscite in the
Borneo territories in five years' time, mirroring the Indonesian commitment in West Irian, could be the face-saving device needed to resolve the
dispute. Regarding Sukarno,

however cavalier he is with American sensibilities, he is demonstrably anxious
to retain United States friendship. He wants and needs our aid; he relishes the
prestige of dealing with us as an 'equal'; and he certainly senses the manifold
disadvantages to Indonesia of a serious breach with the world's most powerful
nation. But if given no alternative other than a humiliating public defeat, he
would probably be willing to break with us. Our leverage thus is substantial but
limited.[23]

If the Attorney General could bring about a cessation of Indonesian
guerrilla forays into the Borneo territories, this would certainly be very
welcome to the Malaysians and their British allies, but steps towards
a negotiated settlement that included any meeting between the principal protagonists before diplomatic recognition had been extended was
a different matter altogether. Policy-makers in London feared that the
Tunku had staked his credibility on his professed preconditions and entering a talks process without recognition would undermine his domestic position, both among leaders in the Borneo territories anxious over
any sell-out of their interests and with Lee Kuan Yew, who could be

[21] Harriman–Forrestal telephone conversation, 7 January 1964, box 582, Harriman papers.
[22] 'Outline of Plan for Attorney General's Trip', 9 January 1964, Indonesia/Malaysia
1963–4, box 2, Hilsman papers.
[23] 'The Attorney General's meeting with Sukarno,' n.d. (c. 9 January 1964), Attorney
General's Far East Trip, box 5–6, Hilsman papers.

expected to seize on any sign of weakness in the Tunku to enhance his own leadership credentials. As was seen in the previous chapter, there was concern in some circles over the Malaysian response to the losses suffered during the engagement at Kalabakan in late December 1963. The Tunku's initial reaction to Kalabakan had been to discount any consideration of new Thai proposals for a cease-fire and a meeting, but this had been replaced by a more sober realization of what total rejection of a diplomatic route entailed. In early January 1964, the Minister of Defence, Peter Thorneycroft, visited Malaysia, where he conferred with Razak and agreed that though confrontation must be seen through to a conclusion, the 'need to continue to seek a political solution was paramount'.[24] The Minister of Defence was not just pacifying the Malaysians with such comments, for he too was convinced that the costs of confrontation could not be sustained over the long term. Thorneycroft reported to the Prime Minister, 'It is abundantly clear to me that in this as in so many of our problems there is no long-term military solution. Although...I shall have a number of military proposals to make we must continue to press for a political solution.'[25]

Almost simultaneously, however, the apparent feeling building up on the British side behind the need for a negotiated settlement was checked by the conclusions being reached by the Foreign Secretary on policy towards Indonesia. These were circulated by Butler to members of the Cabinet on 6 January, in a paper that had been approved by the CRO and Ministry of Defence, and explored possible offensive options as well as the prospects for negotiations. Intensified military action, it was argued, could not prevent a determined Indonesia from continuing to wage low-intensity guerrilla warfare in Borneo, while escalation was only likely to provoke international censure 'because international opinion generally does not regard fomenting a rebellion in someone else's country (which is all the Indonesians admit to doing) as justifying the victim in openly carrying war into his tormentor's country (cf. international, including UK reactions to the French bombing of Tunisian territory during the Algerian war)'. Reference of the conflict to the UN was seen as risky, given that there was little support among Afro-Asian opinion for a British military presence in South East Asia, and there would be a tendency to see fault on both sides of the dispute. Calls for negotiations could see Malaysia having to relax its preconditions for talks and 'once negotiations are internationalised, Malaysia will be subjected to pressure, as the price of peace with Indonesia, to abandon her defence agreement with us

---

[24] Note of a meeting between Thorneycroft and Razak, 6 January 1964, PREM 11/4905.
[25] Thorneycroft to Home, T.9/64, 7 January 1964, *ibid.*

and to deprive us of the Singapore base'. Moreover, discounting a total
Indonesian climb-down, negotiations would necessarily be problematic
as they could only really lead to a settlement if some form of compromise
was offered by Malaysia, involving perhaps a plebiscite in the Borneo territories, concessions to the Philippines over North Borneo or some deal
regarding British use or tenure of the Singapore base. Hence, 'It would
be useless, therefore, for us to contemplate a negotiated solution unless
Indonesia had first been brought to her knees by a prolonged process of
attrition or unless Malaysia and we were ready to make concessions as
well as receive them.'

The bleak conclusion reached by Butler was that current policy would
have to be continued. This involved keeping up a defensive military posture ('we should avoid as far as possible any extension of the conflict
outside Borneo'), playing down the importance of the dispute in public and maintaining diplomatic and commercial relations with Indonesia.
The hope was that Indonesia would eventually 'weary of the struggle
under the pressure of internal, particularly economic, stresses'. Continuing present policy would allow all other options to be kept open, but
carried with it the danger that 'UK public opinion might lose patience
first and insist on either escalation or negotiation. The impression that
our soldiers have been condemned to fighting an interminable war with
one hand tied behind their backs is, of course, precisely the reaction for
which the Indonesians hope.' There was also the chance that Indonesia
might step up its own level of military action. It was dubiously claimed
that,

As long as our conflict with Indonesia remains unofficial and bilateral, we retain
the initiative. We can choose either to intensify it or to seek a settlement. Once we
either internationalize it or turn it into a war (declared or undeclared) against a
wicked aggressor, Her Majesty's Government will be restricted in their freedom
of action both by public opinion at home and international pressure... Once
we turn the present ambiguous struggle into an open Anglo-Indonesian conflict,
neither of us will be able to withdraw without admitting defeat.

The crucial variable in the whole situation, the Foreign Secretary asserted, was the attitude of the United States. The 'ambivalent attitude of
our major ally' had caused Butler to refrain from recommending any more
forceful action, while 'because the United States Government would only
be too glad to seize upon any opening for a negotiated settlement, in which
a reluctant Tunku might be forced from concession to concession', the
Foreign Secretary was led to hold off pushing initiatives that might lead
to talks to resolve the conflict; there was little optimism that the new
Administration in Washington would undertake any drastic change in

US policy. 'Even though a negotiated settlement may have to come in the long run,' Butler noted,

we should remain wary of well intentioned but misguided initiatives to this end . . . we should continue to attempt to persuade our reluctant allies, the US first and foremost, and the Germans, our other NATO allies, and the Japanese, that the possibility of influencing Sukarno does not rest in pandering to his threat to turn Communist but rather that failure to stand up to him now will only increase the risk of Indonesia becoming Communist later.[26]

Butler's paper tended to overlook several key considerations. The most important was the ability of Britain to sustain her military efforts in defence of Malaysia, given the potentially interminable nature of confrontation. The creation of Malaysia was intended to be a way for Britain to reduce her draining commitments east of Suez by the mid-1960s; instead it was beginning to exert uncomfortable pressures on the defence budget. No real attempt was made to meet American arguments that confrontation was serving the interests of the PKI and driving Indonesia in a more radical direction. There was also the question of the internal stability of Malaysia, whose leaders might well begin to find the strains of the conflict intolerable; the Foreign Secretary had characterized the struggle with Indonesia as 'unofficial and bilateral' when it was palpably multilateral in nature, with the pattern of Malaysian politics frequently influencing the stance adopted by British policy-makers. This last point had at least been appreciated by Thorneycroft, who had realized on his trip to Malaysia that more aggressive action might be needed to reassure and satisfy the Malaysians, including the peoples of the Borneo territories, of British resolve (involving perhaps the possibility of undertaking counter-subversion in Sumatra). Thorneycroft had also recognized, nonetheless, that some negotiating track had to be found out of the conflict.

The Prime Minister had expressed an interest in a political settlement to Butler in December 1963, and Butler's contribution must have seemed disappointing. When the Cabinet came together on 9 January 1964 to discuss the issues, it was noted, in what represented a shift from Butler's line, that the Tunku 'expected that we would now intensify our efforts to promote a political solution of the differences between Malaysia and Indonesia; and it would be necessary to consider the means by which this would best be arranged, since we could not contemplate the indefinite continuance of our present military commitment in the Borneo territories'.[27] A few days later, at a meeting of the Defence and Oversea Policy Committee, Thorneycroft presented his own paper on policy to

[26] 'Policy Toward Indonesia', CP(64)5, 6 January 1964, CAB 129/116.
[27] CM(64)2nd mtg, 9 January 1964, CAB 128/38.

Indonesia, which was itself based on a memorandum from Lord Head. This argued that 'we should do everything possible to reach a political means of stopping [confrontation] as soon as possible', but if the conflict were prolonged 'we must carefully consider and be prepared for the need to adopt a more offensive military policy'. In the short run, however, a defensive posture was favoured as it would continue to allow Malaysia to portray itself as the victim. The Minister of Defence backed up Head's conclusions and emphasized the need 'to persuade opinion in the United States both that we were determined to defend Malaysia and that their own interests would be better served by supporting Malaysia than by relying on Indonesia as a bulwark against Communism in South-East Asia'.[28] Butler agreed, but cautioned that 'we must guard against the risk that the United States Government might seek to promote a compromise settlement which would damage our position in South-East Asia', and mentioned the 'renewed risks which were clearly inherent' in Robert Kennedy's recently announced mission to the Far East, which was likely to push recent Thai proposals for a one-month truce leading to tripartite talks. It was finally concluded:

The main object of any political solution should be to enable President Sukarno to abandon his policy of confrontation without loss of prestige. But he would only adopt this course if he was convinced that his present policy would cause irretrievable damage to his relations with the United States. For this reason the full co-operation of the United States was indispensable; and unless their support was assured, it might be better not to attempt to reach a political solution.

Any political negotiations with the Indonesians should not be left with the Malaysian Prime Minister, but should be conducted by the British and US Governments, while studies should be made, along the lines earlier suggested by Rusk, of military counter-measures that could be taken against Indonesian territory.

These important Whitehall debates of early January 1964 underscored the dilemmas confronting British policy-makers. There could evidently be no military solution to confrontation, yet the path of negotiations carried many perils, particularly as there was little in the way of concessions that Malaysia could offer Indonesia that would not threaten to undermine the very basis of the new federation. When one Foreign Office official floated once more the notion of a plebiscite in the Borneo territories, he was reminded by a colleague that the 'CRO will not look at a plebiscite, which they fear might – at the very worst – lead to a break-up

---

[28] Thorneycroft memoranda, DO(64)5, 13 January 1964; DO(64) 1st mtg, 14 January 1964, CAB 148/1.

of Malaysia'.[29] Control of any negotiating process would also be highly uncertain, and notions of excluding the Tunku from the principal talks showed the anxieties felt at repeating the experiences of the previous summer at the Manila summit. Moreover, limiting discussions with the Indonesians to just the British and Americans was completely at odds with Washington's conception of the need for an 'Asian solution' to confrontation, and sensitivities about the involvement of outside and white powers. It was imperative, from a British point of view, to secure some degree of shared understanding with the Johnson Administration in Washington over confrontation before the momentum behind an unwelcome diplomatic resolution became overwhelming.

The latter prospect moved more prominently into view with the US Attorney General's efforts to arrange for a cease-fire and tripartite talks. There had been no consultation by the State Department with London over Kennedy's trip, and some apprehensive British officials remembered the outcome of his previous visit to the region in 1962, where US policy had begun to swing decisively towards Indonesia in the West Irian dispute.[30] Prior to Kennedy's departure from Washington, Ormsby Gore saw both the Attorney General and the President to express the wish that the Tunku should not be pressed to attend an Asian summit prior to diplomatic recognition, arguing that this could undermine his position within Malaysia. When the Ambassador put British views to Johnson, the President stated that the United States would stand firm against Sukarno's confrontation policy but did not comment on tactics, while McGeorge Bundy maintained that Washington would not try to determine the terms of an 'Asian solution'. Bundy informed Kennedy, in another reflection of US suspicions, that an 'essential element of your visit to Tunku may be to determine what part of his position is his own and what part comes from London. British representations being closely held here to avoid any suggestion of US/UK collusion vs. Asians.'[31] In Tokyo itself, the British Ambassador there made further representations to Kennedy when he arrived on 17 January, leading the latter to comment that he

found the British point of view difficult to understand. He had formed the impression after his conversation with [Ormsby Gore] that the British Government did not welcome this American initiative. He thought himself that it was in our

[29] See J. A. Pilcher minute, 7 January 1964, D1051/41, FO 371/175067.
[30] The South East Asia Department even prepared a memorandum comparing the background to the two missions, highlighting Dutch diplomatic isolation following Kennedy's trip to Jakarta in February 1962, see Chalmers memorandum, 20 January 1964, D1051/3, FO 371/175065.
[31] Bundy to Tokyo (for Kennedy), no. 1829, 17 January 1964, NSF, country file, Malaysia cables, 11/63–3/64, LBJL.

interests and that we should be on the same side. If this were not so, it was our war and we could fight it.[32]

The Attorney General's talks with Sukarno seemed fruitful, and the Indonesian President agreed that he would issue instructions for a cease-fire in military confrontation, and withdraw his forces from the Borneo border area, if the Tunku would agree to attend a summit meeting.[33] Komer was encouraged by developments in Tokyo, telling the President:

Our Malaysian enterprise seems to be going very well, though we're only through the first phase ... Now Bobby goes to Manila to enlist Macapagal's help, and then to work on the Tunku. Perhaps the toughest problem will be to get the Tunku to agree to meet without insisting on prior Indo recognition. Here Ormsby Gore's pitch to you against pressing this on the Tunku is worrisome. But Harriman just had a good talk with Gore, who understands why we want to forestall any such unrealistic preconditions when there's at least a 50/50 chance of success of avoiding another nasty crisis in Southeast Asia.[34]

Harriman and Hilsman had indeed seen Ormsby Gore on 18 January to emphasize US desires that the prior recognition precondition be dropped, pointing out that the Tunku had already conceded that he would be prepared to meet the Philippine President before Manila had recognized the new Federation.[35] This moderation in the Tunku's stance had become apparent to the British a few days before when Head had seen the Malaysian Prime Minister to discuss press accounts of Macapagal's latest offer of a meeting. The High Commissioner reported that the last time he had talked about the Filipinos with the Tunku 'he referred to them as bastards and said he would on no account meet Macapagal until he had accepted the Manila Accord'. Now, however, the Tunku would be ready to see the Philippine President on neutral ground, where Macapagal could accept the Accord (and with it the results of the UN survey in the Borneo territories) and Malaysia would agree to refer the Philippine claim to North Borneo to the International Court of Justice.[36] Arriving in Kuala Lumpur on 21 January, the Attorney General managed to secure the Tunku's agreement that if Sukarno called a cease-fire, he would be prepared to attend a summit, to be preceded by a preliminary meeting of foreign ministers held in early February in Bangkok.[37]

[32] Tokyo to FO, no. 27, 17 January 1964, PREM 11/4906.
[33] See Jones, *Indonesia*, 301–2.
[34] Komer memorandum for Johnson, 18 January 1964, NSF, country file, Malaysia memos, 11/63–3/64, LBJL.
[35] Washington to FO, no. 213, 18 January 1964, PREM 11/4906.
[36] Kuala Lumpur to CRO, no. 107, 14 January 1964, PREM 11/4905.
[37] See Kuala Lumpur to CRO, no. 172, 22 January 1964, PREM 11/4906.

The Kennedy mission brought to a head all the British fears and resentments about American policy towards Indonesia that had built up over the preceding months. The Attorney General, and Howard Jones who had also been present in Tokyo, were both felt by British officials to have been duped by Sukarno, and been impressed with his contention that the documents captured during the destruction of the Embassy in Jakarta proved that the British were determined to unseat him.[38] Wright minuted to the Prime Minister that the Foreign Office thought little of Kennedy's efforts and that he 'appears to be on the verge of selling us down the river but has not actually done so yet'.[39] At the Defence and Oversea Policy Committee on 22 January the Prime Minister announced that Kennedy's mediation efforts had led to Malaysian acceptance of a tripartite meeting provided Sukarno agreed to a cease-fire. Discussion among the gathered ministers revealed deep scepticism that the Indonesian President could be relied on to desist from covert attempts at subversion and that 'it would be necessary to prepare contingency plans to counter these operations by all means short of open hostilities. Merely to remain on the defensive would increasingly forfeit the confidence of the local inhabitants.' Again it is likely that counter-subversion measures against Indonesian territory were the steps being contemplated by ministers. Moreover, the Committee anticipated that tripartite talks would lead to heavy pressure on the UK and Malaysia to make concessions, and that 'it would have to be made clear to the Tunku that, if he were to make concessions, particularly as regards our use of the Singapore base or the maintenance of United Kingdom forces in Sabah and Sarawak, without obtaining the agreement of the United Kingdom Government, we might well be unable to meet our commitments to him under the Malaysian Defence Agreement'.[40] Here was the ultimate sanction that British policy-makers could use to influence Malaysian behaviour: any 'Asian solution' which led to an agreement to change the status of the Singapore base and Britain would revoke its security guarantee to the Federation, leaving Malaysia prey to a revival of Indonesian pressures.

British alarm must have increased when Kennedy met Sukarno once again on 22 January in Jakarta, and the following day it was announced by the Indonesian President at a joint press conference that he had issued instructions for a cease-fire to Indonesian forces in Kalimantan. The Attorney General continued on to Bangkok where he secured Thai

---

[38] See Tokyo to FO, no. 36, 19 January 1964; Tokyo to FO, no. 37, 19 January 1964; and for Gilchrist's vigorous denial of the existence of any such material, Jakarta to FO, no. 141, 20 January 1964, *ibid.*

[39] Wright minute for Home, 20 January 1964, *ibid.*

[40] DO(64)2nd mtg, 22 January 1964, CAB 148/1.

agreement to investigate any breaches of the cease-fire and report back to the parties to the dispute.[41] In London, the Cabinet met on the day that the cease-fire was announced, and discussion among ministers reflected uncertainty over what might be unilaterally arranged by the Malaysians. It was stressed that though Britain and the United States shared the common objective of checking Sino-Soviet influence in South East Asia, there were dangers that their chosen methods might diverge. While the Americans were chiefly concerned with preventing Indonesia from aligning with Communist China, Britain wanted to preserve the integrity of Malaysia; if attempts were made to restrain the Malaysian Government from making concessions to Indonesia, 'we might appear to the United States Government to be deliberately thwarting their own policy...' The alternative approach, however, could be equally damaging, as if the Malaysian Government negotiated a withdrawal of UK forces from the Borneo territories, the security of the Federation might be gravely endangered, and Britain's military presence at Singapore undermined, so fatally unhinging Britain's position as a whole in South East Asia. The conclusion reached was that 'while we must continue to seek a political solution of the differences between Malaysia and Indonesia – if only because the alternative course of maintaining UK forces indefinitely on the Borneo frontiers would ultimately be intolerable – we must be on our guard against allowing the Government of Malaysia to pay too high a price for it'.[42] This was not such a straightforward aspiration to fulfil, however, for we have seen how wary British officials were becoming in offering advice to Malaysia, and 'restraint' of the Tunku might actually involve making the unrealistic threat of removing Britain's protection from the Federation. In retrospect it seems unlikely that the Malaysians would regard such a move as anything other than a rather distasteful bluff, for its implementation would lead to the eventuality the British sought to avoid throughout this period: the loss of unrestricted use of their base facilities at Singapore.

When Kennedy finally arrived in London, stopping off on his way back to the United States from the Far East, his reception was frosty. It had not helped that after the Attorney General's departure from Jakarta, Sukarno had made clear that confrontation must continue, and only as a short-term measure were diplomatic tactics being employed. The British press was almost universally hostile to the mediation effort, and Kennedy's meeting with Butler on 24 January was markedly strained, the Foreign Secretary commenting that the Attorney General was 'obviously on the

[41] Jones, *Indonesia*, 301–2.
[42] CM(64)6th mtg, 23 January 1964, CAB 128/38.

defensive and spoke throughout with an undertone of barely veiled resentment and bitterness'. Kennedy maintained that the British case over Malaysia was not sufficiently understood in South East Asia and that fresh efforts should be made with the Philippine and Thai Governments. In addition, 'Everyone he had spoken to agreed in attributing the primary blame to the British conduct of the negotiations during the period immediately preceding the establishment of Malaysia', with Sukarno, in particular, feeling betrayed by the handling of the UN enquiry. In Kennedy's view, '. . . the trouble was that all concerned (including the Malaysians) felt that Britain was too far out in front on the problem of Malaysia. British officers in Malaysia gave the impression that they still believed they were running the country.' When pressed to give specific examples, the Attorney General declined, but his remarks encapsulated in neat fashion widely held regional suspicions of British neo-colonial influence on Malaysian policies. Butler summed up his exchange with Kennedy with the sour observation that the latter's 'frankness had been more conspicuous than his cordiality'.[43]

Despite the Attorney General's reluctance to give specific examples of criticisms directed against the British role, many had in fact come during his short stay in Kuala Lumpur. Here, the Tunku indicated to Kennedy that he 'was less than pleased with Duncan Sandys' performance last September [sic]' saying, '"Sandys came as a friend and became a nuisance."' The new US Ambassador to Malaysia, James Bell, found the 'same outspoken attitude' was held by many others, and that this was 'not an anti-British attitude but rather reflects a feeling that the era of British advice and counsel is rapidly coming to an end'. This Bell attributed partly to 'general annoyance at unsolicited advice, but it is more likely determination on the part of Malaysian leaders to run their own government'. The Ambassador concluded that

this attitude, plus the Malaysian acceptance of the proposals put forward by the Attorney General, is likely to lead to a feeling of somewhat greater reliance on the United States. Having moved away from political ties with the UK and having developed a reluctance to accept British political advice, the Malaysians may, over the next few months, seek a closer relationship with the United States.[44]

Though David Bruce, the US Ambassador in London, had warned the Attorney General that he 'must stop criticizing Duncan Sandys to the British, as he had in every capital that he had visited', Kennedy introduced himself to the latter during a lunch at Chequers by remarking, 'I have heard a lot about you in my travels and I must say that you are just as

[43] FO to Washington, no. 32, 27 January 1964, PREM 11/4906.
[44] Bell to Hilsman, 28 January 1964, POL MALAYSIA–UK, RG 59.

popular in the Far East as I am in Mississippi and Alabama.'[45] For his
part, on his return to the United States, Kennedy expressed his dismay
at the distrust shown towards his mission by British officials and in the
press: 'He has always shared with his brother an intense dislike of Sukarno
(it therefore irritated him when the Beaverbrook Press referred to him as
Sukarno's friend)', Ormsby Gore reported. He was also horrified at the
lack of State Department consultation with London prior to his visit to
the Far East. Kennedy felt he had been

asked by President Johnson to do a job for his country and was assured that
the objective he was given would also be in the British interest. He had then
been hurriedly briefed by the State Department and in view of the time available
had not unreasonably supposed that the State Department would ensure that we
were fully consulted. He had gone out to the Far East and done what he had been
told to do to the best of his ability and he felt somewhat aggrieved by the acute
suspicion of his motives which had been displayed.[46]

To some British officials it was evident that this divergence of approach
with Washington could not be allowed to continue. More effort was required to see things from an American perspective and to devise arguments that could be used to bring Anglo-American policies into closer
alignment. Oliver Wright advised the Prime Minister, '... we are in danger of developing a Sukarno fixation of our own to match the Castro
fixation which we deplore in the Americans. We seem to show no com-
prehension of the overall American and Western interest in a stable
Indonesia.' The Americans wanted to keep the 'largest country in the
area non-Communist even if quasi Fascist', while the British were necessarily committed to Malaysia 'whether we like it or not, because we
created it (and are now having some doubts about it) ...' Rather than
trying to 'put the screws on the Americans', as Sandys advocated, in
order to convert them to the British point of view, Wright felt it would
be more productive to try to reconcile the different positions, asserting,
'I think we shall find that the Americans really have not done too badly by
us at all. They are looking for a political solution which is what we want.
If they have not got everything we want this is not the least because to
get everything you want is not in the nature of political solutions.' Wright
hoped that the Prime Minister would be able 'to counter some of the
more paranoid ideas prevalent in Whitehall'.[47]

Internal Foreign Office discussion had focussed on such Anglo-
American differences at the beginning of January, where James Cable

---

[45] 'Notes for WAH personal files', 1 February 1964, Subject files, Robert F. Kennedy,
Jan.–June 1964, box 479, Harriman papers.
[46] Ormsby Gore to Butler, 29 January 1964, PREM 11/5196.
[47] Wright minute for Home, 22 January 1964, PREM 11/4906.

254 Conflict and confrontation in South East Asia

had replaced Warner as head of the Foreign Office's South East Asia Department. The crux of the matter, Cable felt, was that the Americans regarded the 'loss' of Indonesia to the Communist camp to be a worse eventuality than the loss of a British military presence in South East Asia based on Singapore (which could be the price for an end to confrontation). Cable's opinion was not, however, shared by Sir Harold Caccia, the Permanent Under Secretary, who doubted whether the Americans had even considered the possible results of a political solution to confrontation in terms of British bases. Caccia believed that the Americans placed a high value both on keeping Indonesia non-Communist as well as on ensuring that Britain could make an effective contribution to the Western defence effort in the region through SEATO.[48]

As Kennedy completed his tour of Asian capitals, Cable and his officials gave more thought to the problem, and at a meeting with the Foreign Secretary on 20 January it was proposed to bring together the topics of the Indonesia/Malaysia dispute and recent calls for an international conference to guarantee Cambodian neutrality (a move which the Americans regarded dubiously, fearing that the precedent might be extended to South Vietnam).[49] The intention was, as Cable explained, 'to try to make the United States Government realise that they cannot hope to defend South Vietnam against the Communist threat from the North while simultaneously tolerating, and even encouraging, the Indonesian threat from the South'. The line suggested was that the defence of Malaysia had a crucial bearing on the struggle in Vietnam through its effect on the whole Western position in South East Asia. It could be held that

An 'Asian solution' for Malaysia leading to a neutralization of that country under the influence of Indonesia would... have such repercussions on Thailand, Cambodia and South Vietnam that it would not long be possible to maintain SEATO. In these circumstances South Vietnam would eventually be reduced... to a precarious American bridgehead in a South East Asia otherwise neutralist or Communist.[50]

The British knew full well that in early 1964 the Americans were thoroughly alarmed by French proposals for the neutralization of the conflict

---

[48] Cable minute, 6 January 1964; Pilcher minute, 6 January 1964; Caccia minute, 7 January 1964, D1051/6, FO 371/175065.
[49] The Americans were keen that the British, as one of the co-chairs of the 1954 Geneva conference, should block the idea of a reconvened conference. For the Cambodia issue see Fredrik Logevall, *Choosing War: The Lost Chance for Peace and the Escalation of the War in Vietnam* (Berkeley, 1999), 85–8, and Smith, *International History of the Vietnam War, vol. II*, 204, 208.
[50] Cable minute, 20 January 1964 and 'Notes for possible discussions between Her Majesty's Ambassador, Washington, and President Johnson or Mr Rusk', D1051/3, FO 371/175065.

in Vietnam.[51] The best way to win their understanding and support could be to link the notion of neutralization, and the withdrawal of Western bases, with the form of settlement that the Indonesians might insist on. The result of these discussions was the despatch of a message from Butler to Rusk, with approval from the Prime Minister, which pointed out the possible damaging consequences of a purely 'Asian solution' to confrontation. Any settlement, it was contended, which involved a 'neutralization of Malaysia under Indonesian influence would have profound effects in mainland South East Asia. Thailand might reconsider her adhesion to the Western alliance. There would be repercussions in Laos and Cambodia. Above all...your problems in South Vietnam would be greatly increased.' Butler argued that on his forthcoming visit to Washington with the Prime Minister, 'we should try to look at Western policy in South East Asia as a whole rather than at the individual problems of Britain over Malaysia or of the United States over Vietnam'. In an encouraging reply, the US Secretary of State fully concurred with this approach, and underlined Washington's 'conviction concerning the importance of a vigorous and effective British presence in Southeast Asia'. Moreover, Rusk suggested preliminary talks between officials in Washington, which might also involve the Australians and New Zealanders, on such mutual problems.[52] The British approached the Americans at an advantageous moment. The removal of Diem in November 1963 had not been followed by the consolidation of a stable and effective administration in South Vietnam. The end of January 1964 had witnessed a further coup by the military in Saigon, and the uncertainties of the political situation were compounded by a renewed drive by the guerrilla forces of the National Liberation Front to undermine the remaining bases of government support in the countryside.[53] Pressures began to mount on the US Administration to take more forceful action in order to reverse these trends, with the JCS, in particular, recommending a programme of direct actions against North Vietnam, including air strikes.[54] On the diplomatic front, there was the task of dealing with French suggestions for neutralization of the region's trouble spots, accompanied by de Gaulle's unwelcome decision to establish diplomatic relations with the PRC. (Indeed, US officials had been informed that the most recent coup in Saigon was necessary to check the attempts of pro-French Vietnamese

---

[51] See Logevall, 'De Gaulle, Neutralization, and American Involvement in Vietnam'.
[52] Butler to Rusk, in FO to Washington, no. 962, 21 January 1964; Rusk to Butler, 24 January 1964, D1051/5, FO 371/175065.
[53] See e.g. SNIE 50–64, 'Short-Term Prospects in Southeast Asia', 12 February 1964, FRUS, 1964–1968, vol. I, Vietnam, 1964 (Washington, 1992), 70–1.
[54] See memorandum from JCS to McNamara, JCSM-174-64, 2 March 1964, ibid., 112–18.

officers to explore the possibilities of neutralization.) William Sullivan, a
senior State Department official who headed the Administration's inter-
agency Vietnam coordinating committee, admitted to British officials in
February 1964 that he was currently 'obsessed with the French, regarded
French activities with deep suspicion and tended to see in French policy some grand design aimed at over-throwing the American position
in South-East Asia and setting up, in co-operation with the Chinese, a
neutralist bloc . . .'[55] With their South East Asian policies under such concerted pressure, the Administration in Washington was glad of friendly
counsel from allies, and looking for support in their drive to oppose all
talk of a solution to the war in Vietnam based on neutralization.

Before the arrival of Home and Butler in Washington, a meeting of the
foreign ministers of Malaysia, Indonesia and the Philippines was held in
Bangkok from 6–10 February 1964, to establish the terms for the cease-
fire in confrontation and to prepare the ground for a subsequent tripartite
summit. Here, Subandrio refused to commit Indonesia to a withdrawal
of guerrillas from the Borneo territories as part of the cease-fire arrangements, but the Indonesians gave no indication of how their grievances
against Malaysia might be satisfied.[56] The inconclusive talks broke up
with the Thais offering to supervise the cease-fire, Subandrio returning
to Jakarta to submit a formula for the disengagement of Indonesian irregular forces to his government, and agreement on a further meeting at
some time in the future.[57] Immediately after, friendly conversations were
held at Phnom Penh between the Tunku and Macapagal. This summit
had resulted from the efforts of Cambodia's leader, Prince Sihanouk,
who may well have been trying to usurp any credit that successful Thai
mediation in the wider conflict might bring.[58] The British had little firm
information on the meeting in Phnom Penh, beyond the official line that
the Philippines had agreed to restore consular relations with Malaysia, but
suspected that the Tunku had given some kind of qualified undertaking
to refer the Sabah dispute to the ICJ.[59]

The British had refrained from any intrusive presence on the fringes
of the Bangkok meeting, hoping to avoid the criticisms that had been
generated by the overbearing attitude associated with the Sandys style
of the previous year. Hence, there was considerable relief in the Foreign
Office that Razak had shown a robust attitude in the negotiations,

---

[55] Record of a meeting on 14 February 1964, D103145/9G, FO 371/175062.
[56] Background is offered in Washington to FO, no. 530, 7 February 1964; Washington to
FO, no. 548, 8 February 1964; Bangkok to FO, no. 102, 9 February 1964; Bangkok to
FO, no. 107, 10 February 1964, D1071/57G, FO 371/175074.
[57] See FO to New York, no. 929, 11 February 1964, D1073/2, FO 371/175090.
[58] See Smith, *International History of the Vietnam War, vol. II*, 217.
[59] 'The Philippines and the Malaysia/Indonesia Dispute: Background Notes', 23 April
1964, D1051/54, FO 371/175067.

helping to allay fears that the Malaysians were prone to make concessions if left to their own devices. Noting the successes being enjoyed by the
British security forces in their counter-guerrilla operations during early
1964, and reports of rice shortages and threatened famine in Indonesia,
Cable felt confident enough to note, 'For once... I think time may be on
our side and that, for the moment at least, we can afford to sit back and
allow the Malaysians to continue playing the hand.'[60] Indeed, the campaign for the Malaysian federal elections that soon ensued further militated against any kind of weakness by the Tunku's Government in Kuala
Lumpur, as it presented itself as a resolute defender of all the interests
represented in the new Federation. Indeed, Malaysian over-belligerence
was seen as a greater problem by early March 1964, when entreaties from
British officials, and a personal telegram from Home were required to dissuade the Tunku from declaring a general mobilization against Indonesia
(a move London saw as motivated by blatant electoral considerations).[61]

Just as greater resilience now seemed more in evidence from the
Malaysians, possible face-saving concessions that could be offered to
end confrontation were once more under active discussion in Whitehall
among senior officials. Caccia and Peck, with the support of Lord
Carrington, felt the time had come when the Tunku should be advised
that he offer a plebiscite in five years' time in Sarawak and Sabah, contingent on the Indonesians carrying out the plebiscite they had promised for
West Irian. But as with previous attempts to use this device, opposition
from the CRO was pronounced. Sandys and his officials maintained that
such an offer could make for an uncomfortable parallel between the free
will exercised by the Borneo peoples in their choice of political future
and the methods Indonesia had employed over West Irian, while only
the Tunku could make a decision on such an initiative in the light of his
estimate of feeling within the Borneo territories, and he might, indeed,
prefer a 'more telling parallel' by claiming a plebiscite in Sumatra. Moreover, the advice from Gilchrist from Jakarta was that the Indonesians were
likely to reject any suggestion of linking the two exercises. Nevertheless,
Caccia was very reluctant to renounce the idea and hoped to keep it in
reserve for a later stage.[62] The debate over a possible plebiscite revealed
in clear fashion that senior officials were anxious over the lack of any
obvious diplomatic solution to confrontation, and the need to win favour
with the Americans by putting forward initiatives that appeared moderate
and had some hope of gaining Washington's backing (a solution based

---

[60] Cable minute, 'Tripartite talks in Bangkok – The Cease-Fire', 10 February 1964,
D1071/73, FO 371/175075.
[61] See CRO to Kuala Lumpur, no. 931, 5 March 1964, PREM 11/4907.
[62] Peck minute, 31 January 1964; Caccia minute, 31 January 1964, D1193/11G,
FO 371/175102.

on the offer of a plebiscite had been mentioned by Robert Kennedy to Gilchrist during his stay in Jakarta).

To prepare for the Washington meetings between President Johnson, Home, Butler and Rusk, the Foreign Office assembled briefs on South East Asia with the theme of saying to the Americans, as Peck put it, 'what South Vietnam is to you, Malaysia is to us', and 'jointly we stand, divided we fall'.[63] As far as British interests in the region were concerned, the Foreign Office noted that returns on economic investments were small (about £30 million a year), constituting less than 7 per cent of total overseas earnings, while only 3 per cent of total trade was done with South East Asia, and concluded that 'with the exception of certain oil interests in Brunei and Indonesia, our material interests are marginal'. About as much was earned and more trade was done with Latin America and the Caribbean. Nonetheless, defence costs in the area were running at about £260 million a year (20 per cent of the operational part of defence expenditure, and 50 per cent more than that spent in the Middle East). The justification for this considerable effort was deemed to be political, deriving from 'Britain's present position as the major partner of the United States in the world-wide effort to contain communist expansion'. If South East Asia were lost to Chinese Communism, 'India, Australia and New Zealand will all be dangerously threatened. Indonesia's strident nationalism is, however, unwittingly abetting the communists. This is why British support for Malaysia has to be regarded as indivisible from US support for Vietnam.' If Britain were evicted from the area through Indonesian pressure, the whole Western position would suffer, and the United States would find it difficult to pursue its containment policies in South East Asia alone. The British had to convince the Americans that their possession of the Singapore base made a direct contribution to the overall Western effort to check the advance of Communism. It was, furthermore, acknowledged that 'the Anglo-American partnership is such a vital element in British foreign policy and to our position as a world power, that we could probably not afford the damage to it which would result if we contracted out of S.E. Asia'.[64]

Quadripartite talks between US, British, Australian and New Zealand officials were convened in Washington on 10 February. Harriman, Hilsman and Forrestal met arguments that Sukarno should be dealt with in a firm fashion with the familiar State Department line that the prime US objective was to prevent Indonesia going Communist, and hence they felt it 'important to minimize rather than stress Sukarno's differences with

---

[63] Peck minute, 29 January 1964, D1073/3, FO 371/175090.
[64] 'The British position in South-East Asia in its international setting', brief by Cable, 5 February 1964, D1073/3, FO 371/175090.

the West'. Discounting concern that both Indonesia and the Philippines were espousing the slogan 'Asia for the Asians', Harriman did not feel there was any threat to the continued presence of US bases in the region, as the British would have it. The United States, it was emphasized, 'did not wish to be parties to any efforts to isolate [Indonesia] or drive her into the communist camp', while existing levels of US aid were so low as to be inadequate as any serious lever on Sukarno. As far as Indonesian objectives went, Hilsman doubted that Sukarno had

anything approaching a clear blueprint. Instead, he appeared to hold a diffuse and contradictory range of ambitions, many of them unclear even in his own mind. On some days ... Sukarno probably daydreamed of a new Indonesian empire, while on others he saw himself in the role of a moderate, responsible statesman. Above all, Sukarno was an opportunist, with little consistency in his objectives.[65]

After a day of talks, the British delegation believed they had little chance they could extract a clear public declaration of US support for Malaysia, or any kind of warning to Sukarno over his future behaviour.[66] In private, although Harriman and Hilsman were showing some signs of increasing exasperation with Indonesian conduct in the dispute, they were not pre-pared to give up on the idea of a negotiated settlement, and remained concerned with British and Australian attitudes.[67]

Nevertheless, on the second day of the talks it was possible for all the participants to sign up to a paper (initially put forward by the Aus-tralians) encompassing areas of mutual agreement. These included the points that withdrawal of all Indonesian forces from Sarawak and Sabah should be secured as soon as possible, that any settlement would have to be negotiated by the three principals and 'must be such as will not publicly humiliate Sukarno or weaken Malaysia', that the preservation of British and US bases and defence agreements in the region was essential, that there would be informal consultations about possible joint action at the UN in the event of an Indonesian resumption of hostilities, and finally that 'any settlement should be an Asian conception but should not adversely affect non-Asian interests in the security and development of the area'. Moreover, Harriman was anxious to dispel any doubts that the Americans were trying to appease Sukarno or condone his attitude to the cease-fire.[68] This outcome represented a considerable advance on

---

[65] 'Quadripartite talks on the Far East, Washington, February 10–11, 1964, Summary of discussions on Indonesia and Malaysia', box 2, Hilsman papers.
[66] Washington to FO, no. 582, 11 February 1964, D1073/2, FO 371/175090.
[67] See the discussion of tactics in Harriman–Hilsman telephone conversation, 10 February 1964, box 582, Harriman papers.
[68] Washington to FO, no. 594, 11 February 1964; Washington to FO, no. 595, 11 February 1964, D1073/2, FO 371/175090.

previous Anglo-American exchanges on the conflict. During the talks, the British had been careful to tone down their previous outright denunciations of Sukarno and extreme views of the direction of Indonesian policy. They had, moreover, taken the chance to explain to the Americans that their main difficulty with a so-called 'Asian solution' to confrontation was that it posed a potential threat to the British base at Singapore, and implicitly the US bases in the Philippines. The Americans, in turn, wanted to reassure the British that they valued and supported their continued presence in the region, and appreciated the backing that London was prepared to give to Washington's Vietnam policies.

These emerging trends in Anglo-American views on confrontation were amplified and considerably expanded when Butler, along with Caccia, Ormsby Gore and Peck, met Rusk at the White House, with Harriman, Bruce and McGeorge Bundy in attendance, on the afternoon of 12 February. Voicing his pleasure at the results of the earlier talks, Peck noted that they had 'dispelled the doubts and apprehensions which the British had previously felt', and the 'agreement reached between the United States and the United Kingdom enabled all to go forward and to be able to prepare for political and military action as the case might require it'. The Foreign Secretary expressed his prior concerns over the position of foreign bases, but now felt that the British and Americans had the same view on the need to maintain their position in the region. Concurring, Harriman now argued that he regarded the concept of Maphilindo as 'a face-saver with no immediate substance. The United States had no intention of giving its members a free hand to remove United States or British bases.' Butler then went on to say it would be very valuable to have a reference to US support for Malaysia in the communique following the British visit. Though pointing out that the USA did not have a 'direct' commitment to Malaysia in the same sense as the British, Rusk was prepared to make such a public statement and would welcome a 'balanced' reference that coupled British support for US goals in Vietnam with US backing for Malaysia. After a depressing overview of the situation in South Vietnam and Laos, with the Secretary of State noting that the Americans were looking at the question of 'carrying the battle to the other side ... Otherwise Southeast Asia in general would be in jeopardy', Butler repeated support for US policies and the need to 'keep an eye on the French'.[69] The Foreign Secretary concluded this section of their talks by handing the Americans a paper prepared by the Foreign Office which summed up the British approach: 'the West must unite to hold

[69] See Washington to FO, no. 611, 12 February 1964, D1073/2, *ibid.*; memorandum of conversation, 'Southeast Asia', 12 February 1964, Prime Minister Home visit, 2/12–2/13 1964, NSF, countries file, United Kingdom, box 213, LBJL.

both Vietnam and Malaysia. We cannot be certain that the attempt will be successful – much will depend on developments inside both countries – but we can be sure that abandoning either will soon mean abandoning both and, before very long, the whole Western position in South East Asia.'[70]

Although trade with Cuba was a stumbling block in the subsequent encounters between Home and President Johnson, there were no such problems when it came to South East Asia. Lester Pearson, the Canadian Prime Minister, had already told Home when he passed through Ottawa, that at their most recent meeting Johnson had indicated his personal desire to cut off all aid to Sukarno but that the State Department had held him back.[71] Armed with this encouraging information, in Washington the Prime Minister felt able to affirm that both countries had moved closer on policy towards Indonesia. The President indicated agreement, though remembering to maintain the position that

he had not wished to cut off aid from Indonesia completely and immediately because of the risk that this might throw Soekarno right into the hands of the Communists; and he had not wanted to continue aid because that would give Soekarno an inflated opinion of himself and make him very arrogant. The President thought that he had probably achieved about the right balance in telling Soekarno firmly that if he went on with his military confrontation he could expect no help at all from the United States.[72]

Home told Johnson he felt there was no alternative to current US policy in Vietnam and that the British would consider strengthening the British Advisory Mission under Sir Robert Thompson in Saigon. The communique issued at the end of Home and Butler's visit to Washington contained the element of reciprocity that the British desired and noted that, 'The Prime Minister re-emphasized the United Kingdom support for United States policy in South Viet-Nam. The President re-affirmed the support of the United States for the peaceful national independence of Malaysia.'[73]

[70] Draft brief by Cable, 'The Western Position in South East Asia,' 4 February 1964, D1073/3, FO 371/175090.
[71] PM(O)(64)1st mtg, 10 February 1964, CAB 133/247.
[72] Record of Prime Minister's talks with President Johnson, 12 February 1964, D103145/8G, FO 371/175062 and in PREM 11/4794.
[73] Memorandum by Cable, 'Malaysia and Viet-Nam, British and American Commitments and Undertakings', 4 December 1964, D1077/10, FO 371/175095. The Prime Minister could also have pointed out to Johnson that Thompson had arranged for 450 Vietnamese officers to receive training at British facilities in Malaysia during 1964 (including jungle warfare and Special Branch work), see Butler minute for Home, PM/64/16, 6 February 1964, PREM 11/4794.

The British were pleased with the results of their endeavours in the first few weeks of 1964 to bring US policy towards the Indonesia–Malaysia dispute away from the (to them) more dangerous and unpredictable path it had charted in the final year of the Kennedy Administration. After his return to London, the Prime Minister was in a position to tell the Cabinet on 18 February 1964 that the Americans

now appreciated the logic of our policy in relation to Indonesia; and we were assured that, if the Government of Indonesia resumed their aggressive attitude towards Malaysia, we should have the support of the United States Government in seeking to maintain our position in South-East Asia. We, for our part, had undertaken to provide the United States Government with comparable support in implementing their policy in South Vietnam and in resisting the attempt of the French Government to establish neutralism in the area.[74]

In securing this degree of understanding, the British had undoubtedly been helped by US worries over the deteriorating position in Vietnam and Laos in early 1964, and anxieties over the talk of neutralization prompted by the French, but they had also been assisted by the personal preferences of Lyndon Johnson. Forrestal told Peck shortly after the Home visit that the State Department (in what was probably a reference to Hilsman) would have to restrain Johnson from cutting off aid through impatience and 'were afraid of an inexperienced President taking irrevocable decisions about Sukarno'.[75] Other changes from their experience of the Kennedy Administration were discernible to British observers. In his own reflections on the trip to Washington, Oliver Wright told the Prime Minister, 'President Johnson is not at home in international affairs. He will give Mr Rusk a much freer hand: in fact Rusk has virtually taken over the direction of US foreign policy. President Johnson's own approach is a simple one. If he dislikes a man he is against him. He dislikes Soekarno.' Furthermore, 'To have Rusk is no bad thing, since he is sensible, rational and a very good friend of ours . . . One has the impression that he now directs policy instead of reflecting it.'[76] By March 1964, ministers in London had concluded that US aid to Indonesia was now relatively insignificant, and that further pressure on the Administration in Washington should be dropped as likely to be counterproductive.[77]

American sympathy for the British position, and a much sterner attitude to Sukarno in official US policy, was also underlined by Hilsman's removal and the arrival of William Bundy as Assistant Secretary for Far Eastern Affairs. The view from the Washington Embassy was that Bundy

[74] CM(64)12th mtg, 18 February 1964, CAB 128/38.
[75] Record of a meeting of 14 February 1964, D103145/9G, FO 371/175062.
[76] Wright minute for Home, 17 February 1964, PREM 11/4794.
[77] See DO(64)16th mtg, 25 March 1964, CAB 148/1.

was a 'highly intelligent, clear-thinking person with New England virtues' who was unlikely to accept the Jones–Harriman line on Indonesia, while he was also 'very close to his brother who has absolutely no time for the Bung [Sukarno]'. Embassy officials noted that they were 'very conscious of the value of going direct to Bundy, and indeed to Rusk himself, when the occasion warrants it . . . ' and hence by-passing the Indonesia desk officers in the Far East Bureau.[78] When, at the end of April, Rusk and Bundy were told by the Foreign Secretary of the British decisions to allow for counter-battery fire and hot pursuit of Indonesian raiders back into Kalimantan, they raised no objection. Moreover, when Butler told the Americans that a decision in principle had been taken permitting attacks on Indonesian lateral communications over the border, but with the assurance that there was no question of attacks in Sumatra, Rusk commented that 'a little war planning for other areas might usefully be done behind the scenes'. The Americans would, however, prefer that some reference to the UN precede any attacks on Indonesian communications in Kalimantan.[79] Soon after, Butler was seeing Lyndon Johnson and offering British gratitude for the support given over Malaysia since his February visit, to which the President offered what was called 'a most fulsome tribute to Great Britain and expressed his determination that nothing must ever be allowed to break the ties of deep friendship that bound our two countries together'.[80]

Hilsman later avowed that he thought Johnson's handling of Indonesia was bad: 'He sided too heavily with the British. Of course, it was linked to Vietnam. He wanted British support on Vietnam, you see.'[81] With Rusk and the Bundy brothers now in the ascendant it was increasingly difficult for the remaining advocates of a conciliatory and low-key response to Indonesian behaviour to be found. The course charted by Sukarno's regime was also hardly likely to win new friends in Washington. Towards the end of March, after an American magazine had claimed Indonesia was on the brink of economic collapse and called for the United States to end all aid unless Indonesian aggression was halted, Sukarno delivered a speech in Jakarta where he angrily asserted that he would tell any country that tried to attach strings to its aid, 'You can go to hell with your aid.' The outburst (made in English) was widely reported and led

<hr />

[78] See Peck to Greenhill, 13 April 1964; Greenhill to Peck, 15 April 1964, D103145/18, FO 371/175062.
[79] Record of a meeting at the State Department, 27 April 1964, D1051/42G, FO 371/175067. See also Rusk affirming US support for Malaysia, in record of Butler–Rusk telephone conversation, 23 March 1964, PREM 11/5088.
[80] Text of Foreign Secretary's talk with President Johnson at the White House, 29 April 1964, contained in Washington to FO, no. 1614, 29 April 1964, PREM 11/4789.
[81] Roger Hilsman Oral History.

to further sharp criticisms in Congress. Following the debates of January 1964 over whether Johnson should sign a presidential determination on aid to Indonesia, the subject had largely been allowed to lapse, despite the efforts of Forrestal to persuade William Bundy that the issue should be presented to the President, especially as the legal status of the remaining US programmes was far from clear.[82] Bundy's tougher line over Indonesia also prompted disapproval from Harriman, as well as Forrestal, but their views were sought with far less frequency by those concerned with the day-to-day operation of policy towards Indonesia.[83]

As these important shifts in the balance of forces in Washington were being played out, diplomatic attempts to resolve confrontation were making negligible headway. The 'cease-fire' that had seemed the most positive outcome of Robert Kennedy's trip in January existed in name only, with clashes between the security forces and Indonesian intruders in the Borneo territories still commonplace. Most British commanders felt that the comparative lull that accompanied the Bangkok foreign ministers' meeting in February had been used by the Indonesians to infiltrate more men and supplies across the long border with Kalimantan in preparation for a fresh round of fighting. In fact, having first insisted on the right to airdrop supplies to their guerrilla forces in the Borneo territories, the Indonesians then refused to discuss withdrawal when the Tunku made publicly clear that he would not attend a summit while Jakarta's forces remained on Malaysian territory. With the Malaysian federal elections due at the end of April, there was little chance of a compromise formula being found to allow the talks process to resume, let alone any agreement on what might prove an acceptable basis for a settlement. Nevertheless, the Filipinos were anxious that confrontation should not drag on, and Salvador Lopez maintained a dialogue with Jakarta and Kuala Lumpur with the aim of promoting a summit meeting by arranging for a withdrawal of Indonesian forces to begin at the same time that talks were convened. President Macapagal was also working on proposals for a four-nation Afro-Asian Conciliation Commission (three states to be nominated by each of the parties to the dispute, and the other appointed by the chosen three) to mediate and suggest a solution.

When he passed through Manila in early May 1964 these efforts were given some encouragement from Butler, who emphasized British desires to see an Asian settlement, saying that Britain 'supported the long-term

[82] Forrestal memorandum for Bundy, 23 April 1964, NSF, country file, Indonesia memos, box 246, LBJL.

[83] See e.g. Harriman memorandum for Bundy, 30 April 1964, William Bundy file, box 439, Harriman papers; Forrestal memorandum for Bundy, 8 May 1964, Forrestal file, box 461, *ibid.*; Jones, *Indonesia*, 303, 321–2.

concept of Maphilindo. They were not an Asian power.'[84] However, any initiative for talks was welcome only as long as it did not prejudice the Tunku's position, hence there was considerable concern in London at the news that, following his election victory, the Malaysian Prime Minister had to be firmly dissuaded by Razak from lowering his preconditions, before attending a summit, merely to Indonesian agreement in principle to withdrawal from the Borneo territories.[85] By late May it had been agreed through Philippine mediation that a withdrawal of guerrillas would commence simultaneously with the staging of a summit in Tokyo, with Thai observers to verify Indonesian compliance at a number of checkpoints on the Kalimantan border. Interminable wrangles followed about the details of the arrangements, cloaking the whole process with mistrust, suspicion and some degree of confusion. After several delays, the Tunku finally joined Sukarno in Tokyo on 20 June, while a token group of Indonesian guerrillas passed through a checkpoint at Tebedu, having only just entered Sarawak shortly beforehand. At the summit, there seemed no room for compromise, Sukarno avowing he could not accept Malaysia and revisiting old arguments about the establishment of the Federation the previous year, while the Malaysians pressed for an Indonesian commitment to end confrontation and withdraw all its forces. Macapagal's proposal for an Afro-Asian Conciliation Commission was accepted by the Indonesians, but the Tunku, although agreeing in principle to the framework, insisted that all aggression against Malaysia should cease before taking the idea further. The principals left the Japanese capital after two days of acrimonious exchanges and counter-charges, the final communique simply stating the opposing positions that had been adopted.[86]

It appears clear in retrospect that by this stage both sides had been going through the motions of participation in negotiations with no real expectation of a successful outcome. The Indonesians were probably hoping to bargain gradual withdrawals of their forces from the Borneo territories against Malaysian concessions over the forward deployment of British forces and a further self-determination exercise in Sarawak and Sabah. By mid-1964, it would appear, Sukarno had gone too far in confrontation to pull back without substantial loss of domestic prestige, even had he wished to do so. From the Malaysian perspective, while standing firm against Indonesian pressure, it was important to show that it was prepared to look at diplomatic solutions if it was to win sympathy and support from the wider body of international opinion, including non-aligned states in

---

[84] Record of a meeting between Butler and Macapagal, 6 May 1964, D1051/4, FO 371/175067.
[85] See Kuala Lumpur to CRO, no. 829, 11 May 1964, D1071/139, FO 371/175078.
[86] See Mackie, *Konfrontasi*, 230–5.

the UN (especially when that forum might eventually have to consider the dispute). There was also some genuine anxiety to put an end to confrontation with a vastly more populous, powerful and unpredictable neighbour, combined with a fatalistic belief that any settlement was only likely to be temporary while the current Indonesian regime remained in power. The inauspicious result of the Tokyo summit spelt the end of serious diplomatic attempts to resolve confrontation, at least until a cease-fire agreement was reached in the summer of 1966 under markedly different circumstances. Initiatives to revive the idea of an Afro-Asian Conciliation Commission were overtaken both by internal political changes in Malaysia and Indonesia from the middle of 1964 onwards, and by a dramatic escalation in confrontation by Indonesian attempts to land troops on the Malayan peninsula and which appeared at the time to be the prelude to the full-blown war that many had feared for so long.

The British had been under no illusions that Sukarno's willingness to engage in talks was a sign that he was prepared to renounce confrontation, indeed while the Tokyo summit was in progress the security forces had registered a serious increase in guerrilla activity. Yet from the point of view of Anglo-American relations, the first six months of 1964 had seen a reassuring and steady improvement in the situation, as Washington's view of the appropriate response to Indonesian policies began to coincide with that held by London. In this respect, Home and Butler's Washington talks in February 1964 marked a watershed in that Britain and the United States now agreed that there was a joint threat to Western interests in South East Asia through Indonesia's international behaviour and the inability of the authorities in Saigon to suppress the Communist insurgency in South Vietnam. A tough British reaction to Jakarta's provocations was no longer viewed with doubt and scepticism by the Americans; at the end of June 1964, Rusk was again suggesting to Menzies, when the latter was visiting Washington, that if Indonesia reverted to overt attacks, the British should take positive steps in reply (perhaps by making trouble in the Indonesian Outer Islands), and that there was a need for four-power planning talks to look at this eventuality.[87] The necessary *quid pro quo* had been an affirmation of strong diplomatic backing for American policies in Vietnam, but in early 1964 this was doing no more than renewing the kind of gestures that had been offered since 1961. More problematic was the issue of what level of support to give to the Americans if they chose to expand their operations to include direct action against North Vietnam.

There were already many rumours in London that the Johnson Administration was contemplating more forceful measures and, at the

<hr />

[87] See Washington to FO, no. 2361, 26 June 1964, PREM 11/4908.

end of February, Butler had asked Rusk for the latest information about future US plans in view of the likely questions that might be asked in Parliament. The Foreign Secretary held that he would have to respond to enquiries by saying that his recent statements in Washington involved the 'present defensive policy in South Viet Nam' just as the American commitment was to support 'our present defensive policy in Malaysia. If either of us were to change our policy, a new situation would arise and our two Governments would of course want to consult further.' On this occasion, the US Secretary of State was able to reassure Butler that the present course of policy was 'to do everything possible to assist the South Viet Namese to win their own war' and that escalation of the fighting to place more direct pressures on Hanoi would only be adopted with the greatest reluctance.[88] Nevertheless, calls for a more intensive programme against North Vietnam were becoming more widespread at this time in Washington, and the Administration had already sanctioned a series of covert actions at the beginning of the year, involving South Vietnamese intelligence and sabotage teams with US back-up working north of the 17th parallel.[89] It would not be long before the expansion of the war in Vietnam would provoke much greater unease among British officials, and the Americans called on their SEATO allies for more forthright support. Increasingly, when such requests began to arrive in London, British ministers and officials would come to use their commitment of troops and resources in confrontation as a reason why they could not contemplate extending more active help in Vietnam, superseding their earlier arguments that a tough policy towards the Indonesians contributed to the overall Western effort to defeat threats to stability in South East Asia.

[88] See FO to Washington, no. 3205, 28 February 1964; FO to Washington (containing Rusk's reply), no. 3294, 2 March 1964, PREM 11/4759; see also Logevall, *Choosing War*, 123–4, 150–1.

[89] See memorandum from Bundy to Johnson, 7 January 1964, *FRUS, 1964–1968, I*, 4–5.

10   Escalation, upheaval and reappraisal, July 1964–October 1965

The period between the summer of 1964 and the autumn of 1965 saw the position of the Western powers in South East Asia transformed once more. From the British perspective, they now approached the region no longer as a power with formal colonial interests and responsibilities, but as one tied to the area by treaty commitments, a sense of obligation to regional friends and the need to preserve and show solidarity with the Americans. British relations with Kuala Lumpur were subject to the kind of strains experienced in 1963, but in even more pronounced fashion, as the Malaysian Government ran the affairs of the new Federation in ways that offended London's sensibilities and seemed to threaten the fragile sense of national unity that had been established by the conflict with Indonesia. Indeed, the old colonial ties and patterns of thinking were being supplanted in Malaysian official circles by a greater willingness to demonstrate independence from the overbearing advice and presence of the British (though the need to maintain close ties for the purposes of security was still widely and uncomfortably acknowledged). This was a situation the British did not relish but had anticipated since at least the late 1950s, having never taken the preservation of a moderate and pro-Western UMNO leadership for granted. By the mid-1960s, that conservative leadership still held sway under the Tunku, but its future disposition could not be assured, leading many to question how long the obtrusive British bases could be maintained before local hostility was generated and they were driven out.[1]

Such assertive local nationalism, nevertheless, was also viewed in British official circles as the key to states within the region being able to withstand attempts by the Communist powers to expand their influence. By the end of 1964, in fact, the Foreign Office was looking forward positively to a time when the predominant pattern in South East Asia would be one of non-alignment and self-reliance, allowing for the retreat of an

---

[1] See e.g. Head to Commonwealth Secretary, no. 9, 'Malaysia: Will it Succeed and How Long Will We Stay?', 21 July 1965, PREM 13/430.

overt Western presence. However, it was not considered possible to envisage or work for such developments until the North Vietnamese had been decisively held back in Indochina, and Indonesian ambitions thwarted. Animated by the first goal, the United States had meanwhile embarked on a massive expansion of its military efforts, marked by the initiation of air strikes against targets in the north in February 1965, soon followed by the deployment of ground troops equipped with new counter-insurgency roles. By June 1965 there were 54,000 American military personnel in South Vietnam with nine combat battalions active, and late the following month the Johnson Administration approved a request to increase the number of US battalions to 34, bringing total troop strength up to 175,000 by the end of the year.[2] As the stakes of the Vietnam War were raised, Washington considered it all the more important both that their transatlantic ally retain their presence in South East Asia, and that Indonesia should remain free from Communist control. The point at which American convictions that the British should remain to bolster Western power in the region intersected with London's increasing reluctance to stay, in view of the costs being incurred, was reached in the summer of 1965 when the whole basis of Malaysia was shaken by the abrupt departure of Singapore from the Federation.

The chances of internal and external strains causing some kind of rupture in the fragile political structures of both Indonesia and Malaysia looked increasingly likely as confrontation continued into 1965. In both societies a turning point was reached in the period August–October 1965, first when the bonds tying together the federal framework of Malaysia were broken in dramatic fashion, and then when Indonesia underwent domestic upheaval which resulted in the decimation of the PKI and the rise to ascendancy of a new conservative army-based leadership. It was these developments which were fundamental in understanding how confrontation was eventually terminated and a less volatile climate in relations between the two states created. Communal tensions in Malaysia had been raised by the PAP's open attempt to turn the urban Chinese of Malaya away from the MCA during the campaign for the federal elections in April 1964. The PAP's efforts were countered by the hard-line so-called 'ultras' of UMNO, who began to agitate on behalf of Malays within Singapore who were allegedly suffering discrimination, while vehemently denouncing Lee Kuan Yew. The resulting communal conflicts came to a head on 21 July 1964 in the form of serious rioting in Singapore, which left

---

[2] See Smith, *International History of the Vietnam War, vol. III*, 149. The July 1965 decisions have been subject to exhaustive analysis, but one of the earlier attempts is still the most useful, Larry Berman, *Planning a Tragedy: The Americanization of the War in Vietnam* (New York, 1982).

22 dead and over 500 injured.[3] This was a major blow to any notion of Malaysian national unity, and alongside their concern over the role of UMNO officials in inciting violence in Singapore, British officials were also troubled by the heavy-handed way that Kuala Lumpur handled the affairs of Sarawak and Sabah, prompting the Prime Minister to take up such matters directly with the Tunku when he visited London in early August.[4] Yet, in another sign of how British influence was on the wane, these overtures had little impact. Relations between the constituent parts of the Federation continued to deteriorate and expatriate officers who had remained in the Borneo territories after 1963 found themselves eased out of any significant positions of responsibility.

Attention was temporarily diverted from these internal troubles, when on 17 August 1964, in a significant expansion of the tactics of confrontation, over one hundred Indonesian infiltrators landed along a stretch of coast around Pontian in south west Johore on peninsular Malaya. These raiders were rapidly dealt with by local forces, but this was followed in the early hours of 2 September by a potentially more serious incident, when a group of almost one hundred paratroopers were dropped near Labis in north Johore, apparently with the intention of attracting support from the local Chinese population (Labis had been the centre of much insurgent activity during the Communist insurrection) and setting up a guerrilla base in the Malayan interior.[5] Although again the security forces killed or captured all the intruders, and the Indonesian operation was notable chiefly for its incompetence, no-one could be sure that the Labis landings would not herald more substantial attacks on Malaya itself, and the Malaysian Government decided to declare a state of emergency and refer the incident to the UN Security Council. On the part of the authorities in London and Kuala Lumpur there was an awareness that this new Indonesian escalation was probably designed to take advantage of the recent evidence of communal tensions in Malaysia; Indonesian agents were believed to be connected to a further flare-up of street violence in Singapore in early September. The landings could also have had the aim of drawing British forces away from their primary task of resisting incursions in the Borneo territories. In any event there was a shared view that more incidents of a similar kind could not be allowed to go unanswered, if for no other reason than to bolster Malaysian morale that they could not be attacked with impunity.

[3] See Lau, *Moment of Anguish*, 160–200; Mackie, *Konfrontasi*, 255–6.
[4] See material in PREM 11/4904.
[5] Details of these incidents are conveyed in *Indonesian Aggression Against Malaysia, vol. II* (Kuala Lumpur, 1965).

British ministers therefore agreed a number of phased responses to any recurrence, as long as an initial request came from the Malaysians themselves and the issue was simultaneously referred to the UN.[6] Possible actions included commando raids on the islands of the Riau archipelago and a retaliatory air strike against Indonesian airfields, with target selection and local authority delegated to the High Commissioner in Kuala Lumpur and the Cs-in-C Far East (though this was soon rescinded following concern from Australia and New Zealand that their own forces could easily be drawn in without the chance of prior consultation with London).[7] Retaliatory action of the sort contemplated was a potentially hazardous course, likely to generate strong pressures within Indonesia for an even more vehement response, while much international opinion might be alienated if the action could not be portrayed as a legitimate act of self-defence under the UN Charter. Anglo-Indonesian tensions were also raised to new heights by Jakarta's objections to the passage of a Royal Navy aircraft carrier, HMS *Victorious*, through the Sunda strait between Java and Sumatra, prompting fears in some quarters that a Gulf of Tonkin-type episode was about to be repeated.[8] In the event, no more attacks were launched by Indonesia on the scale of those at Pontian and Labis, though some nuisance raids and sabotage were still directed from across the straits of Malacca, leading some to conclude that the deterrent effect of British counter-measures had worked.

The debate in the UN Security Council, where the Indonesian delegate made no effort to conceal culpability in the parachute landings, culminated with the Russian veto of a draft resolution 'deploring' the Labis incident and calling on both sides to refrain from the use of force and respect each other's territorial integrity (voting in the Council was nine to two in favour of the resolution).[9] This was not seen as a great diplomatic victory in Whitehall, and the UN debate coincided with the extension of a secret approach from Sukarno to the Tunku, offering to meet at any time in order to secure a deal that would call off confrontation in return for a face-saving plebiscite in the Borneo territories.[10] The Indonesian President may have been gambling that the most recent Indonesian incursions had so rattled the Tunku that a negotiation was possible, but if so it was a miscalculation for the Malaysians reacted coolly, and by the

[6] See CRO to Kuala Lumpur, no. 2087, 3 September 1964, PREM 11/4909.
[7] See CRO to Kuala Lumpur, no. 2096, 3 September 1964, *ibid.*; DO(64)36th mtg, 16 September 1964, CAB 148/1.
[8] See DO(64)35th mtg, 7 September 1964, *ibid.*
[9] See *Malaysia's Case in the United Nations Security Council: Documents reproduced from the official record of the Security Council proceedings* (Kuala Lumpur, 1964).
[10] See Kuala Lumpur to CRO, no. 1712, 16 September 1964, and Wright minute for Home, 18 September 1964, PREM 11/4910.

middle of the following month Sukarno was denying the claims coming from Kuala Lumpur that he had begun an initiative to end confrontation. Unilateral feelers were also made to the British by Jakarta at this time, but they were not pursued with any great enthusiasm, London being wary of an Indonesian attempt to expose any negotiation on a purely bilateral basis as a prime example of neo-colonialism and of jeopardizing relations with the Malaysians. Moreover, it was improbable that British ministers would undertake such a delicate task in the middle of a close election campaign at home (the general election eventually held on 15 October 1964 gave the Labour Party an eventual parliamentary majority of only four seats), where any suspicion of a move to meet Indonesian conditions could be seized on by the Opposition and the press. In the event, the installation of a Labour Government in London brought a fresh determination from new ministers that they should not appear weak in comparison with their Conservative predecessors.[11]

In retrospect, it is possible to see the events of September 1964, which had seemed to threaten the start of full-blown hostilities, as the high-water mark of confrontation. A later Indonesian build-up in Kalimantan opposite Kuching at the end of 1964 spread some alarm that an overt attack was imminent. However, in very public manner, two more British battalions were sent to Borneo in January 1965, bringing the total there to a peak of thirteen (about 20,000 men), while British commanders were given permission to extend their deniable cross-border operations up to 10,000 yards.[12] These 'Claret' raids, conducted by British and Gurkha companies, allowed for forceful domination of the frontier region.[13] With concerns mounting about the threats to their security from the north, it was also at this time that the Australian government, linking the menacing situation in Vietnam to the threat from Indonesia, finally sanctioned the use in the Borneo territories of its battalion from the Commonwealth Brigade, rotating with British forces completing their front line tours.[14] As the Indonesian Army showed every sign that their enthusiasm for the task was waning, and with the British holding complete air and sea supremacy, the military side of the struggle increasingly came to occupy a background role, and the dispute reverted to the ideological polemics and rhetoric so favoured by Sukarno. Indeed, following the Indonesian President's announcement of his 'Year of Living Dangerously' in August 1964, the

[11] Thus, for example, the new Defence Secretary, Denis Healey, was quick to confirm the delegated authority and 'credibly deniable' operations that had been sanctioned by the previous government, see OPD(64)2nd mtg, 9 November 1964, CAB 148/17.

[12] See CRO to Kuala Lumpur, no. 142, 14 January 1965, PREM 13/428.

[13] See Pocock, *Fighting General*, 205–14. By the summer of 1965, most contacts with Indonesian troops were actually taking place on the Kalimantan side of the border.

[14] See Edwards, *Crises and Commitments*, 340–3.

tone of his revolutionary romanticism became ever more strident. This was complemented by the forging of much firmer links with Beijing and Hanoi, as part of Sukarno's conception of Indonesia being in the vanguard of the 'New Emerging Forces'. Such was Sukarno's annoyance with the traditional procedures of the UN, and the fact that Malaysia was shortly due to assume a seat on the Security Council, that he even withdrew Indonesia from that organization in January 1965.[15]

Meanwhile, within Malaysia surface relations between the PAP and UMNO appeared to have been patched up somewhat by the autumn of 1964, although the Tunku's suspicions that Lee harboured long-term ambitions to usurp his own position as Prime Minister, possibly through a broader appeal to the non-Malay peoples of the entire Federation, were undiminished. At the end of the year, alarmed by PAP parliamentary opposition to recent federal budget plans, the Tunku began to toy with the idea of revising the Malaysia constitution to make for a looser federation, in which Singapore would enjoy complete autonomy, except in foreign affairs and defence, and forego its seats in the Federal Parliament. Both the PAP and UMNO would necessarily also close down their campaign efforts in Malaya and Singapore, respectively. Lee seemed receptive when private discussions were held in February 1965, but the British (who had not been kept officially informed of these ideas, though had their own confidential sources in Kuala Lumpur) voiced strong reservations, foreseeing a full break-up of the Federation and the loss of international support in confrontation.[16] It was the Tunku, however, who dropped further talk of constitutional changes, as pressures within UMNO for a tougher line against Lee mounted, and it became apparent that the PAP were lobbying for pan-Malaysian support in the Borneo territories. In fact, Lee had decided on a full-scale campaign against the communal politics of the Federation, and by April 1965 was calling for a 'Malaysian Malaysia' rather than one which featured special privileges for some of its peoples. The Malay ultras of UMNO responded with inflammatory rhetoric of their own, and calls on the Tunku to take action, and even to arrest Lee, increased. After a bitter parliamentary debate, the Malaysian Prime Minister travelled to London in June 1965 for a Commonwealth Prime Ministers' meeting, and there, while convalescing from a bout of shingles, he resolved that complete separation of Singapore from the Federation was the only solution. The following month, the Cabinet in Kuala Lumpur approved the Tunku's decision, and preparations went ahead for a public announcement; no indication of what was planned was given to the British

[15] See Mackie, *Konfrontasi*, 276–7
[16] Lau, *Moment of Anguish*, 217–27.

High Commissioner. When informed of the Tunku's intentions, Lee tried to persuade him that a looser federation was preferable, but he and other leading PAP figures finally signed the separation agreement on 7 August having been warned by Federal ministers that more communal strife and bloodshed in Singapore was likely if the present situation continued. Two days later, a bill was quickly passed by the Federal Parliament providing for the separation and complete independence of Singapore, and Lee Kuan Yew held an emotional press conference where he told reporters of his 'moment of anguish' at signing an agreement annulling a merger that he had spent most of his political life struggling to attain.[17]

Singapore's ejection from Malaysia in August 1965, barely two years after the Federation had come into existence, appeared to vindicate Indonesian claims that the whole structure was an artificial creation, designed more to satisfy British neo-colonial aims and Malayan ambitions than to accommodate the wishes of the local populations it encompassed. It was indeed impossible to overlook the sharp communal divisions that had all along made any merger between Malaya and Singapore problematic in the extreme, but which the political circumstances of 1961–3, where fears of a Barisan government predominated, had helped counteract. Once the left-wing threat to Singapore's stability had subsided – an important by-product of the arrests of Operation Cold Store and the PAP victory in the September 1963 elections – then it was likely that more deep-seated tensions and suspicions would resurface. Lying at the heart of the incompatible elements of merger was the Malay conviction that Malaysia would be more in the nature of an enlargement of the existing Federation, allowing a perpetuation of their privileged social and political position, rather than seeing it as a distinct new entity requiring different attitudes and policies. In September 1963, Selkirk had warned the Prime Minister that the leadership in Kuala Lumpur was

all too prone to look at Malaysia as being no more than an extension of Malaya, instead of envisaging it as a united whole to be dealt with on a common basis. Moreover, Malays have great difficulty in handling sensibly and with understanding other Asian races whom they tend to regard as little more than a form of aberration from the Malay ideal.[18]

Although often looked on as a moderate, as compared to the Malay ultras of UMNO, the Tunku can often be found giving vent to his private feelings that the only language the Chinese supporters of SUPP understood was force, or that political opponents had to be 'brought to heel'. There was an expectation that the PAP would confine its energies to Singapore, while

---

[17] *Ibid.*, 246–65; Lee Kuan Yew, *Singapore Story*, 628–40.
[18] Selkirk to Macmillan, 9 September 1963, PREM 11/4183.

the UMNO Alliance badly misjudged the basic non-communal and pan-Malaysian dynamic of the PAP (a party founded in 1954, it must be recalled, on a platform that wanted to see Singapore an integral part of Malaya).[19]

Fears that Jakarta would capitalize on the domestic disharmony so evidently on display within Malaysia in the summer of 1965 were confounded by the fact that Indonesian internal tensions were also coming to a head at this time against a background of virtual economic collapse, with unchecked inflation and severe food shortages in many parts of the country. As we have seen, the most important domestic development since about the middle of 1964 was the steady growth in influence of the PKI, its opponents often isolated and outflanked as anti-imperialist ideology came to dominate everyday political discourse. Sukarno still stood at the centre of the complex patterns of the Indonesian power balance, but his deteriorating health and closer alignment with the demands of the PKI were helping to alienate some erstwhile supporters, particularly in the ranks of the disgruntled and often sidelined officer corps of the Army. Such trends were finally brought to a head in January 1965 when Aidit, the PKI leader, with Sukarno's tacit backing, began a major and open call for the arming of workers and peasants, in order to create a 'fifth force' to rival the traditional armed services, which were also to have political advisers attached to their territorial commands. Sukarno later claimed that the proposals had initially come from the Chinese, and by the summer a showdown with the Army clearly seemed to be in the offing, with coup rumours widespread and an atmosphere of crisis in the capital.[20] In the early hours of the morning of 1 October 1965, a small group of rebel armed forces officers, including members of Sukarno's palace guard, made a bid to seize power with the pretext that they were themselves forestalling an imminent Army coup aimed at the Indonesian President. The details surrounding the coup attempt are still decidedly murky, with the later 'official' Indonesian version alleging deep PKI involvement throughout being contradicted by those commentators who see Communist participation as only marginal in what was at heart a factional struggle within the Army (and the armed services as a whole, with elements in the air force giving the coup plotters explicit support). The coup itself was distinguished by a suspicious level of incompetence, and no mass PKI rising accompanied its execution. By the end of the day, mainline units of the Army, directed by General Suharto, the commander

---

[19] Among one of many ironies from the early period of the PAP's life was the presence of the Tunku at its inauguration in November 1954, see Lee Kuan Yew, *Singapore Story*, 179.

[20] See the excellent analysis in Mortimer, *Indonesian Communism Under Sukarno*, 381–7.

of the strategic reserve, had quickly moved to restore control in Jakarta, their sense of outrage intensified by the murder of several senior anti-Communist generals (and a botched attempt to kill Nasution) by followers of the coup.[21] With the leaders of the PKI fleeing the capital, it proved impossible for Sukarno to protect the party from the bloody backlash that followed. During October, mobs began to attack PKI buildings with impunity, and throughout the provinces local Army commanders suspended the party and began to round up its members and their sympathizers. Subsequent mass killings in the countryside allowed many old scores to be settled, as farmers and religious groups who had previously been chosen as targets by the Communists in their land reform campaign turned on their enemies with a vengeance; the most reliable accounts put the resulting death toll at close to half a million.

The destruction of the PKI left the field clear for the Army, under Suharto's leadership, to assume the dominant place in the constellation of political forces now taking shape in Indonesia. Although Sukarno remained in nominal control as President, his influence over key parts of the decision-making process was in steady decline. The Army moved cautiously at first, but in March 1966 Sukarno was eventually coerced into vesting Suharto with virtually full executive powers. Confrontation could not be renounced overnight (indeed the Army's credibility was in some ways associated with its progress), but Indonesia's new leaders realized they had to change tack if they were to ease their crushing economic problems through receipt of foreign aid and tackling the burden of overseas debt. Moreover, it was now possible for Suharto's regime to embark on a new pro-Western course in foreign policy, a counterpart to the repression of all left-wing political influence at home. Conciliatory statements about the chance for a settlement of the dispute with Malaysia were soon emanating from the new Foreign Minister, Adam Malik, leading to direct ministerial-level talks with Razak at the end of May in Bangkok. Haggling over terms still continued, but it was clear that both sides were not prepared to let such niceties stand in the way of repairing their relationship, and military units in Kalimantan and Borneo were quietly stood down. On 16 August 1966, Razak signed an agreement in Jakarta that terminated hostilities and provided for the opening of diplomatic relations between Indonesia and Malaysia. The Malaysian Government also agreed to give an opportunity for Sarawak and Sabah 'to reaffirm in a free and democratic manner, through general elections, their previous decision about their status in Malaysia'.[22] This commitment fell some way

---

[21] See Legge, *Sukarno*, 386–92; Mackie, *Konfrontasi*, 309–14.
[22] See Mackie, *Konfrontasi*, 317–22.

short of a plebiscite for the territories, and merely gave Kuala Lumpur the chance to highlight support for pro-Malaysia parties in the next state elections as a demonstration that popular will had been reflected in the original incorporation of the territories into Malaysia.

The decisive intervention by the military in Indonesia during the autumn of 1965 and the removal of any prospect that the PKI could assume control in that country marked the point at which confrontation became of far less concern to the Western powers in South East Asia. Particular relief was felt in Washington at this turn of events, as well as a degree of satisfaction that their long-term approach of nurturing anti-Communist elements in the Indonesian Army appeared to have finally paid a handsome dividend. This has even led some scholars of modern Indonesia to conclude that the CIA must have had an active hand in the events of October 1965, though the evidence for such an interpretation does not yet seem convincing.[23] Rather what one sees from the summer of 1964 onwards is disengagement by the United States from Indonesian affairs, coupled with the belief that it was best not to respond provocatively to the anti-American polemics adopted by Jakarta. With the Vietnam War to deal with there was no wish to spark a potentially more onerous conflict with Indonesia. Instead the preference was to work quietly for an increase in tensions between the Army and the PKI.

The key moment in the process of US–Indonesian estrangement seems to have been the official visit made to Washington by Tunku Abdul Rahman in July 1964, when Johnson agreed to extend limited military assistance and economic aid to Malaysia in a very public show of support for the Federation. In his Independence Day speech of 17 August 1964, Sukarno roundly denounced the United States, while Washington's deepening involvement in Vietnam became for many Indonesians the most obvious manifestation of Western imperialism in the region. Congressional moves to cut off all aid to Indonesia were once again mooted in the summer of 1964, and US officials finally resolved to terminate the very small amounts of residual military assistance still flowing to Jakarta, to wind down all training programmes but to keep open channels through a number of minor civilian projects.[24] When mobs attacked United States

---

[23] See H. W. Brands, 'The Limits of Manipulation: How the United States Didn't Topple Sukarno', *Journal of American History*, 76, 3, December 1989, 785–808; H. W. Brands, *The Wages of Globalism: Lyndon Johnson and the Limits of American Power* (New York, 1995), 155–82; Kai Bird, *The Color of Truth: McGeorge and William Bundy: Brothers in Arms* (New York, 1998), 351–2.

[24] See Komer memorandum for Johnson, 19 August 1964; Thomson memorandum for Bundy, 25 August 1964; Thomson memorandum for Bundy, 26 August 1964; Bundy memorandum for Johnson, 31 August 1964, NSF, country file, Indonesia memos, 5/64–8/64, box 246, LBJL.

Information Service libraries in Jakarta and Surabaya at the end of 1964, breaking into the buildings and burning books in scenes widely reported to an outraged American domestic audience, a point of no return seems to have been reached.[25]

With Howard Jones imploring that the United States use all its remaining influence to restrain Sukarno and hold back the PKI, and with Indonesian forces massing in Kalimantan, Johnson considered the radical step of despatching a personal message to Sukarno inviting him to visit Washington, a proposal opposed by both Rusk and William Bundy.[26] When consulted, the British flatly rejected any such initiative, even though it was designed to open up splits between the Indonesian President and the PKI, and in retrospect it appears highly improbable that Johnson would have been prepared to take the strong domestic and congressional criticism that receiving Sukarno would have attracted.[27] Soon after, at the beginning of March 1965, the CIA was reporting that Sukarno had issued instructions for the sustained harassment of American officials in Indonesia, as well as for the takeover of American-owned rubber estates, while preparations were also being made for seizure of US oil interests. The CIA's sources maintained that Sukarno felt the United States, faced with the prospect of all-out war with China in Vietnam, could not afford to see Indonesia swing any closer to Beijing and would take steps to support Jakarta's position in confrontation.[28] If this was the Indonesian President's estimate, it was grossly mistaken; a few days after receipt of such information, Rusk was letting it be known to the British that Johnson had come to the conclusion that 'at the end of the day, should it become necessary, he would be ready for major war against Indonesia, if she raises the stakes too high'.[29]

As an evacuation of dependants and a complete break in diplomatic relations was discussed in Washington, Johnson decided to despatch Ellsworth Bunker as a personal envoy to Sukarno in order for a final

[25] See Jones, *Indonesia*, 344–8; Brands, *Wages of Globalism*, 165–8.
[26] See Marshall Green, *Indonesia: Crisis and Transformation, 1965–1968* (Washington, 1990), 13.
[27] See Johnson to Wilson, T.36/65, 26 January 1965; Wilson to Johnson, T.40/65, 29 January 1965, PREM 13/429.
[28] See CIA Intelligence information cable, TDCS DB–315/00716-65, 2 March 1965; CIA Intelligence information cable, TDCS–314/02882-65, 4 March 1965, NSF, country file, Indonesia cables, 3/65–9/65, box 247, LBJL.
[29] This message was conveyed to Patrick Gordon Walker, the former Labour Foreign Secretary, with the express intention that it be passed to the Prime Minister, Harold Wilson. When asked if this was because of the ANZUS treaty, Rusk replied in the affirmative but continued, 'and because of our relationship with you. We will back you if necessary to the hilt and hope for your support in Vietnam.' See Robert Pierce (ed.), *Patrick Gordon Walker: Political Diaries, 1932–1971* (London, 1991), entry for 6 March 1965, 303–4.

reading of the situation to be made. Having spent two weeks in Indonesia in April 1965, where the Indonesians stressed that the root cause of the breakdown in relations with Washington was US support for Malaysia, Bunker returned with an essentially pessimistic report foreseeing no likelihood for improvement under the existing regime, and which recommended a reduction in local American personnel and 'visibility' (including Peace Corps activity) but maintaining a few projects, including a commitment to help the Army with a new communications system.[30] At the end of May, Marshall Green, a State Department official with no great opinion of Sukarno, arrived in Jakarta as a replacement for Howard Jones, whose long assignment as Ambassador had finally come to an end. Attacks on the US consulates in Medan and Surabaya in early August led to more calls for a total break in relations and at the end of the month Indonesia announced its withdrawal from the IMF and World Bank, a further move towards economic isolation. The failed coup on 1 October came as a surprise to US officials, but they were soon passing encouraging messages to Army leaders with a pro-Western inclination (and allegedly provided information on PKI members and supporters). No protests or objections followed from Washington at the subsequent killings carried out throughout the Indonesian countryside, and with the military facilitating and participating in the whole process. Indeed, beside the morass of Vietnam, events in Indonesia were seen as one of the few encouraging developments in South East Asia as Washington reviewed the year.[31]

Some have argued that the Johnson Administration's decisions over escalation in Vietnam during 1965 were related to the situation in Indonesia, and were partly designed to bolster the anti-Communist forces present in the Army and bureaucracy. There is little documentary evidence to support such a precise link, but it is still possible to see significant connections between US policy in the two areas.[32] When Indonesia seemed to be slipping to Communist control and alignment with the PRC, it may well have been felt even more necessary to adopt a robust response in Vietnam, and subsequently to feel vindicated by the outcome in the form of PKI defeat in a state of major strategic value. On the other hand, it is more probable that internal Indonesian developments were entirely unrelated to the greatly increased commitment of American forces that was decided on in July 1965, making the basis for such a decision seem even more

[30] See Ball memorandum for Johnson, 18 March 1965, NSF, country file, Indonesia memos, 3/65–9/65, box 247, LBJL; Thomson/Bundy memorandum for Johnson, 8 April 1965; Bundy memorandum for Johnson, 26 April 1965, NSF, memos to the President, McGeorge Bundy, box 3, LBJL.
[31] See e.g. Thomson/Ropa memorandum for Bundy, 7 January 1966, memos for McGeorge Bundy 4/64–1/66, box 13, Thomson papers.
[32] See Smith, *International History of the Vietnam War, vol. III*, 19, 167, 185.

fragile than the contemporary arguments suggest. However, in a wider and overall sense, since early 1964 the war in Vietnam helped to impel the United States into a closer alignment with Britain and Malaysia in their conflict with Indonesia. By mid-1964, Vietnam was the dominating concern of the President and his leading foreign-policy advisers, a 'joint obsession', in Nancy Tucker's phrase, providing the framework which 'governed choices made, expenditures apportioned, challenges accepted in . . . disparate parts of the globe'.[33] Attitudes towards states would be determined by their response to the American effort to prop up the regime in Saigon. From this perspective, Malaysia's strong anti-Communist stance, and the symbolic training assistance it was extending to Vietnamese personnel, was appreciated by the Administration, easing the Tunku's important passage to Washington in July 1964, when Kennedy had previously shunned offering direct assistance to Kuala Lumpur. For her part, Britain was a reliable and useful ally, with a team of counter-insurgency experts providing valuable advice to the South Vietnamese, while its diplomatic backing for the American war effort was a valuable international commodity coming from one of the Co-Chairs of the Geneva Conference on Indochina, and made a pointed contrast with the critical position adopted by France. This was perhaps even more the case under Wilson's Labour Government, as McGeorge Bundy was quick to remind an occasionally sceptical Johnson in June 1965.[34] Events since early 1964 had made US officials increasingly conscious of the importance of Britain retaining a military presence in South East Asia as a contributor to the Western effort to restore and uphold regional stability.

It was only to be expected, therefore, that Washington would react negatively to any signs that Britain planned to pull back from its defence role centred at Singapore. Yet as we have seen, the whole Malaysia scheme had been designed to allow Britain to wind up its colonial empire in South East Asia, and reduce its commitments (particularly to SEATO land operations), permitting savings in resources and the promotion of a more unobtrusive presence. In August 1963, Macmillan had written to Selkirk of his longer-term wish that

our interests will not be entirely dependent upon a continuing British military presence once Malaysia has been successfully launched. We are . . . anxious to effect significant economies in our defence expenditure in South East Asia and I would hope that, as the Federation comes to be established and accepted and as its defence forces are built up, we should be able to realise this ambition.

---

[33] Warren I. Cohen and Nancy B. Tucker (eds.), *Lyndon Johnson Confronts the World: American Foreign Policy, 1963–1968* (Cambridge, 1994), 314.
[34] See Bundy memorandum for Johnson, 3 June 1965, NSF, memos to the President, McGeorge Bundy, box 3, LBJL.

The Prime Minister compared the £300 million of British financial investment in India with the £400 million in Malaysia, and pointed out it had not 'proved necessary to defend it through a military presence. Indeed, the amount of money we spend to keep British troops in South East Asia over a few years probably comes to substantially more than our financial stake there.'[35] The confrontation had helped to put any plans to cut back the British military presence into abeyance, and added a new layer of commitment. By 1964, this was a cause of real concern to government ministers, but they could find few answers to the dilemmas that the conflict with Indonesia produced. Escalation of hostilities held no prospect of yielding a long-term political solution, and would involve a far greater expenditure of resources than could safely be contemplated, while the risk of full-scale war could not be entirely discounted. On the other hand, a negotiated settlement was equally unpromising, as short of a complete Indonesian climb-down, Malaysia's room for manoeuvre was severely constrained; any meaningful concession that might be offered, it was feared, could threaten the whole basis and stability of the fragile Federation. During 1964, British forces in the Far East were augmented in response to the Indonesian threat, creating major strains in the defence establishment, especially when other emergencies in South Arabia and East Africa placed a simultaneous call on resources.[36] Particularly hard hit was the regular army, which had seen its strength shrink since the abolition of national service in 1960 to about 170,000, and whose infantry battalions were frequently under establishment.[37]

Despite its costs, however, the sense of a British mission east of Suez still held an important place in mainstream political thinking on defence and foreign policy, not least among the leadership of the Labour Party, which under Harold Wilson developed a strong attachment to Britain's role in Asia that lasted beyond their election victory in October 1964. Part of this was undoubtedly defensive, Labour politicians not wanting to provide easy targets for Conservatives ready to level accusations of 'scuttle' at any sign that commitments were being abandoned, while there was also some prestige value to be drawn from the government still being seen as a main player on the world stage. But leading Labour politicians were also reacting to the obvious signs of instability that were present throughout the area east of Suez and the calls for assistance that were being generated. There was also the vital matter of relations with Washington to consider, Wilson putting great store on a close transatlantic connection.

[35] Macmillan to Selkirk, 5 August 1963, PREM 11/4188.
[36] See Darby, *British Defence Policy*, 236–40.
[37] *Ibid.*, 272–5.

The Americans, for their part, were more than ever keen not to see any reduction in British forces deployed in the arc extending between Cyprus and Singapore via Aden. Within a month of taking office, Wilson was telling David Bruce, the American Ambassador in London, that 'In his view the most important role for Britain for the future would be in the defence of Western interests east of Suez.'[38] Nevertheless, the Prime Minister's rhetoric regarding British pretensions to world-power status collided with economic imperatives which demanded some retrenchment in overseas roles in order to allow significant savings to be found in defence spending (the Treasury being hopeful that the soaring costs of the latter could be capped at £2,000 million from 1965 onwards).

During the summer of 1964, long-term thoughts at the Foreign Office were already turning to the idea of a large-scale reduction of an overt British presence in South East Asia, prompted by the belief that the prolonged maintenance of a British military base at Singapore could only prove steadily more problematic, and might be detrimental to preserving influence. The newly established Foreign Office Planning Staff produced an agreed paper on British policy towards South East Asia in September, but the change of government delayed its submission to ministers, and it was only in November 1964 that it was finally approved by the Defence and Oversea Policy Committee, and subsequently circulated to diplomatic posts.[39] This document highlighted that South East Asia was of 'relatively little economic importance to Britain'. Indeed, barely 3 per cent of Britain's world trade was done with the region, while Malaya, which had brought in a net balance of foreign exchange to the Sterling Area of £43 million in 1955, was now in deficit. Set against this was the unpalatable fact that the defence effort in the Far East was costing in the order of £300 million a year, or 15 per cent of the total defence budget. Rather than using any commercial measure of the British stake in South East Asia, it was argued that in political terms 'we have a substantial interest in preventing its absorption by Communism, and we need to maintain our effort in the area if we are to keep our position as a world power and the United States' principal partner'. Singapore was after all Britain's largest overseas military base, controlling fifteen major land units in the theatre, as well as air and naval forces, with communications extending round to the six units still garrisoned in Hong Kong, while 'successive United States Governments have always attached great political importance (mainly for domestic reasons) to British association with their military commitments in this area. As long, therefore, as our

---

[38] Note of conversation between Wilson and Bruce, 27 November 1964, PREM 13/103.
[39] See Cable circular letter, 1 May 1964, D1051/43, FO 371/175067; see SC(64)46, 31 December 1964, PLA18/9, FO 371/177824.

military presence in South East Asia enables us to exercise a major influence on United States policies, it is worth retaining for this reason alone.'

Nevertheless, there was also a realization among the Foreign Office planners that an overt military posture and maintenance of alliance blocs was not the most effective way to secure Western goals in the region:

Communist absorption of South East Asia can best be avoided by working for the ultimate neutralization of the area, in agreement tacit or formal between the West and the Communist powers. This means a recognition by the West that any excessive desire to retain a military presence and direct political influence in the area is likely to encourage an unnatural alliance between local nationalism and communism. In the long term, Britain and her allies must accept that only a genuine non-alignment in South East Asia can make the containment of communism an attainable objective.

This vision necessarily involved the demise of SEATO and a withdrawal from the Singapore base. It was emphasized, however, that pragmatic considerations and immediate circumstances allowed for no such readjustment. Britain was absorbed in a prolonged conflict with Indonesia which required the use of the very bases and military forces that were seen as detrimental to long-term goals. Hence, it was further argued that 'a delicate balance has to be struck between the dangers of staying too long and the opposite dangers of withdrawing too fast. Any Western "defeat" in South East Asia will equally render impossible the long term objective described above. Military measures will therefore remain essential until the prospects of eventual agreement emerge clearly.'[40]

Such thoughts about the anomalies of the British position had been circulating for several years as the political situation in Singapore had deteriorated and membership of SEATO had carried an attendant risk of being drawn by American policy into military intervention in Laos. In November 1961, Fred Warner had reflected that apart from Hong Kong there was not really any direct British interest in the Far East that required military protection. The then head of the South East Asia Department had also pointed to the crux of the ambiguity surrounding British policy in the Malaysia area:

Singapore is not an interest in itself but a means of defending our interest. This being so our posture seems rather ridiculous. We have 14 major units in the area but all of this only permits us to put one British battalion into the field at present if we have to defend Laos, Vietnam and Malaya, and the machinery by which we deploy this tiny military force (SEATO) commits us to all sorts of adventures which we can ill afford.

[40] 'British Policy Towards South East Asia', OPD(64)10, 19 November 1964, CAB 148/17.

Peck had much sympathy with such views, but judged that it was still necessary to retain some military strength 'to give us a say in American policy in the area'.[41]

The same logic, that Anglo-American relations required a British military presence in South East Asia, applied in 1964, though by now British ministers were keener to impress on their American counterparts that meeting the Indonesian threat to Malaysia was contributing to Washington's efforts in Vietnam. The problem by the mid-1960s was that a British military presence did not necessarily offer London any real say in the conduct of the war in Indochina, as Washington moved to extend the scope of the conflict. In many quarters there was a growing awareness that Americans policies in Vietnam were making no headway, and that frustrations were mounting.[42] In May 1964, after William Bundy had told Butler that the Administration in Washington felt it was necessary to retaliate against North Vietnamese targets if diplomatic efforts to persuade Hanoi to reduce its interference in Laos were unproductive, the Prime Minister commented that he found the news 'sinister', the suspicion always being that electoral considerations weighed heavily in Washington's choice of action.[43] The implicit agreement reached between London and Washington in February 1964 over mutual support, in British eyes at least, was based on an understanding that backing would be given to American defensive policies in South Vietnam (to match a defensive British posture in Malaysia). An offensive policy created awkward dilemmas if Britain was to fulfil its duties as a Co-Chair of the Geneva Conference on Indochina.

In fact the adoption by London of firmer counter-confrontation measures against Indonesia in the spring and summer of 1964 did not allow the British to press home the point about the need to maintain a defensive posture with any real conviction, while their overall need for American support muted their private criticisms of US methods in Vietnam. In August 1964, following the Tonkin Gulf incident, Britain offered full backing in the UN Security Council for American retaliatory action against North Vietnam. The following month, the Americans were able to return the gesture with their supportive voice in the Security Council debates over the Labis parachute landings, while in private indicating that they would understand if the British felt compelled to launch a retaliatory

---

[41] Warner minute 'Britain and Indochina', 1 November 1961; Peck minute, 1 November 1961, D10113/9, FO 371/159722.

[42] See Lord Carrington's revealing report on his tour of South East Asia, 24 April 1964, D1051/39, FO 371/175066.

[43] Note for record of discussion between Foreign Secretary and Prime Minister, 29 May 1964, PREM 11/4759.

air strike against Indonesian targets in the event of a similar provocation. The Labour Government inherited the connections between Western policies in the region, but did not feel altogether happy with the possible consequences, particularly if the Americans chose to escalate their involvement even further. Before Wilson's first visit to Washington as Prime Minister in December 1964, the new Foreign Secretary, Patrick Gordon Walker, had expressed the hope that British officials could 'endeavour, so far as possible, to avoid presenting our support for US policy in Viet-Nam as a quid pro quo after support in Malaysia', preferring to defend American action on its merits.[44]

Such a sharp departure from the previous approach of the Foreign Office prompted James Cable, head of the South East Asia Department, to point out to both the Prime Minister and Foreign Secretary that the Americans would expect to receive British diplomatic support if they had to undertake limited offensive action against North Vietnam. The only alternative to such action, Cable argued, was negotiations, which under present conditions 'could only lead to a settlement gravely adverse to Western interests and deeply humiliating to the United States ... Not least because we need American support over Malaysia, we probably have no option but to give diplomatic support, as long as we can, to whatever policy the US Government choose to adopt.'[45] In a further submission, Cable highlighted the element of reciprocity in British backing for American actions in Vietnam, as against American support for Malaysia, which had been implicit throughout the year, and that American public opinion 'will probably regard our attitude to Viet-Nam as the touchstone of Anglo-American relations, not only in S.E. Asia, but in general'.[46] Peck was also in Washington at this time for talks with William Bundy, and added his voice to the recommendation that ministers support American 'limited and controlled' offensive action against North Vietnam 'which has resemblances to what we may have to do against Indonesia in certain eventualities'.[47]

By late 1964, far from de-coupling the issues of Vietnam and Malaysia, the Americans were ready to stress even further the interconnections. Knowing that the President was keen to see enhanced 'third country' contributions to the American effort in Vietnam, McGeorge Bundy advised Johnson in early December that Wilson would find it very difficult

[44] 'Washington Talks on Indo-China', South East Asia Department minute, 1 December 1964, D1077/6, FO 371/175095.
[45] Cable minute for Wilson and Gordon Walker, 1 December 1964, D1077/9, *ibid.*
[46] 'Visit of Prime Minister and Foreign Secretary to Washington', Cable minute, 4 December 1964, D1077/10, *ibid.*
[47] Washington to FO, no. 3987, 3 December 1964, PREM 13/692.

politically to increase the British contribution in the short term beyond sending a few more police advisers to Saigon. However, if US troops needed to be deployed in any numbers, then it might be possible to ask the British to send a contingent, Bundy acknowledging that the

reciprocal price for this would be stronger support on our part for Malaysia and perhaps closer participation in naval and air deployments designed to cool off Sukarno. This kind of bargain in this part of the world makes a good deal of sense, and Rusk and McNamara will be ready to go forward with the British in detailed discussions on this basis.[48]

In his subsequent talks with Wilson, Johnson went no further than mentioning that a few British soldiers in uniform on the ground in South Vietnam would have a great political and psychological significance. The Prime Minister demurred, citing British responsibilities as one of the Co-Chairs of the Geneva Conference.[49] When Gordon Walker and Denis Healey, the Defence Secretary, outlined the overstretch being encountered by British forces, Rusk quickly countered by saying that the 'American Administration would look with the greatest concern on any plan for a deliberate withdrawal of British influence from any part of the world. British Guiana, East Africa, Cyprus, and Malaysia formed a pattern of major contributions to the defence of the free world.' Reiterating the point, McNamara asserted that, 'What the United States most required from Britain was the maintenance of the British policy of playing a world power role.'[50] On the following day, Rusk again raised the subject of American eagerness to see more British personnel in South Vietnam. The Foreign Secretary instead

urged the importance of viewing the problems of the area as a whole: Malaysia must be taken into account as well as Vietnam. There were 8,000 British troops in Borneo and a total of 20,000 in Malaysia. The United Kingdom's commitment was comparable to the USA's in Vietnam . . . he was emphatic that the United Kingdom could not have troops on the ground in Vietnam.[51]

Hence, the argument over the trade-off between Vietnam and Malaysia was now no longer a question of offering British diplomatic support to the American effort (assumed as virtually automatic), but rather using the

---

[48] Bundy memorandum for President, 5 December 1964, *FRUS, 1964–1968, I*, 981–2; see also CIA memorandum from Assistant Deputy Director (Policy Support) to Bundy, 4 December 1964, NSF, country file, Prime Minister Wilson visit (I), 12/7–8/64, United Kingdom, box 214, LBJL.
[49] Record of meeting at British Embassy, Washington DC, 7 December 1964, PREM 13/104.
[50] PMV(W)(64)2nd mtg, 7 December 1964, CAB 133/266.
[51] PMV(W)(64)4th mtg, 8 December 1964, *ibid.*; account also in D1077/8G, FO 371/175095.

British commitment to Malaysia as a way to fend off American pressures to provide a more active contribution on the ground.

In February 1965, following Viet Cong attacks against US installations in South Vietnam, and reprisal bombings of targets in the north that were a harbinger of a full-scale American air campaign, another Anglo-American exchange took place that demonstrated the limits of British influence. Concerned that the scale of US counter-action should be restricted and directly related to further incidents, Wilson telephoned Johnson to ask if he could make a quick visit to Washington for consultations, but the President brusquely turned the suggestion aside as too alarmist. The Prime Minister nevertheless professed full public support for American actions, leading Johnson to observe pointedly that the British had full US support over Malaysia, but that he did not trouble the British Ambassador when a flare-up occurred with Sukarno: 'I won't tell you how to run Malaysia and you don't tell us how to run Vietnam.'[52] The President's contention of early 1965 that both Britain and the United States should concentrate on each other's conflicts was, however, to prove difficult to maintain as Washington's own concerns about Indonesian behaviour and domestic political trends reached a peak at the same time as Malaysian internal tensions came to a head.

The departure of Singapore from Malaysia in August 1965 immediately threw British policy-makers into a hasty reappraisal of their whole approach to confrontation, and had important implications for Anglo-American relations. The 'Little Malaysia' (of Malaya, Sarawak and Sabah) that some had seen as a possibility in June 1963, when the talks leading to the London Agreement seemed on the verge of failure, had now come into existence. At that time, Foreign Office officials had speculated that such an eventuality could saddle Britain with a commitment to defend the Borneo territories for no real purpose, as Singapore would not lie within the protective umbrella of Malaysia, and a radical government there was likely to insist on speedy eviction of British bases and spell the end of any serious role in South East Asia. The most logical course in such a scenario would be to search energetically for a negotiated solution to the dispute with Indonesia, leading to the independence of the Borneo territories and the restoration of harmonious relations in the region. Such a settlement might allow for a planned withdrawal of British forces from the area. When rumours of a spilt between Malaysia and Singapore surfaced in early 1965, the Cabinet Secretary once again suggested that London should be thinking more seriously about negotiations with Sukarno and

---

[52] Record of telephone conversation between Wilson and Johnson, 11 February 1965, PREM 13/692, and see Harold Wilson, *The Labour Government, 1964–70: A Personal Record* (London, 1971), 116.

departing from Singapore.[53] The events of August allowed British officials to raise these radical ideas in a setting where they appeared to make
even more sense, while among ministers Healey, in particular, was keen
that the confusion surrounding the future of Malaysia should be seized
on as an opportunity to scale back British commitments, writing to the
Prime Minister: 'The key issue is not whether or when we leave Singapore,
but how to get out of Borneo: i.e. how to end our commitment under
confrontation as soon as possible.'[54] At the end of the month the Oversea
Policy and Defence Committee approved a paper which concluded recent
developments made it impossible to envisage UK forces being allowed to
retain their position in either Singapore or Malaysia beyond 1969/70, and
concluded that the best option was to begin a diplomatic initiative to end
confrontation and to be ready to pull out of the Borneo territories in exchange for the offer of a plebiscite in Sarawak and Sabah. In order to begin
contingency planning on such lines, the Americans, Australians and New
Zealanders would have to be approached for preliminary consultations.[55]

Having just committed themselves to a major escalation of their ground
presence in Vietnam, Johnson Administration officials were aghast at
British ideas of making peace with Sukarno and retreating from South
East Asia. After quadripartite talks held in London in early September,
where American representatives, along with the Australians and New
Zealanders, had voiced strong opposition to British ideas about starting
negotiations with Indonesia or pulling back from Singapore, George Ball,
the Under Secretary of State, was despatched from Washington to take
matters up directly with Wilson.[56] Financial assistance was the key bargaining counter that the Americans could wield in the summer of 1965,
as the British Government grappled with another major sterling crisis.[57]
In early August, responding to signs that devaluation was being considered, Ball had recommended that sterling should be given support,
but on condition that the British agreed to fully maintain their world-
wide defence commitments, and that every effort was made to attract a
multilateral financial rescue package, rather than one that relied on the
Americans alone. A devaluation by the British would probably lead them
to cut back on their global commitments and 'This would be disastrous

---

[53] See Trend minute for Wilson, 4 February 1965, PREM 13/429.
[54] Healey to Wilson, 13 August 1965, PREM 13/431. See the records of MISC 75, the
official working-party that looked at the consequences of Singapore's departure from
Malaysia and policy options in August 1965, at CAB 130/239.
[55] See OPD(65)37th mtg, 31 August 1965, CAB 148/18. The approved paper was
OPD(65)123, 25 August 1965, CAB 148/22.
[56] For the quadripartite talks see Blouin memoranda for McNaughton, 7 and 13 September
1965, NSF, country file, Singapore memos, box 281, LBJL.
[57] See Wilson, *The Labour Government*, 169–74.

politically since it would leave us more than ever the policeman of the world.'[58] At the same time President Johnson was resisting McGeorge Bundy's suggestion that a rescue package for sterling could be linked to a token commitment of British forces to Vietnam.[59] The great concern of the Americans was that by stressing how unacceptable they viewed the notion of devaluation, they would commit themselves to sustaining the pound on a unilateral basis and absolve Wilson's Government of its need to take the unpopular domestic measures required to remedy the balance of payments problems of the British economy.

Within the space of a month, and faced with the crisis of a possible British pull-out from Singapore, Washington now moved to bring togther in more explicit fashion the two issues of finance and British overseas commitments. In talks with the Prime Minister and Foreign Secretary in London on 8 and 9 September, Ball outlined American opposition to any reduction of the British presence in South East Asia, or any attempt to reach a compromise solution to confrontation. Calling the recent quadripartite meetings 'premature and hazardous', Ball drew attention to the 'disastrous consequences if the word should be spread that Western power might be withdrawn or diminished'. When Wilson was pressed as to his position, he denied that his government intended to follow a policy of scuttle, avowing that, 'this was not in our minds at all. Such a policy would be contrary to everything he ... had ever said and would make him eat a great number of his own words', while over confrontation Britain 'should do nothing for the time being but soldier on'. Having been told of US proposals to prop up sterling through 'aggressive intervention' in world financial markets, the Prime Minister had a final and private conversation with Ball, where the latter made clear that 'it would be a great mistake if the UK Government failed to understand that the American effort to relieve sterling was inextricably related to the commitment of the UK Government to maintain its commitments around the world'. Wilson stated that 'Her Majesty's Government were quite clear that finance, foreign policy and defence must hang together particularly East of Suez. It would be a tragedy if present economic stringency made us pull out of places to which we could never hope to return. He was quite clear that there was no misunderstanding on this point.' The talks were

[58] 'British Sterling Crisis', Ball memorandum, 6 August 1965, NSF, country file, UK Balance of Payments Crisis, 1965, box 215, LBJL.
[59] Bundy had wanted to tell the Cabinet Secretary that 'a British Brigade in Vietnam would be worth a billion dollars at the moment of truth for Sterling', see Bundy memorandum for Johnson, 28 July 1965, NSF, memos to the President, McGeorge Bundy, box 4, LBJL, and Bundy memorandum for Johnson, 2 August 1965, *ibid.* In general, see John Dumbrell, 'The Johnson Administration and the British Labour Government: Vietnam, the Pound and East of Suez', *Journal of American Studies*, 30, 2, 1996, 211–32.

concluded by Ball again stressing the need for the British and Americans to act in concert and support one another, 'if the US was not to appear to be dominating the world by trying to become "another Rome" '.[60]

Facing the concerted opposition of their principal allies in the region, British ministers had quickly retreated from the notion of a rapid withdrawal from South East Asia, and confirmed that they would seek no early negotiated solution to confrontation.[61] Bundy had reported in satisfied fashion to Johnson that Ball had 'really put it to the British on Singapore and our support of the pound . . . it took two talks for Wilson to agree the association between our defense of the pound and their overseas commitments'.[62] Nevertheless, the British had managed to extract crucial financial support from the Americans, and the Chancellor of the Exchequer was soon able to announce a further short-term stabilization loan from the IMF to help fend off the immediate crisis, giving the government a good chance of electoral success in 1966.[63] Moreover, the fundamental British analysis, that an eventual ending of confrontation would remove the main justification for British bases in Singapore and Malaysia, and domestic political pressures in both states would make their retention beyond about 1970 highly problematic, had not changed. In late September, the Cabinet Secretary was highlighting that while American short-term support for sterling made it difficult to discuss steps to reduce British commitments in the region, the recent exchanges had shown that London had some useful cards to play in future financial discussions:

We need not regret having brought our allies up against . . . [the situation's] realities; and the violence of their reaction to any suggestion that we should 'pull out of the Far East', still more that we should take any initiative to end confrontation, is a measure of the strength of our bargaining position if we meet the desire that we should remain East of Suez.[64]

This was also a position the Americans had not been slow to appreciate, and by the end of the year a lively debate was under way in Washington about whether the kind of operation undertaken in the summer of 1965 could or should be repeated, with Henry Fowler, the Secretary of the

[60] See record of conversation between Wilson and Ball, 4 pm, 8 September 1965; note of a meeting at 10 Downing Street, 10.25 pm, 9 September 1965; note of a meeting at 10 Downing Street, 11.15 pm, 9 September 1965, PREM 13/2450; London to DOS, SECUN 5, 9 September 1965, NSF, country file, United Kingdom cables, 7/65–9/65, box 208, LBJL.
[61] OPD(65)41st mtg, 23 September 1965, CAB 148/18.
[62] Bundy memorandum for Johnson, 10 September 1965, NSF, memos to the President, McGeorge Bundy, box 4, LBJL.
[63] See Kenneth O. Morgan, *Callaghan: A Life* (Oxford, 1997), 225–6.
[64] Trend minute for Wilson, 21 September 1965, PREM 13/431.

Treasury, and Ball arguing that the British had to be encouraged to put their own economic house in order (including a possible pull-back from Asia) against the standard Rusk/McNamara line that the British should be pressured to stay. By 1967, in fact, faced with their own major financial difficulties due to the war in Vietnam, the Johnson Administration had decided that there could be no further unilateral US guarantees for sterling.

For decision-makers in London, the dramatic events in Indonesia in early October 1965, and the rapprochement between Kuala Lumpur and Jakarta that followed, eased the way to give further consideration to an eventual withdrawal from the region. In June 1966, with the Bangkok cease-fire agreement still to be formally ratified, Healey, who had just returned from a Far Eastern tour, recommended that over the next six months troops should be withdrawn from the Borneo territories and concentrated on the 'mainland' of South East Asia in peninsular Malaysia and Singapore. Meanwhile, studies should be made of the long-term future role of forces in the area.[65] The end of confrontation in the summer of 1966 coincided with continuing problems in the balance of payments and another sterling crisis, while in September George Brown was appointed as Foreign Secretary. Brown was described to the Prime Minister as

inclined to question whether it is really in the long-term British interest for us to be physically present in [South East Asia] more or less indefinitely. He fully recognises that we have to honour our present commitments and that we cannot just pull out and leave Australia and New Zealand and all our other allies in the area (to say nothing of the Americans) to their own devices. But he wonders whether... we should not accept as our eventual objective that we should get right out of South East Asia, and pending this becoming possible we should not undertake commitments or plans to keep us on the hook rather than let us off it.[66]

By early 1967, Healey and Brown had begun to discuss the idea of making drastic reductions in the Far East, involving a total withdrawal from the mainland by 1975–6, with only the retention of a minimal maritime and air presence based in Australia. Force declarations to SEATO would necessarily have to be revised and the Anglo-Malaysian Defence Agreement renegotiated to reflect the new realities, and consultations initiated with allies. The Foreign Secretary told the Oversea Policy and Defence Committee: 'Our aim should be to remove our forces from the mainland of Asia as soon as possible and not to retain commitments for which our forces were inadequate. This would best be done by moving to a peripheral strategy based on naval and air forces.'[67] Despite

[65] Healey minute for Wilson, MO/25/2/71, 19 June 1966, PREM 13/1454.
[66] Wright minute for Wilson, 3 September 1966, *ibid.*
[67] OPD(67)14th mtg, item 2, confidential annex, 22 March 1967, CAB 148/30.

apprehension over likely American reactions, it was resolved by ministers that the decision to leave Singapore should be vigorously defended, and Wilson confirmed British determination to implement the policy when he travelled to Washington to meet Johnson at the beginning of June 1967.[68]

American reactions were not as dramatic as some had feared.[69] Indeed, the principal concern of US officials, having registered their familiar protests, was that any announcement not be made public (though here again the British proved unwilling to comply feeling that a public commitment to leave had to be made if firm planning for departure was to proceed). Expectations of what could be asked of the British were lowering throughout the period, and were coupled with a clear grasp of the domestic economic problems faced by the Wilson Government. Though this was implicit, one can also detect some resentment on the part of American observers, that after earlier promises to remain east of Suez, the British might now be using the threat of a withdrawal to extract more guarantees from the Americans over the position of sterling. There was no wish to go down that road again, and in private US officials acknowledged that if the Prime Minister remained intransigent, they would have no alternative but to accept an eventual British withdrawal.[70] In a memorandum prepared for the President prior to Wilson's visit in June, Rusk suggested that the British, 'after years of indecision, appear to have arrived at a conscious decision as to Britain's future role in the world. The decision is to liquidate most of the overseas commitments remaining from the Empire and to become an integral part of the European movement.'[71] On the part of the Americans, as Wright summarized it for the Prime Minister, there was an 'odd mixture of indignation, incomprehension and resignation' and that 'in their heart of hearts, they believe that Britain is pulling out of her world role and that nothing they can do or say will do more than delay this'.[72]

In July 1967, Healey finally came forward with a public declaration that British forces in the Singapore/Malaysia area would be halved by 1970/1 and withdrawn completely by the mid-1970s. Yet another sterling crisis in November 1967, and the devaluation that followed, overtook

---

[68] See record of conversation between Brown and McNamara at the Pentagon, 18 April 1967; Rusk to Brown, 1 May 1967; Wright minute for Wilson, 12 May 1967, PREM 13/1455; record of conversation between Wilson and Johnson at the White House, 2 June 1967, PMV(W)(67), PREM 13/1906.

[69] See Wilson's comments to the Cabinet, CC(67)36th mtg, 6 June 1967, CAB 128/42.

[70] 'East of Suez', State Department background paper, 29 May 1967, NSF, country file, UK: Wilson Visit, 6/2/67, box 216, LBJL.

[71] Rusk memorandum for Johnson, 31 May 1967, *ibid.*

[72] Wright minute, 'My Washington Reconnaissance', 1 June 1967, PREM 13/1906.

these announcements, and led to the final decision in January 1968 to quicken the timetable and pull all forces out of Malaysia, Singapore and the Persian Gulf by the end of 1971.[73] There would be no provision for a substitute base in Australia, as so many officials had wistfully imagined in the late 1950s and early 1960s, leading British force-level declarations for SEATO contingency planning devoid of any further meaning, and no special capability was to be developed allowing for rapid redeployment to the region; American attitudes were once again resigned, once emotional appeals and protests had been made.

Indeed, the time for such language, extolling a shared Anglo-American duty to police the world and uphold stability, was long past. In May 1967, when American officials were first being informed about the decisions to withdraw from east of Suez, David Bruce can be found telling Rusk that the 'so-called Anglo-American special relationship' was 'little more than sentimental terminology'.[74] Britain in the 1960s, turning more (if reluctantly) to a European-centred future, no longer had the will or resources to match the kind of American effort being conducted to check the spread of Communism in the Far East. When Rusk complained to George Brown in January 1968 that he 'could not believe that free aspirin and false teeth were more important than Britain's role in the world', he demonstrated how the priorities of British governments, hamstrung by an economy losing global competitiveness and an electorate expecting adequate standards of social provision, had changed over the previous two decades.[75] Moreover, with the massive application of American power on display in South East Asia by 1967–8 compared to the dwindling British presence, there was little room for London's voice to be heard in the deliberations of the Johnson Administration (as Wilson's floundering efforts in February 1967 to mediate in the Vietnam War demonstrated so graphically).[76] Arguing that American objections should not stand in the way of British decisions to pull out of the region, Oliver Wright noted in May 1967 that, 'One can understand and sympathise with US preoccupations about their future peace-keeping role in Asia. But, in the last analysis, US decisions will not depend on what *we* do; but on how they assess their *own* interests (and quite right too).'[77]

From the American perspective, a British presence at Singapore had somewhat less importance in 1968 considering there was now a firmly

---

[73] See Darwin, *British and Decolonisation*, 291–3.
[74] Bruce to Rusk, 8 May 1967, quoted in John Dumbrell, 'The Johnson Administration and the British Labour Government', 219.
[75] See record of a meeting at the State Department, 11 January 1968, PREM 13/2081.
[76] See Philip Ziegler, *Wilson: The Authorised Life* (London, 1993), 324–6.
[77] Wright minute, 13 May 1967, PREM 13/1455.

anti-Communist, military-led government in Jakarta, and with upwards of half a million US military personnel active in South Vietnam, the levels of contribution that the British could make to wider regional security must have appeared negligible. Nevertheless, the sense of isolation as another Western power departed from the region must have increased in Washington. It was also significant for the future posture of the West in South East Asia that the Wilson Government's decisions of early 1968 to withdraw from the area on a shortened timescale should almost coincide with the Tet Offensive, the point at which the United States had to begin to come to terms with the limits of its capacity to bend indigenous and complex forces to its own flagging will.

Conclusion: The Western presence in South East Asia by the 1960s

In 1945, the Western powers had secured an overwhelming but in many ways ambiguous victory over Japan, and it remained to be seen how long they could preserve their formal presence in South East Asia faced with the assertive forces of nationalism that had been unleashed by that conflict. Among the Europeans, the Dutch retreated from their East Indies Empire in 1949, and had their assets seized and remaining citizens driven out of Indonesia in December 1957, while the French had the even more painful experience of defeat on the battlefield and eviction from Indochina in 1954. The British, by contrast, felt they had achieved the right balance through progressive colonial policies and the prudent exercise of force, with a benevolent United States to support them. The Malayan settlement of 1957 was the model to be emulated; a conviction existed that new Asian states could be directed towards stable Western-derived models of economic development and a foreign policy that was alert to the dangers of Communist domination. 'South East Asia is ... politically adolescent with teenage weaknesses of exuberance, xenophobia, inexperience and irresponsibility', Sir Robert Scott condescendingly remarked to Macmillan in May 1959, 'Guiding the strong new forces of nationalism into constructive channels and coping with the hydra of communist penetration in all its forms demand patience and perseverance.'[1] Radical social change or close relations with the states of the Communist bloc were to be eschewed, while friendly advice, counsel and assistance, it was thought, would create lasting bonds between post-colonial indigenous elites and their Western diplomatic, military and commercial contacts.

By the early 1960s, it is possible to see how difficult such aspirations were to implement in practice. Political leaders in newly independent countries were acutely sensitive to the charge that Western tutelage had not ended, but had merely taken on another form, less direct, but just as pervasive and corrosive. Signs that foreign bases were being retained to serve Western ends were seized on by political agitators, and held

---

[1] Scott to Macmillan, 6 May 1959, PREM 11/2661.

295

up as examples of continued dependence on the old masters. At the same time, metropolitan resources were not up to the task of sustaining a presence so far from the home base, when direct material interests were increasingly deemed as peripheral. After a brief swan-song in 1963–5, partly derived from the demands of the conflict with Indonesia, the British had finally come to accept and make policy decisions that reflected the fact that they were no longer an Asian power which should try to meet its commitments through means that now served only to lose regional influence and antagonize local peoples.

This process was encapsulated by the experience of the confrontation itself, a conflict that straddled the line between a rapidly receding Asia of colonial influence and European entanglement, and the emergence of independent and increasingly assertive regional powers anxious to show their domestic audiences that they could handle their own affairs. This is perhaps best shown by looking at relations between Britain and Malaysia. Indonesian arguments that Malaysia represented a way for Britain's neo-colonial presence to be maintained appeared to hold a large degree of validity, bearing in mind the policy considerations in London and Singapore that gave the scheme so much of its impetus. Yet an analysis of the process by which the Federation was constructed between 1961 and 1963 reveals that decision-makers in London had repeatedly to respond to the priorities of local actors in Kuala Lumpur and Singapore, who were able to set the agenda and force the pace of change. After Malaysia came into existence in September 1963, the ability of Britain to shape events was even more constrained by their loss of formal powers, and the determination of the Federal Government to conduct its own foreign policy. During 1964, the British found that while their advice was patiently listened to by Malaysian ministers, there was no guarantee that it carried sufficient weight to clinch an argument, except in defence matters. The diplomacy of confrontation was often conducted by the principal regional participants with little reference to British interests and concerns in the hunt for an 'Asian solution'. When it was known that the British would disapprove strongly of a proposed course of action, as over the restructuring of the Federation in 1965, the tendency was simply not to keep them informed.

In April 1964, Lord Carrington was still remarking on the 'undeniable "neo-colonialist" atmosphere in Kuala Lumpur. One has only to visit the place to understand, if not excuse, the strictures about an over-obvious British presence made by Mr Robert Kennedy during his visit to London in January.'[2] But the influence of British expatriates, and the kind of

---

[2] Report by Lord Carrington on tour of South East Asia, 24 April 1964, D1051/39, FO 371/175066.

atmosphere that Carrington had noted, was on the wane. In the summer of 1964, the Tunku began to criticize the numbers of British officers still serving in the Borneo territories, and in July the last British
members of the Sabah Cabinet (including the State Secretary) were removed; these were tendencies said to reflect the Tunku's belief that such
expatriate officers were encouraging the territories to pursue an independent line and were hostile to Kuala Lumpur.[3] Conversely enough,
it was confrontation above anything else that heightened the sense of
Malaysian dependence on Britain, and helped to increase any residual leverage British officials might still possess over decision-making in
Kuala Lumpur. In such difficult circumstances, the British could feel
great resentment that the effort they were putting into defending the
Federation against Indonesia was not receiving sufficient recognition,
and that they were being taken for granted. Their only recourse when
faced with Malaysian action that prejudiced their interests was to threaten
to withdraw their counter-confrontation commitment, clearly a measure of last resort and a threat which it was difficult to take at face
value given what had already been invested. Increasingly, these dilemmas led British officials back to reconsider the fundamental question
of what real benefits were derived from their presence in a South East
Asia that was determined to reject overt signs of Western power and
domination.

Even a government as close to the West as that in Kuala Lumpur had
to distance itself from London to some degree. The hopes that British
officials had entertained in 1957 that Malaya might eventually consent to
join SEATO had all but disappeared by the early 1960s. Although the optimists in London felt that UMNO might just be able to hold on to power
until the end of the 1960s, there were also many analyses which doubted
the prolonged electoral viability of its moderate leadership. The only alternative that could be envisaged was a government even more deeply
imbued with Malay nationalism, and perhaps with a stronger Islamic
identity. Whatever the case, it was unlikely that Kuala Lumpur would
tolerate forever the close identification with British defence interests that
lay behind both the 1957 Anglo-Malayan Defence Agreement and the
extended version of it that came into force to cover Malaysia in 1963.
Several key figures were adamant that it was unrealistic to anticipate that
military bases could still be operated in conditions where the local government was opposed to their use, and alternative forms of exercising
influence in the region would have to be found. In April 1964, Head was

[3] See CRO brief for Prime Minister's talk with Tunku Abdul Rahman, Annex II,
31 July 1964, PREM 11/4904; Kuala Lumpur to DOS, no. 1289, 23 June 1964, POL
18 MALAYSIA, RG 59.

writing to Sandys from Kuala Lumpur, in an echo of Selkirk's warnings to Macmillan of 1963, that

in my view it is extremely unlikely that white, foreign, Western bases will continue to be acceptable in South-East Asia for an indefinite time. All our experience since the war argues against this . . . in the councils of the Afro-Asian countries the presence of a Western base on an independent country's territory is the supreme badge of the stooge.

The great mistake, the High Commissioner considered, was to 'outstay our welcome' and to generate an anti-Western political atmosphere upon forced departure.[4] But the removal of the bases was difficult in the short term when Malaysia was under such a direct threat. Indonesia's policies of confrontation, though partly aimed at removing the presence of British bases in the region, had generated new commitments and pressures on London to remain in the area with a significant military capability.

The nature of the Commonwealth commitment to the defence of Australia and New Zealand was also being called into question by the even more pronounced orientation of both states towards their ties with Washington by the mid-1960s. To some extent, both Canberra and Wellington were reading the writing on the wall, indicated by the Macmillan Government's application for entry into the EEC and the plans to scale back British involvement in the region through the establishment of a Greater Malaysia. However much British officials might try to allay Antipodean fears that they could no longer rely in the long term for a British contribution to their immediate defence needs in the Western Pacific, it made better sense to lean even more on the ANZUS connection, especially with the vast expansion of the American military presence in the region as a result of the Vietnam War. The steps taken by the Australian Government in April–May 1963 to substantially boost its own defence capabilities, and the later decision in April 1965 to offer a ground-force contingent for service in South Vietnam was illustrative of such trends, while the end of Robert Menzies's long tenure as Prime Minister in 1966 also symbolized the passing of the Anglophile period.[5]

The Malaysia experiment, and the unforseen commitments involved in confrontation that developed from it, were a temporary interlude in the long process of British decline as an Asian power that can be traced back to the conclusion of the Anglo-Japanese alliance in 1902. The termination of that alliance following the Washington Conference of 1921–2 left Britain standing alone in defence of its interests against the expansionism of Japan and revolutionary Chinese nationalism. After the Second

---

[4] Kuala Lumpur to CRO, no. 3, 14 April 1964, D1051/43, FO 371/175067.
[5] See Edwards, *Crises and Commitments*, 269–71, 361–2.

World War, the arrival of the Americans and the imperatives of the Cold War helped to sustain a British presence despite the debilitating effects of that global conflict. Tradition, sentiment, commercial opportunities and colonial responsibilities helped to perpetuate the Far Eastern role far beyond the time when it seemed appropriate to retain permanent military resources in the region. From at least the mid-1950s, the key consideration playing on London's unwillingness to embark on a major shift in policy away from an expensive defence commitment (when constitutional change in Malaya and Singapore raised the issue in pressing terms) was the dynamic of the Anglo-American relationship and the desire to present a united front to the Communist threat in South East Asia. After the Geneva Conference and Manila Treaty of 1954, it was the SEATO obligation to help provide for the collective defence of South East Asia that underpinned the whole British defence system centred on Singapore. Some officials were occasionally inclined to question the underlying purpose and utility of the commitment. It was, after all, American power that was manifestly resisting further Communist encroachments in Vietnam and Laos, rather than any collective security arrangements. There seemed little likelihood of a conventional cross-border attack that would lead to SEATO being wheeled into action, while British ministers had always resisted attempts to include instances of 'indirect aggression' within the terms of the original Treaty. In 1962, the British Government had finally taken the decision that ground troops could not be permitted to take part in any future SEATO incursion into Laos, leaving the purpose of the forces arrayed at Singapore and in Malaya ambiguous beyond the immediate close defence of Malaysia and the base itself.

There was also the question of whether the 'loss' of Vietnam, Laos and Cambodia would have any real impact on the overall Western position in the Cold War. In November 1961, Fred Warner can be found suggesting that Britain had no real interest in Indochina and 'although it would undoubtedly be disastrous, I think that Britain could accept the whole of Indochina going Communist'. As far as SEATO was concerned, it involved Britain 'constantly being dragged by the hair into the more aggressive anti-Communist schemes of the Americans and the Thais'. The organization had been created 'at a time when military blocs were fashionable' and since the onset of the Laotian crisis in 1959 had 'come to life and grown into a rather dangerous and disagreeable force'. Any Western input into SEATO was seen by most neutral Asian opinion as inherently aggressive, while it gave

unscrupulous and irresponsible governments like that in Thailand the perfect means to blackmail the Americans into ill-considered policies because they can always threaten the collapse of the Organization if they do not get what they want. But its most dangerous feature is that as members we have to consider the possibility of war-like action in a number of contingencies which are not perhaps of vital interest to us (e.g. the loss of Laos).[6]

Although British officials were sometimes inclined to doubt the importance of holding the Western position in Indochina, preferring to fall back on the line of the Mekong river along the northern borders of Thailand, they certainly believed that keeping Indonesia out of Communist hands was important for the security of Malaya, Singapore and the Borneo territories. Nevertheless, they were not prepared to elevate this concern above the creation and preservation of Malaysia. The British, in fact, probably had a more realistic view of the prospects of the PKI and were more concerned about the basic impetus of Indonesian nationalism leading in an expansionist direction. In contrast was the great over-estimation by the Americans of the ability of the PKI to achieve its goals in the face of the adamant opposition of important elements in the bureaucracy and, most crucially, the Indonesian Army, which showed conclusively in 1965 that it was willing and able to act decisively to extinguish the internal threat from the left. The resistance to Communist ideas of powerful conservative social and religious elites in the countryside might also be noted here, and also the distrust and suspicion reserved by many Indonesians for ethnic Chinese (making the PKI's alignment with Beijing by 1964–5 an easy target for its enemies). At least by late 1964, Washington policymakers seem to have appreciated that a lower profile and visibility for the Western presence offered the best chance of reducing the opportunity of anti-imperialist agitation by the PKI and its supporters, but an unwillingness to disengage completely still characterized American attitudes. This kind of fundamental ambivalence over whether to leave newly independent states and societies well alone, or to engage in forms of interventionism in the hope of preventing their succumbing to Communist influence was indicative of several overall trends in US foreign policy in the 1950s and 1960s. While diversity might be a laudable goal in the struggle against the monolithic conception of an ordered society commonly associated with Communism, states which drifted too far from the American-conceived norm were always treated with a healthy dose of suspicion in Washington as it endeavoured to mould the international system to its own devices.

Another paradox running through the heart of American policies was the desire to be seen as different and apart from the old European colonial powers in their approach to Asian problems, while at the same time

[6] Warner minute 'Britain and Indochina', 1 November 1961, D10113/9, FO 371/159722.

realizing that in some respects their interests and outlook were similar to the Europeans. Hence, in the final analysis, while they might disagree in policy approaches to Asian problems (notably towards contacts with Communist China), both the United States and Britain wanted to prevent the Soviet Union and the PRC making significant gains, and hoped to forestall the spread of indigenous Communist movements. Both considered that Western influence of one variety or another was necessary to keep a watchful eye over the states of South East Asia and give assistance and advice. The British could offer the Americans diplomatic experience, intelligence sources and a potentially useful military capability. Furthermore, in psychological and domestic political terms, it was often important for decision-makers in Washington to show they could attract allied support for their policies and that they were not acting in isolation. There was a strong wish to see the British stay on in South East Asia, partly in the expectation that the Americans would have to pick up the responsibilities that were left behind by any British departure. Nevertheless, and at the same time, traditional anti-colonial sentiment within American political culture, coupled with the belief that association with suspect British policy could cause the United States to forfeit popularity among independent or non-aligned Asian states, sometimes militated against forging close ties with London (when straightforward policy differences did not also impede effective cooperation).

This latter consideration was particularly prevalent during Kennedy's presidency, where a new relationship was sought with the developing world. The key to achieving Kennedy's goals for stability in South East Asia lay in reaching a Laotian settlement, countering the Communist insurgency in South Vietnam and improving the credibility of the Diem regime, and steering Indonesia away from its links with the Communist world onto a path of moderate economic development with Western financial assistance. The resolution of the West Irian issue in the summer of 1962 was a significant step along the way to securing that last goal, but British and Malayan plans for the creation of Malaysia introduced a new level of turbulence to South East Asia in 1963, while US policies in Vietnam entered a downward spiral from which they were never to recover. As Washington tried to reconcile the conflicting priorities that the arrival of confrontation generated, the initial impulse was again to avoid being identified with British colonial policy, for fear of contamination in the eyes of Asian opinion. There was throughout an implicit racial dimension to the attitudes of American officials. Both President Kennedy and Averell Harriman evinced a desire during 1963 not to be seen to be ganging up on Jakarta with the other 'white' powers with interests in the region. From September 1963, Washington had pressed for an 'Asian solution' to the conflict, rather than one which carried the appearance of being imposed or even mediated by the West.

In a similar fashion, during the late 1950s, the Americans had resisted the efforts of the British, Australians and New Zealanders to engage in four-power military planning for the Far East, wary that if knowledge of such discussions should leak, the Asian members of SEATO would feel by-passed by a white, Western inner circle. Many Americans regarded SEATO as useful primarily because it associated Asian states with the containment of Communism in the region, and helped to counteract the notion of a United States simply dictating its containment policies throughout the area. British observers tended to regard such American attitudes with wry humour, knowing that there was never any real doubt that Washington possessed the decisive voice, and feeling, for example, that the Americans consistently underrated the extent to which SEATO had become reviled during the 1950s as an aggressive instrument of the Western powers, and as the potential cause of conflict through its inter-ventionist approach to the affairs of Indochina. Reflecting on the Organization's unpopularity in September 1963, Selkirk noted that

Admiral [Harry] Felt [the US C-in-C Pacific] believes that he's alright [sic] so long as he stays out of the 'white man's club'. I doubt if he realizes that in fact in most countries in South and South East Asia, SEATO itself is regarded as a 'white man's club' and the presence of representatives from Pakistan, Thailand and the Philippines does not really alter this situation.[7]

Indeed, in a direct inversion of American attitudes, many British officials felt it was association with bellicose hard-line anti-Communist American policies, particularly towards China, that was doing their own efforts to cast off an image of over-bearing Western imperial power no good whatsoever. This attitude was combined with a belief that it was they who had a special knowledge and understanding of Asian nationalism, derived from their recent past experience, that contrasted with the short-sighted and naive American approach found so deficient in Indochina. In May 1961, Selkirk was noting with regard to Laos that, 'The United States still find it very difficult to grasp the sort of Asian settlement which we were able to obtain in India, Burma and Malaya, and find it hard to get away from their belief that guns and dollars are the only solution.'[8] In similar vein, David Ormsby Gore, then a Foreign Office minister, argued in July 1961 that

Up to now the policy of successive American Administrations has been to give political and above all military support to corrupt right-wing dictatorships. The

---

[7] Selkirk to Home, 9 September 1963, FO 800/897.
[8] Selkirk to Macmillan, 9 May 1961, PREM 11/3737.

Americans have never been able to resist backing anyone who claimed to be a good anti-communist; such a sentiment is one they can understand, while any less simple statement of intent seems to them suspect and dangerous. They have thus completely ignored the true nature of Asian nationalism and failed to realise that it is a force which the Communists will find it very difficult to overcome provided the governments of the countries concerned are genuinely native products and cannot be smeared as American puppets. We ourselves have come to understand this as a result of disagreeable experiences in such countries as Egypt, Iraq and Cyprus but it is to be feared that the Americans have not yet realised the need for a fundamental reappraisal of their policies and will repeat on a more expensive scale in Vietnam and Thailand the mistakes which they have already made in Laos and Korea.[9]

By 1964–5, such warnings appeared to be on the way to fruition, with the overt and heavily militarized US presence in the Far East doing much to alienate much Asian, and indeed international opinion; within Vietnam itself the United States was committed to the support of a series of governments notable only for their chronic instability, unrepresentative character and total reliance on American aid.

During much of the 1950s, Britain's attempt to preserve influence in such regions as the Middle East had provoked tensions and difficulties with the Americans, particularly as the United States tried to avoid too close an association with the policies of a fading imperialist power. Rather than emphasizing its world role (somewhat taken for granted anyway), Washington had encouraged the British to adopt a more positive approach to moves towards European integration then under way, and pressed for an enhanced contribution to NATO. These were trends that were continued by Kennedy, but American initiatives to work with the forces of non-alignment and greater sympathies for anti-colonialism were given prominence as the ideological struggle with the Soviet Union in the developing world entered a new stage. Yet by 1963–4 Kennedy's policies had only enjoyed a limited success and the old anti-Communist imperatives of the containment doctrine, coupled with an aversion to domestic instability and possible revolutionary change, were resurfacing in a strengthened manner. This was most obviously seen over Vietnam, but can also be discerned in the Middle East and Africa. The temptation in such beleaguered times was to turn to old friends and allies, and to argue that their assistance was still needed as the only other Western power with global interests and responsibilities. Only too aware of their dependence on the United States when it came to their various difficulties as they shed their imperial burdens, whether it be with Sukarno and Malaysia, or Nasser and the South Arabian Federation, the British were ready to concert their

[9] FO to Washington, no. 291, 3 July 1961, D103145/11, FO 371/159712.

responses with the Americans and argue that they shared common problems as 'Western' powers faced with threats to their continuing influence. Lying at the heart of Anglo-American relations in the 1960s was the paradox that as Britain disengaged from its old colonial commitments and tried to refashion its international position according to its limited resources, pressure from Washington to maintain a global role was actually on the increase. Following the Prime Minister's visit to Washington in February 1964, Oliver Wright noted that the Americans now seemed to appreciate the value of Britain's worldwide outposts, particularly in areas such as Cyprus, Aden and Singapore, while there was no apparent resentment at the colonial past. As long as Britain maintained its posture in such critical regions, then goodwill in Washington could be expected: 'In short, the unspoken special relationship has if anything been strengthened, chiefly because the Americans have come to realise and accept that we are the only ally with a presence in all parts of the world and one upon which they can rely.' But this development also carried with it the potential for further, perhaps onerous obligations, Wright commenting that alignment with US policy might lead Britain to 'acquire a reputation which will need some living up to. There seems to be plenty of scope in the future for adding to our responsibilities as a world power: none for reducing our commitments.'[10] This was the uncomfortable dilemma that the Labour Government found when it arrived in office later in the year, when domestic imperatives dictated that it find ways to cut back on its overseas obligations as the Americans led the final Western crusade in South East Asia. Washington was keen for London to despatch some recognizable military contribution to Vietnam, but American pressure was effectively met by the argument that British resources were already fully stretched meeting the demands of confrontation. By closing down the option of a more active British involvement in the escalating war in Vietnam during 1964–5, Indonesian policy, though it created immediate dilemmas and problems of its own, may also have saved Britain from a far more costly exercise in containment in the jungles of South East Asia.

[10] Wright minute for Home, 17 February 1964, PREM 11/4794.

Bibliography

UNPUBLISHED DOCUMENTS

Public Record Office, Kew, London
CAB 21, Cabinet Office registered files.
CAB 128, Cabinet minutes.
CAB 129, Cabinet memoranda.
CAB 130, Cabinet committees (GEN and MISC series).
CAB 131, Defence Committee.
CAB 133, International and Commonwealth conferences.
CAB 134, Cabinet committees.
CAB 148, Defence and Oversea Policy Committee.
CO 1030, Colonial Office, Far Eastern Department, original correspondence.
DEFE 7, Ministry of Defence, registered files.
DEFE 11, Chiefs of Staff Committee, registered files.
DEFE 13, Ministry of Defence private office papers.
DEFE 32, Secretary's standard files.
DO 169, Commonwealth Relations Office, Far East and Pacific Department, registered files.
FO 371, Foreign Office, general political correspondence.
FO 800, Private collections, ministers and officials.
FO 1091, Commissioner General for South East Asia, registered files.
FO 1109, Papers of R. A. Butler.
PREM 11, Prime Minister's Office, 1951–1964.
PREM 13, Prime Minister's Office, 1964–1970.

Churchill College, Cambridge
Papers of Sir Andrew Gilchrist.
Papers of Patrick Gordon Walker.

Trinity College, Cambridge
Papers of R. A. Butler.

Bodleian Library, Oxford
Papers of Harold Macmillan.

Rhodes House Library, Oxford
Papers of Sir William Goode, MSS. Indian Ocean s.323.
Papers of Sir Alexander Waddell, MSS. Pacific s.105.
Nigel Fisher Oral History, MSS. British Empire, s.452.

United States National Archives, College Park, Maryland
RG 59, Department of State Records, Central Decimal, Subject-Numeric and Lot Files.

Library of Congress, Manuscripts Division, Washington DC
Papers of W. Averell Harriman.

Dwight D. Eisenhower Library, Abilene, Kansas
Ann Whitman File, NSC series.

John F. Kennedy Library, Boston, Massachusetts
National Security File.
President's Office File.
Papers of Roger Hilsman.
Papers of Robert F. Kennedy.
Papers of Arthur M. Schlesinger Jr.
Papers of James C. Thomson.
Oral Histories: Charles Baldwin, Richard M. Bissell, Lord Harlech (David Ormsby Gore), W. Averell Harriman, Roger Hilsman, Robert Komer, U. Alexis Johnson, Robert Johnson, Howard P. Jones, Carl Kaysen, J. Herman Van Roijen, Walt W. Rostow, William H. Sullivan.

Lyndon B. Johnson Library, Austin, Texas
National Security File.
Special Files, tapes and transcripts of telephone conversations, 1963–4.

PUBLISHED DOCUMENTS

United States
Congressional Record, 1963, vol. 109, part 6 (Washington, 1963).
Foreign Relations of the United States, 1952–1954, vol. XII, East Asia and the Pacific, part 1 (Washington, 1984). Volumes in the *Foreign Relations of the United States* series are hereafter indicated by *FRUS.*
FRUS, 1958–1960, vol. XVI, East Asia–Pacific Region; Cambodia; Laos (Washington, 1992).
FRUS, 1958–1960, vol. XVII, Indonesia (Washington, 1994).
FRUS, 1961–1963, vol. I, Vietnam 1961 (Washington, 1988).
FRUS, 1961–1963, vol. II, Vietnam 1962 (Washington, 1990).
FRUS, 1961–1963, vol. III, Vietnam, January–August 1963 (Washington, 1991).
FRUS, 1961–1963, vol. IV, Vietnam, August–December 1963 (Washington, 1991).
FRUS, 1961–1963, vol. VIII, National Security Policy (Washington, 1996).

FRUS, 1961–1963, vol. XXIII, Southeast Asia (Washington, 1994).
FRUS, 1961–1963, vol. XXIV, Laos Crisis (Washington, 1994).
FRUS, 1964–1968, vol. I, Vietnam, 1964 (Washington, 1992).
FRUS, 1964–1968, vol. II, Vietnam, January–June 1965 (Washington, 1996).
FRUS, 1964–1968, vol. III, Vietnam, June–December 1965 (Washington, 1996).
The Public Papers of the Presidents: John F. Kennedy, 1961 (Washington, 1962).
The Public Papers of the Presidents: John F. Kennedy, 1962 (Washington, 1963).
The Public Papers of the Presidents, John F. Kennedy, 1963 (Washington, 1964).

Great Britain

Hansard, Parliamentary Debates, 5th series, vol. 650.
Hansard, House of Lords Debates, 5th series, vol. 253.
Report of the Commission of Enquiry, North Borneo and Sarawak, 1962, Cmnd 1794 (London, 1962).
Malaysia, Report of the Inter-Governmental Committee, 1962, Cmnd 1954 (London, 1963).
Malaysia: Agreement concluded between the United Kingdom of Great Britain and Northern Ireland, the Federation of Malaya, North Borneo, Sarawak and Singapore, Cmnd 2094 (London, 1963).
Supplementary Agreement Relating to Malaysia, supplement to Cmnd 2094 (London, 1963).

Malaysia

Malaya/Indonesia Relations, 31st August 1957 to 15th September 1963 (Kuala Lumpur, 1963).
Malaya/Philippine Relations, 31st August 1957 to 15th September 1963 (Kuala Lumpur, 1964).
Malaysia's Case in the United Nations Security Council: Documents reproduced from the official record of the Security Council proceedings (Kuala Lumpur, 1964).
Indonesian Aggression Against Malaysia, vol. 2 (Kuala Lumpur, 1965).

British Documents on the End of Empire Project

Goldsworthy, David (ed.), *The Conservative Government and the End of Empire, 1951–1957, Part I: International Relations* (London, 1994).
The Conservative Government and the End of Empire, 1951–1957, Part II: Politics and Administration (London, 1994).
Stockwell, A. J. (ed.), *Malaya, Part I: The Malayan Union Experiment, 1942–1948* (London, 1995).
Malaya, Part II: The Communist Insurrection, 1948–1953 (London, 1995).
Malaya, Part III: The Alliance Route to Independence, 1953–1957 (London, 1995).

Other

Boyce, Peter (ed.), *Malaysia and Singapore in International Diplomacy: Documents and Commentaries* (Sydney, 1968).
Gullick, John M. (ed.), *Malaysia and its Neighbours* (New York, 1967).

Mansergh, Nicholas (ed.), *Documents and Speeches on Commonwealth Affairs, 1952–1962* (London, 1963).

BOOKS

Abramson, Rudy, *Spanning the Century: The Life of W. Averell Harriman, 1891–1986* (New York, 1992).
Aldous, Richard, and Lee, Sabine (eds.), *Harold Macmillan: Aspects of a Political Life* (London, 1999).
Allen, J. de V., *The Malayan Union* (New Haven, 1967).
Allen, Richard, *Malaysia: Prospect and Retrospect* (Oxford, 1968).
Anderson, Benedict O., *Imagined Communities: Reflections on the Origin and Spread of Nationalism* (London, 1991).
Ball, George W., *The Past Has Another Pattern* (New York, 1982).
Barclay, Glen St J., *Friends in High Places: Australian–American Diplomatic Relations since 1945* (Melbourne, 1985).
Berman, Larry, *Planning a Tragedy: The Americanization of the War in Vietnam* (New York, 1982).
Beschloss, Michael R., *Kennedy v. Khrushchev: The Crisis Years, 1960–1963* (London, 1991).
Bird, Kai, *The Color of Truth: McGeorge and William Bundy: Brothers in Arms* (New York, 1998).
Bowles, Chester, *Promises to Keep: My Years in Public Life, 1941–1969* (New York, 1971).
Brands, H. W., *The Wages of Globalism: Lyndon Johnson and the Limits of American Power* (New York, 1995).
Buszynski, Leszek, *SEATO: The Failure of an Alliance Strategy* (Singapore, 1983).
Cable, James, *The Geneva Conference of 1954 on Indochina* (London, 1986).
Cady, John F., *Post-War South East Asia* (Washington, 1974).
Chang, Gordon H., *Friends and Enemies: The United States, China, and the Soviet Union, 1948–1972* (Stanford, 1990).
Chin Kin Wah, *The Defence of Malaysia and Singapore: The Transformation of a Security System, 1957–1971* (Cambridge, 1983).
Chin Ung-Ho, *Chinese Politics in Sarawak: A Study of the Sarawak United People's Party* (Oxford, 1996).
Clark, Ian, *Nuclear Diplomacy and the Special Relationship: America and Britain's Deterrent, 1957–1962* (Oxford, 1994).
Clutterbuck, Richard, *Riot and Revolution in Singapore and Malaya, 1945–63* (London, 1973).
Cohen, Warren I., *Dean Rusk* (New Jersey, 1980).
Cohen, Warren I., and Iriye, Akira (eds.), *The Great Powers in East Asia, 1953–1960* (New York, 1990).
Cohen, Warren I., and Tucker, Nancy B. (eds.), *Lyndon Johnson Confronts the World: American Foreign Policy, 1963–1968* (Cambridge, 1994).
Colbert, Evelyn, *Southeast Asia in International Relations, 1941–1956* (Ithaca, 1977).
Colby, William, and Forbath, Peter, *Honourable Men: My Life in the CIA* (London, 1978).

Conboy, Kenneth, and Morrison, James, *Feet to the Fire: CIA Covert Operations in Indonesia, 1957–1958* (Annapolis, 1999).
Crouch, Harold, *The Army and Politics in Indonesia* (Ithaca, 1978).
Dallek, Robert, *Lone Star Rising: Lyndon Johnson and His Times, 1908–1960* (New York, 1991).
Flawed Giant: Lyndon Johnson and His Times, 1961–1973 (New York, 1998).
Darby, Philip, *British Defence Policy East of Suez, 1947–1968* (London, 1973).
Darwin, John, *Britain and Decolonisation: The Retreat from Empire in the Post-War World* (London, 1988).
Dunbabin, J. P. D., *The Post-Imperial Age: The Great Powers and the Wider World* (London, 1994).
Edwards, Peter, *Crises and Commitments: The Politics and Diplomacy of Australia's Involvement in Southeast Asian Conflicts, 1948–1965* (Sydney, 1992).
Feith, Herbert, *The Decline of Constitutional Democracy in Indonesia* (Ithaca, 1962).
Gaddis, John L., *Strategies of Containment* (Oxford, 1982).
Galbraith, John K., *Ambassador's Journal* (Boston, 1969).
Gardner, Lloyd C., *Approaching Vietnam: From World War II through Dienbienphu* (New York, 1988).
Gardner, Paul F., *Shared Hopes, Separate Fears: Fifty Years of US–Indonesian Relations* (Boulder, 1997).
Giglio, James N., *The Presidency of John F. Kennedy* (Lawrence, 1991).
Green, Marshall, *Indonesia: Crisis and Transformation, 1965–1968* (Washington, 1990).
Gullick, John M., *Malaysia* (London, 1969).
Guthman, Edwin O., and Shulman, Jeffrey (eds.), *Robert Kennedy In His Own Words* (London, 1988).
Halberstam, David, *The Best and the Brightest* (London, 1972).
Hanna, Williard A., *The Formation of Malaysia* (American Universities Field Staff, 1964).
Harper, T. N., *The End of Empire and the Making of Malaya* (Cambridge, 1999).
Healey, Denis, *The Time of My Life* (London, 1989).
Herring, George C., *America's Longest War: The United States and Vietnam, 1950–75* (London, 1979).
Hess, Gary R., *The United States' Emergence as a Southeast Asian Power, 1940–1950* (New York, 1987).
Hilsman, Roger, *To Move A Nation: The Politics of Foreign Policy in the Administration of John F. Kennedy* (New York, 1967).
Hogan, Michael J. (ed.), *America in the World: The Historiography of American Foreign Relations since 1941* (Cambridge, 1995).
Horne, Alistair, *Macmillan, 1957–1986* (London, 1989).
Howard, Anthony, *RAB: The Life of R. A. Butler* (London, 1987).
Immerman, Richard H. (ed.), *The Diplomacy of John Foster Dulles* (Princeton, 1990).
Isaacson, Walter, and Thomas, Evan, *The Wise Men: Six Friends and the World They Made: Acheson, Bohlen, Harriman, Kennan, Lovett, McCloy* (New York, 1986).
Jackson, Robert, *The Malayan Emergency: The Commonwealth's Wars, 1948–1966* (London, 1991).

Jones, Howard P., *Indonesia: The Possible Dream* (New York, 1971).

Kahin, Audrey R. and Kahin, George McT., *Subversion as Foreign Policy: The Secret Eisenhower and Dulles Debacle in Indonesia* (New York, 1995).

Kahin, George McT. (ed.), *Major Governments of Southeast Asia*, 2nd edn (Ithaca, 1963).

Kaplan, Lawrence S., Artaud, Denise and Rubin, Mark R. (eds.), *Dien Bien Phu and the Crisis of Franco-American Relations, 1954–1955* (Wilmington, 1990).

Karnow, Stanley J., *Vietnam: A History* (New York, 1983).

In Our Image: America's Empire in the Philippines (New York, 1989).

Kennedy, John F., *The Strategy of Peace* (New York, 1960).

Knapp, Wilfrid, *A History of War and Peace, 1939–1965* (Oxford, 1967).

Kunz, Diane B. (ed.), *The Diplomacy of the Crucial Decade: American Foreign Relations During the 1960s* (New York, 1994).

Lamb, Richard, *The Macmillan Years, 1957–1963: The Emerging Truth* (London, 1995).

Lau, Albert, *The Malayan Union Controversy, 1942–1948* (Singapore, 1991).

A Moment of Anguish: Singapore in Malaysia and the Politics of Disengagement (Singapore, 1998).

Lee Kuan Yew, *The Singapore Story: Memoirs of Lee Kuan Yew* (Singapore, 1998).

Legge, J. D., *Sukarno: A Political Biography* (London, 1972).

Leifer, Michael, *The Philippine Claim to Sabah* (London, 1967).

The Foreign Relations of New States (Camberwell, 1974).

Indonesia's Foreign Policy (London, 1983).

Leifer, Michael (ed.), *Constraints and Adjustments in British Foreign Policy* (London, 1972).

Lev, Daniel S., *The Transition to Guided Democracy: Indonesian Politics, 1957–1959* (Ithaca, 1966).

Logevall, Fredrik, *Choosing War: The Lost Chance for Peace and the Escalation of the War in Vietnam* (Berkeley, 1999).

Louis, Wm Roger and Bull, Hedley (eds.), *The 'Special Relationship': Anglo-American Relations since 1945* (Oxford, 1986).

Lowe, Peter, *Containing the Cold War in East Asia: British Policies towards Japan, China and Korea, 1948–53* (Manchester, 1997).

Mackie, J. A. C., *Konfrontasi: The Indonesia–Malaysia Dispute, 1963–1966* (Kuala Lumpur, 1974).

Macmillan, Harold, *Pointing the Way, 1959–1961* (London, 1972).

At the End of the Day, 1961–1963 (London, 1973).

Maga, Timothy P., *John F. Kennedy and the New Pacific Community, 1961–63* (London, 1990).

John F. Kennedy and New Frontier Diplomacy, 1961–1963 (Malabar, 1994).

McMahon, Robert J., *Colonialism and Cold War: The United States and the Struggle for Indonesian Independence, 1945–1949* (Ithaca, 1981).

The Limits of Empire: The United States and Southeast Asia since World War II (New York, 1999).

Means, Gordon P., *Malaysian Politics* (London, 1970).

Milne, R. S., *Government and Politics in Malaysia* (Boston, 1967).

Mohamed Noordin Sopiee, *From Malayan Union to Singapore Separation: Political Unification in the Malaysia Region, 1945–65* (Kuala Lumpur, 1974).

Morgan, Kenneth O., *Callaghan: A Life* (Oxford, 1997).

Mortimer, Rex, *Indonesian Communism Under Sukarno: Ideology and Politics, 1959–1965* (Ithaca, 1974).

Nagai, Yonosuke, and Iriye, Akira (eds.), *The Origins of the Cold War in Asia* (Oxford, 1977).

Osborne, Milton E., *Singapore and Malaysia* (Ithaca, 1964).

Paterson, Thomas G. (ed.), *Kennedy's Quest for Victory: American Foreign Policy, 1961–1963* (Oxford, 1989).

Pickering, Jeffrey, *Britain's Withdrawal from East of Suez: The Politics of Retrenchment* (London, 1998).

Pierce, Robert (ed.), *Patrick Gordon Walker: Political Diaries, 1932–1971* (London, 1991).

Pluvier, Jan M., *Confrontations: A Study in Indonesian Politics* (Kuala Lumpur, 1965).

South-East Asia from Colonialism to Independence (Kuala Lumpur, 1974).

Pocock, Tom, *Fighting General: The Public and Private Campaigns of General Sir Walter Walker* (London, 1973).

Ponting, Clive, *Breach of Promise: Labour in Power, 1964–70* (London, 1990).

Porritt, Vernon L., *British Colonial Rule in Sarawak, 1946–1963* (Kuala Lumpur, 1997).

Prados, John, *The Keepers of the Keys: A History of the National Security Council from Truman to Bush* (New York, 1991).

Ratnam, K. J., and Milne, R. S., *The Malayan Parliamentary Election of 1964* (Singapore, 1967).

Reeves, Richard, *President Kennedy: Profile of Power* (New York, 1993).

Rostow, Walt W., *The Diffusion of Power: An Essay on Recent History* (New York, 1972).

Rotter, Andrew J., *The Path to Vietnam: Origins of the American Commitment to Southeast Asia* (Ithaca, 1987).

Rubinstein, Alvin Z. (ed.), *Soviet and Chinese Influence in the Third World* (London, 1975).

Rust, William J., *Kennedy in Vietnam: American Vietnam Policy, 1960–63* (New York, 1985).

Sampson, Anthony, *Macmillan: A Study in Ambiguity* (London, 1967).

Schlesinger Jr, Arthur M., *A Thousand Days: John F. Kennedy in the White House* (London, 1965).

Robert Kennedy and His Times (London, 1978).

Schoenbaum, Thomas J., *Waging Peace and War: Dean Rusk in the Truman, Kennedy, and Johnson Years* (New York, 1988).

Shapley, Deborah, *Promise and Power: The Life and Times of Robert McNamara* (Boston, 1993).

Sharma, Archana, *British Policy Towards Malaysia, 1957–67* (London, 1993).

Sheehan, Neil, *A Bright Shining Lie: John Paul Vann and America in Vietnam*, (London, 1988).

Short, Anthony, *The Communist Insurrection in Malaya, 1948–1960* (London, 1975).

Singh, Anita Inder, *The Limits of British Influence: South Asia and the Anglo-American Relationship, 1947–56* (London, 1993).

Smith, R. B., *An International History of the Vietnam War, vol. I: Revolution versus Containment, 1955–61* (London, 1983).
An International History of the Vietnam War, vol. II: The Struggle for South-East Asia, 1961–65 (London, 1985).
An International History of the Vietnam War, vol. III: The Making of a Limited War, 1965–66 (London, 1991).
Sorenson, Theodore, *Kennedy* (London, 1965).
Steinberg, David J. (ed.), *In Search of Southeast Asia: A Modern History* (Honolulu, 1987).
Stockwell, A. J., *British Policy and Malay Politics during the Malayan Union Experiment, 1942–48* (Kuala Lumpur, 1979).
Subritzky, John, *Confronting Sukarno: British, American, Australian and New Zealand Diplomacy in the Malaysian–Indonesian Confrontation, 1961–5* (London, 2000).
Tarling, Nicholas (ed.), *The Cambridge History of Southeast Asia, vol. II* (Cambridge, 1992).
Taylor, Jay, *China and Southeast Asia: Peking's Relations with Revolutionary Movements* (London, 1976).
Thorne, Christopher, *Allies of a Kind: Britain, the United States and the War Against Japan, 1941–1945* (London, 1978).
The Issue of War: States, Societies, and the Far Eastern Conflict of 1941–1945 (London, 1985).
Turnbull, C. M., *A History of Singapore, 1819–1975* (Kuala Lumpur, 1977).
White, Mark J. (ed.), *Kennedy: The New Frontier Revisited* (London, 1998).
Wilson, Harold, *The Labour Government, 1964–70: A Personal Record* (London, 1971).
Yahuda, Michael, *China's Role in World Affairs* (London, 1978).
Ziegler, Philip, *Wilson: The Authorised Life* (London, 1993).

ARTICLES

Ball, Simon J., 'Selkirk in Singapore', *Twentieth Century British History*, 10, 2, 1999.
Beckett, Ian F. W., 'Robert Thompson and the British Advisory Mission to South Vietnam, 1961–1965', *Small Wars and Insurgencies*, 8, 3, 1997.
Brands, H. W., 'The Limits of Manipulation: How the United States Didn't Topple Sukarno', *Journal of American History*, 76, 3, 1989.
Bunnell, Frederick P., 'The Central Intelligence Agency – Deputy Directorate for Plans 1961 Secret Memorandum on Indonesia: a Study in the Politics of Policy Formulation in the Kennedy Administration', *Indonesia*, 1981.
'American "Low Posture" Toward Indonesia in the Months Leading up to the 1965 "Coup"', *Indonesia*, 1990.
Dumbrell, John, 'The Johnson Administration and the British Labour Government: Vietnam, the Pound and East of Suez', *Journal of American Studies*, 30, 2, 1996.
Holland, Robert F., 'The Imperial Factor in British Strategies from Attlee to Macmillan, 1945–63', *Journal of Imperial and Commonwealth History*, 12, 1984.

Jones, Gareth, 'Sukarno's Early Views on the Territorial Boundaries of Indonesia', *Australian Outlook*, 18, 1964.

Jones, Matthew, ' "Maximum Disavowable Aid": Britain, the United States and the Indonesian Rebellion, 1957–58', *English Historical Review*, 114, 459, 1999.

'Creating Malaysia: Singapore Security, the Borneo Territories and the Contours of British Policy, 1961–63', *Journal of Imperial and Commonwealth History*, 28, 2, 2000.

Kahin, George McT., 'Malaysia and Indonesia', *Pacific Affairs*, 37, 3, 1964.

Leifer, Michael, 'Anglo-American Differences over Malaysia', *The World Today*, 20, 4, 1964.

Logevall, Fredrik, 'De Gaulle, Neutralization and American Involvement in Vietnam, 1963–1964', *Pacific Historical Review*, 41, 1992.

Louis, Wm. Roger, and Robinson, Ronald, 'The Imperialism of Decolonization', *Journal of Imperial and Commonwealth History*, 22, 3, 1994.

Mohamed Noordin Sopiee, 'The Advocacy of Malaysia before 1961', *Modern Asian Studies*, 7, 4, 1973.

Paterson, Thomas G., 'Bearing the Burden: a Critical Look at John F. Kennedy's Foreign Policy', *The Virginia Quarterly Review*, 54, 2, 1978.

Scott, Peter Dale, 'The US and the Overthrow of Sukarno, 1965–1967', *Pacific Affairs*, 58, 2, 1985.

Sodhy, P., 'Malaysian–United States Relations during Indonesia's Confrontation against Malaysia, 1963–1966', *Journal of South East Asian Studies*, 19, 1, 1988.

Stockwell, A. J., 'Colonial Planning during World War Two: the Case of Malaya', *Journal of Imperial and Commonwealth History*, 2, 3, 1974.

'British Imperial Policy and Decolonisation in Malaya, 1942–52', *Journal of Imperial and Commonwealth History*, 13, 1, 1984.

'Malaysia: the Making of a Neo-Colony?', *Journal of Imperial and Commonwealth History*, 26, 2, 1998.

Tilman, Robert O., 'Elections in Sarawak', *Asian Survey*, 3, 10, 1963.

Warner, Geoffrey, 'The United States and Vietnam: from Kennedy to Johnson', *International Affairs*, 73, 2, 1997.

OTHER WORK

Bunnell, Frederick P., 'The Kennedy Initiatives in Indonesia, 1962–1963', unpublished PhD thesis, Cornell University, 1969.

Easter, David, 'British Defence Policy in South East Asia and the Confrontation, 1960–66', unpublished PhD thesis, London School of Economics and Political Science, 1998.

Index

Vietnam War
  and developments in, 58–9, 135, 235,
    266–7, 269, 280
  and Great Britain, 25, 261–2, 266–7,
    284–5, 289, 304
  and Kennedy, 205, 207
  and links with confrontation, 254–5,
    258, 260–2, 263, 266, 279–80, 284–5,
    284–7
  and 'neutralization' proposals, 254,
    255–6, 260, 262
  and USA, 21, 25, 37, 52, 58–9, 135–6,
    205–7, 255–6, 260, 267, 269, 279–80,
    284, 303
Victorious, HMS, 271

Waddell, Sir Alexander,
  and Brunei revolt, 112
  and Cobbold Commission, 80
  and Greater Malaysia scheme, 66, 72
Warner, Fred, 221
  on appointment of Harriman as
    Assistant Secretary for the Far
    East, 25
  and British attitude towards Sukarno,
    172
  and British military presence in South
    East Asia, 283
  and quadripartite talks of February
    1963, 131–2, 135, 136
  and Philippine claim to North Borneo
    (Sabah), 104
  on SEATO and Indochina, 299–300
  and US policy in West Irian dispute,
    101
  and US policy towards Malaysia,
    136–7
  and US policy towards Indonesia, 208

  and US pressure on Tunku Abdul
    Rahman, 216
Watherston, Sir David,
  as member of Cobbold Commission, 80,
    85, 86–7
West Irian, 5, 13–14, 33–5, 39–54,
    100–3, 104–5, 106
White, Sir Dennis,
  and Brunei revolt, 111
Wilson, Harold,
  and British east of Suez role, 281–2
  visit to Washington, December 1964,
    285–6
  and Johnson and Vietnam, 287
  meetings with George Ball of September
    1965, 289
  meetings with Lyndon Johnson of June
    1967, 292
Wong Pow Nee,
  as member of Cobbold Commission,
    80, 81, 86
Wright, Oliver,
  and British 'Sukarno fixation', 255
  and British global commitments,
    304
  and Lyndon Johnson's view of Sukarno,
    262
  and Robert Kennedy confrontation
    mediation mission, 250
  and need for political solution to
    confrontation, 230
  and US reactions to British withdrawal
    from South East Asia, 292, 293
Wyatt, Wilson,
  and oil negotiations with Indonesia,
    153, 155–6

Yong, Stephen, 166